Cognitive Development and Learning in Instructional Contexts

James P. Byrnes
University of Maryland

Allyn and Bacon
Boston • London • Toronto • Sydney • Tokyo • Singapore

For Julia and Tommy

Vice President, Education: Nancy Forsyth
Marketing Manager: Kathy Hunter
Production Administrator: Marjorie Payne
Editorial Assistant: Kate Wagstaffe
Cover Administrator: Suzanne Harbison
Composition/Prepress Buyer: Linda Cox
Manufacturing Buyer: Aloka Rathnam
Editorial-Production Service: Chestnut Hill Enterprises, Inc.

Copyright © 1996 by Allyn & Bacon
A Simon & Schuster Company
Needham Heights, Massachusetts 02194

Library of Congress Cataloging-in-Publication Data

Byrnes, James P.
   Cognitive development and learning in instructional contexts /
James P. Byrnes.
     p. cm.
   Includes bibliographical references and index.
   ISBN 0–205–15950–8
   1. Educational Psychology.   2. Cognition.   3. Learning, Psychology
of.   4. Child psychology.   I. Title.
LB1051.B95
370.15′2—dc20   95-34912
                                                        CIP

Printed in the United States of America

10 9 8 7 6 5 4 3 2 1   00 99 98 97 96 95

Contents

Preface

In 1989, I developed a course at the University of Maryland called *Cognitive Development in School Contexts* in which I organized the psychological literature on reading, writing, math, science, and social studies into a developmental perspective. I wanted preservice and working teachers to see how thinking changes with age in each of these subject areas. I also wanted them to be familiar with contemporary theories of learning, higher-order thinking, and motivation. Finally, I wanted teachers to be knowledgeable about gender, ethnic, and other differences among students so that they could begin to think about why these differences exist. Because I could not find a text that covered all of these topics, I had to resort to copying bits and pieces of other texts and journal articles every time I taught this course. This process soon became too cumbersome for me and expensive for students, so I was motivated to write this book.

Goals of the Book

I want to equip teachers, parents, and students with the knowledge they need to be effective problem solvers. I say more about this in Chapter 1, but my premise is that one can only solve a learning or motivation problem is one knows the cause of this problem. Informing teachers about the inner workings of the mind is identical to teaching a car mechanic about the inner working of engines or teaching physicians about the inner workings of the body. Car mechanics need to be intimately familiar with the workings of an engine in order to know how to fix a problem when it occurs. Physicians cannot cure an ailment if they do not know how various organs and tissues work. My premise is that teachers cannot solve learning and motivation problems without knowledge of how the mind works.

Of course, there are many other students and professionals who would benefit from the information contained in this book. For example, most developmen-

v

tal psychologists are generally unfamiliar with the research that has examined cognitive development in school subjects. Thus, the present book is the perfect complement to traditional books on cognitive development, which generally do not cover academic learning. In addition, any college student or graduate student could benefit from knowing what goes on in someone's mind when they write, read, or solve problems in math or science. I think reading this book will improve a student's metacognition (i.e., knowledge of how the mind works). Knowing more about how the mind works will in turn help students know how to increase their own chances of success in school.

Scientific Basis of the Work

The view of the mind presented in this book is grounded firmly in research; that is, I have only included claims about the mind that are supported by sound, empirical studies conducted by developmental, educational, or cognitive psychologists. Too often, educators are swayed by approaches that "sound good" but are not supported by the data. At times I had to go against the prevailing consensus of the educational community because I came across studies that did not support the consensus. In most cases, however, the educational community has created important reforms based on the very research that I describe.

Acknowledgments

I have the good fortune of working in a college of education that is filled with talent. I owe intellectual debts to John Guthrie, Jamie Metsala, Judith Torney-Purta, Allan Wigfield, and Kathy Wentzel who are colleagues in my own Human Development Department. They have taught me much about reading, motivation, and social studies learning. In our Curriculum and Instruction Department, I have benefited from my discussions with the math education group (Jim Fey, Martin Johnson, Pat Campbell, Anna Graeber) and faculty in the science (John Layman, Bill Holliday) and social studies areas (Joe Cirrincione, Bruce Van Sledright). From the Department of Special Education, I have learned much from Karen Harris and Steve Graham. I also wish to thank Nancy Forsyth at Allyn & Bacon for her encouragement and for securing expert advice from the following reviewers: Karen Block, University of Pittsburg; Harold Jones, Lander University; Michael Piburn, Arizona State University; Alice Corkhill, University of Nevada Las Vegas; Robert Slavin, Johns Hopkins; Shari Tishman, Harvard University; Jay Blanchard, Arizona State University; Dale Schunk, Purdue University; and Peter Oliver, University of Hartford. Finally, I want to thank my wife Barbara for many illuminating hours of conversation about education and for her support while I wrote this book.

C h a p t e r **1**

Introduction

The goal of this introductory chapter is to give you a sense of what this book is about. To accomplish this goal, this chapter is divided into four sections. In the first section, you will be told the reasons this book was written and also learn about the diagnosis approach to problem-solving. In the second section, you will learn about two constructs that are used to organize the studies reported in this book: cognitive development and individual differences. In the third section, you will be told about the importance of developmental and individual differences in cognition. In the final section, you will be presented with the themes that emerge from nearly every chapter in this book.

Why This Book Was Written

There are four reasons this book was written:

1. To help successful students understand why they are so successful.
2. To help students who are dissatisfied with their performance in school understand how they can improve their performance.
3. To help teachers or teachers-in-training understand the nature of learning and motivation.
4. To equip individuals who look after the needs of students with the knowledge they need to evaluate current instructional practices and have a clear sense of how things should change when ineffective practices are discovered.

For the readers of this book who are interested in learning or motivation problems, this book can be thought of as either a self-help book or how-to book (depending on whether you, or someone else, is experiencing the problems related to classroom learning or motivation). The approach taken here, however, is not one in which the readers of this book will be given a series of prescriptions or recipes for success. Instead, readers will be given the information they need to effectively *diagnose* the causes of learning problems *on their own* and figure out how to solve these problems *on their own*.

To help you appreciate the utility of this diagnosis approach to problem-solving, consider the following analogy. Car mechanics would not be in business very long if they engaged in a try this/try that approach to engine repair. Usually, the same engine problem (e.g., stalling) can have two or more possible causes (e.g., insufficient air getting to the carburetor; water in the fuel line; etc.). The mechanic will be able to repair the problem only if he or she can identify which possible cause is the culprit (e.g., insufficient air) and then somehow deal with this cause (e.g., turns a screw on the carburetor, which lets in more air).

Implicit in this analogy is the idea that effective problem-solving begins with a firm understanding of the domain in question. Good car mechanics know all of the parts of the car and how these parts work. This knowledge helps them comprehend failures because they understand how things disrupt the normal functioning of the part in question. By the end of this book, you will learn a lot about the components of the mind and how these work when people learn information. This knowledge will help you understand how things can interfere with the optimal functioning of the mind and give you an idea of how to deal with these interferences.

To get a sense of some of the diagnoses that you will be able to make after reading this book, consider the following list of questions:

1. Why are some school subjects so difficult for young children to understand? Why is it that older children learn the same material more easily?
2. Why do people seem to forget so much of what they learn in school? Why do younger children forget more than older children?
3. Why are so many high school graduates unable to apply what they learned in school to the real world?
4. Why is it that not all students in the same grade learn the same material equally well?
5. Why do so many students lose their motivation to do well in school as they grow older?
6. In any given grade, why are some students more motivated than others?

Regardless of whether you are a teacher, parent, policy-maker, or student, you are probably interested in finding answers to these questions. The goal of this book is to provide the best possible answers to them. You will note that whenever this book provides an answer to one of these questions, you will be given a diagnosis.

Two Central Constructs

As a second way of coming to know the content of this book, let's next examine two central constructs that organize many of the ideas you will learn about. As the title of this book implies, the primary focus of this book is cognitive development in instructional contexts. To get a clearer understanding of this focus, we first need to define what is meant by the phrase *cognitive development*. The word *cognitive* is used to imply that we shall be focusing on mental processes such as thinking, learning, remembering, and problem solving (as opposed to other psychological constructs such as emotions, friendships, and personality traits). The word *development* is used to imply that cognitive processes *change* with age or experience (usually for the better). In sum, then, we shall be examining how cognitive processes such as thinking change with age. However, we shall limit our literature review to the research that has examined school-related learning (e.g., children's learning of math, science, and social studies). This limitation explains the second part of the title and makes this present book distinct from other cognitive development texts that devote little attention to school subjects (e.g., Flavell, Miller & Miller, 1993; Siegler, 1991).

In addition to examining developmental differences in cognitive performance, this book also examines so-called *individual differences*. To get a good sense of the meaning of this construct, it is helpful to compare it to the notion of developmental differences. When researchers examine developmental differences in performance, they usually compare the average student in a grade to the average student in another grade (e.g., the average sixth grader compared to the average third grader). By considering the average student in a grade, developmental researchers intentionally ignore differences that might exist among children in the same grade. In contrast, researchers who study individual differences try to reveal differences between one child in a grade and another child in that same grade (e.g., one sixth grader compared to another sixth grader). So, if you return to the questions posed in the first section of this chapter, you will see that whereas questions (1), (2), and (5) focus on developmental differences, questions (4) and (6) focus on individual differences. In nearly every chapter, we shall examine both developmental and individual differences in cognitive performance on school-related tasks.

Why Study Developmental and Individual Differences?

Any experienced teacher will tell you that there is no such thing as an instructional technique that works well for all students in all grade levels. There are always groups of students who benefit more from a certain technique than others. Research has consistently confirmed this experience-based conviction (Pressley et al., 1994; Snow, 1994). Similarly, successful teachers would tell you that you should not teach a topic to first graders the same way that you would teach it to sixth graders. One of the main goals of this book is to help readers understand *why* instruction has to be catered to the needs of different groups of students. Such information will not only help teachers become more flexible, adaptive problem-solvers in the classroom, but it will also help consumers of instruction (e.g., parents, students) pose counterarguments to an instructor's claim that a student's learning problems could not be due to the way a particular instructional technique was implemented because the technique is "known to work."

In addition, as Vygotsky noted a long time ago, the best way to understand the current state of a group of learners is to know where they have come from and where they seem to be going (Wertsch, 1985). An unfortunate aspect of much of the work in Educational Psychology is that researchers do not always take a developmental perspective. It can be quite informative for a high school teacher to know how his or her students used to think when they were in the sixth grade. Similarly, it can be equally useful for this teacher to think about what his or her students are capable of in time so that instruction can be geared toward moving students in that direction.

Common Themes across Chapters

The final way to provide an overview of the contents of this book is to present the issues or themes that seem to arise in almost every chapter. Four themes stand out:

1. *The contrast between rote learning and meaningful learning.* In every subject area (e.g., math, science, social studies), there are a whole host of facts to be learned and skills to be acquired. For example, students are asked to learn facts such as "$6 \times 7 = 42$" and "water is made up of hydrogen and oxygen," as well as skills such as knowing how to add fractions and knowing how to conduct a good experiment. Most educators and students recognize that these facts and skills could be learned in either a meaningless, rote way or a meaningful way. We shall see in the chapters on math, science, reading, and social studies that there is a strong push these days to engage students in meaningful as opposed to rote learning. In addition, the contrast between rote and meaningful learning plays an important role in the discussions of higher-order thinking in Chapter 3 and in discussions of memory in Chapter 4. Finally, the contrast between Thorndike's theory and other theories of learning (e.g., Schema theory) also hinges on the distinction between rote and meaningful learning (see Chapter 2).

2. *The emphasis on the constructivist view of learning.* The constructivist view of learning stands in sharp contrast to what can be called the objectivist view of learning (Cobb, Yackel & Wood, 1992; Pirie & Kieren, 1992; Stofflett, 1994; Roth, 1994). Objectivists believe that knowledge can exist outside the mind of the knower and that learning is simply the process by which this externally real knowledge is transferred rather directly to the knower's mind. In this immediate acquisition conception, there is no reason students should have trouble learning anything. Moreover, it is assumed that what students get out of a lecture or lab is what is contained in the lecture or lab (fact for fact) and that all students will acquire the same information (Pressley et al., 1994). In other words, the relationship among ideas (e.g., that between money and base-ten arithmetic) exists in real objects, is obvious, and can be immediately seen by all students.

In contrast, constructivists believe that knowledge has no existence outside someone's mind and that students always *interpret* what is presented to them using their preexisting knowledge, histories, and typical ways of perceiving and acting (Pirie & Kieren, 1992). Because students often have unique experiences and histories, constructivists expect that students will develop idiosyncratic understandings of the same material that differ from the understandings of experts in a field. For example, it is conceivable that in a class of 15 students, 15 different interpretations of the same lecture on gravity could ensue. Moreover, it is likely that each of these "alternative conceptions" of gravity would differ from that of someone who has a doctorate in physics. Finally, constructivists believe that students take what they can from a lecture or experience and use the partial understandings that are gleaned to build more complete and accurate understandings over time with repeated encounters with the same material.

The first place constructivism appears in later chapters of this book is in the discussion of Piagetian and Schema theory in Chapter 2. But constructivist themes emerge repeatedly in the chapters on math, science, social studies, and reading. It is fair to say that among leading educators in each of these fields (i.e., math educators, science educators, etc.), the constructivist approach is widely accepted and advocated. As we shall see, constructivists and objectivists teach very differently.

3. *The existence of developmental and individual differences in cognitive performance.* In addition to recognizing a recurrent emphasis on meaningful learning and constructivism, you will also see that important developmental and individual differences exist for all subject areas. In particular, you will see that certain topics or skills are quite difficult for children to learn before they have mastered other ideas first (e.g., ideas such as *rational number, freedom of speech,* or *atomic structure*). The existence of developmental differences in the ability to comprehend ideas or express a skill confirms the impression of experienced teachers that you cannot teach the same topic the same way to all different age groups.

In addition, you will see that for all subject areas, there are gender differences or ethnic differences in performance as well as motivational differences between students in the same class. Such findings support the contention that not all students benefit from standard instruction and that the needs of some students are not being met. The last chapter in this book attempts to diagnose the causes of gender and ethnic differences so that problem-solvers can get clues as to how to eliminate these differences. The other chapters report the nature and extent of these and other individual differences in specific subject areas.

4. *Student achievement is disappointing in nearly every subject area.* When one looks at national achievement data to determine the existence of developmental or individual differences in performance, it is easy to miss the point that most students perform at levels far below what is desirable. On many National Assessments of Educational Progress, for example, whereas students can score as high as 500, the top scorers on the math, science, reading, social studies, or writing tests get scores of only 350. Thus, even the top scorers (who represent only a small fraction of students and who often are high school seniors) only obtain mediocre scores. What is equally disturbing is the fact that most students score below that mediocre level. It is possible to dismiss such data based on a general suspicion of standardized tests, but something seems to be amiss when so many different types of standardized and experimenter-made tests imply low levels of knowledge and skill in many students. Moreover, even if a reader believes that scoring at the 350 level is not so bad, few would disagree with the claim that there is room for improvement in the way we teach.

In nearly every chapter, suggestions are made as to how best to teach children given what we know about the nature of the mind. It will be important to compare these suggestions to the standard approach to teaching a subject that is described in the same chapter to begin to diagnose the reasons few students attain the top levels of performance on a variety of tests.

5. *We still do not fully understand the causes of success and failure in school.* Although, as you will see, a great deal of research has been conducted with respect to children's learning of school subjects, we still have a long way to go in order to fully understand why some students succeed and others do not. Part of the reason for this slow pace of progress is that we have been applying well-founded psychological models of cognition and research to educational subject matters for just 30 years. As a result, the field of Educational Psychology is still in its infancy relative to fields such as medicine, chemistry, or physics. Moreover, every time we conduct a new experiment, the data may help us answer one question, but also causes us to ask five more. Nevertheless, the fact that it is possible to find five common themes across most chapters is quite telling, because it means that we are moving in the right direction.

As you read the rest of this book, set the goal of using the information you learn about the nature of learning and motivation to form your own diagnoses of what is right and wrong with our educational system. In addition, keep an eye out for the themes of meaningfulness, constructivism, and the importance of developmental and individual differences. Finally, come back to this chapter when you finish this book to see if you can answer the questions posed earlier.

Chapter 2

Theories of Cognitive Development and Learning

Summary

1. Thorndike described knowledge in terms of associations between situations and responses; Knowledge grows according to the laws of exercise and effect; Students are viewed more as "other regulated" than "self-regulated."

2. Piaget pioneered the notion of constructivism and described knowledge in terms of schemes, concepts, and structures; Knowledge is manifested in four levels of thought and grows through processes of abstraction, assimilation, and accommodation; equilibration is an illustration of how students adapt to the demands of the classroom.

3. Schema theorists argue that although schemata sometimes cause us to misunderstand or misremember things, they make us better problem-solvers and are helpful for categorizing, understanding, and remembering things; schemata are formed through an abstraction process and can change in response to experience; adaptive students acquire schemata and modify them based on experience.

4. Information Processing theorists posit the existence of two forms of knowledge: declarative and procedural; knowledge acquisition is described as information passing through three memory stores; adaptive students use strategies to create permanent memories and monitor their performance.

5. Vygotsky described knowledge in terms of concepts and functions; knowledge acquisition is described as a process of internalizing the words and actions of teachers, parents, and more competent peers; adaptive students use egocentric speech and inner speech to help themselves stay on track.

6. Three themes emerge from the theories: practice is important; learning should be meaningful; and the knowledge children bring to the classroom can greatly affect what they learn.

Over the last 100 years, many theories of cognitive development and learning have been proposed. We obviously cannot examine all of these views, so we need to limit the selection in some way. Given the goals of this book, we shall examine only those theories that have shaped contemporary research in the areas of math learning, scientific reasoning, social studies learning, reading comprehension, or writing. By *shaped* it is meant that educational researchers have recently used the theories to (a) interpret developmental or individual differences among students or (b) design new experiments.

The two requirements that the theories be educationally relevant and currently driving research limit the selection to just four theories. Two of these theories are associated with individuals (Piaget, Vygotsky) and two represent groups of researchers who share certain assumptions about the nature of the mind (Information Processing theory, Schema theory). For contrastive purposes, we shall also examine Thorndike's theory to see how the newer approaches differ from older approaches. The theories shall be presented in an order that largely mirrors the order in which they historically influenced educational researchers: Thorndike, Piaget, Schema theory, Information Processing theory, and Vygotsky.

For each of the five theories, we shall see how it provides answers to four questions:

1. *The "Nature of Knowledge" Question*: What form does knowledge take in a student's mind?
2. *The "Learning and Knowledge Growth" Question*: How do students acquire knowledge and skills?
3. *The "Self-regulation" Question*: How do students help themselves stay on track and adapt to the demands of the classroom?
4. *The "Educational Applications" Question*: How might the theory explain student successes and failures or help teachers provide more effective forms of instruction?

After all theories have been presented, the themes that are common to all approaches will be described.

Thorndike's Theory

Although Thorndike's (1913) classic theory is out of favor (and has been since at least the 1960s), it is still useful to examine it for two reasons: (a) many teachers seem to implicitly rely on Thorndike's principles when they teach, and (b) many contemporary theories can explain aspects of learning that Thorndike's theory cannot explain. By comparing the newer approaches to Thorndike's view, we get a better sense of the value of the newer approaches.

In what follows, Thorndike's theory shall be summarized in four subsections. Each subsection corresponds to one of the four questions listed earlier.

The Nature of Knowledge

What form does knowledge take in a student's mind? If we could somehow open up a student's head and "see" his or her knowledge, what would it look like? Thorndike felt that all knowledge consisted of a network of associative *bonds* between situations and responses. Some examples of pairings between situations and responses are shown in Table 2.1.

TABLE 2.1   Thorndike's Theory: Examples of Situation-Response Pairings

Situation 1: A student is in Mrs. Jones's classroom with his classmates; Mrs. Jones says, "3 × 3 = ?" (with rising intonation)
Response 1: The student responds, "9!"

Situation 2: A student is in the first seat of a row; Mr. Johnson says, "Class, this is your seat work for today," as he hands a pile of papers to the student.
Response 2: The student takes one and passes the pile to the student behind her.

Situation 3: A student is walking home and approaches a crosswalk. She looks up and sees that the traffic light is red.
Response 3: She stands at the corner and does not try to cross.

Thorndike assumed that a student's brain could encode and store mental traces of individual aspects of a situation (e.g., the blackboard, the desks, the teacher, etc., in Situation 1). When these aspects are perceived, they activate the mental traces corresponding to them. The mental traces in turn are collectively associated with a specific response. When the association is fully formed, every time a student is in Situation 1, he or she responds with Response 1. Every time the student is in Situation 2, he or she responds with Response 2 (not Response 1 or 3).

Thorndike felt that associations were realized in the brain by way of connections among neurons. In particular, he felt that there were neurons corresponding to perceived aspects of the situation and other neurons corresponding to responses. When an association is created, these two groups of neurons (one group for the situation and one for the response) become connected to each other through an additional neuronal pathway. Thorndike's connectionism is the forerunner to modern day connectionism (see Chapter 5 for a description of modern connectionism).

For Thorndike, all knowledge, no matter how complex, consisted of associative bonds between situations and responses. Thus, whether we are talking about answering a question with a simple multiplication fact or solving calculus word problems, students know what to do or say in a given situation by virtue of having a response (e.g., a formula for a derivative) associated with that situation (e.g., seeing a calculus word problem).

Learning and Knowledge Growth

How do students acquire knowledge as Thorndike described it? Thorndike proposed two main laws of associative learning: the law of exercise and the law of effect. These laws can be paraphrased as follows:

- *The Law of Exercise*: The bond between a situation and a response increases in strength every time the situation and response co-occur in close spatio-temporal proximity.

- *The Law of Effect*: The bond between a situation and response gets "stamped in" (i.e., dramatically increased and "hard-wired" in the brain) when the response is followed by a satisfying state of affairs; when it is followed by an annoying state of affairs, it is "stamped out."

The strength of an associate bond refers to the speed and regularity with which a response comes to mind when a student is in a particular situation. For example, a weak bond would be in evidence when nothing comes to mind when the teacher says, "$3 \times 3 = ?$" in Situation 1 (see Table 2.1). Similarly, if the response "9" comes to the student's mind on only three out of the ten days in which the teacher asks the question, we would have further evidence of a weak bond.

Self-regulation

How do students help themselves stay on track and adapt to the demands of the classroom? Thorndike did not have much to stay about how students regulate themselves as much as how *teachers* can regulate students. You may have noticed a strong resemblance between Thorndike's views and those of B. F. Skinner. Thorndike preceded Skinner in time, and Skinner used Thorndike's theory as a starting point for his own.

Nevertheless, Thorndike believed that forming associative bonds through repetition and rewards was part of our natural equipment as animals. Adaptation consisted of developing a repertoire of responses that lead to positive things and eliminating responses that could bring about harm. Thus, adaptive students increase responses that yield reinforcement and decrease responses that yield punishment.

Educational Applications

Thorndike wrote several books in the areas of educational psychology and arithmetic learning. Given his two laws of learning, he had two main suggestions for teachers:

1. Use lots of repetition in order to build up associate bonds between situations and responses (e.g., flashcards, choral responding, etc.).
2. Be sure to follow correct responses with rewards (e.g., stickers, praise) and incorrect responses with punishments (e.g., low grades, public corrections).

There are many teachers who even today rely heavily on rote repetition and reward systems to build up factual knowledge in their students. As we will see later in this chapter and throughout the rest of this book, many people dispute the idea that students should engage in large amounts of fact-learning when they are in school.

Piaget's Theory

During the 1960s and early 1970s, Piaget's theory was the dominant theory of cognitive development in the fields of developmental psychology and education. Whereas interest in and acceptance of Piagetian theory has decreased sharply since that time for developmental psychologists, a number of educational researchers still advocate many of Piaget's views. Let's examine how Piaget would answer our four questions.

The Nature of Knowledge

What form does knowledge take for Piaget? When Piaget referred to children's knowledge, he used one of three terms: scheme (plural = schemata), concept, and structure. A *scheme* can be either physical or mental and may be described as actions or processes that are used repeatedly by a child to attain goals or solve problems (Piaget, 1952). An example of a physical scheme would be the "grasping" scheme that infants use to pick up and familiarize themselves with the physical properties of objects (e.g., Is it hard? Does it make noise? etc.). An example of a mental scheme would be the "isolation of variables" scheme (see Chapter 9) that adolescents use to figure out such things as what factors cause a pendulum to swing fast or slow (e.g., Is it the length of the string? Is it how hard I push?).

Schemata are enduring action sequences that a child or adolescent uses across a wide range of objects and situations. In describing this quality, Piaget (1952) said that schemata are "transposable" and "generalizable." Thus, an infant might use the grasping scheme in two completely different situations involving two completely different objects for the very same purpose: to see what the objects are like. The tendency to use schemes across situations makes them different from the singular, situation-bound responses described by Thorndike. A second important difference concerns the fact that whereas schemata are used to accomplish goals, Thorndike's responses are not linked to goals.

In addition to studying the role of schemes in development, Piaget also focused on a variety of *concepts* such as time, space, causality, number, conservation, and classes (i.e., categories of things such as *dog* and *triangle*). Concepts differ from schemata in that concepts are not goal-directed procedures as much as forms of understanding that involve *relations* among things or aspects of things (Byrnes, 1992). For example, the concept of time involves understanding the relation between speed and distance (Piaget, 1969). Causality involves understanding the relation between causes and effects (Piaget & Garcia, 1974). Classes involve both the membership relation between things and the categories to which they belong (e.g., Rover is a dog) and the class-inclusion relation between one category and another (e.g., dogs are kinds of animals) (Inhelder & Piaget, 1964).

For Piaget, a second difference between schemata and concepts concerns the fact that whereas children at all age levels possess schemata of one form or another (physical or mental), only older children, adolescents, and adults possess concepts. Concepts are formed by way of abstraction across different objects and situations. For example, the category of dog describes what is true of all dogs despite subtle differences in appearance or differences in location. Similarly, the five-minute disparity between 12:05 and 12:10 is true for all clocks not just some clocks. This disparity is also identical to the disparity between 12:13 and 12:18. Finally, the number five is an abstraction across all sets of objects that have five objects in them no matter what these objects look like or where they can be found. For Piaget, the abstraction process takes some time and requires lots of experience with objects in many situations. It is for this reason that Piaget argued that concepts emerge slowly over time. In his studies, he found "true" concepts (as he defined them) only in older children, adolescents, and adults.

This emphasis on the abstract and relational quality of concepts makes for another difference between the views of Piaget and Thorndike. Whereas Piaget spoke of many different types of mental relations (e.g., "before/after"; "in front of/behind"; "caused/not caused"; "greater than/less than"; "is a kind of"; etc.), Thorndike spoke of only one kind: associations. For Piaget, temporal, spatial, causal, numerical, and categorical relations are imposed on the world of objects by children in order to imbue it with meaning (i.e., make it make sense). Associations are devoid of meaning.

Besides *scheme* and *concept*, the third term that Piaget used to describe knowledge was *structure*. A structure is something that has both form and content (Piaget, 1970). The form of a knowledge structure is the organization of ideas (Byrnes, 1992). Piaget endeavored to show how many different knowledge domains have the same form (i.e., organization) despite having different content. For example, the class-inclusion relation can be found in domains as different as biology ("the pancreas is an organ . . . "), math ("a square is a parallelogram . . . "), and social studies ("a republic is a form of government . . . "). Piaget liked to describe such recurrent structures using formulas. For the class-inclusion relation, he used the formula "$A + A' = B$" where A stands for a subordinate class (e.g., "pancreas"), B stands for the superordinate class (e.g., organ) and A' stands for the rest of the subordinate categories that make up the superordinate class (e.g., all other organs besides the pancreas).

Learning and Knowledge Growth

How do students acquire schemata and concepts? When Piaget first started out in the 1920s, there were only two possible explanations of where knowledge comes from: empiricism and nativism. *Empiricists* such as philosopher John Locke and psychologist Edward Thorndike believed that people's minds are "blank slates" when they are born. Their natural biological endowment allows them to form associations between things that they perceive through their senses. Thus, most empiricists are happy with Thorndike's two laws of association for explaining how students acquire knowledge. The world has a natural regularity to it that imposes itself on our minds (e.g., the day-night cycle of the day). Thus, we would develop a concept of time by merely observing the cycles of days, months, seasons, and so forth (Byrnes, 1992).

Nativism is the polar opposite of empiricism. Nativists such as Immanuel Kant and Noam Chomsky believe that the world is not terribly regular or organized. As a result, concepts cannot be acquired through exposure to the world. Nativists suggest instead that many important concepts such as causality, time, space, number, and linguistic concepts (e.g., *verb*) are inborn. No one teaches these ideas to children; they are present at birth in a fully formed state or unfold with maturation. Thus, just as a child naturally goes through puberty, he or she just naturally develops sophisticated ideas. We are born with these ideas in order that we might impose them on the world and make sense of stimulation that makes no inherent sense.

After much reflection, Piaget found problems with both empiricism and nativism. As a result, he created a third alternative: *constructivism*. He agreed with the nativistic view that people have concepts that they impose on the world to make sense of it but disagreed with the belief that these ideas were inborn. He agreed with the empiricist view that the world has a certain regularity and structure to it that children come to know through experience but disagreed with the idea that concepts are learned immediately through exposure to the world. His middle-ground stance was that exposure to the world and children's activities cause them to create mental precursors to more fully developed ideas. He felt that children's minds take these precursor components and build more sophisticated ideas out of them (Piaget & Inhelder, 1969).

For example, when children are born, they lack voluntary control over their arm and hand movements. Everything is reflexive. Soon, however, they gain some voluntary control and begin creating grasping and pushing schemes out of reflexes (hence, reflexes serve as precursors to the schemes). Early on, the grasping and pushing schemes are not interconnected. By around eight to twelve months, however, a child who wants an attractive toy hidden behind a barrier can combine the grasping and pushing scheme together in order to retrieve the toy. Children are not born with this knowledge of how to put the two schemes together, nor can they be taught this earlier in the first year even though they have the two schemes. Children *themselves* think of putting the two schemes together to attain a goal (i.e., get the toy). Later on, the act of counting objects will serve as a precursor to the mathematical idea of sets, and grouping actions will serve as a precursor to mental addition and subtraction. Still later, children will combine addition and subtraction together with the insight that subtraction is the opposite of addition.

Perhaps an analogy will help clarify the differences between empiricism, nativism, and constructivism. Imagine that a student's knowledge is like a brick wall. Each brick is a piece of information that is interconnected to other pieces of information. Empiricists think that a child's mind is merely a receptacle for a teacher who builds the wall inside the child's head. As they teach something, they metaphorically lay another brick in just the right spot. In contrast, nativists think that the wall is already built when children are born. All teachers do is help students turn inward and see what they already know. Or, they can wait for the wall to build up by itself much as we stand back and watch a child grow taller.

Constructivists think that teachers do provide the bricks, but they merely toss them to students who try to lay the bricks themselves. Sometimes students do not understand a brick, so they drop it or lay it in the wrong place. Sometimes they have not built the wall up high enough to be able to lay a certain kind of brick (e.g., a really abstract idea).

A problem with empiricism is that it is cannot explain student misunderstandings. If a teacher explains things properly, there is nothing that would interfere with the brick's being properly laid in a student's mind. Moreover, ideas could be learned at any age in a fairly direct manner. In contrast, nativism can account for children's failure to understand by saying that certain ideas have not unfolded yet. However, nativists cannot explain interesting errors on the part of children in which they seem to put existing ideas together on their own in a creative way. Moreover, nativism cannot explain misconceptions and distortions in fully mature individuals (i.e., adults).

Piaget's theory can explain the slow progression of understanding that we find with many educational concepts as well as misconceptions. He used the notion of *assimilation* to describe the process of a student taking some experience or piece of information and finding a home for it in his or her existing knowledge structure (i.e., finding a spot in the wall for a brick that was just tossed). Sometimes an idea is so discrepant from what a child believes that it cannot be assimilated. He used the notion of *accommodation* to describe the process of changing the existing configuration of knowledge in order that the troublesome idea can be assimilated (Piaget, 1952).

To illustrate assimilation and accommodation, let's examine a few examples. Young preschoolers who are driving at night with their parents often think that the moon is following them (it certainly looks that way). The physics of the explanation is too abstract for them to comprehend, so they could not assimilate this explanation if it were provided. Ultimately, this knowledge of the physical world will change enough that they will understand such ideas (see Chapter 9). Similarly, somewhat older students think that numbers are positive amounts derived from counting. The idea that numbers can be negative quantities or various configurations of components (e.g., 3 = 1, 1 & 1; 1 & 2; 2 & 1; 3 & 0; etc.) is discrepant from their current ideas so such ideas are not easily assimilated (see Chapter 8). Eventually, children can grasp such ideas because their knowledge has accommodated.

Piaget argued that confronting discrepant ideas is absolutely essential for knowledge growth (Piaget, 1980). If children never had experiences or heard information that contradicted the erroneous ideas they construct by themselves, they would never develop the correct conceptions. Thus, the readiness idea of waiting until a child's mind matures enough is actually an implication of nativism, not Piaget's constructivism.

Moreover, Piaget argued that assimilation and accommodation work in opposition to each other. When we assimilate something, our mind metaphorically says, "The current organization and accuracy of my ideas is fine. Find a place for this new information somewhere." When we accommodate, our mind says, "The current organization is not fine. Reorganize things and create new space." You cannot keep things the same and change them at the same time. Thus, only one of assimilation or accommodation wins out in a given situation. This battle between these processes means that change in children's misconceptions can be frustratingly slow for teachers. Once again, empiricists cannot explain the slow change in wrong ideas. When the battle is resolved over some idea (Piaget called this resolution *equilibration*), children's understanding usually moves to a higher plane, a higher level of insight. It often becomes more abstract as well. For example, in order for a child to come to understand that dogs and people are both animals, they have to change their concept of *animal* in such a way that it is more abstract (e.g., "a living thing that can move itself" from "furry four-legged things").

When he conducted his experiments with many children ranging from infants to adolescents, Piaget observed that children's experience and the process of equilibration seemed to promote the emergence of four levels of thought: the sensorimotor level, the preoperational level, the concrete operational level, and the formal operational level. Each level is characterized by how children view the world.

When the world is viewed from the standpoint of *sensorimotor* thinking (birth to about 18 months of age), things are understood with respect to what actions can be performed on them. For example, a bottle, a toy, and a finger are all the same because they are suckables. In addition, sensorimotor thinking is limited to the here-and-now. Children who can reason only at the sensorimotor level (e.g., infants or severely retarded older students) cannot think about the past or things that might happen in the future. They simply perceive things in current view and try to use a physical scheme to interact with these things.

After physical schemes have been repeated many times to attain goals, children's minds form abstract, mental versions of these schemes. As a result, children can imagine themselves doing something before they do it. Once children can think in this representational way, they have moved into the *preoperations* level (beginning around 18 to 24 months of age). In addition to being able to imagine future events, children can also think about things that happened to them in the past. Thus, preoperational children are freed from the here-and-now.

Although preoperational thinking is more advanced and more adaptive than sensorimotor thought, it is limited in four ways. First, it has overly strong ties to perception, perceptual similarity, and spatial relations. For example, my daughter, when she was three, believed that a family exists only when the family members hug. When they are spatially separated, the family no longer exists. Similarly, many preschoolers think that an arrangement of five pennies spread out in a row contains more pennies than a pile of five pennies.

When they mentally group things, preschoolers rely heavily on perceptual similarity. For example, they think that dogs and horses are both "doggies" and that goldfish and whales are both "fishies." Grouping things by perceptual similarity, of course, is not a good idea because few categories are defined this way. Do we define the category of *doctor* by how doctors look? How about *country, dictator, polynomial,* or *acid?* Most categories in fields such as science, mathematics, and social studies are defined in a nonperceptual, abstract way. As a result, these categories can be hard for preschoolers to grasp.

The second limitation of preoperational thinking is that it is *unidimensional*; that is, they can think about only one aspect of something at a time. For example, when they are asked to sort objects into categories, they use just one dimension (e.g., big versus small) rather than multiple dimensions (e.g., size and color). In addition to studies of categorization, Piaget revealed unidimensionality in his many studies of conservation. In his classic beaker task, for example, preschoolers attended only to the height of the glasses and not the width in judging which of two glasses has more juice in it. It is easy to show how many concepts in school are multidimensional (e.g., the definition of a square or a republic), so this second limitation would cause problems for students if it persisted after preschool. The tendency to focus on just one dimension has been called *centration* (Piaget & Inhelder, 1969).

The third limitation of preoperational thought is that it is *irreversible*; that is, preschoolers often cannot mentally imagine something that has just been done (e.g., a ball of clay being rolled into a sausage) being undone (e.g., the sausage being rolled back into a ball). Piaget likened this limitation to a movie projector that cannot play movies in reverse. Again, most subjects in school contain ideas that involve reversibility. In math, for example, we have the fact that addition is the opposite of subtraction and that –5 is the opposite of 5. In history classes, it is common to speculate whether some trend could ever be reversed (e.g., Russian citizens going back to repressive communism after tasting freedom and capitalism).

The fourth limitation of preoperational thinking is that children *have difficulty distinguishing between reality and fantasy*. For example, they sometimes have difficulty telling the difference between real people and TV characters (so do many soap opera fans).

These four limitations of preoperational thinking are overcome when children develop the concrete operational mode of thought around age five or six. In particular, concrete operational children are no longer limited to using perceptual similarity when they group things. However, although children can understand somewhat more abstract properties, these properties still must be something one can point to or concretely describe (e.g., *warm-blooded* for *mammals*). In addition to going beyond mere perceptual similarity, concrete operational children also do not confuse spatial arrangements with actual quantities (e.g., a squashed clay ball has the same amount of clay as a ball that has been rolled into a sausage). In addition, children can think about two dimensions at once and can also mentally undo a real event that has happened. Finally, concrete operational children do not confuse reality with fantasy. In fact, they are overly concerned with the way things are.

In some cultures, thinking that is (a) freed from perceptual relations, (b) reversible, (c) two dimensional, and (d) realistic would be sufficient for full adaptation to that culture. In our culture, however, we apparently need more than that. For example, many things in school require comprehension of more than two dimensions and the ability to go beyond reality to think about hypothetical possibilities (e.g., Would the Vietnam war have ended earlier if Kennedy had not be assassinated?). Moreover, some ideas cannot be defined by pointing to something or using concrete descriptions (e.g., the fourth dimension, conservatism, the limit of a function, etc.). Students who can think about multiple dimensions, hypothetical possibilities, and abstract properties have entered Piaget's *formal operations* level of thinking (begins usually around age ten or 11).

The idea that children are limited to a particular type of thought when they are in a particular age range has prompted many researchers to criticize Piaget's theory and conduct a number of studies to refute the notion of stages (see Brainerd, 1978). Children have been shown to grasp ideas earlier than Piaget found and many studies show that students rarely demonstrate the same level of thought (e.g., concrete operations) across a range of tasks. Thus, most of us are preoperational for some topics (e.g., computers), concrete operational for others (e.g., economics), and formal operational for others (e.g., math). These and other problems with the theory led many psychologists to lose interest in Piaget's theory.

Self-regulation

How do students help themselves stay on track and adapt to the demands of the classroom? For Piaget, the mind is naturally predisposed toward self-regulation (or "auto-regulation" as he called it). In particular, he felt that it is maladaptive for the mind to be out of sync with reality. When students try out an idea on the world and find that it is wrong, it is natural for their minds to modify this idea so that it becomes more in line with reality. This tendency for the mind to be self-modifying and self-correcting is, of course, what Piaget had in mind when he described the relation between assimilation and accommodation. Piaget (1952) wrote that the mind's tendency to be adaptive is embodied in the form of equilibration.

To see the adaptive value of the schemata and concepts that Piaget described, consider what would happen if (a) a 16-year-old understood numbers the way a five-year-old does; (b) an adult could not tell the difference between things that are caused and things that happen by chance; and (c) a three-year-old did not understand that things continue to exist even when they are not in view. Concepts such as these are fundamental to reality. No one could survive in our culture without them.

Educational Applications

The applications of Piaget's theory to educational practice can be stated in the form of two principles:

> *Principle 1*: In order for students to create mental structures, they must first internalize action schemes by repeatedly performing them to attain a goal.

This principle derives from Piaget's views about how preoperational thought arises out of the internalization of sensorimotor schemes. It implies that if a teacher wants students to be able to read silently or perform mental computations, they need lots of practice performing these actions overtly to reach a goal.

Principle 2: Thinking at each developmental level has unique features to take into consideration when designing educational programs.

Preoperational thought is unidimensional, irreversible, and based on a mixture of concrete reality and fantasy. Concrete operational thought is two-dimensional, reversible, and exclusively based in concrete reality. Formal operational thought is multidimensional, reversible, and can function in both concrete reality and hypothetical possibilities. In making a decision regarding when and how to present some topic, teachers can ask three questions: (1) how many dimensions or issues do students have to consider at once? (2) Does understanding the topic require reversible thought or an understanding of opposites? (3) Are there things I can point to in order to illustrate the idea sufficiently? If a topic seems to require a certain level of thought (e.g., concrete operations), teachers can use the ages of their students for a rough guess as to whether students would be capable of understanding this topic. For example, between age five and nine, children are generally limited to concrete operations. If the topic requires formal operations, teachers may elect to present it when students are about eight or nine in order to challenge their thinking and promote growth. In addition, teachers should distill precursory ideas from the topic, which could be grasped and ultimately put together by students. For example, to help students be able to understand algebraic functions later, a teacher could have them form charts in which one value (e.g., the height a ball is dropped) is paired with another (e.g., the height it bounces). Over time, children will get a sense of systematic links between values.

Schema Theory

About the same time that Piaget's theory began to decline in popularity (i.e., the early 1970s), researchers began to gain interest in Schema theory. Psychologists liked the interesting memory distortions that Schema theory could explain. Educational researchers found Schema theory to be extremely useful for explaining such things as reading comprehension and scientific thinking. Let's now see how Schema theorists would answer our four questions.

The Nature of Knowledge

What form does knowledge take in a student's mind? As might be inferred from its name, Schema theory posits the existence of knowledge structures called *schemata* (singular = schema). Schemata come in two forms: one type for objects (e.g., a schema for *dog* or *house*) and another type for events. The latter have been commonly called *scripts* (e.g., a restaurant script or a birthday party script; Nelson, 1986). Regardless of whether we are talking about objects or events, a schema can be defined as a mental representation of what all instances of something have in common. For example, your house schema represents what is common to all of the houses that you have been in and your restaurant script represents what is the typical sequence of events when you have gone to a restaurant (Anderson, 1990; Smith, 1989). To illustrate these notions, Table 2.2 presents the contents of many people's schemata for houses and restaurants.

The House schema shown in Table 2.2 is depicted using the slot-filler convention. Here, "slots" such as "parts" specify the values that the object has on various attributes (e.g., values = wood, brick, and stone). An alternate and, perhaps, more popular way of depicting someone's knowledge (especially among educational researchers) is to use the node-link format. Figure 2.1 provides a node-link depiction of the "House" schema. The node-link convention is useful because it shows the relations among ideas. Each relation is depicted with an arrow (e.g., the "is-a" link for the superset relation) and each idea is represented by an oval (the node for "house").

Schemata serve four functions in your mind. First, they *categorize* your experiences (Smith, 1989). Creating categories makes for a more efficient use of your memory capacity than storing each individual experience that you have as a separate memory. To see this, assume that there are exactly 10,000 types of things in the world (e.g., dogs, cats, trees, people, restaurants, etc.) and that you have personally encountered 100 instances of each type of thing (e.g., 100 different dogs in your lifetime). That would make for one million separate, specific, and unrelated memories. If your mind were a filing cabinet, you would have one million separate folders for each experience. In contrast, if you categorized things as you

TABLE 2.2   Contents of Most People's "House" Schema and "Restaurant" Script

"House" Schema
    Superset: building
    Parts: rooms
    Materials: wood, brick, stone
    Function: human dwelling
    Shape: rectilinear, triangular
    Size: 100–10,000 sq. ft.

Restaurant Script
    Enter → give reservation name → be seated → order drinks → look at menu → discuss menu → order meal → talk → eat salad or soup → eat food → order dessert → eat dessert → pay bill → leave tip → leave

The "house" schema comes from Anderson (1990); the "restaurant" script comes from college student responses in Bower, Black & Turner (1979).

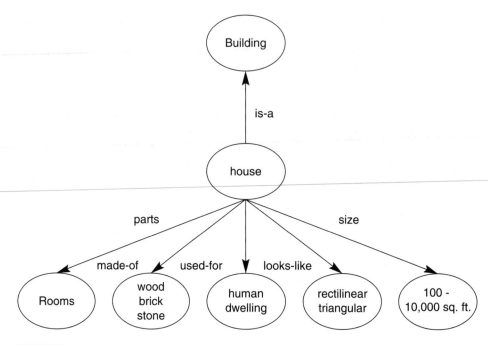

FIGURE 2.1

encountered them (e.g., "Here's another dog") your experiences would be grouped together in far fewer folders (i.e., 10,000) that could be searched more quickly for relevant information (e.g., a single folder for all of your encounters with dogs).

But schemata improve the efficiency of memory in another way as well. Instead of storing all details of an experience (much the way a videotape does), a schema is more like a sheet of paper that contains your notes about the experience. You write down only what was common to an experience with a specific object (e.g., what happened with Rover) and other previous experiences with the same type of object (e.g., what happened with Spot, Fido, and Fifi). All other details are lost and, therefore, do not use up space in your memory.

The other advantage of categorizing things is that your mind sets up expectations (Smith & Medin, 1981). When you have a category for dogs for example, you do not say, "Oh, what's that?" when you encounter a dog (expressing surprise and wariness about an unknown thing). Your mind says, "Oh, it's just another dog. He'll probably wag his tail or bark." Similarly, people who have a well-established restaurant script do not get intimidated and confused when they enter a restaurant, because their script tells them what to expect and what to do when certain things happen (e.g., expect a host or hostess to give you a menu; see Table 2.2).

The categorizing function of schemata is very much related to two other roles they play in the mind: helping us to *remember* and *comprehend* things. When you create a schema for something and attach a label to it (e.g., *dogs*), you can retrieve what you know about this type of thing using the label. Using the label or hearing someone else use it is like having a label on a folder in your mental filing cabinet that you can use to find and pull out the folder pertaining to that type of thing to see what you know about it. Similarly, other aspects of the thing that are stored in memory (e.g., what it looks like, its parts, etc.) can be used to retrieve the entire schema. For example, if you see a wagging tail under a friend's kitchen table, you retrieve your dog schema based on that clue.

By *comprehension*, it is meant that you understand what is going on. As we shall see in Chapter 6, schemata help us understand what is happening in a story and what to expect next. When an author writes, "Mary heard a croaking sound under the bush. She picked the small creature up and felt its bumpy skin . . . ,"we use our schema for *frog* (as well as those for *bush, creature*, etc.) to form a mental representation of what just happened in the story. People who have croaks and bumpy skin as part of their frog schema would know immediately that the character found a frog under the bush.

In addition to helping us to categorize, remember, and comprehend our experiences, schemata are also an important constituent of our *problem-solving* ability. In elementary school, children are presented with four main types of arithmetic word problems (Riley, Greeno & Heller, 1983). After solving many individual problems of each type, children are said to form a schema for that type. Similarly, in high school algebra and physics classes, students encounter repeated cases of the same types of problems and likewise form schemata for these problems (Clement, 1982; Mayer, 1982). Schemata help students know what to do when they encounter specific problems much the way schemata help people know what to do when they enter a restaurant (see Chapters 8 and 9 for details). Table 2.3 lists three instances of the same type of problem as well as a schema that might form for this type of problem.

TABLE 2.3   A Schema for the Same Type of Word Problem

Individual Problems
1. John had three apples. Mary gave him two more. How many does he have now?
   Solution: Add John's amount to Mary's
2. Bill had two hats. Charley gave him three more. How many does he have now?
   Solution: Add Bill's amount to Charley's
3. Jessica has three brothers and sisters. Her mom just had a baby. How many brothers and sisters does she have now?
   Solution: Add the two amounts together

A Schema for Them
   Person 1 has a certain amount of things. Person 2 gives Person 1 a certain amount more. How many does Person 1 have now?
   Solution: Add the two amounts together

Learning and Knowledge Growth

How do students acquire knowledge according to Schema theorists? There are three ways to answer this question. The first involves explaining how schemata are formed in the first place. The second involves explaining how existing schemata affect the storage of incoming stimulation. The third involves describing three types of schematic change.

Schemata are said to be formed through the process of *abstraction* (Adams, 1990; Hintzman, 1986). As alluded to earlier, children find themselves in multiple situations involving the same object. For example, the first time that a child sees a vacuum cleaner, it might be when her mom vacuums her family room. The next time it might be Dad using it in her bedroom. The next time it might be Grandma at Grandma's house. Over time, what is retained in her vacuum cleaner schema will be just those aspects of the experience that are common to all situations involving it. She will see that it does not matter who uses it, what room it is used in, what color it is, or what shape it has. What is common is the fact that it is used to clean rugs and that it makes a characteristic noise. The latter information will make up her schema for the object.

The emphasis on abstraction makes Schema theory simultaneously similar to Piaget's theory and distinct from Thorndike's theory. In particular, whereas Thorndike emphasized highly specific memory traces for specific situations, Piaget and Schema theorists argue that specific details are lost when schemata and concepts are formed. Schema theory is also similar to Piaget's theory in its emphasis on meaningful relationships among ideas (the links in a node-link structure) and constructivism (Paris, 1978). However, Schema theory is distinct from Piagetian theory because it does not emphasize the existence of stages, levels of understanding, or levels of abstraction.

Once formed, schemata affect what is remembered about an experience through three processes: selection, gist-extraction, and interpretation (after Alba & Hasher, 1982). As mentioned earlier, a major tenet of Schema theory is that the mind does not encode and store all aspects of an experience. Rather, it uses schemata to *select* just those aspects of the situation that are schema-relevant. At a baseball game, for example, you will not remember every single aspect of the experience (i.e., all of the sights and sounds at the park); you will remember only those aspects of the experience that are consistent with your baseball game script (e.g., who won, important plays, etc.). Similarly, students will not remember all aspects of a class (e.g., the tie Mr. Nelson had on during his history class); they will remember only those aspects that are consistent with their script for that teacher's typical class (e.g., the normal sequence of events that happen during Mr. Nelson's fourth period history class).

Those aspects of the experience that are selectively encoded and stored are initially specific, accurate, and verbatim traces of those aspects. For example, on any given day, Mr. Nelson's students may use their script for his class to expect that he will end the class for that day as he usually does: by telling them about the quiz for the next day. This expectation causes students to selectively attend to his description of the quiz (and not attend to his earlier, atypical description of a TV show that he watched). After he informs them about the quiz, his words are stored in their verbatim form.

Soon, however, the second process of *gist-extraction* begins. During gist-extraction, Mr. Nelson's exact wording (i.e., the verbatim trace) is replaced by the gist of what he said. For example, if Mr. Nelson actually said, "The quiz will cover the sections of the chapter that describe the accomplishments of Louis XIV and XV," the gist-extraction process might leave a student with the memory that they had to read sections about two kings.

Together, the processes of selection and gist-extraction mean that it would be hard for someone to give an accurate and detailed description of some experience. They could give only a short account of generally what happened. If true, these limitations on memory mean that people could not be very reliable witnesses in trials. Unless they are interviewed almost immediately after they witness a crime, it would be impossible for them to give an accurate description of details such as what people were wearing, what color car they drove, and what exactly was said.

These memory problems could be further compounded by the third process affecting what is retained from an experience: *interpretation*. As alluded to earlier, schemata help the comprehension process by filling in things that are not said or seen. For example, the lines above about Mary do not say that she picked up a frog, but people would nevertheless *infer* that she did. Similarly, if you read the lines, "She spoke to the manager about the meat prices," you might infer that the woman was complaining that the prices were too high. Although inferences are important to the comprehension process, they are merely probabilistic and could be incorrect. Returning to the legal aspects again, consider the situation in which you saw man and a woman interacting in front of a parked car. What behaviors would lead you to infer that they were together or knew each other? What would lead you to infer they were unacquainted and that the man might be bothering the woman? If the woman were attacked and you were later questioned by the police about what you saw, you might say, "They seemed to know each other." Such a statement might lead the police to limit their pool of suspects to someone who knew the victim. Note, however, that your inference might be incorrect.

This emphasis on distorted, nonveridical memories has recently prompted many psychologists to lose interest in Schema theory. Studies show that people are quite capable of accurate, verbatim recall when they put their mind to it (Alba & Hasher, 1982). Moreover, other studies show that sometimes people do not make extremely obvious inferences (Schacter, 1989). Thus, whereas Schema theory can account for some aspects of memory, categorization, and comprehension, it cannot account for all aspects of learning.

So far we have answered the learning and knowledge growth question by considering how schemata are formed and the three processes that affect your memory of experiences (i.e., selection, gist-extraction, and interpretation). We now turn to the issue of how schemata change. Rumelhart (1984) proposed that schemata are modified by one of three processes: accretion, tuning, or restructuring. Both *accretion* and *tuning* involve modifying an existing schema so that it becomes more flexible. Tuning involves a somewhat larger structural change than accretion. An example of accretion would be adding the value *adobe* to the materials slot in the house schema (see Table 2.2). In simply adding values, you should note that the basic structure of the schema stays the same.

An example of tuning would be adding a new slot to an existing schema. For example, let's say that early in life you did not have the slot for size in your house schema. Over time, however, you realized that there are many different kinds of buildings besides houses and that the size of these buildings is one clue that helps you determine what kind of building it is. In response to this environmental feedback, you add the slot for size to your house schema.

In contrast to accretion and tuning which basically modify portions of existing structures, *restructuring* involves more substantial changes. One such change would be a wholesale modification of the basic relations that make up a schema. Another would be the process of creating entirely new schemata by way of making analogies to old schemata. A good illustration of the former process is the shift from preoperational categories (based on perceptual similarity) to concrete operational categories (use of more abstract features). When this occurs, all of the slots that would make up a preoperational schema for something would be replaced by entirely different slots. A good example of the second type of restructuring would be the case of a college student who transfers to a new university. This student could use his or her script for registering for courses in the former university to create one for registering for courses in the new university.

Self-regulation

How do students help themselves stay on track and adapt to the demands of the classroom? Schema theorists have not had much to say about self-regulation except to say that successful problem-solvers have a large repertoire of flexible, accurate schemata. It can be presumed that they would say that adaptive (i.e., successful) students are more likely to develop such schemata in response to feedback than maladaptive (i.e., unsuccessful) students. But again, it is quite adaptive for individuals to create schemata, because they help reduce the surprise value of the world and equip an individual with ready-made responses that do not require a great deal of reflection.

Educational Applications

There are three main implications of Schema theory for educational practice:

1. Teachers should view learning as the acquisition and modification of schemata rather than as the acquisition of rote-learned, isolated facts. To form schemata, teachers should present multiple instances of something (e.g., a word problem) and have students identify the common features of the instances. To form scripts, teachers should have students experience the same type of event and have them abstract commonalities across these events.

2. Teachers should expect that without various study aids (e.g., notes), students will sometimes retain only a small, selective portion of an experience or lesson; they might also elaborate or distort what they have retained using inferences.

3. Meaningful learning occurs when students can incorporate new information into an existing schema or when they can create new schemata by way of analogy to old schemata; To facilitate these processes, teachers should evoke appropriate schemata before presenting a topic in lecture or before students read about the topic. If the topic is new and students lack a schema for the material, teachers can use *advance organizers* to promote analogical reasoning (Mayer, 1979). An advance organizer is a short introductory statement that details the similarities between a new topic and a topic that students already know. For example, a science teacher can use a row of dominoes to illustrate how electricity passes through a wire. Similarly, a social studies teacher can use the American Congress as an example to help students understand the British Parliament.

Information Processing Theory

Information Processing theory began to influence educational researchers around the same time that Schema theory did (i.e., the mid 1970s) and continues to influence their thinking now. Here's how Information Processing theorists would answer our four questions:

The Nature of Knowledge

What form does knowledge take in a student's mind? Information processing theory has its roots in the field of Artificial Intelligence (AI). Over the last 40 years, AI researchers have endeavored to create computer systems to simulate human cognitive skills (e.g., mental computations, language comprehension, chess playing, etc.) and have equipped these computer systems with two main types of knowledge structures: one that models human *declarative knowledge* (e.g., Collins & Loftus, 1975; Newell & Simon, 1972) and another that models human *procedural knowledge* (Newell & Simon, 1972). Declarative knowledge or "knowing that" is a compilation of facts such as "a bird can fly," "triangles have three sides," and "Harrisburg is the capital of Pennsylvania." Procedural knowledge or "knowing how to" is a compilation of linear action sequences that people perform to attain goals. Examples of procedural knowledge include knowing how to tie shoes, knowing how to write the alphabet, knowing how to count, knowing how to drive, and so forth. This dichotomy between facts and actions is similar to Piaget's distinction between concepts and schemes, as well as to the distinction in Schema theory between schemata for objects and schemata for events.

On computers, declarative knowledge has been modeled using *semantic nets* (also called *propositional networks* because facts are often stated in the form of propositions such as "birds have feathers."). A semantic net is a node-link structure similar to that shown in Figure 2.1, which specifies the relations among facts. In most models, the relations among ideas are associative in nature. The more often you encounter a fact such as "birds have feathers," the stronger the associative bond between the constituents *birds* and *feathers* becomes. The label *semantic* is used because words (e.g., bird) are often associated to facts and these facts give meaning to the words.

Procedural knowledge has been modeled using *productions*. In its original form (e.g., Newell & Simon, 1972), a production was an if-then statement that linked an action to certain antecedent conditions. Usually these antecedent conditions specify two things: some state of the environment and the goals of the individual. Some examples of productions would be:

1. *Condition:* IF (the numbers are fractions) AND (the goal is to add), THEN
2. *Action:*   (use the least common denominator).
3. *Condition:* IF (the shoe is on) AND (the goal is to tie it), THEN
4. *Action:*   (make two loops and . . .).

Productions are said to "fire" when the conditions described in the IF part are met (e.g., the person perceives $\frac{1}{2} + \frac{1}{4}$ and has the goal of wanting to add these fractions). The speed and regularity with which productions fire depends on the strength of an associative bond between conditions and actions. Information Processing theorists call a set of productions a production system.

The discerning reader will recognize a strong similarity between productions and Thorndike's description of situation-response pairs. The difference between situation-response pairs and productions is that the latter often include more general notions (e.g., concepts such as *fractions*) as well as goals (Singly & Anderson, 1989).

Before moving on to the issue of learning and knowledge growth, it is important to note that not all researchers who align themselves with Information Processing theory think that semantic nets and production systems are good models of human knowledge. Some think that all knowledge is procedural and suggest dropping declarative knowledge (Winograd, 1975). Others prefer to use flowcharts and rules to describe performance rather than use productions (Siegler, 1991). Still others spend most of their time describing important skills and processes (e.g., intelligence, analogical reasoning) and only occasionally focus on the nature of knowledge (Sternberg, 1985). Thus, the issues of (a) whether we have one or two kinds of knowledge and (b) how best to model knowledge, have yet to be resolved.

Learning and Knowledge Growth

How do students acquire this knowledge? At the heart of Information Processing theory is an account of how information from the environment becomes stored in memory. The most influential model of this storage process was originally proposed by Atkinson and Shiffrin in 1968. In this model, human memory is conceived of as three *stores*. Information (i.e., stimulation in the environment) is said to pass first through the *sensory store*, then through the *short term store*, and finally ends up in the *long term store*. These stores are characterized by structural features such as how much information they can hold (*capacity*) and how long they can hold it (Siegler, 1991).

When stimulation is detected by sensory receptors, it gets into the sensory store in the form of an *icon*. To get a sense of a visual icon, stare briefly at an object and close your eyes. You will see an image of this object with your eyes closed. Note, however, how quickly it fades. Experiments have shown that the capacity of the sensory store is not terribly large. For example, when a 12-item matrix is flashed, subjects only retain about 40 percent of the items. It has also been found that icons will form even for stimuli that are exposed for only $1/_{20}$ of a second (Siegler, 1991).

Icons, however, will last only for one second, unless you attend to them (Atkinson & Shiffrin, 1968). *Attention* causes information in the sensory store to be passed along to the short-term store. The size of the average person's short-term memory has been determined to be a fixed capacity of seven chunks of information. Thus, when presented with seven pieces or less of information (e.g., seven shopping items, a phone number, etc.), people are able to retain all items. If more than seven items are presented, some of the items will not enter the short-term store and will, therefore, be forgotten.

The term *chunk* does not refer to just a single piece of information. Rather, it can refer to a meaningful grouping of items. Thus, whereas the list of eight numbers—1 7 9 4 2 8 6 5 0—requires eight chunks, the list of eight letters—N I N E T E E N—requires only one chunk because these eight letters make up a single meaningful grouping. In essence, by grouping the items in any long list into meaningful clusters, one reduces the number of short-term memory chunks required to retain this information.

If nothing is done to the information in short term memory within 15 to 30 seconds, it will be lost or forgotten (Siegler, 1991). For example, if someone tells you his or her phone number, you will probably forget it in 15 seconds unless you do something else. Clearly, phone numbers and most of the information presented in school are important to remember for longer than 15 seconds. Ideally, one would like to get information into one's longterm memory because storage is permanent there. In order for information to pass from the short-term memory to the long-term memory, it is typically necessary to use a memory *strategy*. What would you do in the case of a phone number? Probably rehearse it over and over. Using a strategy like rehearsal is like pressing the *save* button on a personal computer. One's short term memory is like a computer's buffer, which temporarily holds textual information and puts it on the screen while you work on it. One's long-term memory is like a floppy diskette or a hard disk. Once information is written on them by the save function, it is there permanently. The experience of forgetting really indicates that you are having a problem of *retrieval* (i.e., getting information out of long-term memory); it does not indicate that there has been a genuine decay or loss of information.

Besides the assumption of permanence, Information Processing theorists make two other assumptions about long-term memory. First, they assume that unlike the short-term memory, the capacity of the long-term memory is unlimited. That is, a person's long-term memory will never run out of space. Second, they believe that information about objects is held in a fragmentary way. For example, information such as the name of an object (how it sounds, how to spell it), what the object looks like, the kind of thing it is, and so on are all held in separate places in long-term memory. This assumption explains the tip-of-the-tongue phenomenon in which one can recall only portions of some information (Siegler, 1991).

Thus, *learning* for Information Processing theorists is all about attending to information in the environment and using strategies to transfer it from short-term storage to long-term storage. As we shall see in the next chapter, children become more skilled at using their attentional and strategic capacities as they grow older. In effect, they become more efficient and effective information processors with age. These increased skills help them overcome the processing limitations imposed by the sensory store and short-term store so that they gain knowledge more quickly and efficiently than younger children.

Having answered both the "nature of knowledge" and "learning and knowledge growth" questions, we are now in a position of seeing how the answers to these questions interface. The statement that people have declarative and procedural knowledge really means that they store factual knowledge and procedures in long-term memory. Both kinds of knowledge get into long-term memory by way of memory strategies such as rehearsal. The more often information is rehearsed, the stronger the associative bonds between individual segments of knowledge.

Self-regulation

How do students help themselves stay on track and adapt to the demands of the classroom? Information Processing theorists would answer this question by appealing to two aspects of performance: *strategies* and *cognitive monitoring* (Brown, Ferrara, Bransford & Campione, 1983; Flavell, Miller & Miller, 1993; Pressley, Borkowski & Schneider, 1987). Strategies are actions that you perform to attain goals. Two examples of strategies would be (a) using rehearsal to learn a set of vocabulary words and (b) writing a summary of a chapter to make sure that you have all of the main points. Cognitive monitoring involves processes such as deciding which strategies you will use to attain a goal (rehearsal or something else?), monitoring how well things are going as you make your way toward the goal (Am I learning this stuff? Do I understand?), and then evaluating how things went after you reach your goal (Could I have learned this a better way?). To see the difference between strategies and cognitive monitoring, consider the following manufacturing example. A strategy is like a worker who tries to make something and cognitive monitoring is like a supervisor who picks a worker for a certain job, tells the worker what to make, wanders by to see how the worker is doing, and then inspects the product after the worker is finished.

We need strategies because the world throws more information at us than our memories can handle. That is, we frequently experience information overload. Strategies help us retain far more information than we would without them. But we could not acquire, use, or switch strategies without having the ability to plan, monitor, and evaluate our performance. That is why true adaptation to the world requires both strategies and cognitive monitoring.

Educational Applications

Information Processing theory has two main implications for educational practice:

1. Teachers need to recognize that students are naturally limited in the amount of information they can process and remember. One way to circumvent their capacity limitations is to divide information into smaller segments and give them ample time to learn the segments. A second way would be to provide explicit strategy instruction (see Chapter 3). A third way is to organize individual pieces of information so that groups of these items will form chunks.
2. Building up a large repertoire of declarative and procedural knowledge that can be easily accessed requires lots of exposure and practice. Teachers should provide these opportunities for their students.

Vygotsky's Theory

Vygotsky was a Russian psychologist who conducted his most important work during the 1920s and 1930s. Because behaviorism dominated American psychology until the late 1950s, however, Americans did not learn of his ideas until about 1962. Overshadowed first by Piaget's theory and then by Information Processing theory, it was not until interest in both of these theories started to wane (i.e., the late 1970s) that a large number of psychologists and educational researchers used Vygotsky's theory to study learning. Let's see how Vygotsky would answer our four questions.

The Nature of Knowledge

What form does knowledge take in a student's mind? In his writings, Vygotksy (1962, 1978) referred to two kinds of cognitive entities: *concepts* and *functions*. Though we have seen from Piaget's work that there are many different types of concepts (e.g., time, space, causality, etc.), Vygotsky limited himself to studying the type of concepts known as categories. A concept, for Vygotsky, was a class of things that had a label (e.g., *square*) and could be defined by a set of criteria (e.g., four sides, equal sides, etc.). In his view, a child demonstrated a mature understanding of a concept when he or she (a) seemed to know all of the defining criteria for that concept (e.g., four sides, equal sides, etc. for squares) and (b) understood that the word for the concept (e.g., *square*) is arbitrary and conventional (Vygotsky, 1962). Children who demonstrated a mature understanding of many categories were said to comprehend "true" concepts (also called *scientific concepts* by Vygotsky).

In his studies, Vygotsky found that children did not seem to understand "true" concepts until early adolescence. Prior to that time, children only seemed to be capable of lower-level *pseudoconcepts* and so-called *spontaneous concepts*. A pseudoconcept is in evidence when a child can use the label for the concept correctly (e.g., uses *square* to refer to squares) but seems to be unaware of the defining criteria. A spontaneous concept is a concept constructed by a child that is largely based on his or her own experience. Thus, the definition of *dog* might include criteria such as "brown with white spots" and *grandmother* might include the criteria "has a soft lap" (Vygotsky, 1978).

In contrast to the idiosyncratic, personalized quality of spontaneous concepts, true concepts are marked by their generality. This generality derives from the fact that true concepts are defined in an abstract and context-independent way. For example, unlike the words *that* or *him,* which often mean different things in different contexts (e.g., *him* could mean Bill in one context and Fred in another), concepts such as *atom, democracy, fraction,* and so forth are defined in ways that make the specifics of contexts irrelevant. For example, the definition of *democracy* is meant to apply to all democracies, not just one that someone happens to be talking about in a particular context. The discerning reader will note that in emphasizing the abstract character of true concepts, Vygotksy is similar to Piaget and Schema theorists. He was, moreover, one of the first people to criticize Thorndike's view that knowledge consists of nonabstract situation-response pairs.

Besides concepts, Vygotsky was also interested in the development of five main cognitive functions: language, thinking, perception, attention, and memory. He did not, however, describe the nature of these functions in any great detail. Instead, he described them briefly using examples and tried to show how success in problem-solving and memory tasks depended on the *integration* of one or more of these functions in development. For example, when confronted with the task of obtaining a treat from a cabinet that was out of reach, Vygotsky found that successful children used language to plan a strategy and talk themselves through to solution. In Vygotsky's mind, they combined the language, perception, and attention functions together.

Vygotsky (1978) felt that the integrations involving language were particularly important because they separated us from lower animal species. When an animal tries to solve a problem, it relies on genetically determined responses or on responses that have been reinforced by the environment. Its decisions are either under the control of genetic predispositions or of stimuli in the environment. When humans solve problems, in contrast, they can use their language skills to invent new strategies or get ideas from other humans. The language function, then, helps humans break the stimulus-response cycle and gain control over the environment. In Vygotsky's mind, symbols in language mediate between stimuli and responses.

Learning and Knowledge Growth

How do students acquire knowledge and skills? Vygotsky and his followers have answered this question in three ways. First, they assumed that the tendency to use symbols (e.g., speech) during problem-solving is something that children acquire by way of social interaction. Vygotsky (1978, p. 57) argued that "Every function in the child's cultural development appears twice: first on the social level, and later on the individual level; first *between* people (*interpsychological*) and then *inside* the child (*intrapsychological*)." So, for example, prior to a child's using verbal rehearsal to learn a list of vocabulary words, something analogous to verbal rehearsal must have occurred between the child and a teacher or parent (e.g., a teacher helping a class to rehearse information).

It is important to note, however, that children do not merely imitate the actions of a teacher and immediately employ symbols and signs in their problem-solving behavior. Vygotsky (1978, p. 46) argued that ". . . *sign-using activity in children is neither simply invented nor passed down by adults*; rather, it arises from something that is originally not a sign operation and becomes one only after a series of *qualitative* transformations."

The second answer pertains to concept development. For Vygotskians, one of the primary goals of instruction is to change children's spontaneous concepts into their scientific counterparts. Vygotsky noted, however, that this shift may take many years to accomplish because children do not give up their spontaneous concepts that easily. Using a description quite similar to Piaget's constructivist account of assimilation and accommodation, Vygotsky argued that after instruction, spontaneous concepts "grow up" and scientific concepts "grow down"; that is, spontaneous concepts give children an intellectual foothold to which they can partially assimilate a scientific definition. Over time, grappling with a scientific concept causes their spontaneous concepts to become ever more accurate, general, and abstract.

Both the first and second answers to the "learning and knowledge growth" question show the necessity of adult intervention in children's thinking. Vygotsky argued that without adults modeling symbolically mediated problem-solving or providing instruction on scientific concepts, children's thinking would remain in a lower-level state. Vygotsky's stance differs from Piaget's in this regard because Piaget suggested that children invent many ideas on their own.

The third answer, which also entails social interaction, appeals to the notion of the *zone of proximal development*. According to Vygotsky, intellectual skills are progressively mastered by children. When they first learn a skill (e.g., reading), they make many errors and rely heavily on teachers for corrective advice. After large amounts of practice and feedback from teachers, however, children ultimately reach a point at which they can perform the skill well on their own. In between the absolute-novice level and the complete-mastery level, there is a point at which a child could perform well if someone were to give him or her just a little help (e.g., a hint). For Vygotsky (1978, p. 86), the zone of proximal development is ". . . the distance between the actual developmental level as determined by independent problem solving and the level of potential development as determined through problem solving under adult guidance or in collaboration with more capable peers."

Teachers and peers foster intellectual growth by providing instruction within a student's zone of proximal development. Some of Vygotsky's followers (e.g., Wood, Bruner & Ross, 1976) have used the notion of *scaffolding* to describe how teachers and more capable peers lend a hand to students to help them advance to the next level of performance. Scaffolds are those structures that masons climb on to lay higher and higher layers of bricks. When we described Piaget's theory, we used the analogy of children being masons. Whereas Piaget felt that teachers were needed merely to toss bricks to students, Vygotsky implied that without teachers and peers acting as scaffolds, students would be unable to climb up and lay higher levels of knowledge.

Self-regulation

How do students keep themselves on track and adapt to the demands of the classroom? Vygotksy answered this question by describing three components of the language function: communicative speech, egocentric speech, and inner speech. *Communicative speech* and *egocentric speech* are both forms of "external" speech that we can hear children using. As the name implies, communicative speech is that form of speech the child uses in order to communicate with someone else. Egocentric speech, in contrast, is speech to oneself. *Inner speech* is the internalized version of egocentric speech.

Vygotsky argued that the function of egocentric and inner speech is to focus your attention and guide your own behavior. You may find yourself using egocentric speech in situations such as when you are going to the store and ask a friend if he or she needs anything. When you are at the store, you engage in egocentric speech when you say, "Let's see, what did she want me to pick up?" Or, when you are first learning something (e.g., driving a stick shift car), you might say "Okay, to back up you push it this way." Vygotsky found that children used egocentric speech the most when they were performing a hard task and adults were not present to help.

Educational Applications

Vygotsky's theory has four main educational implications:

1. Teachers should act as scaffolds in which they provide just enough guidance so as to help children make progress on their own. For example, instead of intrusively telling a child how to solve a problem step-by-step, a teacher should do such things as start problems and ask children to finish them, or give hints that help students discover a solution on their own.

2. Instruction should always "be in advance" of a child's current level of mastery. That is, teachers should teach within a child's zone of proximal development. If material is presented at or below the mastery level, there will be no growth. If it is presented well beyond the zone, children will be confused and frustrated.

3. In order for children to internalize a skill, instruction should progress in four phases. In the first phase, teachers should model the skill and give a verbal commentary regarding what they are doing and why. In the second phase, students should try to imitate what the teacher has done (including the verbal commentary). Early on, children will perform poorly, so teachers need to give verbal feedback and correct errors. In the third phase, teachers should progressively fade from the scene as children gain more and more mastery over the skill. Palincsar & Brown (1984) used this technique to teach children four reading strategies and were highly successful. They called their approach *reciprocal teaching*. To the standard Vygotskian approach, they added the element of teachers and students repeatedly taking turns. Everyone would take a turn playing the teacher until everyone reached mastery. That way, students got sufficient practice to internalize the skill and they also got to see the teacher model expert behavior multiple times.

4. Children need to be repeatedly confronted with scientific conceptions in order for their spontaneous concepts to become more accurate and general. According to Vygotksy, all fields (i.e., math, science, social studies, the arts, etc.) have scientific concepts, not just science, so this implication is true for all subject areas.

Common Themes

Though the five theories differ, there were three issues that most emphasized in one way or another. First, all five theories emphasized the role of practice and repetition. For Thorndike and Information Processing theorists, practice increased the strength of associative bonds. For Piaget, Schema theorists, and Vygotsky, practice helps students internalize skills and form abstractions. Second, three theories emphasized the fact that knowledge consists of meaningful relations (Piaget, Schema theory, Information Processing theory). Third, three theories emphasized the constructive nature of learning (Piaget, Schema theory, Vygotsky). That is, children interpret reality and instruction; they do not merely internalize it.

Chapter *3*

Memory

Summary

1. The major components of the human memory system include sensory buffers, rehearsal systems, records, cues, working memory, and permanent memory.

2. The process of creating permanent memories or records is called encoding; encoding can involve simple repetition or elaboration (i.e., the imposition of meaningful relations to embellish what we are experiencing). When experiences are elaborated, they are processed more deeply.

3. Memories can be easy to retrieve (high strength) or hard to retrieve (low strength); one important factor that affects the strength or retrievability of a memory is practice.

4. There are three main ways to retrieve a memory: recall, recognition, and inferential reconstruction.

5. There are three main views of forgetting: decay theory, interference theory, and loss of retrieval cues theory. Decay theory places a heavy emphasis on the passage of time and lack of practice as reasons for memory failures; the other two place greater emphasis on the strength of the connection between cues and stored memories.

6. Various memory strategies work because they involve practice, the imposition of meaningful relations, and visual imagery; People only use strategies when they realize the need for and value of these strategies.

7. Younger children remember far less than older children and adults because the former (a) use strategies less, (b) are less likely to see the need for strategies, (c) have less knowledge, and (d) process information less quickly than the latter.

Although the focus of the previous chapter was on learning (i.e., how information gets into our minds), we often touched upon issues involving memory (i.e., how we remember what we learned). In this chapter, we will focus mostly on memory, though we will often touch upon issues involving learning as well. It turns out that learning and memory are inextricably intertwined, because what we remember about some information is often a function of how we learned that information in the first place (Brown et al., 1983).

The present chapter is divided into five sections. In the first, the components of the human memory system will be described. The goal of the first section is to give you a sense of how we are able to retain information in memory. In the second section, you will learn about the opposite of retention, namely, forgetting. In the third section, you will learn about things you can do to increase the chances that you will remember information (i.e., memory strategies). In the fourth section, you learn why older children remember things better than younger children. In the fifth and final section, the instructional implications of the research on memory will be drawn.

The Nature of Human Memory

The human memory system is described below in two phases. First we shall consider the basic components of this system and then we will consider the main processes that occur within these components.

Components of the Memory System

The question "How does our memory work?" is analogous to the question "How does a car engine work?" The most helpful answer to either question is one that describes the parts of the system (e.g., "The engine consists of a battery, carburetor, . . ."). The key elements of our memory system include: sensory buffers, rehearsal systems, records, cues, working memory, and permanent memory. Let's examine each of these components in turn.

Sensory Buffers

When we experience something (e.g., go to a party, attend a lecture, read a book, etc.), our sensory detectors (located in our eyes, ears, noses, tongues, and skin) and the perceptual systems corresponding to these detectors (located in our brains) register this stimulation, interpret it, and retain it for a brief period. The visual system, for example, retains (or echoes) visual patterns for only about one second and the auditory system retains speechlike patterns for only about two to three seconds (Anderson, 1990, 1995). To get a sense of this phenomenon, look at the matrix of numbers below, close your eyes, and say as many as you can remember seeing:

2	9	3	7
5	1	6	4
8	2	5	3

If you are like most people, you probably registered all of the numbers in the matrix but were unable to name them all because the image of the matrix seemed to fade by about one second.

The sensory buffer is useful in that it retains stimulation long enough that your mind can interpret it (e.g., "I see a cat"; "I hear music"), but it would not be very good if we could retain our experiences only for one second. At the very least, students would retain nothing from lectures and would fail every exam they take. Fortunately, our memory system includes other components and processes besides sensory buffers.

Rehearsal Systems

If someone told you a phone number and you could not write it down, what would you do? If you are like most people, you would probably say the number over and over to yourself. Each time you do, the number stays alive for another two to three seconds. If you wanted to remember a visual pattern instead of an auditory pattern (e.g., where some office was located in a building; what something looked like), you would probably revisualize it to yourself over and over. In each case, you are using a particular sensory system as a rehearsal system (Anderson, 1995). Based on the work of Alan Baddeley (e.g., Baddeley, 1990) we now call the system for rehearsing verbal information the *phonological loop* and the system for rehearsing visual or spatial information the *visuo-spatial sketch pad*.

At one time, we used to think that the phonological loop had a fixed capacity of between five and nine units (e.g., "the magic number 7"; Miller, 1956). Thus, if someone has a span of, say, seven units and heard someone else call out six letters, she could recall all six of them. Similarly, if this person heard someone call out 12 letters, she would probably fail to remember about five of them. These days, we recognize that it is not the number of items per se that influences what we recall, it is how many we can *rehearse* before the sensory trace for each item fades that matters. For example, since we can say *wit, sum, harm, bag, top* in two seconds, we could recall all five of these words if they were called out. However, we typically cannot say *university, opportunity, expository, participation, auditorium* in two seconds, so we would probably recall only about two or three of these words (Baddeley, 1990).

Baddeley likens the process of rehearsal to that of a circus performer spinning plates. Each time we rehearse, we "spin the plate" for that item of information to keep it going. If we have many items (e.g., 12) or items that take a lot of time to spin (e.g., five-syllable words), the plates for those items will stop before we can keep them going. A plate stopping is analogous to a sensory trace fading.

Records

A prominent cognitive psychologist named John Anderson uses the term *record* to refer to a mental representation of an item of information that we store permanently in our memory (Anderson, 1995). In Anderson's view, when we say that someone knows a lot of things, we are really saying that he or she has many records in his or her memory. You have records for such things as your middle name, the town in which you were born, what the answer to "2 + 2" is, and so on.

Over the years, researchers have learned three important things about records. First, we have records corresponding to two types of knowledge: declarative and procedural (Anderson, 1983; 1995; Squire, 1987). Your *declarative knowledge* or "know that" is a compilation of all of the facts you know. Often, declarative knowledge can be stated in the form of *propositions* and, as such, some researchers contend that our records corresponding to declarative knowledge are propositional in nature (e.g., Kintsch, 1974). A proposition is an assertion that can be either true or false (e.g., Harrisburg is the capital of Pennsylvania; there are three cups in a quart). Many studies have shown that declarative knowledge exists in the form of associative networks such as those described in Chapter 2 in the section on Schema theory. In such networks, there are central notions (e.g., *bird*) that are connected associatively to facts you know about the central notion (e.g., can fly; lays eggs; etc.).

Your *procedural knowledge* or "knowing how to" is a compilation of all of the skills you know. You probably have records for tying your shoes, performing arithmetic, riding a bike, using a word processing package, frying an egg, and so forth. Unlike declarative knowledge, in which ideas are interconnected in a network, studies have shown that procedures do not seem to form an associative network among themselves (Anderson, 1993).

Although many psychologists dispute the idea that we need to posit declarative and procedural knowledge (see Winograd, 1975), brain research has supported the distinction. In particular, certain brain injuries impair the person's ability to retrieve declarative knowledge (e.g., names such as *stickshift, steering wheel*, etc.) while leaving his or her procedural knowledge intact (e.g., being able to drive). Similarly, brain injuries in some other part of the brain may impair procedural knowledge while leaving declarative knowledge intact (Squire, 1987).

Besides recognizing that there are two types of records (declarative and procedural), the second thing researchers have learned about records is that they can be stored in two types of *codes* or formats: visual or verbal (Anderson, 1995; Paivio, 1971). For example, your declarative knowledge that German shepherds have pointy ears could be stored as a mental image of what these dogs look like, or stored as the factual proposition "German shepherds have pointy ears." Similarly, your procedural knowledge of how to fry an egg might be stored as a nonverbal sequence of imagined actions or as a verbalized set of instructions (e.g., "First, turn on the burner. Next, put butter in the pan . . .").

Third, researchers have developed two constructs to explain why we have an easier time remembering some things instead of others: strength and activation level (Anderson, 1990; 1995). The *strength* of a record is the degree to which it can be retrieved from memory and made available to consciousness. High-strength records are well-learned facts or procedures that come easily to mind when you try to remember them (e.g., your middle name; how to tie your shoe). Low-strength records are facts or procedures that you have not learned as well and are difficult to recall (e.g., remembering certain presidents or dates; remembering how to factor an equation). Many studies have shown that the amount of *practice* that you engage in affects the strength of a record. Generally speaking, skills or facts that are practiced regularly attain higher levels of strength than skills or facts that are not practiced to the same degree. We'll consider strength again later in the section on forgetting.

The *activation level* of a record corresponds to its current degree of availability. Making a record sufficiently active to the point that you can think about it is analogous to using a fishing pole to lift a fish close enough to the surface that you can see it. This analogy implies that records need to attain a certain threshold value of activity in order that you have the experience of remembering something.

Records that are in a high state of activation are, then, conscious and available. Records that are in a low state of activation are not quite conscious or available (Anderson, 1990; 1995). Readers familiar with word processing packages know the process of retrieving a document from a floppy diskette or hard drive. Some packages require you to highlight the title of a paper and then press *1* to retrieve it (some ask you to merely click it with a mouse). When it comes up on the screen, you have made your paper available for inspection and revision. Hence, you have put your paper in a high state of activation. When it is just sitting there on the diskette, it is in a low state of activation. The human mind is such that when you press *1* to retrieve a memory (e.g., who wrote *Death of a Salesman?*), sometimes the memory record comes up on your mental screen and sometimes it does not. High-strength items come up quickly and right away. Low-strength items do not.

Putting strength and activation together, then, we can say that whereas activation level has to do with the current state of a record, strength has to do with the potential to be activated. High-strength records are easier to make highly active (i.e., available to consciousness) than low-strength records.

Research has shown that when a given record is activated, the activation of this record can spread to other records associated with it. For example, consider the case in someone has records associated in the following way: the record for Lincoln is associated to both the record for president and the record for Civil War. When he or she hears the word *Lincoln*, two things happen. First, the record for Lincoln becomes more active than it was. Second, some of the activation of the Lincoln record spreads to the records for president and Civil War. The results of some memory experiments suggest that activation spreads out throughout an associative network of records and becomes weaker the farther it travels along the network. If Lincoln is only remotely associated with Robert E. Lee, but immediately associated with Civil War, the record for the latter will receive greater indirect activation than the record for the former.

Cues

Cues are things in the environment or items in a rehearsal system that are connected to records. More specifically, cues can cause records to shift from being in a state of low activation to a state of higher activation. If the level of activation is high enough, the record is available to consciousness. For example, if you read the question "Who wrote *Death of a Salesman?*" each of the words in this question (e.g., *death, salesman*) could serve as a cue if it is associated with the record of the author. Or, an additional cue might be the prompt "Arthur ——— wrote *Death of a Salesman*".

When you repeat a question to yourself, the cues are no longer in the environment but are now items in a rehearsal system. Using our fishing analogy again, cues are like the rod, reel, and bait. When we cast cues, they sometimes help us pull up a record and make it highly active. Using our word processing analogy, perceiving a cue is like pressing the *1* to retrieve a document.

Working Memory and Permanent Memory

Working memory is a concept used to refer to any information that is currently available for working on a problem (Anderson, 1995). Thus, items in the sensory buffers or rehearsal systems are in working memory as are permanent records that are in a highly active state. *Working memory* is a concept that has replaced the notion of *short-term memory* in contemporary cognitive psychology.

We have already seen how information in sensory buffers can fade within a few seconds. Moreover, there is no guarantee that information that is in a rehearsal system will be turned into a permanent record (see Main Processes section below). In addition, records that are in a highly active state can easily return to a state of low activation if a person is distracted or stops thinking about the idea. It is for this reason that working memory is considered to be a form of *transient* memory (Anderson, 1995).

In contrast, permanent memory pertains to our storehouse of records. At one time, we used to call permanent memory long-term memory and call working memory short-term memory based on several classic models of memory (e.g., Atkinson & Shiffrin, 1968). These models have proved to be somewhat incorrect and misleading, so many cognitive psychologists no longer use the terms associated with them.

Summary

The main components of the human memory system include sensory buffers, rehearsal systems, records, cues, working memory, and permanent memory. Returning to our car example, these components are analogous to engine parts such as carburetor, battery, and so on. Having described the main parts of our memory engine, we can now examine important processes that take place within these parts.

Main Processes of the Memory System

Having described the main parts of the memory system, we can now turn to a more dynamic description of the operations or sequence of events that take place within this system of parts. Some of these processes relate to the initial formation of records and some relate to retrieving them from permanent memory. Let's examine these two sets of processes in turn.

Forming Permanent Records

Researchers have examined three main processes related to getting information into permanent memory: encoding, rehearsal, and elaboration. *Encoding* is the general term for the process of taking sensory information and transforming it into a permanent record. Said another way, encoding is the process of forming a mental representation of something we experience (Anderson, 1995; Newell & Simon, 1972; Siegler, 1991). Rather than being photographic or complete, encoding is viewed by theorists from a variety of perspectives as being *selective* and *interpretive*. By selective, it is meant that records include only certain aspects of an experience. By interpretive, it is meant that our orientation toward stimulation determines how we encode it. A good example of this phenomenon is how viewers of a presidential debate often think that their candidate won the debate.

Rehearsal is a process that we described above when we examined rehearsal systems. It is the process of repeating or reexperiencing some stimulation over and over. Thus, repeating a phone number over and over is an example of rehearsal. There is a large body of literature that shows that repetition and practice determine the strength of a record. In fact, researchers recently revealed the existence of the *power law of learning* (Anderson, 1995; Newell & Rosenbloom, 1981) that can be stated as such:

Strength = Practice[b]

This is an exponential equation, which means that learners improve their recall the most during the first few study trials. After that point, they can still increase the strength of a record, but the increases will not be so much. For example, if a student studies the material for a test for ten straight days, he or she might recall only 40 percent of the material if tested after the first study day, but 80 to 90 percent of the material if tested after the second study day. Between the third and tenth days, the student might increase from 90 to 95 percent, but note how the increase during the last eight days of 5 percent is much less than the 40 to 50 percent increase between the first and second days.

The fairly straightfoward implication of the power law of learning is that teachers should do whatever they can to increase the strength of permanent records through practice. By increasing strength, a record becomes more easily accessed.

The third process related to forming a record, *elaborating* pertains to the process of going beyond the information given and embellishing a raw experience with additional details. For example, if you read the sentence, "The boy was crying," you could encode the sentence in a fairly impoverished way or embellish your encoding somewhat. We can represent the impoverished encoding using the graphic convention:

Boy

crying

Or, we could ask ourselves questions such as "Who is this boy?" "Why is he crying?" As will be explained more fully in the chapters on reading (Chapters 5 and 6), the minds of skilled readers usually ask such questions automatically. When they do, readers make inferences such as "It is a little boy who fell." Such an inference would modify the impoverished encoding to be:

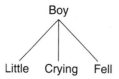

As we saw in the previous chapter in the section on Schema theory, such embellishments may make it hard for students to remember what they actually saw and what they inferred. Thus, a reader might falsely recognize the sentence "The little boy was crying because he fell" as the one they read earlier.

Some researchers have put the notions of encoding and elaborating together to form the construct of *depth of processing* (Anderson, 1995; Craik & Lockhart, 1972). In this view, any experience can be encoded shallowly or deeply. To see this, imagine that you are in class listening to someone with a very unusual accent. When the speaker says something like, "Einstein may have been dyslexic," you may pay little attention to the meaning of this sentence and focus mostly on the person's strange way of pronouncing the words. If so, you have processed this sentence shallowly. On the other hand, if you try to understand the meaning of the sentence, make inferences, and relate the information to what you already know, you have processed it more deeply. Studies show that students have better retention of material when they process information deeply (e.g., Benton, Glover, Monkowski & Shaughnessy, 1983; McDaniel, Einstein, Dunay, & Cobb, 1986).

To get students to process information deeply, teachers can ask questions that encourage them to think more about it. For example, after reading the second amendment to the U.S. Constitution ("A well regulated militia, being necessary to the security of a free State, the right of the people to keep and bear arms, shall not be infringed"), a teacher could ask a question that requires students to process the information either shallowly (e.g., "What right does the Constitution provide regarding guns?") or more deeply (e.g., "Why did the authors of the Constitution think it was necessary to give people the right to bear arms?").

Retrieving Records from Permanent Memory

Creating permanent records by way of encoding, rehearsal, or elaboration is not all there is to remembering information. Even after you put information into memory, you still have the task of getting it out. To get a sense of this problem, note that putting an important paper in your desk drawer is not the only thing you have to do to be able to find it later. Putting it in the drawer is only helpful if (a) doing this helps you remember where it is (e.g., because you always put papers there) and (b) the paper is easy to find once you start looking in the drawer. If you randomly toss it into a disorganized mass of other papers, it may take you a while to find it. If we thought of our minds as such desk drawers, we would have similar difficulty retrieving a record if care was not taken with respect to storing an experience.

There are three main ways we retrieve information from permanent memory: recall, recognition, and inferential reconstruction. *Recall* is the process that is involved when you are presented with cues and you try to retrieve information associated with the cues (Flavell, Miller & Miller, 1993). For example, if on a test a student is asked, "Who was the third president of the United States?" the cues *third* and *president* could prompt him to retrieve the name Thomas Jefferson from permanent memory. Similarly, someone's face might serve as a cue for his or her name.

Recognition is the process involved when you see, hear, smell, touch, or taste something and have the feeling that you encountered this sight, sound, smell, feeling, or taste before. In this case, you are matching a stored representation of something to the real thing in the world (Flavell et al., 1993). For example, a student might have the fact that Thomas Jefferson was the third president of the United States stored as a permanent record. When presented with the item "Jefferson was the third president" on a true-false test, the student recognizes this fact as being true. Similarly, you have permanent records for many familiar faces. When you see a person that you know, you match the face to the stored representation and recognize him or her. Unlike recall in which cues activate something merely associated with it, in recognition, cues directly match records.

The third retrieval process, *inferential reconstruction*, is used when cues cause you to retrieve only a few fragments of a more complete record. Upon retrieving these fragments, you build up a plausible story around the fragments that seems to be a close approximation of the original record (Anderson, 1995). To get a sense of this, think of a TV show that you have not seen in many years and try to recall the plot (e.g., "Frosty the Snowman"). If you tried to tell the story to a friend who has not seen it, what would you say? Now think of a show that you saw last week and try to recall its plot. Notice the difference between the two memories. The latter is probably more complete and more similar to the experience of watching the show.

Forgetting

What happens to our memories as time passes? Why is our memory of some things better than our memory of others? Answers to these questions center around the notion of forgetting. After many years of experimentation, three views of forgetting have been proposed: decay theory, interference theory, and the loss of retrieval cues view. Let's examine each of these views next.

Decay Theory

Decay theory is the oldest view of forgetting and one that is quite consistent with the view of the average person on the street (Anderson, 1995). The main premise of this view is that the strength of a record weakens over time if no further practice ensues or if it has not been activated for some time. To get a sense of this notion, let's use the convention that the strength of a record is the probability that it can be recalled. For example, if there is a 40 percent chance that you will give the right answer to the question "What is the square root of 256?", let's say that the strength of the answer "16" is .40. The decay view suggests that a record that starts out with a strength of 1.0 would ultimately weaken to .80, then .60, then .40, and so on with the passage of time.

If our personal computers followed a similar law of decay, a paper we have written and tried to retrieve would be less likely to come up on a screen as each day passes. But, of course, a paper comes up right away no matter how long it has resided on a floppy disk (assuming no damage has occurred), so computers do not follow the law of decay.

Research has shown that, indeed, the passage of time does seem to affect the retrievability of a record in a strikingly regular way. Across many different types of memories (e.g., for nonsense syllables, TV shows, factual sentences, etc.), studies show that most of what you forget is lost very early in the game. You continue to forget additional information after this point, but the rate of loss slows. This general trend has been called the *power law of forgetting* (Anderson, 1995). For example, one study showed that people remember 80 percent of canceled TV shows one year after they are canceled. Between the first and eighth year after cancellation, retention drops somewhat quickly from 80 percent to about 58 percent (a 22 percent loss). Between the eighth and fifteenth year, however, retention drops only 3 percent further (from 58 percent down to 55 percent) (Squire, 1989).

So the passage of time is an important factor in retrievability. But it has also been found that the amount of practice affects forgetting as well. As we already learned, practice affects the initial strength of a record. Research has shown that at any point, people who have engaged in more practice show a greater likelihood of retrieving a memory than people who have not practiced as much. Nevertheless, even people who practice a lot show the same *rate* of forgetting as people who practice less (Anderson, 1995). So, for example, if Person A practiced something 50 times, she might show a drop from 80 percent correct to 50 percent right away (a 30 percent drop) and then level off to 45 percent over time (a 5 percent drop). If Person B practiced something 100 times, he might go from 100 percent correct down to 70 percent (a 30 percent drop) and level off at 65 percent (a 5 percent drop). Thus, the rate of loss is the same, but at each point Person B would recall more than Person A. Anderson (1995) has put the two factors of time and practice together in the same schematic function:

$$\text{Strength} = A \times \text{Practice}^b \times \text{Delay}^{-c}$$

The *A* is simply some constant. Notice that the superscript for practice is positive (meaning that more practice yields greater strength) and the superscript for delay is negative (meaning strength is less as time passes). By multiplying these factors together, we see that practice can ameliorate some of the effects of time.

If we apply this notion to a classroom setting, we can see that much of the material that children learn early in an academic year will continually lose strength over the course of the year. To minimize the loss, it would be important to have students engage in considerable practice of the early material.

What is interesting about the power law of forgetting is that our minds seem to be naturally equipped to retain only those events that repeat on a regular basis. That is, our minds seem to be saying, "This event keeps happening, so I'd better remember it; that event has not happened for some time and did not repeat very much when it did—I'd better forget it." Researchers have found that there is a strong correlation between the frequency with which things occur in the environment (e.g., the number of times a person's name is mentioned on a daily basis in the newspaper) and the likelihood that people can recall this information (Anderson & Schooler, 1991).

Interference Theory

Although time and practice do seem to affect how much we forget, these factors are not the whole story. Sometimes an *interference* relation can develop between information already in memory and information that we are just learning. When newly learned information causes students to have trouble remembering old information, that is called retroactive interference. For example, first and second graders spend a lot of time learning the fact that "3 + 4 = 7." When they learn a new multiplication fact in third grade such as "3 x 4 = 12," the new associative relation between 3, 4, and 12 may interfere with the old associative relation between 3, 4, and 7. Thus, when asked, "What is 3 + 4?" they may answer "12." In this case, the 3 and 4 are acting as retrieval cues that activate the record for 12 instead of the record for 7. To overcome this problem, students need to form a four-way association between 3, 4, x and 12 as well as between 3, 4, + and 7.

When old information interferes with retention of new information, that is called proactive interference. An example of proactive interference would be the case of a third grader responding "7" when asked "What is 3 x 4?" Another example would be an adult giving an old phone number when asked his or her new number. In the latter case, the phrase *phone number* is a retrieval cue that is associated with both numbers, but is associated more strongly with the old number than it is with the new number.

At this point it is worth noting that from the standpoint of both decay theory and interference theory, forgetting is not seen as information evaporating out of memory. Instead, both views consider forgetting to be a problem of pulling up information that is still there (i.e., activating a record to a high enough level). Where these views differ is in how they explain *why* a record fails to attain a high enough level of activation.

To illustrate the decay view, let's assume that retrieval cues increase the probability of recall. For example, if the record for *Truman* is at .50 strength, assume that the words in the question, "Who was president after Roosevelt?" temporarily increase the strength of Truman by .30 to .80. If the threshold of remembering is .70, then the question would easily evoke the answer. However, if the strength of the record for Truman has dissipated to just .30, then the cues in the question might only increase the strength to .60, which falls short of the .70 threshold.

To illustrate the interference view, let's again consider the Truman example, but assume that the cue *Roosevelt* is associated to both the record *Taft* and the record *Truman*. Research suggests that a given cue can send only a fixed amount of activation across a set of records (Anderson, 1995). If we split the .30 increase in strength among Taft and Truman (giving .15 to each) and assume that Truman is again at .50 strength normally, then its strength is temporarily increased to .65 by the question. Note, however, that if the threshold is .70, we once again get a memory failure. Thus, we can still have trouble activating a record even when it is at high strength if the cues we give are associated to many other records.

Loss of Retrieval Cues

The third explanation of forgetting involves the weakening of associations among retrieval cues and records (Anderson, 1995; Tulving & Psotka, 1971). Sometimes we see a face out of context and have the curious feeling that we know that person. For example, I might see one of my students at the grocery store. When this student is currently in one of my classes, the student's face is still strongly associated to the classroom context and other things, such as his or her name. So I can ask myself, "Is this one of my students?", imagine my classes, and then "see" the student in one class. These cues together help me then recall the student's name. However, when I see a student from many years ago, the associations among the face, classroom, names, and so forth weaken to the point that I am not even sure that the familiar face is a student I have had!

The readers of this book have also probably had the experience of trying to remember something in the middle of taking a test. Sometimes contextual cues such as the place you wrote something in your notes can serve as a retrieval cue to help you remember. Although such contextual cues may help you right after studying, they will lose their association to information over time. When asked the same test question many months later, you probably will be unable to recall the information.

As was the case for the decay and interference views, the loss of retrieval cues view also assumes that forgetting is the problem of activating a record that is still there in memory. Again, though, it differs from the other views in terms of how it explains retrieval problems. To illustrate the latter view, let's return to our Truman example. Whereas the words *President* and *Roosevelt* were said in earlier examples to temporarily increase a strength by .30, let's assume that these cues lose their activating potency over time. Instead of increasing a strength by .30, an old cue might only increase strength by .10. Thus, a record at .50 would only be increased to .60, which falls short of the .70 threshold we have been assuming. The discerning reader will recognize that the loss of retrieval cues view is simply a decay theory that focuses on a dissipating association between cues and records (rather than a view that focuses on the dissipating strength of a record).

Memory Strategies and Metamemory

At this point, you should have a good sense of the nature of retention and for-getting. In what follows, we will examine some things that students can do to help themselves remember information better. As we shall see, certain memory strategies work because they exploit the properties of memory that were de-scribed in the last two sections of this chapter. Although students use many dif-ferent strategies, we shall focus on five that have received the most attention from researchers: rehearsal, organization, elaboration, the method of loci, and the key-word method. After describing the five strategies, we shall explore a component of the memory system that plays an important role in whether we use strategies: metamemory.

Rehearsal

As mentioned earlier, rehearsal is the strategy of repeating information over and over. At one time, it was thought that rehearsal was absolutely necessary for long-term retention; that is, it was thought that repetition would inevitably in-crease the strength of a record and that records could not attain a high degree of strength without repetition (Anderson, 1995; Atkinson & Shiffrin, 1968). How-ever, many studies have shown that repetition does not always increase the strength of a record and that sometimes people learn after a single exposure to information. Thus, it is best to say that repetition is important for better retention, but it is not the only route to success.

Why does repetition work? As mentioned earlier, it seems that our minds are naturally sensitive to the statistical properties of the environment. We are built to remember things that we are likely to encounter again and to forget rare events. Consistent with this claim is the work that has examined *spacing* effects (Ander-son, 1995). One way to study material is to engage in *distributed practice* in which you spread out your studying over time (e.g., one-third of the material over each of three days). A second way to study is to cram (i.e., studying everything at once just before an exam). Research shows that people who engage in distributed prac-tice show better long-term retention of material than people who cram. However, the relative value of one method over the other depends on how much time will elapse between when you finish studying and when the test will occur. If you study once per week for four weeks and a week intervenes between the day you stop studying (e.g., October 1) and the test day (e.g., October 8), you will re-member more than a student who crams on the first and studies no more. How-ever, if you stop on the first and a crammer studies on the seventh, the crammer will do better. So, if you want to not only do well on a test and remember the ma-terial long after the test, it is best to combine distributed practice with studying intensively the night before.

Two other findings that have relevance for studying are those that pertain to primacy and recency effects. It is common for students to study material in the order that it appears in their notes (i.e., material in the first class studied first, material in the second class studied second, etc.). Research shows that when people study material in this way, they tend to remember the material at the beginning and end of the sequence and tend to forget the material in the middle (Greene, 1986). The obvious implication of this work is that the material in your notes should be studied in a variety of orders to even out primacy and recency effects across all of the material.

Organization

Organization is the strategy of arranging to-be-remembered material into subgroups and hierarchies of subgroups. To get a sense of this strategy, how would you study the following list of items?:

carrot, truck, cake, broccoli, bike, bus, ice cream, peas
train, potato, candy, pudding, plane, squash, soda

Instead of rehearsing them as a single set of 15 items, you probably would form three groups of five items (e.g., veggies, vehicles, and sweet stuff) and rehearse them in groups. Then, at the test time, you can use the labels of these groups as retrieval cues (e.g., "Okay, there were five veggies . . ."").

If a teacher presents students with an unordered array of material to study, then it is highly sensible for students to impose some organization on this material. Doing so has two main advantages. First, students will encode the material in a more elaborative way than would be the case with simple rehearsal. Figure 3.1 illustrates the node-link schema corresponding to the encoding for the list of

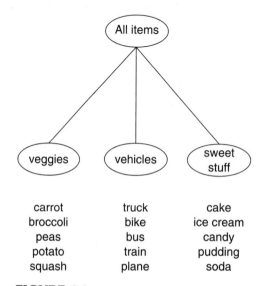

FIGURE 3.1

items above. Notice how all ideas are interconnected and how a person has to use his or her existing knowledge of categories to form these groups. Second, the student gives himself or herself additional retrieval cues to recall the material later (i.e., the category labels) (Anderson, 1990; 1995).

But even when teachers present material in a highly organized way, the organization strategy comes into play because students can use the teacher's organization to help themselves elaboratively encode the material and use their teacher's headings and groupings as retrieval cues. For example, if a biology teacher uses the grouping *endocrine glands* to discuss all of the endocrine glands in the body all at once, students can use this label to help themselves recall all of the endocrine glands at the test.

It is interesting, however, that when students create their *own* organization, they often show better recall than when teachers give an organization to students. This finding has been called the *generation effect* (McDaniel, Waddill & Einstein, 1988). Teachers have to decide whether their students are capable of imposing the right organization on material before letting them construct such an organization. If students lack the necessary background knowledge or have many misconceptions, they are likely to impose an incorrect grouping on the material. Thus, they will remember a lot but what they remember will be wrong.

Having said that, I find it useful at this point to discuss the issue of the intention to learn. A large number of studies have shown that as long as students encode material in an elaborative way, they will show good memory of the material even if they are not trying to remember the material (Anderson, 1995). That is, if you compare (a) people who are told they are in a memory experiment and who encode material elaboratively to (b) people who are unaware they are in an experiment and who nevertheless are made to process information deeply, you find that the intention to learn does not matter. The reason there is a generation effect in many experiments is not that people are trying to remember as much as they usually are given unorganized, impoverished ideas to work with.

Elaboration

Elaboration is the general term for imposing meaning of any kind on material. We just learned that organization is one form of elaboration, but the prototypical example of elaboration comes from experiments involving paired-associates learning. If you were presented with the following list of word pairs and told that your job is to learn the pairs, what would you do?:

> cat-ribbon
> elephant-pin
> giraffe-scissors
> monkey-sewing machine
> etc.

Most people tend to form mental images that link one term to another. For example, you may have imagined the cat wearing the ribbon or the elephant getting stuck by the pin. Either way, this interactive imagery has been found to be highly effective for learning the pairs (Weinstein & Mayer, 1986). Whereas it may seem at first that you have never had to engage in such paired associate learning, consider the fact that the pairing of states with their capitals is paired associate learning. So is the pairing of faces with names, and so on. Elaboration is useful because it creates meaningful relations when none exists.

There are three reasons elaboration works as a strategy. First, as the name implies, elaboration involves the creation of an elaborative encoding of the material. Second, when students are free to make up their own images, we have the generation effect (moreover, the image serves as an additional retrieval cue for either word). Third, we have learned from dual code theory that we are naturally equipped to retain visual information more easily than verbal information. By taking the purely verbal input and linking it to images, we are drawing on one of our natural strengths.

Method of Loci

The method of loci involves linking up a familiar routine with a series of items that you are trying to learn. Typically, researchers ask students to take a list of facts and mentally attach each fact to a route that is very familiar to them. For example, students who have driven to school the same way every day for four years are highly familiar with this route and can imagine it easily. When given a list of, say, 20 facts to learn for a test, students can divide their route into 20 landmarks along the way (e.g., their neighbor's house, the grocery store on the corner, the church on the next corner, etc.). Then, they can imagine each fact plastered on each of the landmarks. When test time comes, they merely think about their route and the material can be read off this image.

The method of loci works for a variety of reasons. Once again, we have elaborative encoding of the material. In addition, students are exploiting their natural capacity to remember visual material better than verbal material. Third, in selecting which route to use and which landmarks, we have the generation effect again. Fourth, the fixed sequence of events imposes an organization on material that may not have an organization. Fifth, each landmark or its label can serve as an additional retrieval cue.

The Keyword Method

The keyword method is particularly useful for learning verbal material such as new vocabulary words. In this approach, a student takes a new word and finds a portion that may be a familiar-sounding, easy-to-imagine term within the word. For example, with the word *caterwaul* a student might identify both *cat* and *wall* (notice that homonyms can be used). When it is learned that *caterwaul* means a noisy fight, the student can imagine two cats fighting and screeching on a wall. Or, with the Spanish word *carta* (meaning *letter*) a student could see the term *cart* and imagine a letter being transported by a shopping cart. Research shows that the keyword approach can be highly effective for vocabulary and other similar tasks (Pressley, Levin & Delaney, 1982).

Let's use a little constructivist learning here. Why is the keyword method effective? The reader should be able at this point to say why, given what has been said about the other approaches.

Metamemory

Of the five strategies described above, which do you think would be most effective for studying for a test? Do you use any of these strategies? Would you be more likely to use a particular strategy (e.g., organization) for an essay test than for a multiple choice test? The answers that you give to these questions derive from your metamemory. The term *metamemory* refers to a person's knowledge and beliefs about how his or her memory works (Flavell, Miller & Miller, 1993). Perhaps the two most important aspects of metamemory concern: (a) the recognition that your memory is not flawless and (b) knowledge of what strategies to use in particular circumstances.

Strategies are things that you do to avoid forgetting something important. But in order to use a strategy, you have to first recognize that there is some likelihood that you might forget something unless you engage in a strategy. At an even more basic level, strategy-users are people who recognize that they sometimes forget. In contrast to good rememberers who know when they are likely to forget something (e.g., they say "I'd better write that down"), poor rememberers think that they never forget. As a consequence, poor remembers never use strategies and forget a great deal (though they do not recognize this).

Besides recognizing that they forget, good rememberers know which strategies are effective for them and which are not. For example, a good student might discover that the method of loci never works for her but the keyword method does. Upon learning this, she stops using the method of loci. Similarly, a good student might also recognize that rehearsal works well for learning lists of facts, but that various imagery techniques work better for remembering textbook material. Thus, this student would flexibly shift from rehearsal to imagery as his tasks changed from learning lists to reading textbooks.

A third important aspect of metamemory concerns note-taking. Instead of writing everything down that a teacher says, most students write down things that they think they might forget by test time. Good students are adept at writing down notes in such a way that they can use the notes as effective study aides. Poor students, in contrast, misjudge their memory abilities. As a result, they either take too few or too many notes.

Now that you have learned about the components of the memory system (e.g., records, encoding, strategies, etc.), you probably have a different view of memory from the one you had before you read this chapter. If so, that means your metamemory beliefs might have changed. If your beliefs have changed, you might be likely to use strategies you never used before because you now understand why they might be effective.

The Development of Memory

Few people would dispute the claim that older children, adolescents, and adults all seem to remember better than younger children. The question remains, however, as to why memory improves with age. In this section, we will attempt to answer this question by focusing on six key aspects of memory performance: recognition, recall, strategy use, metamemory, prior knowledge, and speed of processing.

Recognition and Recall

Two questions have dominated the developmental work on recognition and recall: (a) When do children first show evidence of recognition and recall? and (c) How do these memory processes change with age? With respect to the first question, studies show that even infants are capable of recognition and recall. To test the former, researchers have relied on the *habituation* technique. In this technique, infants are repeatedly presented with the same stimulus over and over (e.g., a face) and then a new one is introduced (e.g., a different face). When the first stimulus is presented for the first time, infants demonstrate an *orienting response*, which is simply sustained attention to the novel stimulus. After the stimulus is repeatedly flashed, however, infants look less and less. Decreased looking is assumed to reflect recognition memory. In particular, infants only look for a long time at a novel stimulus. By looking less and less, they are showing that the stimulus is no longer novel to them (i.e., that they recognize it). Even four-month-olds have been shown to habituate to a repeated visual stimulus and show a new orienting response when the stimulus is changed (Bornstein, 1989).

Unlike recognition memory, which emerges almost immediately after birth, recall ability does not seem to emerge until the end of an infant's first year. As implied earlier in this chapter, recall is the ability to think about something that was encountered before but is no longer present. When it is defined in this way, a student of Piaget's theory will see that the classic object permanence task is really a recall task. In the object permanence task, infants are shown an attractive stimulus and then watch the stimulus being placed under a blanket. Children who know that the stimulus still exists when out of view and who move the blanket to retrieve the stimulus have object permanence (Piaget, 1952).

Thus, we see that even infants have rudimentary recognition and recall skills. Given this fact, it cannot be said that age changes in memory are the result of one age group having these basic competencies and the other group not having them. Instead, age changes in memory must be due to other aspects of memory performance such as strategy use, metamemory, and so on. As we shall see, these latter aspects help children *execute* recognition and recall better than younger children.

Strategy Use

In the earlier section on strategies and metamemory, we saw that strategies improve memory when they function to increase the strength of a record (e.g., rehearsal), promote more elaborate encodings of stimuli (e.g., organization, elaboration), or link up verbal material with imagery (method of loci, key-word method). Developmental researchers who have examined memory have asked, "When do children first use strategies such as rehearsal, organization, or elaboration?"

The results of many studies reveal that children progressively acquire such strategies between the first grade and high school levels (Flavell et al., 1993; Kail, 1991; Ornstein & Naus, 1985). The acquisition of any given strategy can be seen to roughly follow four phases (Flavell et al., 1993):

1. *Strategy not available phase*: At first, children do not use a strategy sponta-neously and cannot be taught it very well.
2. *Production Deficiency phase*: Children still do not use a strategy spontaneously but can be taught it; when they use it, their performance improves. However, they need to be prompted to use the strategy after they are taught it.
3. *Utilization deficiency*: Children start to spontaneously use a strategy without prompting but accrue little or no benefit from doing so. They have to devote so much attention to using the strategy that they have little resources left for concentrating on the material.
4. *Mature Strategy Use*: Children spontaneously use a strategy and do so very well. There is no need to prompt them to use it and their recall is substan-tially higher than children in the *strategy not available, production deficiency*, or *utilization deficiency* phases.

Besides saying that all strategies seem to be acquired in four phases, a second way to summarize the developmental research on strategies is to say that older "Mature Strategy Users" often execute a strategy more effectively than younger "Mature Strategy Users." To illustrate, take the case of rehearsal. When eight-year-olds hear ten items read one by one (e.g., "cat . . . tree . . . truck . . . fence," etc.), many are likely to rehearse only the most current item (i.e., the one just said by the experimenter). In contrast, a 13-year-old would be likely to engage in the more effective *cumulative* rehearsal in which all prior items are rehearsed as a group. The schematic below illustrates the difference between cumulative and noncumulative rehearsal:

Experimenter says:
 "cat . . . . . tree . . . . . truck . . . . . etc."
eight-year-old says:
 "cat,cat,cat . . . tree,tree,tree . . . truck,truck,truck . . . etc."
13-year-old says:
 "cat,cat,cat . . . cat-tree,cat-tree,cat-tree . . . cat-tree-truck,cat-tree-truck,cat-tree-truck . . . etc."

Finally, research suggests that certain strategies are acquired before others. In particular, children seem to acquire rehearsal between the ages of 6 to 8, orga-nization between the ages of 8 to 10, and elaboration between the ages of 10 to 13.

When a child increases his or her repertoire of strategies, he or she can use multiple strategies to study the same information. For example, a child may take a group of 20 pictures and first sort them into five categories (i.e., use organization). Then, she may rehearse them by group. Finally, she may use some form of imagery that links each of the four items in a group together (i.e., use elaboration).

Thus, there is development in terms of (a) the tendency to use a strategy, (b) how well a given strategy is executed, and (c) how many strategies are used in combination. The net result is that older children tend to recall far more information than younger children.

Before moving on to the issue of metamemory, this section should not leave the reader with the impression that younger children never use strategies. In fact, clever experimentation shows how even three-year-olds will engage in strategy-like behaviors to help them remember things (Flavell et al., 1993). For example, when told that they will earn a prize if they can remember where a Big Bird toy is hidden in a room, three-year-olds will repeatedly stare at the location while engaged in another distracting activity. But these protostrategies are not as effective as strategies such as rehearsal or organization, because protostrategies generally do not increase the strength of a record, promote elaborated encodings, or link up stimulation with imagery.

Metamemory

Besides strategy use, a second important factor that accounts for developmental differences in recall and recognition is metamemory. In the previous section on metamemory, we learned that people are likely to use strategies if they (a) recognize that they sometimes forget and (b) know a lot about strategies (e.g., which strategies to use in which contexts). We just learned that older children are more likely to use strategies than younger children, so it seems reasonable to hypothesize that the reason they are more likely to do so is that the former are more likely to appreciate the limited nature of their memories and know more about strategies than the latter.

Research generally has supported this hypothesis. In particular, younger children often think they have better memories than they actually have (Kreutzer, Leonard & Flavell, 1975; Schneider, 1985). Moreover, although preschool children show some insight into the relative effectiveness of protostrategies and comprehend basic ideas about studying (e.g., studying ten items would be harder than studying five items), older children clearly have more insight about the nature and effectiveness of strategies such as rehearsal, organization, or elaboration (Flavell et al., 1993).

Prior Knowledge

Earlier we learned that someone would be more likely to remember a sentence (e.g., "Fred shot Bill") if he or she elaborated this sentence with an inference (e.g., "Bill had an affair with Fred's wife"). A little reflection shows that an individual cannot elaborate on an encoding in this way unless he or she has a certain amount of knowledge. For the sentence above, for example, the person would have to have stored knowledge of the things that prompt people to commit murder.

Most of the chapters in this book document the many ways in which children gain knowledge with age. Given this pervasive trend, it would be reasonable to assume that older children would be more likely to form elaborative encodings than younger children because the former have more knowledge than the latter. This assumption has been born out in many studies (Flavell et al., 1993).

In a classic study (Paris, 1975), for example, children read passages such as the following:

> Linda was playing with her new doll in front of her big red house. Suddenly, she heard a strange sound coming from under the porch. It was the flapping of wings. Linda wanted to help so much, but she did not know what to do. She ran inside the house and grabbed a shoe box from the closet. Then Linda looked inside her desk until she found eight sheets of yellow paper. She cut up the paper into little pieces and put them in the bottom of the box. Linda gently picked up the helpless creature and took it with her. Her teacher knew what to do.

When asked a question such as "Did Linda find a frog?" older children were more likely than younger children to say "No" because they were more likely to infer that the creature was a bird. Notice how the word *bird* is never stated above. Paris (1975) and many others have shown that inference-making such as this helps children remember the content of the passage better because they create more elaborative encodings of the information.

Speed of Processing

The final factor that helps explain why older children recall more than younger children is speed of processing. To see the importance of speed in memory, let's return to our plate-spinning metaphor for working memory. Someone who takes a lot of time to spin each plate could keep, say, only three plates spinning simultaneously. If we added a few more plates, some would stop spinning before he or she could get to the new plates. In contrast, someone who spins plates quickly and who runs fast could keep many more plates spinning at once.

In working memory, it is important to perform operations quickly before the information in working memory fades. To see this, try solving the following problem:

> Look at the following list of seven numbers, then look away, and then add them all up in your head:
>
> 7   2   5   6   1   4   7

If you are someone who normally can rehearse a maximum of seven numbers, being asked to add them up as well causes you to not pay attention to some before they fade. Notice how you might be able to perform this task better if you were extremely fast at adding.

Researchers have shown that across a variety of tasks and mental operations, older children can perform faster than younger children (Kail, 1991). Thus, it can be assumed that when they are placed in the same situation requiring the same skills, older children would be able to remember more than younger children because they can simultaneously pay attention to more things than younger children.

Summary

In sum, older children can often remember more than younger children because the former (a) have a wider repertoire of memory strategies and competence in using them, (b) have more insight into the nature of their memory and memory strategies, (c) have more knowledge, and (d) can perform mental operations faster than the latter.

Instructional Implications

A reasonable way of stating the instructional implications of memory research is to provide the following list of suggestions:

1. *Teachers should view their job as helping students to form permanent records of the information that is presented in class.* To accomplish this goal, teachers need to (a) maximize the number of opportunities that students have to practice newly learned material (to increase strength), and (b) promote elaborative encoding of the material (through "why" questioning, use of imagery, and other techniques).

2. *When creating tests, teachers should provide sufficient cues in their questions to maximize the chances that students will retrieve the information.* One way to do this is to arrange questions to follow the same order that material was presented in class. That way, students can use various episodic cues (e.g., where something was located in their notes; things that happened that day in class) to help them recall something. Another way is to use examples that are highly similar to those presented in class.

3. *Teachers should use multiple methods to promote "deep" processing of the material.* In addition to asking "why" questions, other methods include asking students to solve problems with the information or apply it to the real world in some other way (e.g., after giving the definition of *republic,* send students to the library to find examples of republics in the world). In addition, teachers should explicitly teach students about the nature of memory (to alter their metamemories) and also teach them how to engage in rehearsal, organization, elaboration, and other strategies that promote long-term retention. The developmental work, however, suggests that strategy instruction would be

most beneficial when children are in the "production deficiency" stage (because less advanced children could not learn the strategy and more advanced students already use the strategy). Of course, younger children in the "mature strategy use" phase could always be taught how to use a strategy more efficiently (e.g., shown how to engage in cumulative rehearsal).

4. Because all information seems to be susceptible to the power law of forgetting, spacing effects, and interference effects, *teachers should ameliorate the effects of forgetting through increased distributed practice and occasional reminders of information throughout a school year*. The more things repeat, the less likely they are to be forgotten. The more things are spaced, the less likely they will interfere with each other. Interference can also be minimized through increased practice and elaborative strategies that help information link up with imagery.

Higher-Order Thinking

Summary

1. Theories of higher-order thinking take either a developmental or definitional focus. Developmental theories assume that (a) there is a continuum of thinking ranging from lower forms to higher forms and (b) students have to master the lower forms of thought before they are capable of the higher forms. In contrast, definitional theories assume that students at all levels can engage in higher-order thought.

2. Adjectives that the developmental theorists use to describe higher-order thinking include *abstract, logical, self-regulated, conscious*, and *symbolic*. These theorists suggest that higher-order thought is evident when students engage in cognitive processes such as classification, hypothesis-testing, analysis, synthesis, and evaluation.

3. Definitional theories share a common emphasis on nonroutine, intelligent problem-solving. Among other things, intelligent problem-solving involves (a) knowing what exactly is at issue, (b) a reflective analysis of one's options, (c) implementation of the best option, and (d) an evaluation of outcomes.

4. Discussions of higher-order thinking and transfer usually go hand in hand. Students rarely transfer what they learn in school to real-world settings. Transfer is more likely if students can (a) partially decontextualize skills and develop conditional knowledge about their application, (b) cast their knowledge in the form of principles, (c) develop a conceptual understanding of procedures, and (d) approach their learning in a mindful way.

Observations of classrooms show that most teachers seem to fall into one of two camps: (a) those who emphasize fact-learning over thinking and (b) those who emphasize thinking over fact-learning. Historically, there have been times when many teachers have fallen into the first camp and times when the opposite was true. Let's call the former time an "emphasis-on-facts" phase in our history. We can call the other periods of time an "emphasis-on-thinking" phase. It turns out that there have been far more emphasis-on-facts phases than emphasis-on-thinking phases in our history. Moreover, the former phases have lasted considerably longer than the latter. As a result, we can safely say that an emphasis on facts is the norm for our country (Newmann, 1990) and the emphasis on thinking represents an occasional deviation from this norm.

What causes schools to occasionally shift toward emphasizing thinking? The main catalyst seems to be public dissatisfaction with the standard approach of emphasizing facts. More specifically, increases in dissatisfaction seem to occur right after some major technological advance has taken place (e.g., the Soviets launched the *Sputnik* satellite; computers became commonplace in the work world; etc.). Technological advances make the workplace much more complex than it had been up to that point and many people start noticing that workers do not deal with the increased complexity very well. Soon after, many people start complaining that "I wish our graduates could think better."

If enough influential people complain (e.g, the secretary of education), school systems ultimately respond by altering the curriculum to focus more on thinking. After the curricular changes are put in place, however, schools usually lapse back into the standard approach of emphasizing facts over thinking. When some new technological advance takes place, the cycle begins again.

An examination of our recent history shows that after a brief interlude in the 1960s in which we emphasized thinking, we lapsed back into a mode of emphasizing fact-learning again. Not surprisingly, many people have started calling for reform again. Leaders in the field of teacher education have heard the most recent calls for reform and have responded in two ways. First, researchers and other experts have proposed standards for specific content areas such as math or science (e.g., National Council of Teachers of Mathematics, 1989). These standards almost always suggest that thinking should take precedence over fact-learning. Second, school systems have used these standards to alter the curriculum to foster so-called higher-order thinking.

Most school systems, however, have defined higher-order thinking in their own way. As a result, there is no standard curriculum for promoting thinking skills and there are a large number of distinct definitions of higher-order thinking floating around classrooms (Cuban, 1984; Newmann, 1990). Given this somewhat confusing state of affairs, the primary goal of the present chapter is to clarify the nature of higher-order thinking. More specifically, the discussion shall center around the following questions: What is higher-order thinking and how can it be fostered?

These questions are answered in the four sections of this chapter. In the first section, you will learn about theories of higher-order thinking that place it within a developmental framework (Developmental Approaches). In the second section, you will learn about approaches that define higher-order thinking but do not place it within a developmental framework (Definitional Approaches). In the third section, the research on the transfer of skills is summarized. In the fourth and final section, the instructional implications of the research on higher-order thinking are drawn.

Developmental Approaches

As a starting point, we shall examine four approaches that suggest that thinking progresses from lower forms to higher forms with development: (a) Piaget's approach, (b) Vygotsky's approach, (c) Bloom's approach, and (d) the novice-expert approach. As we shall see, whereas each of these approaches implies that teachers can do a great deal to help students progress toward the highest forms of thinking, each one also suggests that it would be unwise to ask students to engage in the highest form of thinking before they have mastered many of the lower-order forms first.

Piaget's Approach

There are two overarching assumptions of Piaget's theory that can be used to characterize his view on higher-order thinking: (a) thinking becomes increasingly *abstract* with development and (b) thinking becomes increasingly *logical* with development. For Piaget, higher-order thinking is abstract and logical. Let's examine this definition further by "unpacking" the two assumptions above.

Assumption 1

By *abstract,* Piaget meant "removed from immediate perception and action" (Piaget, 1965; Piaget & Inhelder, 1969). Thinking that is closely tied to perception or action is lower-order thinking (e.g., sensorimotor or preoperational thought). Thinking that is less tied to perception and action is higher-order thinking (e.g., concrete and formal operational thought). Moreover, as a child moves between one level of thought and the next, his or her thinking becomes more abstract because each stage transition produces thinking that is one step further removed from immediate perception and action. Thus, preoperational thought is more abstract than sensorimotor thought because the former is one step removed from immediate perception. Similarly, concrete operational thinking is more abstract than preoperational thinking because it is two steps removed from immediate perception, and formal operational thought is more abstract than concrete operational thought because it is three steps removed (Overton & Byrnes, 1991).

When children reach the concrete operations level for some content area, they are capable of reasoning with symbols that do not resemble their real-world referents. For example, the symbol 3 does not resemble a collection of three objects and the word *animal* does not look like any particular animal. In freeing the mind from *particular* concrete referents, children can think about the symbols themselves. Thus, although the symbol 3 can refer to a set of three apples or three trucks, one can ignore *which* objects it refers to in, say, judging that when one takes away one object from any set of three objects, one is always left with two objects (no matter what those objects are). Then, when children reach the formal operations level, symbols can stand for sets of symbols. For example, *X* can stand for 3 or 4 or whatever.

In order to be ultimately capable of abstract reasoning, Piaget argued, children need to interact with objects or actual content. For example, preoperational children need to count actual sets of objects and form many sets of three things in order for their minds to create structures that help them comprehend symbols such as *3*. In particular, through the process of *reflective abstraction,* children's minds abstract across sets of objects to form schematic representations of set size. Similarly, they need to work on many sets of arithmetic problems (e.g., "3 + 4 = 7") before their minds will abstract a schema that would promote an understanding of algebraic formulas (e.g., "x + y = z"). In essence, experiences with objects, arithmetic sentences, and so forth are the grist for the schema-abstraction mill. Thus, Piaget would not argue that nothing should be done to promote abstract thinking until children reach a certain age. Abstract thinking will not emerge on its own without ample experiences.

Assumption 2

By *logical,* Piaget meant that thinking literally conforms to the canons of logic. Long before Piaget did his experiments, philosophers devised laws and theorems that were argued to be universal truths. One such theorem was the assertion that "If $A > B$ and $B > C$, then $A > C$." Piaget was well versed in logic and was quite surprised to see that seven-year-olds could make such transitive inferences long before students are exposed to the idea of transitivity in logic or math courses. Whereas a preoperational child would have to examine each item mentioned in a transitive statement in order to reach the correct conclusion (e.g., look at all three of a set of colored sticks that decrease in size to know that the first stick is larger than the third), concrete operational children would know the answer without actually comparing the first and third item (e.g., the first and third stick).

In addition to transitive inferences, concrete operational thought conforms to logical analyses in two other ways. First, philosophers have claimed that logical thinking requires that things be classified in such a way that valid inductive and deductive inferences can be drawn. To ensure the validity of categorical inferences, it is important to have correct definitions of categories such as *squares* or *mammals.* The definition of *squares* is correct if it properly includes all of the things that are squares and properly excludes all of the things that are not squares. According to many philosophers, the best way to create correct definitions is to use lists of "necessary and sufficient" attributes (Smith, 1989). For squares, for example, the necessary and sufficient attributes are that the thing have (a) four sides, (b) equal sides, (c) opposite sides parallel, and (d) 90-degree angles. Anything that has all four attributes is a square and anything that lacks one or more of these attributes is not a square. Inhelder and Piaget (1964) argued that whereas preoperational children categorize things together if they merely look similar (e.g., a trout and a whale are both fish), concrete operational children categorize things using necessary and sufficient criteria. Thus, once again concrete operational thought is more logical than preoperational thought.

The third way that concrete operational thought is more logical pertains to the notions of negation and reversibility. Concrete operational children connect categories and operations to their opposites. For example, all of the things that are dogs are grouped together with all other animals that are not dogs through the superordinate category of animals. This hierarchical grouping allows a child to fully comprehend class-inclusion relations (e.g., that dogs and cats are both animals). In addition, each mental operation is linked to an opposite operation that undoes the former. For example, addition is linked to its opposite, subtraction. By linking things to their opposites, children gain a sense of *logical necessity.* That is, they feel that their deductions must be true. Thus, when asked, "If all of the dogs in the world were to die, would there be any animals left?", concrete operational children would say, "Of course. Dogs are not the only kind of animals."

Formal operational thinking extends the logical aspects of concrete operational thinking in new ways. In the first place, inductive, deductive, and transitive inferences can now be applied to both real things and hypothetical ideas. In addition, children become capable of performing valid experiments, because formal operational students examine combinations of variables and use the isolation of variables technique to test their hypotheses (see Chapter 9).

Summary

Piaget argued that with age and experience, children's thinking becomes increasingly abstract and logical. As a result, they can classify things properly and arrange things in terms of increasing magnitude. Once their knowledge is arranged in this way, children can test hypotheses and draw valid inductive, deductive, and transitive inferences. Although preoperational and sensorimotor children also form hypotheses and draw inferences, these inferences are not always correct or valid. For example, children might infer that a horse is a dog because it has four legs. The main source of their reasoning errors is the fact that their knowledge is: (a) often incorrect, (b) not sufficiently abstract, and (c) not fully interconnected (e.g., ideas connected to their opposites).

Before moving on to Vygotsky's view, it is worth noting that many of the higher-order-thinking curriculum packages on the market specify that teachers should promote inference-making, hypothesis-testing, and classification skills. Piagetian theory suggests that children at all ages are capable of these operations but are unlikely to *correctly* apply them to real-world content until they have been able to interact sufficiently with things in the world and form abstractions across their experiences.

Vygotsky's Approach

Vygotsky shared Piaget's belief that there is a progression from lower forms of thought to higher forms of thought with development. However, Vygotsky defined higher-order thinking differently from Piaget. For Vygotsky, a given cognitive activity reflects higher-order thinking when: (a) there is a shift of control from the environment to the individual ("other-regulation" to "self-regulation"), (b) an individual has conscious access to this cognitive activity (i.e., the individual is aware of and can articulate what he or she is doing), (c) the cognitive activity has a social origin, and (d) the individual uses symbols or signs to mediate the cognitive activity (Wertsch, 1985). Let's examine each of these aspects of higher-order thinking in turn.

For any given cognitive process such as memory or attention, *self-regulation* means that students are intentionally using the process to learn something or adapt to the environment. In essence, children control their own memory skills or direct their own attention in the service of some goal (e.g., getting an A on a test). *Other-regulation* means that someone else (e.g., a parent) is remembering for children, or that something (e.g., a TV) is controlling their attention. As we learned in Chapter 3, there are developmental differences in the extent to which children use memory strategies. We saw that such developmental changes in strategy use produce developmental differences in how much children learn and remember. Vygotsky would characterize these developmental differences by saying that older children are self-regulated and younger children are other-regulated.

The second aspect of higher-order thinking, that is, conscious access, is a logical prerequisite to the former one regarding control. It is not possible to control some process unless one can consciously think about the activities that subserve this process (e.g., memory strategies). Researchers have shown that when children are in the process of mastering a cognitive activity such as language, memory, or attention, there is a point at which they can perform the activity well but are unable to consciously reflect on what they are doing (Piaget, 1976; Karmiloff-Smith, 1984). After a period of successful execution of the activity, however, children ultimately become able to reflect on what they are doing. For Vygotsky, the activity is only higher-order thinking when it becomes accessible to consciousness.

The third requirement that a skill has to have a social origin is a hallmark of the Vygotskian perspective. Vygotsky believed that the best forms of human thought are passed on generation by generation through interchanges between more competent individuals (e.g., parents and teachers) and less competent individuals (e.g., children). More specifically, skills that become internalized in a child (e.g., using the strategy of rehearsal) start off as a form of social interaction between competent and less competent members of society (e.g., a mother rehearsing something with her child).

A good illustration of how cognitive activities can have a social origin is the form of instruction known as *reciprocal teaching* (Palinscar & Brown, 1984). Reciprocal teaching consists of four steps. In the first step, a teacher creates a small group of children. Then, each person in the group takes turns playing the teacher. On the first day, the teacher models the skill that she wants to teach (e.g., a reading strategy such as summarizing) and describes what she is doing and why. On the second day, one of the children tries to imitate what the teacher did the day before. Early on, children do not perform the skill as well as the teacher, so it is necessary for the teacher to give a lot of verbal feedback and corrections. This process of modeling the skill for the others cycles through the group until all members achieve mastery.

In addition to illustrating how a skill can have a social origin, reciprocal teaching also illustrates the fourth aspect of higher-order thinking: The skill is mediated by symbols and signs. When one talks about what one is doing, one's actions become regulated by the most common form of symbol use, viz., language. That is, self-talk helps you direct your attention and plan your behaviors in such a way that you meet your goals. Moreover, early on in the process, a teacher's verbal feedback can play an important role in children's learning of the skill. In order for children to gain control of the skills, however, it is necessary for teachers to progressively intervene less and less as they see children mastering the skills (a process commonly known in educational circles as *fading*).

Summary
For Vygotsky, any skill is a lower form of thought if (a) something or someone in the environment is totally controlling an actor's performance of the skill, (b) the actor cannot consciously reflect on what he or she is doing, (c) the skill was not acquired through interaction with more competent individuals, and (d) the activity is not mediated by symbol systems such as language. In contrast, the same skill becomes a higher form of thought once the performer controls its execution, has conscious access to it, and uses self-talk to direct his or her performance. For Vygotsky, social interaction is the key to shifting a skill from the lower-order version to the higher-order version.

Bloom's Approach
A number of years ago, Benjamin Bloom and his colleagues devised a hierarchy of instructional objectives that had a profound effect on educational practice (Bloom et al., 1956). Each objective within the hierarchy specifies what a teacher would want his or her students to know and be able to do. By indexing types of knowledge, cognitive processes, and skills within each objective, Bloom et al.'s model is as much a theory of learning and cognition as it is a model of instructional objectives.

As the notion *hierarchy* implies, some types of knowledge are logical prerequisites to others. As a result, Bloom's approach is similar to Piaget's and Vygotsky's approach in the assumption that certain forms of complex thinking are not attainable until other, simpler forms are mastered first.

Bloom's taxonomy describes six levels of knowledge:

1. The Knowledge Level: *Knowing information in a merely associative or rote-learned way* (e.g., knowing your times tables without understanding the process of multiplication; a three-year-old counting to ten in French without knowing what she is doing; etc.);
2. The Comprehension Level: *Understanding information in a deeper, more elaborative way* (e.g., being able to explain an answer and fit it into a "big" picture; getting the main idea of a passage; etc.);

3. The Application Level: *Taking definitions, formulas, principles, and so forth and using them to identify things in the world or solve real-world problems* (e.g., using Piaget's definition of preoperational thinking to identify the level of thought demonstrated by a given child; using the formula "F = ma" to predict the acceleration of a real object that has been dropped from a certain height; etc.);

4. The Analysis Level: *Breaking complex information down into its component parts and seeing how the parts interrelate* (e.g., dividing the Civil War into "key" battles and relating the battles to each other; identifying and interrelating the major themes of a book; identifying the constituent sounds in a word; etc.);

5. The Synthesis Level: *Taking a set of components and creating something more complex out of them* (e.g., blending separate sounds together to form a word; putting Piaget's theory together with information processing theory; etc.).

6. The Evaluation Level: *Judging something against a standard of quality* (e.g., rating the quality of a painting, play, or novel; arguing that one theory explains some phenomenon better than another theory; explaining why one governmental policy is better than another; etc.).

A little bit of reflection shows that a student could not apply, analyze, synthesize, or evaluate some information before he or she knew and understood the information fairly well. Thus, the first two levels of Bloom's taxonomy are logical prerequisites to the remaining four. Similarly, there are good applications of information and there are poor applications. Moreover, there are good analyses or syntheses and there are poor ones. Thus, application, analysis, and synthesis are prerequisites to evaluation.

Given the logical dependency between one level and the next, Bloom's approach suggests that teachers should not attempt to foster higher-order thinking in a group of novices by immediately getting them to think at the highest levels. Rather, instruction should begin with the lower-order skills and move through the higher levels in sequence. It should also be noted that the higher four levels are genuinely higher forms of thought when students perform these processes on information *themselves*. Teachers can apply, analyze, synthesize, or evaluate ideas for students in their lectures, but notice how students are passive learners in this process.

The Novice-Expert Approach

Whereas the approaches of Piaget, Vygotsky, and Bloom have been around for some time, the novice-expert approach is a fairly recent addition to the fields of cognitive development and education. Researchers who espouse the novice-expert approach have the goal of identifying the nature of expertise in some area (e.g., math, chess, computers). To reveal the nature of expertise, researchers usually observe experts and novices as they try to solve problems. Then, the problem-solving approaches of novices are compared to those of the experts. The guiding question behind such work is "What is true of experts that is not true of novices?"

Recent summaries of this line of research (e.g., Anderson, 1990; Glaser & Chi, 1988) suggest that there are seven main dimensions of expertise:

1. *Domain-Specificity:* At one time, it was thought that chess experts or computer experts are highly skilled and knowledgeable in many domains. In effect, the belief was that experts tend to be very smart. Research shows, however, that there is very little evidence that a person who is highly skilled in one domain (e.g., chess) can transfer this skill to another domain (e.g., math). Thus, genuine expertise seems to be limited to a single domain.

2. *Greater Knowledge and Experience:* One of the largest differences between novices and experts is that experts have acquired considerably more knowledge and skills in an area than novices. Thus, given a list of the possible ideas that one could have for an area and some way to inspect the contents of someone's memory, we would find that an expert's memory would contain many more items on the list than a novice's memory. Moreover, by virtue of using skills many times, the expert ends up practicing them to the point that they can be performed quickly and automatically. But it is important to note that experts not only have more knowledge and skills than novices, they also interrelate this information in more complex, elaborate, and abstract ways (Chi et al., 1989).

3. *Meaningful Perception:* When experts and novices look at the same situation, experts tend to see the situation as a meaningful whole and novices tend to see it as a collection of discrete elements. In the earliest demonstration of this phenomenon, chess experts were found to see an arrangement of, say, 15 chess pieces on a chessboard as a single meaningful pattern. Novices, in contrast, saw it as 15 unrelated units of information. If chess is played repeatedly for many years, certain arrangements will recur many times. Experts recognize the recurrent patterns as ones they have seen before. In an analogous way, expert teachers will recognize recurrent classroom situations, and expert car mechanics will recognize recurrent engine problems.

4. *Reflective, Qualitative Problem Analysis:* Research shows that experts begin their problem-solving attempts with a period in which they pause to understand a problem. Novices, in contrast, do not take the time to analyze a problem very deeply. Instead, they are very quick to jump right in and deploy stereotypical responses. For experts, a good portion of the problem-analysis phase consists of trying to recognize the problem, elaborating or imposing constraints on possible solutions, and building a workable mental representation of the problem.

5. *Principled Problem Representation:* An expert's mental representation of a problem is more workable than that of a novice because whereas the expert would understand a problem in a deep (i.e., principled) way, the novice would understand it in a superficial way. For example, a novice might think that two physics problems are similar because both involve an inclined plane. An expert, in contrast, might think they are not very similar because one pertains to Newton's first law and the other pertains to Newton's third law. Similarly, a novice teacher might think that a classroom disturbance is similar to an earlier one simply because the same two students are involved. In contrast, an expert teacher might think that the two situations are dissimilar because one was precipitated by student boredom and the other was precipitated by a student's anger over a grade.

6. *Effective Strategy Construction:* Some studies have found that novices and experts use the same tactics when they solve parts of the problem, but they arrange these tactics in different orders. Thus, once again we have a qualitative difference rather than a quantitative difference.

7. *Post-Analysis Speed and Accuracy:* Although experts spend more time than novices on the analysis phase, they nevertheless are much faster than novices in their execution of problem-solving strategies. Undoubtably, the former's greater speed derives from the greater amount of practice that experts have (Anderson, 1990). Moreover, unlike novices, who would make many errors if they tried to speed up their responding, experts are found to be quite accurate even when they are given little time to respond.

These seven dimensions of expertise provide two further enhancements to the expert's ability. The first is that experts can make better use of their working memory capacity than novices because of three aspects of their expertise: knowledge, speed, and automaticity (Glaser & Chi, 1988). In particular, knowledge, speed, and automaticity improve memory ability by freeing up available working memory slots. To see this, recall that greater knowledge helps an expert mentally group a large amount of information into a single chunk. If all of the information can be grouped into, say, two chunks, an expert may have five slots of working memory available to encode additional information. But thanks to increases in speed and automaticity, even the two slots required by the chunked information may be available as well. Thus, with the same number of slots, an expert can attend to and store a larger amount of the same situation.

The second enhancement is that experts demonstrate greater self-monitoring skills than novices; that is, the former are more likely to know when they are confused or make an error than the latter. This enhanced capacity for self-monitoring appears to accrue from the fact that experts form more accurate mental representations of a problem than novices. These more accurate representations, in turn, derive from an expert's greater knowledge and tendency to spend more time analyzing a problem qualitatively.

Research shows that expertise seems to emerge only after an individual gains considerable knowledge and skill in an area and has had sufficient time to practice skills until they are automatic. In fact, several researchers have found that it seems to take about ten years until someone becomes a true expert in an area (Hayes, 1985; Ericsson & Smith, 1991). Given these time constraints, it follows that students should not be asked to think like experts from the start of their exposure to an area. For example, we would not expect a third grader who is exposed to math word problems for the first time to be helped by someone saying, "Now, don't jump right in. Take a few minutes to really understand the problem and then solve it really fast." In the absence of prior knowledge and problem schemata (see Chapter 8), increased reflection and forced speed may have little benefit.

Summary of Developmental Approaches

Perhaps the best summary of the four developmental approaches would be a recapitulation of the major terms used to describe higher-order thinking so far. For Piaget, the main attributes of higher-order thought are that it is *abstract* and *logical*. The four major cognitive processes include *classification, inference-making* (deductive, inductive, and transitive), *hypothesis-testing,* and *experimentation.* These four processes only reflect higher-order thought when they are applied to knowledge that is abstract and logically organized.

For Vygotsky, higher-order thinking must have a *social origin* as well be *self-regulated, conscious,* and *symbolically mediated.* For Bloom, higher forms of thought involve *understanding, application, analysis, synthesis,* and *evaluation.* For researchers in the novice-expert tradition, the central aspects of expertise include *domain-specificity, substantial knowledge and skill, meaningful perception, reflectivity, principled understanding, speed, enhanced memory,* and *enhanced self-monitoring.*

All of the developmental approaches have emphasized the fact that there is a natural progression in thinking from lower forms to higher forms with age or experience. This developmental progression implies that students need to have a certain amount of education, experience, or practice before they can become capable of the highest forms of thought. Hence, each approach implies that it is unwise to ask beginners to engage in the highest forms of thought right away because the tasks that require this type of thought would either be over their heads or be performed incorrectly. And yet, each approach also reveals that it is wrong to assume that teachers should do nothing to promote thinking until students reach a certain age.

Definitional Approaches

In this section, we shall examine three approaches to higher-order thinking that define it but do not place it within a developmental framework. That is, there is very little in the following definitions that would limit higher-order thinking to only those individuals who have progressed sufficiently along a developmental continuum.

Sternberg's Approach

Overview
In the 1980s, Robert Sternberg proposed an information-processing theory of intelligence (e.g., Sternberg, 1985). Close inspection of Sternberg's theory shows that it is a description of how intelligent people solve problems and acquire

information. Soon after his theory was proposed, many people started to ask, "Could I teach my students how to approach problems more intelligently?" In essence, they were asking whether students could be taught how to think better. In many people's minds, there is no real difference between thinking well and higher-order thinking, so Sternberg's theory of intelligence soon became viewed as an approach to higher-order thinking (e.g., Vye, Delclos, Burns & Bransford, 1988).

Similar to other intelligence theorists who came before him, Sternberg devised his theory in two main steps. In the first step, he identified the key skills and processes involved in intelligent problem-solving and learning. In the second step, he tried to form clusters of skills that seemed to perform similar functions in the mind. In essence, for each skill or process he asked, "What job does this skill or process play in the mind?" Those skills or processes with similar jobs were grouped together to form a single cluster.

Using this approach, Sternberg identified three clusters of skills. He considered each cluster to be a component of intelligence. The *metacognitive* component mainly consists of the skills involved in thinking about how to solve a problem before you start. The *performance* component consists of the skills that you use in the midst of solving a problem. The *knowledge acquisition* component comprises those skills involved in acquiring new information. In what follows, we shall examine these three components in more detail.

- *Metacognitive Component.* The metacognitive component consists of skills such as (a) problem definition (i.e., thinking about what you are trying to accomplish and what you are allowed to do), (b) planning (i.e., selecting and ordering a set of problem-solving steps), and (c) allocating attentional resources (i.e., thinking about which things you are going to pay attention to and for how long).
- *Performance Component.* The performance component consists of a variety of mental skills and processes that have to do with specific tasks. Each task requires its own key skills and processes. To illustrate, consider analogies such as "Human : Hand :: Animal : (a) Paw, (b) Fur." For Sternberg (1985) analogy problems require the processes of *encoding* (i.e., processing all five terms in the analogy), *inference* (i.e., computing the relation between the first and second term), *mapping* (i.e., computing the relation between the first and third terms), and *application* (i.e., computing a relation between the third and fourth terms that is parallel to that between the first and second terms). Whereas analogies require encoding, inference, mapping, and application, other tasks require a different set of skills and processes.
- *Knowledge Acquisition.* The knowledge acquisition component consists of three primary processes: selective encoding (i.e., encoding only that information which is relevant to the learning task), selective combination (i.e., taking all of the selectively encoded information and putting it together in an effective way), and selective comparison (i.e., comparing what you just learned by way of selective encoding to something you already know).

Higher-Order Thinking

Sternberg (1985) argued that the metacognitive component lies at the heart of intelligence and higher-order thinking because it functions as an "executive"; that is, it coordinates the activities of the performance and knowledge acquisition components. More specifically, the metacognitive component is involved in decisions regarding (a) which performance components should be accessed and performed in a particular context, (b) when it is time to shift to a new problem-solving solution, and (c) when it is time to learn something new. Thus, if one wanted to foster higher-order thinking, one would attempt to enhance the functioning of the skills that comprise the metacognitive component (e.g., planning, problem-definition, monitoring, and allocation of attentional resources).

As indicated in the introduction to this section, there is nothing in Sternberg's theory that suggests that higher-order thinking (as he defines it) could be found only in a group of older, experienced individuals. From what is known about the cognitive abilities of young children, even two-year-olds could approach tasks in the way described by Sternberg.

The IDEAL Problem-Solver Approach

John Bransford and his colleagues have long been interested in the issue of how to teach thinking skills to students. Their thoughtful analysis of many years of research reveals that there are two main components of effective thinking and problem-solving: (a) a set of general problem-solving strategies and (b) specific knowledge that is organized in such a way that it enhances successful performance (Bransford et al., 1986).

General Problem-Solving Strategies

Bransford and his colleagues use the acronym IDEAL to capture the five general strategies that comprise effective thinking and problem-solving: (a) *Identifying* the existence of a problem, (b) *Defining* the nature of the problem, (c) *Exploring* possible solutions to the problem and deciding on a best alternative, (d) *Acting* on this decision by implementing the chosen alternative, and (e) *Looking* at the effects of this decision to see whether the problem was solved. Let's examine each of these five strategies further to see what they mean.

Problem identification. Good thinking begins with the capacity to notice the existence of problems. As implied in the adage "An ounce of prevention is worth a pound of cure," effective problem-solving consists of noticing problems before they get out of hand. People who are highly successful in school, at work, and in their personal lives notice problems early on and work toward solving them soon after they are noticed. Poor thinkers rarely notice problems when they arise. To illustrate, consider how poor readers have been found to be unaware of the fact that they have reading problems (Bransford et al., 1986).

Problem definition.   But simply noticing the existence of a problem does not help much in telling the problem-solver how to solve it. Consider how noticing a problem in a personal relationship (e.g., you are fighting with someone all of the time) does not immediately tell you what is wrong and how it should be solved. Similarly, a poor reader might become aware of having trouble reading but not know exactly what is wrong. That brings us to the next step: defining the problem.

Problem definition is analogous to a physician's diagnosis of a disease, because when you define a problem you indicate what is causing the problem. In fact, diagnosis is just one form of the general process of problem definition. The key step in diagnosis involves unpacking the question "What is wrong?" by thinking about your goals. In most cases, a problem is simply something that is standing in the way of your reaching your goals. With relationships, you might have the goal of interacting harmoniously with your partner as often as possible. Fighting means that you are not meeting this goal. Similarly, a fifth grader might have the goal of getting an A on a math test, so encountering some difficult questions on the test is a problem because she may not meet her goal. Good thinking consists of defining and redefining your goals until you have some that help you maximize your success (Sternberg, 1985). Poor thinkers always seem to define the problem incorrectly; that is, they define it in terms of lower-level, nonessential, or overly constrained goals.

To illustrate, consider the fifth grader who wants an A on her math test. When she encounters the first hard question, she defines her problem (i.e., states her goals) in two ways: (a) I need to get *this* question right in order to get an A, or (b) I need to get 90 percent of all of the questions right in order to get an A. If she defines the problem as in (a), she may waste a lot of time trying to solve that one problem. In contrast, if she defines it as in (b), she might go on to other problems that she can solve.

Exploration.   Our fifth-grader example shows the importance of the problem definition step (the *D* in IDEAL) because strategies relate closely to definitions. Different strategies are considered when one defines problems in different ways (e.g., figuring out the answer to one question versus figuring out the answers to 90 percent of the questions). Thus, the explore step (i.e., the *E* in IDEAL) is dependent on the prior definition step. But even when two individuals define problems in similar ways, a good thinker engages in exploration differently from a poor thinker. In particular, good thinkers would tend to be more reflective and open-minded about possibilities than poor thinkers (Janis, 1989).

Act.   Unlike the identify, define, and explore steps, the act part of the IDEAL model may not be a step that plays a large role in distinguishing good thinkers from poor thinkers. It is conceivable that good thinkers and poor thinkers can perform the actions that lead to success equally well. Nevertheless, poor thinkers are more likely to fail than good thinkers because only the latter identify, define, and explore effectively. Thus, only the latter *think of* doing the appropriate actions (on their own).

Look. The final crucial step in effective thinking and problem-solving is the *L* in IDEAL. Research shows that good problem-solvers are constantly monitoring their performances. They note when actions lead to success and when they do not. When failure occurs, good thinkers go back to the early steps in the process (e.g., define or explore) to try something else. Poor thinkers have been found to pay little attention to their successes and failures. As a result, they are often unlikely to revise their strategies (Bransford et al., 1986).

Domain-Specific Knowledge

Earlier it was noted that the IDEAL approach specifies that there are two aspects of good thinking: general strategies and domain-specific knowledge. We have already examined the five general strategies, so let's now examine the role of knowledge. Bransford et al. note that good thinking cannot operate in a vacuum. We saw in the section on developmental approaches that experts are more likely to notice problems and monitor their performance than novices because of the greater knowledge possessed by the former. Moreover, knowledge helps experts appropriately define problems. Thus, Bransford et al. would agree that having knowledge is a prerequisite to the successful application of the five IDEAL strategies, but they note that students could develop an almost "habit-like" tendency to go through the five steps if teachers of all content areas (e.g., math, science, reading, etc.) used the IDEAL model simultaneously in their classrooms. Moreover, it is possible for students to have sufficient knowledge but nevertheless carry out the IDEAL steps in a suboptimal way. Thus, the IDEAL strategies and knowledge are independent but, hopefully interacting aspects of performance.

Resnick's Approach

Lauren Resnick, an expert on cognition and instruction, was asked by the National Research Council to review the vast literature on higher-order thinking and make recommendations regarding how to foster it in students (Resnick, 1987). She found, as most other reviewers have found, that there is a large number of definitions of higher-order thinking in existence. She quickly recognized that in order to make recommendations regarding how to improve thinking, she would first need to distill a single, unified conception of higher-order thinking from the large number of conceptions that exist. Her attempt at distilling a unified conception generated the following definition of higher-order thinking:

Higher-order thinking is *non-algorithmic* (i.e., the path of action is not fully specified in advance), *complex* (i.e., there are multiple solutions and the total path is not "visible" from any single vantage point), and *effortful* (i.e., there is considerable mental energy devoted to aspects of problem-solving). Moreover, it involves *nuanced judgments*, the application of *multiple* (sometimes conflicting) *criteria*, *uncertainty* about what is known, *self-regulation*, and the imposition of *meaning*. In contrast, lower-order thinking would be algorithmic, simple, reflexlike, transparent, certain, other-regulated, and associative (rather than meaning-imposing).

Similar to Bransford et al., Resnick recognizes the importance of subject-matter knowledge in the ability to demonstrate higher-order thinking. Nevertheless, she argues that many aspects of good thinking are shared across disciplines and situations. Moreover, she contends that the approach of teaching basic skills first and higher-level skills second runs counter to the current thinking of subject-matter specialists. That is, she argues that there is no reason content could not be taught in the midst of solving problems.

Summary of Definitional Approaches

The common thread of Sternberg's approach, the IDEAL model, and Resnick's approach is the conception of good thinking as flexible, reflective *problem-solving*. Contrary to the developmental approaches, the three definitional approaches suggest that the elements of effective problem-solving *can* be fostered early and *should* be fostered across disciplines. Nevertheless, the proponents of the definitional approaches also stress that thinking skills operate best when students have acquired sufficient content knowledge appropriate to a particular context.

Other Approaches

Before moving on to other issues, it is worth pointing out that the developmental and definitional approaches are by no means the only approaches to higher-order thinking. Because of space limitations, it was not possible to describe many other approaches that have their followings, such as Ennis's model of critical thinking (Ennis, 1962), Lipman's philosophy for children program (Lipman, 1985), and the CoRT program (de Bono, 1983). (See Halpern, 1990; Nickerson, Perkins & Smith, 1985; Resnick, 1987; Segal, Chipman & Glaser, 1985, for reviews.)

Transfer of Skills

The term *transfer* is used to refer to the process of extending knowledge acquired in one context (e.g., the classroom) to other contexts (e.g., the workplace). In many ways, the issue of how to promote thinking in students is very much related to the issue of transfer. Why? It turns out that when employers and others complain that students cannot think, they often mean that students show very little evidence of transfer. More specifically, the observation is that students often fail to *use* the facts they learn in school to help them solve problems outside of school. With a few notable exceptions, the casual observation that people rarely transfer their knowledge has been confirmed many times in laboratory studies (Singly & Anderson, 1989; Brown, Collins & Duguid, 1989; Salomon & Perkins, 1989).

If students do not transfer what they learn in school to real-world contexts, it means that our education system is failing miserably. Thus, it is imperative to understand the reasons transfer does or does not happen. In what follows, we shall examine some of these reasons.

Embeddedness in Single Contexts

One reason a skill may not be transferred is that students often tie it to the single context in which it was learned. For example, children who learn how to solve math problems in the context of seatwork seem to call on their arithmetic skills only during seatwork. If they are moved to another context (e.g., the candy store), they have no idea how to use their math knowledge to solve a problem in that new context (e.g., how much money they need to buy several pieces of candy). Many scholars argue that in order for a skill to be transferred, it has to first become disembedded from the original learning context (Singly & Anderson, 1989; Piaget & Inhelder, 1969; Vygotsky, 1962; Brown, Bransford, Campione & Ferrara, 1983). The term *decontextualization* refers to the process of progressively severing links between a skill and irrelevant aspects of the learning context until only the link between one's goals and the skill remain (Singly & Anderson, 1989). For example, word processing skills become decontextualized once a writer realizes that he or she can use essentially any word processing package on any computer to write the same letter.

Lack of Conditional Knowledge

Although decontextualizing a skill increases the likelihood of transfer, it is not enough. Students also need to know when and where a decontextualized skill would be useful (Brown at al., 1983; Gagne, Yekovich & Yekovich, 1993; Garner, 1987). One of the best ways of acquiring such *conditional knowledge* is to connect your skills to goals (Brown, 1989; Singly & Anderson, 1989). For example, if the word processing function *delete* is linked to the goal of eliminating a word, then moving to a different computer will not be a problem if you say to yourself, "I have to delete this word. I wonder how to do it on this computer?"

If people lack conditional knowledge for a skill, then, it probably has something to do with their goals. If, for example, skills were never linked to appropriate goals in the original learning context, there would be no basis for using these skills in the transfer context. In essence, there would be an incompatibility between the goal structures of the two contexts. To illustrate, consider the situation in which the goal of using a skill in the learning context was "to finish my seatwork," but the goal of using the skill in the transfer context was "to know how much money to give the cashier for these four pieces of candy."

Unprincipled Learning

There are two main ways to teach a set of facts. One way is to present each fact as a separate idea that should be learned in a rote way. A second way is to group facts together that represent instances of the same principle. For example, instead of having students learn individual facts such as "the number that comes after 6 is 7" and "the number that comes after 2013 is 2014," we could teach them the general principle that "to arrive at the number that comes after a given number, add 1 to it" (Brophy, 1990; Gage & Berliner, 1991). Similarly, instead of teaching children the separate pronunciations of *cat, mat,* and *hat,* you could teach them a principle about many words that end in *-at.* Studies have shown that whereas transfer rarely happens when a student's knowledge consists of individual facts learned at the rote level, it happens quite often when he or she knows a principle and it applies in a new context (Singly & Anderson, 1989).

Lack of Conceptual Knowledge

Many studies have shown that students are more likely to show transfer when they have a deep conceptual understanding of a skill than when they lack this conceptual understanding (e.g., Mayer, 1989; Resnick, 1980). Perhaps the first demonstration of this phenomenon occurred when Gestalt psychologists tried to show how Thorndike's views on rote learning and transfer were incorrect. In one study, Wertheimer (1945) used two methods to teach children the "drop-perpendicular" method for computing the area of a parallelogram. One group of children was simply shown how to perform the drop-perpendicular technique (i.e., they learned it by rote). Another group was given an explanation of why the method works in addition to being shown how to do it. The explanation consisted of showing them how one could cut off a triangular portion of a parallelogram and reattach it at the other end to make a rectangle (as in Figure 4.1). Then, it became clear that the drop-perpendicular approach was simply an extension of the familiar "length × width" rule for finding the area of a rectangle. When children were presented with a parallelogram in an unusual orientation, the no-explanation group performed the drop-perpendicular method in an inappropriate way.

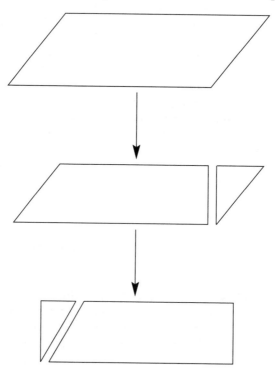

FIGURE 4.1

The explanation group, in contrast, adjusted the method to fit the new orientation and derived the right answer.

At this point, we can form bridges across several sections of this chapter. The reader may have noticed a certain similarity between what was said about learning principles and what was said about conceptual understanding. A conceptual understanding often means having knowledge of principles and what they mean. Moreover, when we examined the novice-expert research, we saw that experts have a deeper, more principled understanding of problems than novices. Given this difference in knowledge, it would be expected that experts are more likely to show transfer than novices. The research confirms this expectation.

Inaccurate Conceptions of the Mind

In the beginning of this chapter, it was noted that many studies have shown that people do not transfer skills across contexts. In contrast, in the two sections that you just read, you saw that people often *do* transfer skills. What accounts for the differences across studies? The main difference seems to be how individuals view the mind. Those individuals who have an accurate conception of how the mind works have been successful in promoting transfer. Those individuals who have an inaccurate conception of how the mind works have not been successful.

To illustrate, consider the early work of E. L. Thorndike on transfer (Thorndike & Woodworth, 1901). Thorndike conducted his studies to disprove an educational approach called the "formal discipline" method. Advocates of the formal discipline method (who still exist today) argue that the mind is composed of a set of faculties such as attention and reasoning that could be exercised in the same way one exercises muscles (Singly & Anderson, 1989). These faculties reign over knowledge and can be applied in any situation. Back in Thorndike's day, it was assumed that by taking courses in, say, Latin or logic, faculties such as reasoning could be exercised. The result was that a student would learn how to generally think better after taking such courses.

Thorndike disagreed strongly with the notion that there are general faculties. He believed that the mind consisted of nothing more than a multitude of stimulus-response bonds. For example, part of your math knowledge would be the associative bond between the stimulus "$3 \times 3 = ?$" and your response, "9." The rest of your math knowledge is a variety of other bonds. Thorndike argued that transfer would happen only when there was a great deal of similarity between a learning context and a transfer context. In this "identity of elements" view, similarity consisted of the virtual identity of aspects of the situation (e.g., the same people or objects present) or behavior (the same response was performed). In support of his view (and against the formal discipline view) he showed that transfer happened only when there was a great deal of similarity in situations and responses. Moreover, he (and many others after him) showed that students who take Latin, geometry, and logic courses do not do better in other subject areas than students who do not take such courses. Moreover, there was no evidence that these students thought better than other students.

Thus, Thorndike's studies showed that the notion of *general faculties* is not a correct view of mind. Unfortunately for him, however, many researchers have shown that his view of the mind is not correct either. As described in the previous two sections, transfer can occur when people know principles or understand what they are doing. Thorndike's theory made no room for notions such as principles, conceptual knowledge, procedural knowledge, schemata, or expertise. Thus, it now makes sense that he did not observe transfer in his studies.

Lack of Metacognition

There are two meanings of the term *metacognition* that are relevant to discussions of transfer. The first has to do with the notion of *mindfulness* (Salomon & Perkins, 1989). Transfer is more likely when an individual makes a conscious attempt to process a situation in a thoughtful, reflective, and analytical way. One way to be mindful is to ask oneself questions such as "Have I tried to solve a problem like this one before?" (Brown et al., 1983).

A second relevant meaning of *metacognition* pertains to the notion of *learning to learn*. Good learners have a better sense of the nature of learning than poor learners; that is, they have a more accurate "theory of mind" (cf. Wellman, 1990). For example, they recognize that (a) it is normal to be confused sometimes, (b) certain strategies work better in certain situations than others, (c) asking help of an expert can be quite effective, and (d) one's memory is far from fallible. Thus, just as it is important for researchers and teachers to have an accurate view of the mind (see the previous section), it is important for students themselves to have an accurate view of their own minds.

Summary

We have seen that transfer is more likely to occur if students can partially decontextualize skills and develop conditional knowledge about their application. Goals were argued to play a central role in discussions of decontextualization and conditional knowledge. Transfer was also found to be likely if learners cast their knowledge in the form of principles, and also develop a conceptual understanding of procedures and strategies. Finally, transfer is enhanced when students (a) have an accurate conception of the learning process and (b) approach their learning in a mindful way.

Instructional Implications

Having examined seven approaches to higher-order thinking as well as the research on transfer, we are now in a position to examine the instructional implications of all of this work:

1. The developmental approaches stress the importance of following a sequence of fostering lower forms of thought before higher forms of thought. Students need considerable experience interacting with concrete content and solving problems in order to be able to form abstractions and develop mastery over this information. To foster the development of abstractions, teachers can provide many examples and point out the similarities among examples (e.g., present five examples of the same type of word problem and ask students how they are the same; present the government structures of three countries and ask students to say why all are democracies). Moreover, they can provide feedback regarding improper classifications and conceptions. To help students gain mastery over skills, they can use methods such as reciprocal teaching. According to developmental views, then, it is not a problem if preschool or early elementary teachers focus mainly on lower-level skills. The problem is that teachers of *older* students never go beyond fact-learning.

2. It is a maxim that students learn what their teachers emphasize in class. Bloom and his colleagues were quite helpful in pointing out the connection between teaching *objectives* and teaching approaches. In particular, if one wants students to know information at the knowledge level, one can simply use a drill-and-practice approach. In contrast, if one wants students to know information at the comprehension level, they must be taught in ways which help them understand better (e.g., using analogies). Similarly, if teachers want students to be able to apply information, they must show students *how to* apply information and give them multiple opportunities to apply what they know. Students who are just taught facts (e.g., the definition of a democracy) cannot immediately apply this information (e.g., recognize a democracy when they see one; take a nondemocracy and change it into one).

3. Perhaps the main lesson of the theories and research reported in this chapter is that there should be a straightforward connection between school tasks and tasks in the real world. As several prominent researchers have pointed out, the concepts of learning and transfer are very much interrelated (A. Brown et al., 1983; J. S. Brown et al., 1989; Singly & Anderson, 1989). The issue of whether a student will transfer knowledge depends on how the skill was learned. If one wants students to be able to use a skill in real-world contexts, one should simulate these real-world contexts in the classroom. Thus, one should develop real-world problems as content and have students develop solutions to these problems. Moreover, it is important to ensure that the goals of the classroom problems are similar to the goals of real-world problems. For example, a town in Maryland has the highest cancer rate in the country. A teacher in Maryland would be better off to use this example to teach the scientific method to students than more remote content (e.g., have them think of reasons for this high cancer rate and set them out to research these possibilities).

4. To foster decontextualization, teachers should have students solve multiple realistic problems that are superficially dissimilar but identical with respect to strategies and goals. Moreover, it should be noted that the goal is not to present skills in a totally decontextualized form (e.g., decoding words on a flashcard or having a separate class on higher-order thinking, decision-making, or study skills). Rather, the goals of decontextualization are to (a) eliminate associations among skills and *irrelevant* aspects of contexts, and (b) form connections between

skills and the various contexts to which the skills could be applied. Thus, all skills should be contextualized to a degree.

5. Whenever content is presented in class, it is helpful if students can be asked to classify things into categories, arrange things along some dimension, make hypotheses, draw inferences, analyze things into their components, and solve problems. These cognitive processes can apply to any subject matter, but once again, it is important that students know and comprehend basic facts first.

6. Teachers play a vital role in encouraging mindfulness and reflectivity and in promoting an understanding of the learning process. Activities such as allowing a student ample time to think about an answer and rewarding mindfulness would go a long way to increase reflectivity in the classroom. To promote an understanding of the learning process, teachers can use think-aloud to model learning-to-learn strategies or can simply point out to children what they can do to help solve a problem on their own.

In the chapters on reading, writing, math, science, and social studies, you will find case studies of teaching programs that illustrate many of the above principles. Instead of singling out one subject area here (e.g., math) to illustrate how one implements higher-order thinking in the classroom based on these principles, the interested reader can merely turn to the end of each of Chapters 5, 6, 7, 8, 9, and 10 for illustrations. In the meantime, a good constructivist exercise would be to take a topic that you would want to teach to students and make each of the six guidelines above into a checklist. That is, ask yourself, have students had enough practice with concrete content that they can think abstractly about this content? What do I want them to be able to do? (recall the facts? comprehend them? apply them?). Are my examples and exercises related to real-world tasks? Am I asking them to classify things, arrange things along a dimension, make hypotheses, draw inferences, analyze things into their components, and solve problems? The more you answer "yes" to these questions, the more you will engage your students in higher-order thinking.

Chapter 5

Beginning Reading

Summary

1. Although skilled readers process the individual letters in a word, they perceive it as a whole.

2. The connections between written words and their meanings are well established in a skilled reader's mind.

3. Skilled readers connect the phonemes of their spoken language to written words and syllables.

4. Skilled readers create mental models of what they are reading and use these mental models to form expectations.

5. Skilled readers rely on syntactic cues to create a mental representation of a sentence.

6. The best predictors of early reading success are a child's knowledge of letters and phonemic awareness.

7. Children who learn to read the best in the first grade enter first grade already knowing a lot about reading.

8. Children are less likely to rely heavily on context and more likely to decode words quickly and automatically with age.

9. The biggest differences between same-age good and poor readers concerns their abilities to (a) recognize words automatically, (b) recognize words rapidly, and (c) recode print items into a phonological representation.

10. Gender differences in beginning reading are fairly small and inconsistent. In contrast, ethnic differences are fairly large and consistent.

At first blush, reading seems to be a fairly simple act of sounding out words. In reality, however, it is a complex collection of skills that take many years to master. To get an initial sense of the kind of mental tasks that skilled readers perform, read the contents of Table 5.1 in order to answer the following question: "How does the author feel about smoking?"

Let's now consider some of the things that you did when you tried to answer the question above. When you first examined Table 5.1, you mainly focused your eyes on the words in the table, not the other symbols. When you encountered a

TABLE 5.1   Examples Illustrating Levels of Reading

$ $ $ $ $ $ $ $ $ $ $ $ $ $ $ $ $ $

(1) smoked

% %   % % %   % %%%%   @@@@@@@

(2) Mary smoked three packs of cigarettes a day.
. . . . > > > >,,,,,,,,,. . . . .

(3) Mary smoked three packs of cigarettes a day. After she died, her husband sold their Phillip Morris stocks. This was a good thing to do because cigarettes are the scourge of mankind.

# #	$	$
#	# #	#

line that contained more than one word (e.g. line (2)), you read them from left to right. The fact that you looked for words shows that you know that the text carries the message; The fact that you read words from left to right shows that you know the directionality of written English (Clay, 1985). Young, prereading children lack such *concepts of print.*

In addition to illustrating print concepts, Table 5.1 also illustrates certain levels of reading (Carver, 1973; Mayer, 1987). For example, when you read the single word *smoked,* you recognized this cluster of letters and retrieved ideas associated with it (e.g., smoked salmon). In Carver's (1973) model, this is called "level 1 reading." When you finished reading the first full sentence in line (2), you not only tried to recognize the words and access their meanings, you also integrated all of these meanings into a structural representation of the entire sentence. In Carver's (1973) model, this is called "level 2 reading." When you read the three sentences in line (3), you probably made the inference that "she" and "her" refer to "Mary" and that smoking was the cause of her death. Carver (1973) called this "level 3 reading." Finally, some of you may also have formed the opinion that the author of line (3) was a little extreme in his or her characterization of smoking as "the scourge of mankind." Carver (1973) used the label "level 4 reading" to refer to the ability to evaluate or criticize text.

The goal of the present chapter is to convey the nature of beginning reading (i.e., Carver's levels 1 and 2). In the first section of this chapter, you will get a sense of what children need to learn in order to become skilled readers (The Nature of Skilled Reading). In the second section, you will learn how reading skills develop (The Development of Skilled Reading). In the third section, you will learn how good readers differ from not-so-good readers (Individual Differences in Reading Skills). In the fourth section, you will learn how instruction should be designed in order to help children become skilled readers (Instructional Implications).

The Nature of Skilled Reading

In order to know how to help children become good readers, we first need to know what good reading entails. The best way to learn what good reading entails is to examine well-established models of proficient reading (Adams, 1990). Figure 5.1 shows one such model.

This model is based on the idea that when people read, they process many different types of information (e.g., letters, word meanings, syntax, etc.). More important, the model implies two things: (a) that processing is *divided* among relatively autonomous subsystems that perform their own tasks (indicated by the ovals), and (b) that each subsystem *sends* what it knows or has figured out to at least one other subsystem (indicated by the arrows). The former point means that readers have many different clues that they can use to make sense of a sentence. The latter point means that one processor can send its clues to other processors to help them make sense of their own clues; that is, the processors work *interactively* with one another (Perfetti, 1985). With this in mind, let's examine the jobs performed by the orthographic, meaning, phonological and context processors in turn.

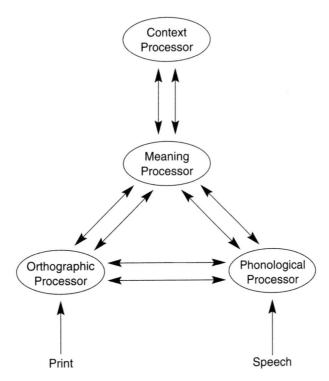

FIGURE 5.1   A Model of Proficient Reading

The Orthographic Processor

Orthographic knowledge consists of knowing the individual symbols of a written language. For example, a child who knows the letters of the English alphabet has orthographic knowledge. The orthographic processor shown in Figure 5.1 can be thought of as a storehouse of orthographic knowledge. More specifically, the orthographic processor has the job of processing and recognizing strings of letters (i.e., words). It accomplishes this feat by means of small units that recognize individual letters (McClelland & Rumelhart, 1981; Seidenberg & McClelland, 1989).

Word recognition occurs when the units for each letter of a word attain a sufficient degree of activation. The main way that each unit becomes activated is through direct perception of the letter it stands for. The second way that units can be activated is through *spreading activation* (see Chapter 3). A unit can spread its activation to another unit if the units are linked in an associative relationship. Associations form between units when certain letters (e.g., *q*) frequently co-occur with other letters (e.g., *u*). Any unit that has been partially activated by spreading activation turns on faster than it would if the letter were presented alone. For example, when someone sees a *q*, and then a *u*, the unit for *u* is turned on faster than it would have been if *u* had been perceived alone. Thus, associations and spreading activation promote faster reading.

Any familiar word, then, is really a highly associated pattern of letters and each letter in the word primes the perception of the others. As a result, the entire word is recognized very quickly and automatically as a result of perceiving all of the letters.

After many years of research using sophisticated technology, we now have a better sense of how the orthographic processor works in skilled readers. Here are some of the findings:

1. Contrary to popular belief, skilled readers process the individual letters of the words they are reading. They are not aware of this because word recognition has become automatic and subconscious for them. However, skilled readers do not recognize the letters of a word independently of one another. Rather, after many years of reading, associations form between the units for one letter in a word and the units for other letters. As a result, a familiar word is perceived as a whole.

2. The strength of the association between the units for letters reflects the frequencies with which these letters co-occur in written texts. For example, when the letter *t* occurs as the first letter of a three-letter word, it is extremely likely that the next letter will be an *h* (Adams, 1990). People who read a lot develop mental associations between letters. Once associations form, they allow the activation from the units for one letter to spread to the units for another. As a result, skilled readers recognize familiar words very quickly and automatically. In contrast, someone who has never read a book and knows only letters would not recognize words as fast as a skilled reader because no associations have formed among the units for letters. Such a person would, however, recognize isolated letters as fast as a skilled reader.

3. Letter associations also help skilled readers process the proper order of letters in a word (e.g., *the* versus *hte*), as well as perceive association-preserving pseudowords (e.g., *Mave*).

4. Finally, letter associations also help a reader divide a word into syllables. For example, whereas *dr* is an acceptable combination of letters that maps onto the sounds of spoken English, *dn* is not. As a result, a skilled reader who encounters the word *midnight* would visually divide this word into *mid* and *night*. In contrast, skilled readers would not visually divide *address* into *add* and *ress*. Moreover, a skilled reader implicitly knows that vowels seem to pull their adjacent consonants into a cluster of association patterns. For example, the first *a* in *partial* pulls the *p* and *r* toward itself. This fact combined with the fact that *rt* is an unacceptable spoken combination means that *partial* would be divided into *par* and *tial* (Adams, 1990).

It is interesting to note that, historically, written language did not use spacing and punctuation to delineate words (Just & Carpenter, 1987). As a result, readers had to rely on their orthographic knowledge exclusively to make sense of a sentence. To see how this might work, consider the following sentence:

THATTOYWASLOST

The Meaning Processor

Overview

Of course, comprehending a sentence requires far more than the ability to determine whether letter strings are orthographically acceptable or familiar. For example, the sentence "Trat distle quas" contains three acceptable combinations of letters, but it is meaningless. Similarly, the sentence "The octogenarian insinuated himself into our organization" would be meaningless to someone who knows she has seen the words *octogenarian* and *insinuated* before, but cannot remember what they mean. Thus, sentence comprehension requires both an orthographic processor to recognize letter strings and a meaning processor to access word meanings.

Two views have been proposed regarding how meanings are assigned to words. According to the *lexical access* view, entire word meanings are stored in a *lexicon*. The lexicon is simply a mental dictionary that organizes word meanings in terms of lists of attributes or schemata (see Chapter 2 for a description of schemata). When a written word is perceived, its meanings are accessed if the resting activation level of these word meanings is high enough (Just & Carpenter, 1987). Moreover, the higher the resting activation level, the faster a word meaning will be retrieved. Word meanings attain a high activation level if the words to which they are attached occur frequently. Thus, the meanings of frequent words are accessed faster than the meanings of infrequent words.

The second view derives from recent *connectionist* theories. According to this view, word meanings are represented in the meaning processor as associated sets of primitive meaning elements, in the same way that spellings of familiar words are represented in the orthographic processor as associated sets of letters (Adams, 1990). A person's experience determines which meaning elements get associated and stored for a given word (Hintzman, 1986). For example, a child who hears the word *dog* applied to a specific dog in a specific context might associate the whole experience with the word *dog*. The next time she hears the word *dog* applied, however, it might be with a different dog in a different context. According to the connectionist view, those aspects of the second context that are similar to aspects of the first context (e.g., both dogs had a flea collar) would become associated and stored with the word *dog*. Over time, a consistent set of meaning elements would be distilled from these repeated encounters with dogs. Each element would be highly associated with the others and would, therefore, prime one's memory for the others. Moreover, some aspects of the meaning of *dog* would be more central to its meaning and reflect consistent correlations of attributes (e.g., "has fur" and "barks"). Such attributes would be accessed the fastest when the single word *dog* is read. Other meaning elements that are somewhat less central (e.g., "has an owner") would also be accessible but would be accessed more slowly if at all when the word is read in isolation.

As Figure 5.1 shows, the meaning processor is directly linked to the orthographic processor. This means that the output of each processor can help the other do its job better. In support of this claim, Whittlesea and Cantwell (1987) found that when a pseudoword is given a meaningful definition, subjects perceived this word faster than they did when it lacked a definition. This improved perceptibility lasted for at least 24 hours, even when the supplied meaning had been forgotten. Thus, the meaning processor helped the orthographic processor do its job better. But the reverse can happen as well. As we shall see in the section on the development of reading ability, students who frequently read text with new words can dramatically increase the size of their vocabularies. Thus, orthographic knowledge can improve the capacity of the meaning processor.

The Phonological Processor

Analogous to the orthographic and meaning processors, the phonological processor consists of units that form associations with each other. Phonological units correspond to *phonemes* in the reader's spoken language. Phonemes such as *ba* and *tuh* can be combined into syllables such as *bat* and also into words such as *battle*. The auditory representation of a word, syllable, or phoneme is comprised of an activated set of specific units in the phonological processor (Adams, 1990).

When skilled readers see a written word, they do not have to translate it phonologically in order for its meaning to be accessed. Many studies have shown that meaning can be accessed simply by a visual pattern of letters (Adams, 1990; Seidenberg & McClelland, 1989). And yet, skilled readers often *do* translate words phonologically when they read.

Why would people perform some operation when they do not have to? The answer seems to be that the phonological processor provides a certain degree of redundancy with the information provided by the other processors. This redundancy can be quite helpful when the information provided by the other processors is incomplete, deceptive, or weakly specified (Stanovich, 1980; Adams, 1990).

More specifically, the phonological processor seems to provide two important services to the overall reading system. In the first place, it provides an alphabetic backup system that may be crucial for maintaining fast and accurate reading (Adams, 1990). This backup system exists mainly because the orthography of written English largely obeys the *alphabetic principle*: written symbols (i.e., graphemes) correspond to spoken sounds (i.e., phonemes). Although this grapheme-phoneme correspondence is not one-to-one or perfectly regular, it is nevertheless fairly predictable (Just & Carpenter, 1987). As a result, the phonological processor could provide helpful information in a variety of situations. For example, consider the case in which a reader knows the meaning of a spoken word but has never seen it written down. There would be no direct connection between (a) the units corresponding to the letters of this word in the orthographic processor and (b) the units corresponding to the meaning of this word in the meaning processor. There would, however, be a connection between the phonological processor units and the meaning processor units for this word. If the word obeys the alphabetic principle fairly well, the person would be able to sound it out and hear himself or herself saying the familiar word. This pronunciation would access the meaning of the word. Over repeated readings, the two-way association between the phonological processor units and meaning processor units for this word would become a three-way association between the orthographic, meaning, and phonological units.

The second service provided by the phonological processor has to do with a reader's memory for what he or she has just read. In Chapter 3, we discussed that portion of memory known as working memory. Within working memory, research has revealed an "articulatory loop" in which verbal information is rehearsed for later processing (Baddeley, 1990). In order to make sense of what they are reading, readers have to take all of the words in a sentence and put them together into a meaningful whole (Just & Carpenter, 1987). This integration requires a certain degree of memory, because when one reads from left to right, only one or two words fall within a reader's visual fixation span. That is, all of the words to the left of a visual fixation point must be retained in working memory. The articulatory loop plays a crucial role of keeping a record of all of the words in a sentence in order that all of their meanings can be integrated together. The phonological processor must be intimately connected to the articulatory loop, because adults with brain injuries in verbal areas show a marked inability to retain words that they just read.

The Context Processor

The context processor has the job of constructing an on-line, coherent interpretation of the text (Adams, 1990). The output of this processor is a mental representation of everything a reader has read so far. For example, upon reading the sentence "When the president came in, the reporters all rose," the context may be a mental image of President Clinton walking up to the podium in the White House press room. Some researchers (e.g., Just & Carpenter, 1987) call this image a *referential representation* of the text and others (e.g. van Dijk & Kintsch, 1983) call it a *situation model*. For simplicity and consistency with Chapter 8, we shall use the latter term.

Semantic, pragmatic, and syntactic knowledge all contribute to the construction of a situation model (Seidenberg & McClelland, 1989). For example, when skilled readers encounter the sentence "John went to the store to buy a ———," they use their semantic knowledge to access the meanings of all of the words in this sentence. In addition, they use their pragmatic knowledge to expect that John will buy something that people usually buy at stores. If the blank were filled in by *savings bond,* readers would likely be surprised when their eyes reached the word *savings.*

Syntactic knowledge also prompts the reader to form certain expectations about what will occur next (Garrett, 1990; Goodman & Goodman, 1979; Just & Carpenter, 1987). To see how the syntactic parser operates, it is useful to describe the linguist's notions of grammatical rules and tree structures.

In contemporary theorizing, language comprehension and production is said to be guided by a set of grammatical rules (Lasnick, 1990). That is, there are certain *types* of sentences and each type can be produced using a specific set of rules. For example, each of the following sentences can be produced by using the same three rules:

1. The fat boy hit the round ball.
2. The girl chewed an apple.
3. A man drew a picture.
4. A woman punched the cop.

These rules are:

R1 Sentence = Noun Phrase + Verb Phrase (i.e., S → NP + VP)
R2 Verb Phrase = Verb + Noun Phrase (i.e., VP → V + NP)
R3 Noun Phrase = Determiner + (optional adjective) + Noun
   (i.e., NP → Det + (adj)+ N)

To depict the hierarchical arrangement of a set of rules, linguists have used so-called tree structures. Figure 5.2 depicts a tree structure for the three rules above. By nesting one component (e.g., a determiner) within another (e.g., a noun phrase), the structure shows how the former is part of the latter.

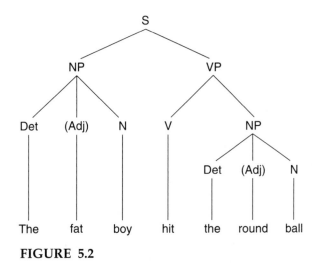

FIGURE 5.2

Given a specific input sentence and knowledge of grammatical rules, the human mind is thought to build up a particular tree structure for the sentence, component by component. For example, upon reading the word *the*, the rule for producing noun phrases gets elicited. Implicitly, the mind says "Okay. A noun phrase must be starting." Given that a determiner has already been encountered, Rule 3 (above) sets up the expectation that either an adjective or a noun will be encountered next. When the word *fat* is read in Sentence 1, it is assigned the slot for adjective. Having organized the words *the* and *fat* together, Rule 3 now sets up the expectation that the next word will likely be a noun, and so on. In order for this system to work, written words (e.g., *fat*) have to be mentally associated with grammatical classes (e.g., *adjective*).

Over the years, various researchers have doubted the existence of a mental parser, grammatical rules, and grammatical classes. Although these doubters have made some good points, there is considerable evidence that syntactic knowledge is an important aspect of sentence comprehension. In the first place, there is the syndrome called *Broca's Aphasia*, which results from injury to the Broca's area of the cerebral cortex. Individuals who have this disorder are able to comprehend the meanings of individual words but have trouble with the syntax of sentences (Just & Carpenter, 1987). For example, they see no difference between the following two sentences:

1. They fed her the dog biscuits.

2. They fed her dog the biscuits.

Although these two sentences have the same words, they have different tree structures and, therefore, different meanings.

In addition, there are many well known "garden-path" sentences such as the following:

3. The old train the young.

4. Since Jay always jogs a mile seems like a short distance to him.

5. The horse raced past the barn fell.

These sentences show that your syntax analyzer constructed one kind of tree structure until it met a particular word that violated expectations (e.g., the second *the* in (3), and *seems* in (4)).

Further, there are studies that show how syntax affects both the meaning and pronunciation of a word that is encountered. For example, read the following sentences:

6. John said, "Does are in the park, aren't they?"

7. Tomorrow was the annual one-day fishing contest and fishermen would invade the place. Some of the best bass guitarists in the country would come here.

In (6), grammatical rules suggest that *Does* is an auxiliary verb. Instead, it turns out to be a noun. The noun and the auxiliary have different pronunciations and meanings. In (7), grammatical rules and prior context suggest that *bass* is a noun that labels a type of fish. Instead, it turns out to be an adjective. The noun and adjective have different meanings and pronunciations.

Finally, grammatical rules are evident when a reader encounters ambiguous sentences such as:

8. Visiting relatives can be a nuisance.

9. The burglar saw the cop with binoculars.

The only way someone could see the multiple readings of these sentences is if he or she constructed multiple tree structures for each one.

In sum, then, syntactic, pragmatic, and semantic knowledge all contribute to the construction of a situation model. Once in place, this model prompts a reader to form expectations about what will occur next in the text. As each new segment of text is encountered, skilled readers interpret what is read in a way that makes it consistent with the current situation model.

The model of proficient reading in Figure 5.2 shows the two-way relationship between the context processor and the meaning processor. The model implies that the prior context can influence the meaning assigned to a word and that current meanings influence the construction of a situation model. Thus, when skilled readers process the sentence "John removed the thorn from the rose," they assign a different meaning to *rose* than they would if they read the sentence "The crowd rose to sing the national anthem."

But research has shown that the context-meaning effects are weak relative to the orthography-meaning effects. That is, readers are much better at predicting possible meanings of a word based on its perceived spelling than they are at predicting which word will follow a preceding context (Adams, 1990). When context-meaning links conflict with orthography-meaning links, the latter win out. Thus, skilled reading consists, first and foremost, of learning the correspondences between written words and their meanings. Context effects occur *after* words are perceived and various possible meanings are accessed. But overall, context, orthography, meanings, and phonology all work in concert to help a reader construct the best possible interpretation of a text.

The Development of Skilled Reading

Now that you know what skilled readers do, you have sense of the end point of reading development (but, of course, reading always improves with practice and experience). The beginning point of reading development is that point in a child's life when he or she has no idea what reading involves (e.g., infancy). In this section, we shall examine how children progress from the beginning point to the end point of reading development. In particular, this section focuses on four questions: (a) Which factors predict reading success in the first few grades?, (b) Where do prereading skills come from?, (c) Why isn't preschool vocabulary a good predictor of early reading? and (d) Are there developmental models of reading acquisition?

Predicting Reading Success

At one time, the notion of *reading readiness* was strongly advocated. In this view, a child's mind was thought to develop during early childhood until it reached the point at which it could understand reading instruction. Prior to this "readingness" point, reading instruction was thought to be useless because children would be unable to comprehend it. In apparent support of this notion, several researchers in the 1930s found that children did not seem to benefit from reading instruction until they had a mental age of at least six years, six months. On the basis of such studies, children were thought to know very little about reading prior to the first grade. In addition, reading ability was often equated with intelligence (Adams, 1990; Just & Carpenter, 1987; Stanovich, Cunningham & Feeman, 1984).

While it is true that a child's preschool IQ is correlated with later reading success, this correlation is not as high as the mental age hypothesis would predict. For example, the average correlation between IQ and reading scores for children below the fourth grade is about $r = .45$ (Stanovich, et al., 1984) and the median correlation is $r = .34$ (Stanovich, 1989). Moreover, mental age loses its predictive power when other more predictive factors are included in studies of early reading success. As we shall see next, these other factors include logical reasoning ability, letter knowledge, phonemic awareness, and syntactic awareness.

Logical Reasoning Ability
Several studies have shown that children who enter first grade with more concrete operational skills learn to read better than children with fewer concrete operational skills (Arlin, 1981; Tunmer, Herriman, & Nesdale, 1988). The kinds of skills measured in these studies include classification, seriation, and conservation

(See Piaget's theory in Chapter 2). Apparently, first graders are more likely to benefit from reading instruction if they have a general tendency to (a) "decenter" from the perceptual qualities of objects, (b) categorize objects in terms of multiple dimensions, and (c) arrange objects into specific, sequential orders (e.g., arrange sticks by increasing height). Perhaps children who think about objects in this way also think about strings of letters and sounds in this way as well. But it is important to note that any given Piagetian task is only weakly predictive of reading success. It is only when one combines performance on four or five Piagetian measures that the prediction improves. Based on what we know of Piaget's theory (see Chapter 2), this finding suggests that children who learn to read well either come from enriched environments or tend to be generally more mentally active than their peers (or both).

Letter Knowledge

Starting with Chall (1967) and Bond & Dykstra (1967), a number of studies have shown that children's knowledge of letter names is a very good predictor of their beginning reading achievement (Adams, 1990). Thus, children who enter school knowing that *b* is called *bee* and *t* is called *tee* perform better than children who lack this knowledge on end-of-year reading achievement tests.

If letter knowledge were a causal determinant of reading success, then teaching letter names to children would help them read better. However, such interventions have proved ineffective (Adams, 1990). Why? It seems that knowing letter names is not enough. Children who learn to read well are also *fast* and *accurate* in their letter naming; that is, they are highly familiar with this information. As a result, they are free to use their attentional resources to think about other things. In addition, six-year-olds who are fluent in letter names must differ in important ways from six-year-olds who are not. Fluency only comes from lots of repetition. Someone (e.g., a parent) must present letter names to children in daily interactions, and this same person might also engender a budding "emergent literacy" in them as well (Goodman, 1991; see The Origin of Prereading Skills below).

A second possibility is that children who know letter names may use this information to discover the alphabetic principle (Adams, 1990). In particular, many letter names sound like the way a letter is pronounced. For example, the name of *b* is *bee* and it is pronounced *buh*. Children may exploit this similarity to induce symbol-sound correspondences. Thus, the key to the process may not be letter names per se but the recognition of the connection between letter names, pronunciations, and the alphabetic principle (i.e., that there is a systematic correspondence between letters and sounds). The studies described earlier in which children were taught letter names may not have been successful because they did not tell children how to *use* this knowledge to induce the alphabetic principle. Perhaps instruction that points out the connection between names and pronunciations would be more effective. Again, though, what is it about a child who uses letter names to induce the alphabetic principle on his or her own (without being explicitly taught)? One would think that it is intelligence, given the historical equating of induction ability and intelligence (Jensen, 1987). However, measures of intelligence do not predict early reading success after one controls for children's letter knowledge, and letter knowledge still predicts reading performance even after IQ has been controlled (Adams, 1990; Stanovich, 1988).

To get a sense of how one factor can be a better predictor of reading success than another, consider the following hypothetical example. Look at the association between a student's IQ when he or she is five years old, letter knowledge at five, and reading achievement at the end of first grade:

Name	IQ at 5	Letters at 5	1st Grade Reading
Matt	High*	High*	Very Good
Ryan	High	High	Poor
Steven	High	Low*	Poor
Chris	Low	Low	Very good
Tom	High*	High*	Very Good
Kristen	Low*	Low*	Poor
Tiffany	High	High	Poor
Julia	High*	High*	Very Good
Tara	High	Low*	Poor
Amanda	High*	High*	Very Good

If IQ is a good predictor, then every child who has a high IQ at five years of age should be a good reader by the end of first grade (like Matt above). Conversely, every low-IQ child should be a poor reader by the end of first grade (like Kristen above). If letter knowledge is a good predictor, every child with high letter knowledge at five should be a good reader at the end of first grade and every child with low letter knowledge should be a poor reader at the end of first grade. In the table above, there is an asterisk next to the children who fit these low with low/high with high predictive patterns. If IQ were a perfect predictor, we should see ten asterisks down the IQ column (all eight high-IQ children would have very good reading scores; both of the low-IQ children would have poor reading skills). If letter knowledge were a perfect predictor, we should also see ten asterisks down the letter knowledge column. What we see instead is that whereas five out of ten children fit the pattern for IQ, seven out of ten do for letter knowledge. Thus, it is better to know someone's letter knowledge because it predicts success or failure better than IQ. If we had no other information but IQ, however, we would see that it correctly predicts some of the children. But you should also see that when you know both IQ scores and letter knowledge scores, IQ scores add very little new information. The same five children who fit the IQ pattern (Matt, Tom, Kristen, Julia, and Amanda) also fit the letter knowledge pattern. So, knowing their IQ is redundant information for these five children. Note further that we pick up two additional children by knowing their letter knowledge (that would have been missed by using just IQ).

Phonemic Awareness

Similar to letter knowledge, children's phonemic awareness is an excellent predictor of their early reading success (Adams, 1990 Tunmer et al., 1988; Vellutino & Scanlon, 1991). Phonemic awareness is the ability to reflect on, manipulate, and discriminate among phonemes (i.e., the component sounds in a word).

The connection between phonemic awareness and reading is somewhat more straightforward than that between letter knowledge and reading. Because written English largely obeys the alphabetic principle, there is a correspondence between letter patterns (graphemes) and the sounds of spoken English (phonemes). It should be obvious that someone could not induce this connection unless he or she already knew what a phoneme was (even implicitly). Whereas it is easy to get a child to see the component graphemes of a word by simply writing the sections of the word on a blackboard (e.g., *decompose* = *de* + *compose*), it is quite difficult to get a young child to "hear" the component sounds of a word. In particular, preschoolers seem to acquire phonemic awareness very slowly and progressively (Adams, 1990) and disadvantaged children have particular difficulty with this skill (Wallach, Wallach, Dozier & Kaplan, 1977).

To get a better sense of what phonemic awareness entails, it is helpful to describe some of the ways it is measured. In phonemic *segmentation* tasks, children are asked to indicate the number of phonemes in a word by tapping (Liberman et al, 1974). For *car*, for example, they would tap three times (once for each of *kuh*, *ah*, and *rrr*). In phonemic *manipulation* tasks, children are asked to delete, add, or rearrange the phonemes in a word. For example, they might be asked to say *pink* without the *kuh* sound at the end (Adams, 1990). In *blending* tasks, children are given the phonemes and asked to put them together (e.g., they are given *kuh*, *ah* and *rrr* and are expected to say *car*). In *oddity* tasks, they are asked to say which of three words does not belong (e.g., *doll, hop, top*). In *rime* tasks, they are asked to produce or detect common end-sounds of words such as *-at* for *bat* and *cat*. Finally, in *onset* tasks they are asked to detect common beginning sounds. Alliteration tasks tap into the ability to detect common onsets (Bryant et al, 1990).

A variety of studies have shown that performance on any of these phonemic awareness tasks strongly predicts early reading success even after controlling for IQ (Adams, 1990; Vellutino & Scanlon, 1991). Moreover, whereas direct instruction of letter knowledge has been found to have no effect on later reading performance (as we noted earlier), many studies have shown that explicit instruction in phonemic awareness improves reading performance considerably (Adams, 1990; Stanovich, 1988).

Syntactic Awareness

Syntactic awareness is the ability to judge the grammatical acceptability of sentences. A child is said to possess syntactic awareness if he or she can tell the difference between an acceptable and unacceptable construction. In most studies, unacceptable constructions are formed by violating word order. For example, a child would be asked to listen to sentences such as "Made cookies Mom" or "Why the dog is barking so loudly?" and asked to say whether it is acceptable or not acceptable (Bialystok, 1988; Tunmer et al., 1988). The results of these studies show that the ability to detect grammatical violations is a good predictor of reading comprehension scores.

Why would early syntactic awareness be predictive of later reading success? Earlier we learned that syntactic knowledge plays an important role in the context processor (see Figure 5.1). When students encounter unfamiliar words in texts, syntactic rules may help them identify the grammatical category of these words (e.g., *undulated* is a verb) and subsequently help them acquire the meaning of these words as well. Moreover, as argued earlier, contexts can help students decide among particular pronunciations of words (Tunmer et al., 1988). Finally, prior contexts can prime the meanings of words and promote faster processing (Adams, 1990).

Summary

In this section, we saw that (a) logical reasoning ability, (b) fluency in letter naming, (c) phonemic awareness, and (d) syntactic awareness were better predictors of early reading achievement than mental age. To explain why factors (b) to (d) predict successful reading, we appealed to the model of proficient reading shown in Figure 5.1. In particular, it was argued that letter knowledge and phonemic awareness help a child acquire insight into the alphabetic principle of written English. When we described the model of proficient reading in the first part of this chapter, we said that a reader's knowledge of the alphabetic principle is embodied in the interactive relationship between the orthographic and phonological processors. Putting the claims about skilled reading and predictive factors together, then, we can say that a child who has letter knowledge and phonemic awareness probably forms connections between the orthographic and phonological processors faster than a child who lacks these prerequisite skills.

Teachers and parents who want to promote phonemic awareness and letter knowledge in preschool children can engage in a variety of activities to promote these skills. For example, phonemic awareness can be enhanced through rhyming games such as that presented on an episode of *Sesame Street*: Form a group of four children. One child in the group says a word and other children have to come up with a rhyme to that word. A child who cannot come up with a rhyme is out. The game continues until one child is left. For letter knowledge, the game Concentration can be used in which identical letters can be found by turning over cards.

With respect to syntax, we argued that syntactic knowledge was a key aspect of the context processor and that children who are syntactically aware can use the context processor to help the other processors do their jobs better. Syntactic awareness can be enhanced using puppets who always say things incorrectly. Children help the puppet by telling it how to say things better.

Overall, then, we see that the research on skilled readers squares nicely with the research on predictive factors and that it is easy to develop activities to promote important prerequisite skills. The curious thing about the research on predictive factors, however, is the fact that skills such as phonemic awareness and syntactic awareness are not only prerequisites for learning to read, they also seem to *improve* after a child learns to read. That is, children who have been reading for several years (e.g., third graders) show more phonemic awareness and syntactic awareness than children who are just starting to read (Adams, 1990; Stanovich, 1988). Moreover, having phonemic awareness, syntactic awareness, and insight into the alphabetic principle is a large part of what it means to know how to read. Thus, the research seems to say that children learn to read well in the first grade only if they already know much about reading when they enter first grade (Adams, 1990; Goodman, 1991).

Which children enter school already knowing a lot about reading? All of the research on predictive factors seems to point to differences in the home lives (or preschool experiences) of children that would cause some children to enter school with considerable analytical ability (as indexed by Piagetian tasks) as well as phonemic awareness, syntactic awareness, and insight into the alphabetic principle. In the next section, we shall explore some of these possible environmental differences.

The Origin of Prereading Skills

The *mental age* conception of reading readiness implies that there are two kinds of children: readers and nonreaders. Recently, researchers have questioned the existence of this simple dichotomy. In particular, studies in the area of "emergent literacy" (e.g., Teale & Sulzby, 1986) have shown that children should be viewed as acquiring increasing and progressive insight into the nature of reading throughout the preschool period. The advocates of the emergent literacy perspective have revealed that there are a number of subtle aspects of reading that adults take for granted but children have to learn. For example, young children do not immediately know that (a) the words in a book tell the story and the pictures are just an accompaniment to the words, (b) one reads words from left to right and lines of words from top to bottom, (c) written words correspond to spoken words, (d) one reads all of the words on a page before reading the words on the next page, (e) pages are read in a specific order from the first to the last page, (f) there is someone (i.e., the author) who had the story in his or her mind and decided to write it down so that children could know the story too, and (g) writing is like speaking because it is way of communicating ideas (Clay, 1985; Sulzby, 1991; Teale & Sulzby, 1986). The advocates of the emergent literacy perspective argue that such ideas are just as important as knowledge of the alphabetic principle for beginning reading.

If children are not born with ideas such as the directionality of print and the alphabetic principle, how do they acquire them? The most straightforward explanation involves the notion of exposure to texts (Adams, 1990). Several recent studies have shown that children who receive more exposure to books (e.g., through shared reading) enter school being readier to read than children with less exposure (e.g., Heath, 1983; Teale, 1986). Moreover, children who have the most trouble learning to read tend to come from disadvantaged backgrounds (Slavin, Karweit & Wasik, 1994; Wallach & Wallach, 1979).

However, two findings reveal that disadvantaged children are not doomed to a life of illiteracy. First, careful ethnographic studies have shown that family income matters less than the value parents place on reading. Some disadvantaged children have parents who place a premium on literacy, and these children enter school with a great deal of reading readiness (Heath, 1983). Second, other studies have shown that parents can be taught how to read to their children in a way that significantly increases their children's language skills (Whitehurst et al., 1988). Such findings imply that large-scale parent education programs might increase the reading readiness of disadvantaged children.

How much parental input is needed for early reading success? It is hard to tell at present because too little research has been done on the topic. We can, however, speculate about the role of exposure using a quantitative example. Imagine two children who come from identical middle-class backgrounds. One child (Julia) has parents who read to her every day for 20 minutes. The other child (Emily) has parents who read to her every other day for ten minutes. Whereas the difference between Julia's and Emily's book exposure does not seem that great, consider that in a given year, Julia receives about 120 hours of book reading and Emily receives only about 30 hours. If their book reading started around age one, then by the time they enter first grade, Julia will have received 480 hours of book reading and Emily will have received just 120 hours. Given that the average child receives about 360 hours of reading instruction in first grade (Adams, 1990), we can see that Julia's exposure to books at home exceeds what would happen in the first grade, but Emily's exposure would be far less than what she would encounter at school. However, both children will probably learn to read because reading was emphasized to a certain degree in both households. Children in low-income homes that do not emphasize reading, in contrast, might accumulate only about 40 hours or less of book reading by the time they are six years old (Heath, 1983; Teale, 1986).

Such quantitative differences in exposure would affect early reading performance in several ways. First, in the absence of explicit instruction, children are more likely to induce the alphabetic principle on their own if they encounter more and more books. Second, fluency in letter knowledge develops in response to many repeated encounters with letters. Third, phonemic awareness might be developed in response to exposure to certain kinds of books (e.g., nursery rhymes or Dr. Seuss books). It is likely that high-exposure children encounter such books more often than low-exposure children. Fourth, if children need to interact with books in order to progress along emergent literacy stages, then it stands to reason that high-exposure children will enter first grade with more emergent literacy skills than low-exposure children.

Developmental Models and Trends

In the previous section, we examined reading development from infancy to the point at which children enter the first grade. In this section, we shall extend this analysis somewhat. In particular, this section begins with a description of some general developmental trends in performance. Then, a developmental model of early decoding skill is described.

The general developmental trends can be understood with reference to the model of proficient reading described earlier. In the earliest phases of reading development, children have very little orthographic knowledge but considerable knowledge of meaning-sound relations (i.e., oral vocabulary). Moreover, as mentioned above, successful readers also enter first grade with phonemic awareness, syntactic awareness, and knowledge of the alphabetic principle. Early reading development consists of putting all of this entering knowledge together with written words; that is, it can be characterized as the progressive acquisition of letter-sound correspondences as well as letter-meaning correspondences.

Because word recognition is slow and effortful in the beginning, beginning readers rely heavily on prior context to help them guess words rather than read them phonetically. With lots of repeated practice, word recognition eventually becomes automatic, thereby indicating that the connections between words and meanings are firmly established. Whereas prior context and the pronunciations of words are still involved in reading, they are no longer essential for the beginning reader. Rather, they now serve as backup systems to the primary links between the orthographic and meaning processors. Thus, children rely more on letter-meaning connections and *less* on prior context and pronunciations with age (Adams, 1990; Stanovich, 1988). Furthermore, children who enter first grade with phonemic awareness and syntactic awareness dramatically increase these skills as they read more and more. Finally, rapid, efficient word recognition allows readers to attend to meaning more closely and to develop a variety of comprehension strategies (see Chapter 5; Stanovich, 1986).

In addition to these general trends, early reading development can be cast in terms of Erli and Wilce's (1987) developmental model of decoding. They proposed four stages in the acquisition of decoding skill. During the *nonreading* stage, children cannot read any words from primers or even "environmental words" (e.g., Coke) in isolation. However, many of these children know that print carries information. During the *visual-cue* reading stage, real reading begins because children start attending to the characteristics of words themselves. However, such cues are often limited to the general shape of a word, not letters or letter patterns. During the *phonetic-cue* reading stage, children have partial knowledge of letters and their associations with sounds. For example, they may know the sounds corresponding to *h* and *t*, but not know the sound corresponding to *i*. Even so, when presented with *hit*, their partial knowledge helps them guess the word. During the *systematic phonemic decoding* stage, children know the full alphabet, have phonemic awareness, and have unraveled much of the letter-sound correspondences in their texts. Moreover, they decode with considerable fluency and automaticity.

The Role of Vocabulary

In the section The Origin of Prereading Skills, we saw that there are three proximal causes of reading success (i.e., phonemic awareness, letter knowledge, and syntactic awareness) that may themselves be caused by more distal factors such as exposure to books. Missing in this account is any mention of a child's vocabulary. One would think that children who enter first grade with a larger oral vocabulary would have an easier time developing meaning-grapheme-phoneme associations than children who enter first grade with a smaller oral vocabulary. Why isn't preschool vocabulary predictive of early reading success?

In the first place, we have seen that there is no substitute for the direct connections between the orthographic processor and meaning processor (Adams, 1990). Rapid and accurate word recognition occurs only when these connections are well established. Whereas children with large oral vocabularies have created links between the phonological and meaning processors, they may not have created the crucial links between the orthographic and meaning processors. Second, a child who has a large oral vocabulary may not have developed phonemic or syntactic awareness. That is, a child who recognizes and knows the meaning of spoken words such as *send* and *pretend* may not have noticed that these words have sounds in common. Third, a child who has a large oral vocabulary will only have an advantage over children with smaller vocabularies if their reading materials and assessments contain words that are familiar only to the former child. As we shall see later, basal readers are intentionally constructed to contain words that are highly familiar to most (middle class) children. Moreover, when new words are presented in these texts, about 70 percent of children are already familiar with them (Roser & Juel, 1982). It is only when *sight* vocabularies are developed that having a large vocabulary would give certain children an advantage over their peers. This advantage would have its most conspicuous effects on achievement tests that require knowledge of unfamiliar words (e.g., the SAT).

Further, studies have shown that intensive efforts at teaching children vocabulary words have had only a modest effect on their reading comprehension (Adams, 1990; Calfee & Drum, 1986). Moreover, to teach vocabulary intensely, it is necessary to spend more than the average of two minutes that most teachers spend on vocabulary instruction (Durkin, 1979), and some recent studies suggest that it would not be worth the extra time to do so. For example, McKeown, Beck, Omanson, and Perfetti (1983) taught children 104 new words within 75 30-minute lessons spread out over five months. Although children did learn about 80 percent of the new words (i.e., 81 words), this number pales in comparison to the 3,000 words children normally acquire in a year (Adams, 1990). Moreover, even if McKeown et al.'s lessons lasted all day long for a full year, children would still gain far less than 3,000 words (i.e., about 1,900 words).

Given the fact that teachers spend so little time on reading instruction and the fact that large increases in time do not produce comparably large increases in new words, how do children acquire 3,000 words per year? The answer seems to be that they learn new words by reading them in context (Adams, 1990; Calfee & Drum, 1986). Most of the gains seem to be accrued in out-of-school reading because (a) children encounter more words out of school than in school (Nagy, Herman & Anderson, 1985) and (b) many children read basal readers in school, and basal readers introduce few new vocabulary words. Thus, just as phonemic awareness and syntactic awareness increase through reading, children's vocabulary increases through reading as well. What this means is that extensive reading is a better predictor of vocabulary growth than vocabulary is a predictor of reading.

We close this section by noting that we are not saying that a person's vocabulary is irrelevant to reading success. Quite the contrary. Someone could not read well without having a good oral and sight vocabulary. Thus, a reader's vocabulary is necessary for reading success. Since most kids have the necessary vocabulary for beginning reading, however, vocabulary size is not sufficient for differentiating the more successful readers from the less successful readers (at least not in the early grades). In the next section, we examine the factors that do discriminate good readers from poor readers.

Individual Differences in Reading Skills

If one looks at the reading skills of children in any grade, one will find that some children read well below average, some read at grade level, and some have above-average ability. In this section, we shall explore some of the variables that might account for such individual differences. The first class of variables relates to cognitive processes and the second class of variables relates to demographic factors.

With respect to cognitive processes, there are a number of ways in which good readers could conceivably differ from poor readers. On the one hand, they could differ in terms of general processing factors such as intelligence, working memory capacity, perceptual ability, rule induction, and metacognition. On the other hand, they could differ in terms of reading-specific processes such as word recognition, use of context, phonemic awareness, and comprehension strategies. It turns out that significant differences have been found between good and poor readers for all of these variables (Stanovich, 1980, 1986, 1988). The question is, however, which of these variables seem to most clearly distinguish good readers from poor readers.

Careful reviews of the literature have revealed three particularly important differences between good and poor readers. First, good readers are better than poor readers at recognizing words automatically. When word recognition is automatic, a reader can focus his or her attention on higher-level sentence integration and semantic processing. However, automatic recognition is most important in the first and second grades, because most high-frequency words are automatized to adult levels by the third grade (Stanovich, 1980). Beginning in the third grade, the second and most important difference between good and poor readers emerges: Good readers are able to *rapidly* recognize words and subword units. Speed is important because readers need to be able to operate on information in working memory before it dissipates. The third important difference between good and poor readers concerns the ability to recode print items into a phonological representation. Phonological recoding facilitates reading by (a) providing a redundant pathway for accessing word meaning and (b) providing a more stable code for the information that is held in working memory (Adams, 1990; Stanovich, 1980).

At one time, the ability to use prior context was also thought to be a major difference between good and poor readers. After many years of research, however, this proposal turns out to be incorrect. In fact, poor readers use prior context as much if not more than good readers and are likely to make many substitution errors when they encounter an unfamiliar word (Adams, 1990; Stanovich, 1988). Skilled readers rely much more heavily on direct connections between orthography and meaning than on context. Context only exerts an experimental effect on good readers when the text is artificially doctored or degraded. Thus, whereas good readers rely on context less and less as they get older, poor readers do not show a similar kind of decreasing reliance on context, presumably because they have so much trouble recognizing and deciphering a word. Of course, this is not to say that context is irrelevant to good readers. As mentioned earlier, context serves as an important backup system to the connections between text and meanings.

Why are good readers better at automatic and fast recognition and pronunciation of words than poor readers? From what we know about the nature of skill acquisition and the formation of associations, it seems clear that good readers have had considerably more practice at recognizing and pronouncing words than poor readers. A likely cause of practice differences could be the fact that children are grouped by reading ability starting in the first grade. Children in higher groups are given more opportunities for practice than children in lower groups, and the initial gap between groups widens with age (Stanovich, 1986).

Turning now to demographic factors, we can ask whether there are gender or ethnic differences in beginning reading. With respect to gender differences, there is the cultural belief that girls have better verbal abilities than boys. After all, girls talk earlier and tend to be more verbally expressive than boys (Maccoby & Jacklin, 1974; Hyde & Linn, 1988). But do these tendencies translate into an advantage in reading for girls? Surprisingly few studies have addressed this issue. With respect to vocabulary differences, for example, one recent review of studies conducted since the 1960s uncovered only 13 studies in which gender differences were analyzed (Hyde & Linn, 1988). For children younger than five, the review revealed an average effect-size of .05, which seems to indicate a lack of a gender difference (see Chapter 12 for an explanation of effect-sizes). However, about 40 percent of these studies showed that four-year-old males had slightly larger vocabularies than females and 60 percent showed that four-year-old females had moderately larger vocabularies. Thus, sometimes preschool boys will be found to have better vocabularies and sometimes girls will, but the difference will be small when it is found. For six- to nine-year-olds (i.e., beginning readers), the review revealed just nine studies in which gender differences in vocabulary were examined. Here, the average effect size was −.31, indicating a moderate advantage for boys. Thus, the cultural view that girls have better vocabularies than boys seems to be wrong.

With respect to gender differences in reading comprehension, the review found just two studies of preschoolers and one of these involved disadvantaged children. The effect-sizes for these two studies were .32 and .07, respectively, indicating that female preschoolers have better comprehension skills than preschool boys. For six- to nine-year-old children, the review uncovered six studies yielding an average effect-size of −.14. This average suggests that when children are learning to read, females tend to perform slightly better than males on tests of reading comprehension. However, four out of the six effect-sizes on which this average is based ranged between .01 and .08. Based on such findings, Hyde and Linn (1988) conclude that we should abandon the cultural stereotype regarding gender differences in reading abilities.

A different story emerges when ethnic differences in reading ability are examined. Here, Caucasian students tend to perform substantially better than African-American or Hispanic students. In a study involving first, third, and fifth graders, for example, Stevenson, Chen, and Uttal (1990) found that Caucasian students performed better than African-American and Hispanic students on a nonstandardized reading comprehension test in the first grade. By the time these students reached the third grade, the Caucasian students still performed better than the African-American students. For vocabulary, ethnic differences favoring Caucasian students did not emerge until the fifth grade. Over all measures, the effect-sizes ranged from a low of .42 to a high of 1.05, and ethnic differences still remained even after the effects of family income and parental education were removed. In Chapter 12, we shall explore some of the causes and consequences of ethnic differences in reading.

Instructional Implications

Now that we have a sense of the nature and development of skilled reading, we are finally in a position to consider the best ways to teach children how to read. In this section, we shall examine some current approaches to reading instruction and consider which aspects of these approaches are consistent with the research presented in the first three parts of this chapter. After this discussion of current approaches has been completed, we shall examine a case study of an approach to beginning reading that draws on contemporary theory and research in reading.

Contemporary Approaches

Over the last 30 years (at least), very vigorous debates have been waged about the best way to teach children how to read. These debates have focused on issues such as (a) whether word recognition should be taught via the whole-word ("look-say") approach or the phonics approach, (b) whether basal readers or children's literature should be used to teach reading skills, and (c) whether children's incorrect spelling should be corrected or ignored. Individuals who find themselves on one or the other side of these debates differ in their beliefs about the nature of reading.

On the one hand, there is the *phonics* view, which emphasizes the systematicity of symbol-sound correspondences. Advocates of this perspective argue that children should be directly taught about the regularities of letter-sound mappings and shown how to identify and blend individual sounds together into a whole word. Moreover, they argue that in order to maximize children's learning of symbol-sound regularities, teachers should explicitly point out these regularities in classroom exercises (Stahl & Miller, 1989). Unfortunately, this assumption has led to the practice of children spending most of their time learning various decoding rules via decontextualized drills instead of using decoding rules while reading meaningful text.

Very often (though not always), teachers who believe in the phonics approach use basal readers. Basal readers contain stories in which the rules for decoding words almost always work for the words in the stories. Moreover, the words are selected from frequency norms to be highly familiar, and the sentences containing these words are designed to be short and grammatically simple. The logic behind basal readers is that children will learn to be fluent more quickly by repeatedly reading these artificially constructed stories.

The phonics approach can be contrasted with the *whole language* view. According to this view, reading instruction should begin in a natural manner using the child's own language as a bridge to beginning reading instruction (Stahl & Miller, 1989). At the core of this approach is the idea that children should focus most of their attention on the communicative function of written language rather than its form; that is, children should always be thinking about why the words were written rather than letter-by-letter sound mappings.

With respect to phonics instruction, the whole language view makes four claims. First, they suggest that it is nearly impossible to decompose a word down into individual phonemes without losing something in the translation. Each phoneme sounds different when part of a word than when alone. To see this, try blending the separate sounds for *c, a,* and *r* together and compare this blend with the sound made by the whole word. Second, they argue that drills on decoding rules should not be a regular part of every lesson. Rather, decoding help should only be given as needed (e.g., when a child who is reading meaningful text encounters a word he or she cannot decode). Third, advocates argue that there is not a major difference between written and spoken language. Children learn to speak naturally (without explicit instruction on grammar), so they should also learn to read naturally as well (without explicit instruction on decoding rules). Thus, children should be allowed to induce symbol-sound correspondences implicitly as they read the same way that they induce grammatical rules implicitly as they talk to their parents.

In addition, advocates of the whole language view argue that children's literature should be used instead of the artificial stories in (some) basal readers because the latter alter the natural predictability of texts. Predictability is important because reading is seen to be a "psycholinguistic guessing game" in which a reader uses prior context, semantics, and syntax to forecast upcoming words. This guessing game notion seems to have derived from studies in the 1960s that showed how skilled readers used prior context to help them recognize hard-to-see words.

Furthermore, the whole language view emphasizes children's own writing to help them see that writing, reading, and speaking are all forms of communication. When children write down their own ideas, they will see that written language is functional from the start. Moreover, writing allows a child to see the cyclic communication pattern that evolves from the germ of an idea:

> I can think → I can talk about what I think → I can write down what I say → Others can read what I write (which tells them what I think).

Finally, for beginning readers who cannot yet spell or read fluently, whole language teachers often encourage the use of *invented spelling*. The belief is that if teachers focus too much attention on spelling, they teach children to focus more on the form of what they are writing than on the meaning.

Having briefly defined the phonics and whole language methods, we are now in a position to consider how these views are consistent (or not) with the research described in the first three parts of this chapter. Before doing so, however, it is necessary to point out that it is hard to find a teacher who is a "pure" practitioner of either method. Most teachers use elements of both approaches (Adams, 1990; Chall, 1983). Why? The first reason is that the whole language approach gained its initial momentum after many veteran teachers had been using the phonics approach for several years. Rather than abandoning the phonics approach entirely, such teachers merely added certain aspects of the whole language approach to a foundation of phonics instruction. The second reason has to do with experience. Even teachers who are staunch advocates of the whole language approach find that it is often necessary to explicitly teach children how to decode. Thus, the idea that children will acquire knowledge of the symbol-sound correspondences purely by induction has few believers in the classroom.

The third reason is that basal readers have been modified to include more children's literature than they used to have. To be sure, some of this literature has been doctored by substituting familiar, easy-to-decode words for unfamiliar words or words that do not fit the decoding words. Nevertheless, teachers recognize that one can still follow the basic principles of the whole language approach using the stories in the basal readers.

Thus, it would be hard to find a teacher who practiced the pure phonics approach or the pure whole language approach. Nevertheless, we can consider which aspects of the pure approaches are consistent with the research described earlier.

The primary virtue of the phonics approach is that it focuses attention on individual letters and grapheme-phoneme correspondences. This practice is consistent with the following findings: (a) letter knowledge is an excellent predictor of early reading success, (b) successful readers have phonemic awareness and insight into the alphabetic principle, (c) skilled readers attend to individual letters and letter patterns, (d) skilled readers use phonological information as an important backup system, and (e) good readers primarily differ from poor readers in terms of their ability to rapidly name words and pseudowords out of context. In addition to these findings, we can add that large scale evaluations have found that the most successful reading programs always have included explicit phonics instruction (Adams, 1990).

The second set of consistencies derives from the use of basal readers. In particular, basal readers may help readers acquire early skills by organizing specific grapheme-phoneme correspondences together, using familiar words, and using short sentences. By organizing information together, children can identify correspondences more quickly than a natural induction process would allow. By repeating familiar words, children can develop automatic and rapid recognition of those words and thereby be able to attend to the meaning of what they are reading. By using short sentences, children's working memory capacities will not be overloaded. As a result, they will be more likely to construct a meaningful interpretation of a sentence.

What's wrong with the "pure" phonics approach? Several things. In the first place, although the letter-sound connections that develop between the orthographic and phonological processors are important, the word-meaning connections that develop between the orthographic and meaning processors are much more important. In using isolated drills of letter-sound correspondences, children will not develop the latter type of connections. Second, the largest growth in children's vocabulary occurs when they read new words in context. Because basal readers rarely introduce unfamiliar words, they stifle children's vocabulary growth. Third, the pure phonics approach does not emphasize writing nearly as much as the whole language approach and often does not make an explicit connection between writing and reading.

Turning now to the whole language approach, we can say that its primary virtue lies in the emphasis placed on meaning. As mentioned earlier, there is no substitute for the connections between words and their meanings. Anyone who adheres to the whole language approach will not end up with students who can sound out words well but cannot make sense of what they read. Second, in using children's literature, children will read new words in context and develop larger vocabularies. Third, in emphasizing reading-writing connections, children will begin to consider authors and what they were trying to convey. Fourth, the context processor does play an important backup role in the reading process (especially the role of syntax), and the whole language approach emphasizes context far more than the phonics approach.

The final virtue of the whole language approach has to do with its emphasis on invented spelling. Although the whole language theorists are probably right that deemphasizing correct spelling may help children attend more to the message they want to convey than the form of this message, inventing spelling may play a more important role in helping children gain insight into the alphabetic principle (Adams, 1990). That is, a child can only invent spellings if he or she already knows that letters correspond to sounds.

What's wrong with the "pure" whole language approach? Several things. First, its occasional advocacy of sight-word reading and deemphasis on phonics instruction is not consistent with the research on the nature and development of skilled reading. Second, the claim that skilled readers use prior context more than less skilled readers has been shown to be incorrect. Prior context is far less important than rapid activation of grapheme-meaning correspondences. Third, the "natural" tendency for children to induce symbol-sound correspondences is only natural for children who enter school with considerable emergent literacy. Children from disadvantaged backgrounds have little knowledge from which to make inductions. Fourth, although invented spelling helps a child gain insight into the alphabetic principle, prolonged invented spelling interferes with the process of forming connections between (proper) spellings, meanings, and pronunciations. A child who always spells *tough* as *tuf* will have difficulty learning to rapidly recognize *tough* when it is encountered in a text. Thus, whereas invented spelling has a place in the context of emergent literacy, it loses its value after insight into the alphabetic principle has been gained.

In sum, then, there are aspects of both approaches that are consistent and inconsistent with the research described earlier. Obviously, the best approach to reading will combine the aspects of both approaches that are consistent with the research. The only remaining lesson of this research has to do with the issues of repetition, practice, and exposure: Successful readers have parents who read to them a lot when they were preschoolers. After they learn to read in school, successful readers read a lot in school and out of school.

A Case Study

In recent years, *Reading Recovery* has become a very popular program for improving the reading performance of the lowest 10 to 20 percent of readers in a classroom. It is largely based on the Whole Language approach of Marie Clay (1985) and others. In most school districts, children are placed into the Reading Recovery program if they are identified by their teachers as failing to make sufficient progress after one year of reading instruction (about 10–20 percent of students in some classrooms). Once in the program, children receive one-on-one tutoring until they reach a point at which they can be placed back into standard, small-group reading instruction (i.e., they are "discontinued"). Clay (1985) reports that the method has been highly successful.

As described by Clay (1985), lessons often contain seven activities:

1. *rereading books that are familiar to the child*
2. *independent reading of a new book that was introduced in the previous lesson; the teacher takes notes on the accuracy of the child's reading (called a "running record")*
3. *children identify letters placed on a magnetic board (if they still fail to recognize letters)*

4. *writing of a story (includes phonological awareness training of unfamiliar words in the story)*
5. *cutting up a story up and having the child reassemble it*
6. *introducing a new book*
7. *reading of the new book*

Because it is based on Whole Language philosophy, the standard Reading Recovery program emphasizes reading connected text, not decontextualized phonics drills. All problem-solving on the part of the child (e.g., how to pronounce a word) is done on-line, as the child reads children's literature.

In a recent study, Iversen & Tunmer (1993) attempted to modify the standard Reading Recovery program to include more systematic phonics instruction than normal to see if this combined approach would be even more effective than the standard approach. After some children had been in Reading Recovery for about 15 to 18 lessons and were able to identify at least 35 of the 54 alphabetic characters used in the third segment of the lesson (see above), they were given instruction on phonograms. Phonograms are clusters of letters common to groups of words (e.g., *and* for *and, band, hand,* etc.). Starting with one word (e.g., *and*) children were shown how to make one word into another using magnetic letters (e.g., removing the *b* from *band* to make *and.*). Each time changes in a word were made, children were asked to say the word and practice changes back and forth.

Iverson and Tunmer compared the performance of children in the standard Reading Recovery program to that of children in the modified program and that of a control group who were part of the regular classroom. They found that children in both of the Reading Recovery programs performed significantly better than children not in these programs on measures of letter recognition, word recognition, print concepts, and phonemic awareness. However, children in the modified program were discontinued some 15 lessons earlier than children in the standard program (i.e., they were remediated faster). This study demonstrates the virtue of combining the best of the whole language and phonics approaches.

C h a p t e r **6**

Reading Comprehension

Summary

1. There are both structural aspects of reading comprehension and functional aspects. In terms of structural aspects, comprehension is enhanced when readers have prior knowledge of topics as well as schemata for narrative and expository texts. In terms of functional aspects, comprehension is enhanced when readers set goals for their reading and employ a variety of reading strategies.

2. With age, children seem to develop both structural and functional competencies that help them process what they are reading. In particular, older children are more likely than younger children to have (a) schematized knowledge of topics, (b) schemata for the different kinds of texts,

and (c) knowledge of reading strategies such as inference-making and backtracking.

3. However, it takes considerable time for schemata to develop on their own. Moreover, older children who are capable of using strategies often do not use them. Instruction that has focused on schemata and strategies has been found to speed up the natural course of events and improve reading comprehension in students.

4. Good readers seem to acquire knowledge, schemata, and strategies faster than same-age peers who are poor readers. Similar to young children, older poor readers have comprehension problems because they lack topic knowledge, schemata, and reading strategies.

In Chapter 5, we examined so-called beginning reading and characterized it in terms of Carver's (1973) Levels 1 and 2 (i.e., processing of individual words and sentences). In this chapter, we examine how readers comprehend larger segments of text such as paragraphs (Carver's Level 3).

Before proceeding further, however, it should be noted that the distinction between beginning reading and reading comprehension is somewhat artificial and was made for expository purposes only. Although it has been traditional to characterize the former as "learning to read" and the latter as "reading to learn" (Chall, 1983), this characterization might prompt someone to draw two unwarranted conclusions: (a) that beginning reading never involves the extraction of meaning from text and (b) that beginning reading only involves the proper pronunciation of words. Teachers and publishers who have drawn these conclusions have assumed that young readers do not have to read meaningful text in order to learn how to read (i.e., any text or string of words will do). In contrast, one of the major premises of the Whole Language approach to reading is that any form of reading can, and should be, meaningful (see Chapter 5). I share this view but note that certain skills arise in the context of reading full paragraphs and stories that do not arise when single words or sentences are read. The purpose of this chapter is to examine these emergent skills.

In what follows, we shall examine multisentence comprehension in four sections. In the first section, the component processes of reading comprehension are described. In the second section, developmental trends in the acquisition of these component processes are presented. In the third section, good comprehenders are contrasted with poor comprehenders. In the fourth section, the instructional implications of the research on reading comprehension are drawn and an example of how to implement reading theory in the classroom is presented.

The Nature of Reading Comprehension

A useful way to describe reading comprehension is to first give an overall sense of what it entails, then describe some of its structural aspects, and then describe some of its functional aspects.

Overview

To get an initial sense of what reading comprehension entails, it is helpful to examine the three-way relation between writers, written language, and readers. In the beginning, there are writers who have the goal of creating certain ideas in their readers' minds. To fulfill such a goal, writers ask themselves questions such as, "If I want my readers to have such-and-such thoughts, what words can I use?" Writers choose certain words, phrases, and sentences based on their beliefs about the *conventional* ways to say things and presume that their readers know these conventions. Thus, if the conventional way to state a prediction is to use an "if . . . then" construction and a writer wants her readers to know her prediction, she will use an "if . . . then" construction to make this prediction in print (e.g., "If the economy improves, Clinton will get reelected"). We can say that readers comprehend some written text when they understand what the writer was trying to say. In a sense, then, when a reader comprehends a writer, we have a meeting of minds.

Consider an analogy to illustrate this notion. Imagine a very simple world in which the people in that world can say or write only four things: (a) "blah" (translates as "I'm hungry"), (b) "choo" (translates as "I wish I could find food"), (c) "yipe" (translates as "This looks very tasty"), and (d) "dork" (translates as "Let's eat this"). Next, pretend that someone on this imaginary planet is handed a note from his friend that says "Blah choo." We can say that the former comprehends the note if he gets the idea that his friend is hungry and wants to find food.

What could cause a comprehension failure on this imaginary planet? There are three possibilities. First, the reader may not know the conventions. For example, he may think that *dork* means "I'm hungry." Second, the writer could choose the wrong words because he does not know the conventions. Third, neither person might know the conventions.

Comprehension failures happen for the same reasons on our planet, too. Poor writers often find themselves saying, "What I was really trying to say was . . . " Such statements express the idea that what they had written did not accurately plant the right ideas in the readers' minds. Poor comprehenders, in contrast, often find themselves saying, "I wasn't sure what the author's point was." As we shall see below, this three-way relation between writers, texts, and readers plays a prominent part in discussions of structural and functional aspects of reading comprehension.

Structural Aspects of Comprehension

In Chapters 2 and 3, we learned about cognitive structures called *schemata.* A schema was said to be a mental representation of what multiple instances of some type of thing have in common. For example, a schema for a house specifies the things that most houses have in common. Besides having schemata for things like houses, it turns out that skilled readers and writers have schemata for specific types of texts, too. The two main schemata that have been examined closely are those for *narrative* and *expository* texts. In what follows, we shall see how schemata for specific topics (e.g., houses), narratives, and expository texts help students comprehend and remember what they are reading.

Topic Knowledge
When readers have schematized knowledge for things (e.g., houses) and events (e.g., funerals), they are better able to assimilate the information presented in some text than when they lack this knowledge. In particular, when readers try to process some text, their minds try to find mental spots for each successive idea that is expressed in the text. For example, if you are reading a passage that says "Dogs are one of the most common pets," your mind might metaphorically say, "I knew that because my *dog* node is attached to a *common-pet* node by way of an *is-a* link." But if you next read the line "Dogs were first domesticated by ancient peoples," your mind might say, "I didn't know that; let's add that piece of information to my *dog* schema."

In addition to providing an assimilative base for incoming information, schemata for topics also help readers make inferences when things are not explicitly stated by an author. For example, if you read the line "The suspect handed Ralphy a 'milkbone,' . . . " you would probably use your *dog* schema to make the inference that Ralphy is a dog. Similarly, if you were to read the line "Nobody came to Mary's birthday party" you might use your knowledge of people to infer that Mary became sad as a result.

Schemata for Narrative Texts

Authors of narratives attempt to communicate event-based experiences to their readers. In most narratives, there are (a) *characters* who have goals and motives for performing actions, (b) *temporal* and *spatial placements* in which the story takes place, (c) *complications* and *major goals* of main characters, (d) *plots* and *resolutions* of complications, (e) *affect patterns* (i.e., emotional and other responses to the storyline), (f) *points, morals,* and *themes,* and (g) *points of view* and *perspectives* (Graesser, Golding & Long, 1991).

An individual who writes a narrative, then, has schematized knowledge of the above components of a story and tries to fill in the components as he or she writes a particular story (see Chapter 7). An author does so with the expectation that his or her readers have this schematized knowledge as well. As each part of a story unfolds, readers rely on their narrative schemata to form expectations as to what will come next. Skilled writers play off these expectations to occasionally surprise readers or leave them hanging (as cliff-hangers do). Readers use their schemata for narratives to help them judge whether a story is a good one and also to create a *situation model* of what they have read (see Chapter 8 for a description of situation models).

Schemata for Expository Texts

Whereas the main goal of narratives is to tell a story to entertain readers, the main goal of expository texts is to provide information so that the reader can learn something (Weaver & Kintsch, 1991). Thus, whereas *Snow White* is an example of a narrative text, the present textbook is an example of an expository text (though I hope that this book can be entertaining as well as informative).

Just as good writers and readers have schemata for narrative texts, they have schemata for expository texts as well. The two most cited theoretical models of expository schemata are those of Meyer (1985) and Kintsch (1982). In Kintsch's (1982) model, there are three main relations that make up the schemata for expository texts: (a) *general-particular relations,* which have to do with identifying, defining, classifying, or illustrating things (e.g., "A schema is a mental representation . . ."), (b) *object-object* relations, which have to do with comparing or contrasting things (e.g., "Working memory differs from long-term memory in that . . .", and (c) *object-part relations,* which have to do with causal relations, how the parts of something are put together, and how the parts work individually and collectively (e.g., "There are three types of memory: short-term, working, and long-term . . .").

In Meyer's (1985) model, the ideas in a passage are also said to stand in certain relations to each other. Analyses of many common expository texts show that writers arrange their ideas into five common relations:

1. *Collection*: A relation that shows how things are related together into a group (e.g., "There are seven types of vehicles on the road today. First, there are . . .");
2. *Causation*: A relation that shows how one event is the antecedent cause of another event (e.g., "The tanker spilled all of its oil into the sea. As a result, the sea life . . .");
3. *Response*: A relation that shows how one idea is a problem and another is a solution to the problem (e.g., "A significant number of homeless people have a substance abuse problem. It should be clear that homelessness will not diminish until increased money goes to treatment of this disorder . . .");
4. *Comparison*: A relation in which the similarities and differences between things are pointed out (e.g., "Piaget and Vygotsky both emphasized egocentric speech; However, Vygotsky viewed it more as . . .");
5. *Description*: A relation in which more information about something is given such as attributes, specifics, manners, or settings (e.g., "Newer oil tankers are safer than they used to be. These days they have power steering and double hulls").

Because these relations pertain to how the ideas are arranged in some text, they are said make up the "prose structure" of the text. Writers hope that the arrangement of ideas in their readers' minds is the same as the arrangement of ideas in the text.

An individual who writes an expository textbook, then, has schematized knowledge of the relations identified by Kintsch (1982) and Meyer (1985) and also knows the conventional ways of communicating these relations. The most common way to prompt readers to recognize a relation is to place sentences close together. When one sentence follows another, skilled readers try to form a connection between them. If a writer fears that his or her readers will not make the connection even when sentences are placed in close proximity, he or she can use various *signaling* devices to make the connection explicit. For example, to convey Meyer's (1985) comparison relation, a writer might use the words *In contrast,* . . . To signal causal relations, he or she might use the words *As a result,* . . . Of course, readers do not always need signals to make the connection. Consider the following two passages:

1. There are two main causes of heart disease. Fatty diets promote the formation of placque deposits on arteries. Cigarettes enhance the formation of placque by constricting blood vessels.
2. There are two main causes of heart disease. First, fatty diets promote the formation of placque deposits on arteries. Second, cigarettes enhance the formation of placque by constricting blood vessels.

For most readers, the words *First* and *Second* in the second passage are not needed in order to connect the ideas in the three sentences together into Meyer's (1985) "collection" relation.

Over time, it is assumed that readers gain knowledge of the common relations found in expository texts such as collection, causation, response, comparison, and description. In a sense, their mind unconsciously says, "Okay, how is this sentence related to the one(s) that I just read? Is it a causation relation? A comparison?" If the closest sentence does not provide an immediate fit, people read on until they find a sentence that does.

In addition to helping readers form expectations, knowledge of prose structure helps readers comprehend and retain more of what they read (Meyer, 1985; Weaver & Kintsch, 1991). In particular, the five relations identified by Meyer often serve as an author's main point or thesis. Main ideas are connected by one of these five relations and lesser ideas are subsumed beneath this overall relation. People who first encode the main point and then attach additional ideas to the main point demonstrate superior comprehension and memory of the ideas in a passage. People who treat paragraphs as a string of individual ideas show inferior comprehension and memory.

To illustrate, consider the homelessness passage shown in Table 6.1. The sentences in this passage are numbered so that the arrangement of ideas can be graphically depicted in the figure below the passage. The author's main thesis is the following: Because the problem of homelessness is mainly caused by high

TABLE 6.1   The Prose Structure of the Homelessness Passage

Homelessness in America

(1) Across America, there are millions of homeless people. (2) Although single, unemployed people make up the majority of Americans seeking shelter, the number of homeless families is on the rise. (3) In fact, families make up nearly 40% of the occupants of homeless shelters in some cities. (4) Some estimates suggest that 7 out of 10 homeless families are headed by an individual who abuses alcohol or drugs. (5) It should come as no surprise, then, that the American Psychological Association has lobbied hard for increased funding for treatment centers.

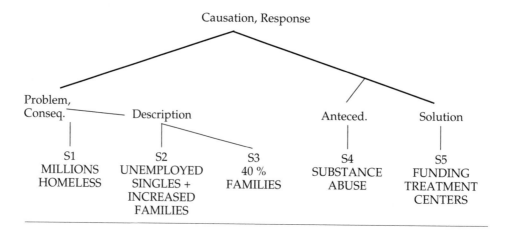

levels of substance abuse, the best way to reduce homelessness is to attack substance abuse (e.g., through treatment centers). In the manner of theorists such as Meyer (1985), the heavy line linking sentences 1, 4, and 5 indicates that these sentences pertain to the author's main thesis. The central ideas are connected by way of a dual causation and response relation. The less important ideas are connected with the thinner lines and can be seen to be subordinate to (i.e., connected below) the main thesis. Research suggests that if an individual were to look for the author's main thesis about homelessness and then connect the other ideas in the passage to this thesis as shown in Table 6.1., such an individual would show superior comprehension and recall of the ideas in the passage.

Functional Aspects of Comprehension

In addition to having structural knowledge of topics and the various kinds of texts (e.g., narrative versus expository), readers also need to engage in a variety of on-line processes in order to enhance their reading comprehension (Paris, Wasik & Turner, 1991; Pressley et al., 1994). These processes are collectively called reading strategies and include: (a) goal-setting, (b) inference-making, (c) identifying the main idea, (d) summarizing, (e) predicting, (f) monitoring, and (g) backtracking.

Setting a goal for reading is the first thing that readers need to do before they read (Pressley et al., 1994). Reading is a *purposeful* activity in that we read things for different reasons (Paris et al., 1991). For example, whereas we usually read a newspaper to find out what is happening in the world, we read spy novels simply to be entertained or take our minds off work. Similarly, sometimes we only want a rough sense of what an author is trying to say, so we only skim the pages for major points. Other times we really want to process everything an author says so we read every line very carefully (e.g., when we read a textbook right before a test). Goal-setting is crucial because the goals we set can either enhance or limit what we get from reading. For example, if someone sets the goal of pronouncing all of the words correctly but fails to set the goal of learning something, he or she is unlikely to engage in any of the remaining strategies.

Inference-making is, perhaps, the most widely studied reading strategy (Paris et al., 1991). Readers make inferences in order to (a) elaborate on the meaning of an individual sentence and (b) integrate the meanings of several sentences in a text (Alba & Hasher, 1982). For example, when readers encounter sentences such as "The man stirred his coffee," many of them elaborate on the ideas presented by inferring that he used a spoon. In addition, when presented with a pair of sentences such as

> Joe smoked four packs a day. After he died, his wife sold her Phillip Morris stocks,

many readers infer that smoking caused Joe to die. Thus, the two ideas of smoking and dying are integrated together through a causal relation. Moreover, inferences play an important role in the construction of a reader's situation model for the text he or she is reading. As mentioned above, the principal source of inferences is a reader's schematized knowledge of topics such as *coffee* and *cigarettes*.

Why do readers make inferences when they read? It seems that a reader's mind is always trying to make sense of what it is encountering. One way of making sense of things is to make the information presented more concrete and specific. So, when people read the sentence above about stirring, their minds naturally ask questions such as, "What kind of thing do people usually use to stir their coffee?" Notice that the inference that a spoon was used is merely probabilistic. People sometimes use whatever is handy such as the handle of a fork.

As to why we make intersentence inferences, it is helpful to repeat a point made earlier: It seems that the mind is always asking, "How does this new sentence relate to the sentences that I already read?" When two events co-occur close in time, it is natural to think that the prior one caused the later one (Bullock et al., 1982). For example, by stating the first sentence above about smoking and then the second one about dying right after it, it is natural to assume that smoking killed Joe. Similarly, if one reads "The floor was just mopped. I fell," it is natural to assume that the speaker slipped on the floor. It is possible, however, that smoking did not kill Joe and that the person fell because of something else (e.g., tripped over a bucket). Thus, once again we see that inferences are not necessary conclusions, they are merely probabilistic guesses.

In addition to causal connections, there are a variety of other intersentence connections that could be made. For example, readers naturally link up a pronoun in a second sentence to a person's name in a first sentence (e.g., "Mary saw the doctor. She said . . ."). Similar to causal inferences, inferences about pronouns are also probabilistic (i.e., The doctor could be a woman).

Besides inference-making, a second important comprehension strategy is *identifying the main idea*. In order to identify the main idea of some passage, readers need to assess the relevance of each idea and then rank-order ideas in terms of centrality or importance (van Dijk & Kintsch, 1983). Consider the following paragraph taken from George Lakoff's (1987) book, *Women, Fire, and Dangerous Things*:

> Most categorization is automatic and unconscious, and if we become aware of it at all, it is only in problematic cases. In moving about the world, we automatically categorize people, animals, and physical objects, both natural and man-made. This sometimes leads to the impression that we just categorize things as they are, that things come in natural kinds, and that our categories of mind naturally fit the kinds of things that are in the world. But a large proportion of our categories are not categories of *things*; they are categories of abstract entities. We categorize events, actions, emotions, spatial relationships, social relationships, and abstract entities of an enormous range: governments, illnesses, and entities in both scientific and folk theories, like electrons and colds. Any adequate account of human thought must provide an accurate theory for *all* our categories, both concrete and abstract (p. 6).

What is the main idea of this paragraph? Is it contained in the first sentence? The last? The fourth? How do you know? If this were an item from the verbal section of the SAT, one of the questions about this paragraph would ask you to say which was the main idea. Apart from the practical reality that important standardized tests require the ability to identify the main idea, readers also need this skill in order the construct the prose structure for a text (see the earlier section Structural Aspects above). George Lakoff rank-ordered the ideas in his paragraph in a particular way and he wanted you to get his point about categorization. To say that you comprehended his paragraph is to say that you rank-ordered ideas the same way that he did. It might be useful to construct the prose structure of this paragraph using Meyer's (1985) five relations in the manner of Table 6.1 in order to try to determine Lakoff's main point.

In addition to determining the prose structure of a passage, a second way to identify main ideas is to locate various signals in the text. Sometimes signals are graphic (e.g., italics), sometimes they are lexical (e.g., using the word *essential*), and sometimes they are semantic (e.g., explicit topic sentences). Readers expect that the main idea will occur early in a paragraph, but location is not always a very good predictor. In fact, studies have shown that as few as 25 percent of children's textbooks have main ideas located near the beginning of paragraphs (Garner, 1987). Thus, it may be a better idea to rely on prose structure relations and prior knowledge to find the main idea than to rely on text signals.

Besides being central to comprehension, an additional reason that identifying the main idea is an important strategy is that it is a prerequisite skill for performing the third important reading strategy: *summarizing*. In order to create a summary, you need to be able to delete unimportant ideas and retain only the gist of what is written. The gist, in turn, is comprised mostly of the main ideas.

To see this, consider the five rules for forming a good summary proposed by Brown and Day (1983). The first two rules specify that readers should delete trivial, irrelevant, or redundant information. The third rule suggests that readers should find a superordinate term for members of a category (e.g., *cars* for Buick, Dodge, and Toyota). Rules four and five specify that readers should find and use the main ideas of a passage in their summary. If main ideas are not explicitly provided by an author, readers should construct their own main ideas. Thus, one could not construct a good summary without being able to identify main ideas.

The fourth important reading strategy is *predicting*. Predicting consists of simply forming expectations regarding what will happen next in a narrative story or anticipating what the author of an expository text will say next. Good writers are skilled at helping readers make predictions and also good at violating expectations in such a way that it is entertaining. To illustrate, consider the following passage taken from the book *Dave Barry Slept Here* written by columnist Dave Barry in 1989:

> While the United States was struggling to get out of the Depression, the nations of Europe were struggling to overcome the horror and devastation and death of World War I so they could go ahead and have World War II. By the 1930s everybody was just about ready, so Germany, showing the kind of

spunky "can-do" spirit that made it so popular over the years, started invading various surrounding nations. Fortunately these were for the most part *small* nations, but Germany's actions nevertheless alarmed Britain and France, which decided to strike back via the bold and clever strategy of signing agreements with Adolf Hitler (p. 117).

Dave Barry's sarcasm works well because readers expect him to say one thing and he frequently says another.

The fifth reading strategy is called comprehension *monitoring*. Simply put, comprehension monitoring is the ability to "know when you don't know"; that is, it is the ability to detect a comprehension failure (Markman, 1981). As was discussed in Chapter 4, reading does not consist of simply knowing how to sound out words. Rather, reading consists of extracting meaning from texts. If a portion of a text does not make sense, readers should recognize that the main goal of reading (i.e., extracting meaning) has not been met.

When readers recognize that something they just read does not make sense, they have two options: (a) they could say, "Oh well! Let's just read on" or (b) they could decide to do something about their comprehension failure. The latter option brings us to our sixth and final strategy, *backtracking*. Backtracking consists of rereading a portion of a text when a comprehension failure occurs. Garner (1987) suggests that readers backtrack in response to four judgments and beliefs:

1. They do not understand or remember what they just read.
2. They believe that they can find the information needed to resolve the difficulty in the text.
3. The prior material must be scanned to locate the helpful information.
4. Information from several prior sentences may need to be combined and manipulated to resolve the comprehension problem.

Summary

In contemporary reading theories, it is assumed that reading comprehension is greatly aided when readers (a) have topic knowledge, (b) have structural knowledge of the different types of texts (i.e., narrative and expository) and (c) employ a variety of on-line strategies such as inference-making, identifying the main idea, summarizing, predicting, monitoring, and backtracking. In the next two sections, we shall examine the extent of these structural and functional capabilities in older and younger readers, and in more skilled and less skilled readers.

Developmental Trends in Reading Comprehension

To summarize the development of reading comprehension skills, we shall first examine the research concerned with developmental differences in children's schemata, and then examine developmental research related to reading strategies.

Development in Structural (i.e., Schematic) Knowledge

In discussing the development of schemata, one asks questions such as "What kind of schemata do young children have?" and "How do the schemata of younger children differ from those of older children?" In what follows, we shall attempt to answer such questions by focusing first on the research on the development of schemata for specific topics, then on the developmental research on schemata for stories, and finally on the research on the development of schemata for expository texts.

Topic Knowledge

In Chapter 2, we learned that children's knowledge for various topics (e.g., animals, fractions, baseball, etc.) is arranged into schemata. Thus, their knowledge of birds might be represented by a node for *bird* connected to a node for *canary* by an *is-a* link, and so on. With age, experience, and increased education, children's schemata for various topics become more and more elaborate. As we will see several times below, this increased topic knowledge greatly facilitates their comprehension.

Story Schemata

Although several theoretical models of schemata for stories have been proposed over the years (Graesser et al., 1991), the models that have generated the most developmental research are those based on the *story grammars* proposed by Mandler and Johnson (1977) and Stein and Glenn (1979). In Stein & Glenn's (1979) classic account, a story grammar is a theoretical description of what most stories have in common. It is not intended to reflect an actual knowledge structure in a young reader's mind. Rather, it is a representation of an *expert*'s knowledge of what all stories have in common (Stein, 1982). To get a sense of the formal, abstract character of a story grammar, consider the following example: If an adult were to sign up for a writing workshop to learn how to write a book for children, he or she would probably be presented with some form of a Story Grammar by the workshop leader. The workshop leader would say things like, "Any successful story has seven parts. The first part is . . ."

Although children do not start out with a formal, explicit story grammar in their minds, they do develop *story schemas* in response to listening to and reading many stories. A story schema contains personalized, implicit knowledge about what most stories have in common (Stein, 1982). Given the personalized nature of story schemas, any two children could develop different story schemas if they listened to very different types of stories during their lives. However, as children read more and more stories and gain increased knowledge about people, their story schemas should become more similar to a formal story grammar.

The original story grammar proposed by Stein & Glenn (1979) specified that stories have seven main components: (a) A *major setting*, which includes the introduction of characters (e.g., "Once upon a time, there was a beautiful young woman called Cinderella . . ."), (b) a *minor setting*, which includes a description of the story context (e.g., "She lived in a castle with her stepmother . . ."), (c) *initiating events*, which include changes in the environment or things that happen to main characters (e.g., "One day, the Prince invited everyone to a ball . . ."), (d) *internal responses*, which include the characters' goals, plans, and thoughts that arise in response to the initiating events (e.g., "Cinderella said, 'Oh, I want to go the ball too!' . . .), (e) *attempts*, which include the character's actions to fulfill the goal (e.g., "So she started to fix an old gown to make it more presentable . . ."), (f) *direct consequences*, which specify whether the goal was attained (e.g., "But her stepmother made her clean the castle instead of fix her gown . . ."), and (g) *reactions*, which include the character's feelings or thoughts about the direct consequences (e.g., "When it came time to go to the ball, Cinderella was sad because she could not go . . ."). The first two elements are usually grouped together to form what is called the *setting* part of a story and the last five elements are grouped together to form what is called the *episode* part of the story. Hence, protopical stories contain both a setting and at least one episode.

Research has shown that when stories conform to the canonical structure specified above (i.e., they have all seven of the components arranged in the same order as above), few developmental differences emerge. In particular, even four- and five-year-olds show good recall of the events in a story when it has all of the components outlined in Stein and Glenn's story grammar. Older children do, however, recall more information in the story than younger children and also make more inferences than younger children. The majority of these inferences seem to be attempts to fill in category information that was missing in the actual text (Stein, 1982). For example, if the *reaction* portion of a story was missing, older children tend to fill in this component in by way of inference.

When noncanonical stories are used, developmental differences become even more pronounced. For example, when a story is artifically disorganized (e.g., the initiating event occurs after the direct consequence), older children are more able to recover the canonical structure of the story in their retellings than younger children (Stein, 1982). Similarly, when children are given the initial portions of a story and asked to complete it, older children are more likely than younger children to add the components that the grammar would suggest are missing (Eckler & Weininger, 1989). Finally, when presented with stories that are missing some of the components specified in the grammar (e.g., direct consequences), older readers (who have well-developed story schemas) are more likely than young readers to say that the story was not a good one (Stein & Policastro, 1984).

Thus, developmental differences are most pronounced when children are asked to comprehend a story that does *not* conform to a story grammar. It would seem that a canonical story minimizes the amount of processing that has to be done in order for the story to be comprehended. This minimization would occur only if children had something like a story schema in their minds. Since older children tend to have greater processing capacity than younger children, the former can take a noncanonical story and mentally fill in components or rearrange them to make it into a more canonical story.

In sum, then, story schemas play two important roles. First, they minimize the processing that has to occur when a story is read. When presented with a canonical story, readers need not devote all of their mental resources to comprehending the basic facts in the story. Instead, readers can use any additional processing resources to perform other mental tasks such as inference-making (Stein, 1982) and metaphor comprehension (Waggoner, Meece & Palermo, 1985). Second, story schemas set up expectations as to what will occur next in a story. For example, if the initiating event component has just occurred in a story, readers tend to expect that the internal response component will be encountered soon. Although older students can make better use of the two roles played by story schemas than younger students, even preschoolers seem to have a rudimentary story schema. In most cases, however, it is necessary to use auxiliary pictures and probing questions to reveal a story schema in children below the age of six (Shapiro & Hudson, 1991).

Many school systems have incorporated the story grammar model into their reading curriculum. In fact, teachers frequently ask students to identify the parts of a story that they just read (e.g., "Who can tell me what the setting is? What is the initiating event?" etc.). Thus, students learn the parts and then get lots of practice finding the parts in actual stories. If schema theory is correct that the mind naturally abstracts common elements on its own, perhaps this explicit instruction would not be necessary. And yet, at the very least, we would expect that this practice would certainly help students acquire a story schema faster than they would on their own. Research supports this expectation (Pressley, Johnson, Symons, McGoldrick & Kurita, 1989).

Schemata for Expository Texts

In its purest form, a developmental study of prose structure would take groups of children at two ages and give them well-organized and poorly organized expository passages to recall (e.g., Danner, 1976). In such a study, one could examine (a) whether older children are more likely than younger children to use the author's prose structure to help their recall (i.e., to find the author's main thesis and use it to organize their recall of subordinate ideas), (b) whether older children are less likely than younger children to need explicit text signals to derive the prose structure, and (c) whether older children are more likely than younger children to derive the prose structure in poorly organized passages. All of these findings would support the idea that, with age and increased reading opportunities, children acquire schemata for expository texts.

Unfortunately, such pure developmental studies are hard to find. Instead of using multiple age groups, many researchers have used just one age group. In addition, many researchers seemed to be more interested in reading ability than age, because when they compared children of two age groups, they usually added reading ability as a variable (e.g., they compared fifth grade poor comprehenders to third grade good comprehenders). Further, many researchers provided instruction on how to derive prose structure to see if children's comprehension could be improved. As a result, few of the existing studies can be used to say whether children naturally acquire schemata for expository texts simply by reading many of them (as seems to be the case for story schemas).

Nevertheless, the existing research suggests that the derivation of prose structure is often not an easy task for children at any age. Meyer, Brandt, and Bluth (1980), for example, found that when given four well-organized passages to remember, only 22 percent of ninth graders consistently used the strategy of using the author's main thesis to organize their recalls. More than 50 percent of these students failed to use the strategy even once. As a result, even the best readers recalled 70 percent or less of the ideas in the passages. Similarly, Zinar (1990) found that fifth graders recalled only about 20 to 25 percent of the content of short prose passages, suggesting that they too failed to use the prose structure to guide their recall.

This is not to say, however, that children's performance is always so deficient. For example, Garner et al. (1986) found excellent knowledge of prose structure in a group of seventh graders. In particular, 75 percent could provide a meaningful description of a paragraph, 98 percent could exclude topically unrelated sentences from a paragraph, 87 percent knew where to place a topic sentence in a paragraph, and 87 percent could arrange a set of sentences into a cohesive whole. Similarly, Spires, Gallini, and Riggsbee (1992) found that fourth graders in a control group recalled 60 percent or more of the content of expository passages arranged in the form of problem/solution or compare/contrast formats.

The finding that children can perform both extremely well and extremely poorly suggests that something other than schemata for expository texts might be at work. One possible explanation for such variable performance is children's knowledge of the passage topic (Roller, 1990). For very familiar passages, being aware of common formats such as problem/solution or compare/contrast may add little to one's knowledge of the topic. That is, a reader might show excellent comprehension of a familiar passage even when he or she lacks knowledge of common formats (i.e., lacks a schema for expository passages). For example, a young child who is enthralled by dinosaurs might show very good comprehension of a passage about the extinction of dinosaurs even though this child lacks knowledge of the format in which the ideas are arranged (e.g., causal relations). Conversely, a reader may show very poor comprehension of an unfamiliar passage even when he or she has known of common formats. For example, an adult who is unfamiliar with computers but familiar with compare/contrast formats might show poor comprehension of a passage about the similarities and differences between two kinds of computers.

If both prior knowledge and schemata for expository texts (SETs) affect comprehension, the effects of SETs should be most pronounced when readers are only moderately familiar with a topic. In reviewing the literature on prose structure, Roller (1990) found two findings in support of this notion: (a) presenting disorganized paragraphs has its strongest effects when readers are moderately familiar with the topic and (b) providing instruction of the different types of prose structures (e.g., problem/solution and so on) has its strongests effects when readers are moderately familiar with a topic. When readers are either very unfamiliar or very familiar with a topic, these effects are considerably weaker.

In sum, then, there is evidence that children in the later grades have at least implicit knowledge of various prose structures. Whether they make use of this structure to aid their comprehension and recall seems to depend on their familiarity with a topic. Because most studies in this area have neither controlled for familiarity nor used a pure developmental design, it is hard to say what the natural developmental course of schemata for expository texts is. Nevertheless, a number of studies have shown that when children are told about the various types of relations in prose passages and asked to identify these relations (e.g., "Look at this paragraph. Where is a collection relation? How about a cause-effect relation?" etc.), they show improved comprehension. So, just as teaching story grammar elements can help improve children's comprehension of stories, so can teaching them the common expository help them comprehend expository passages better. But given the role of familiarity, it would make sense that pointing out expository relations should only be done when the passage contains content that is moderately familiar to students. It would be a waste of time for content that is either highly familiar or highly unfamiliar. One way a teacher could check the familiarity of a topic would be to have students generate a group concept map or "web" prior to reading. Here, students would say everything they know about a topic and the teacher would depict this knowledge using a node-link schema on the board.

The Development of Reading Strategies

In what follows, the developmental research on goal-setting, inference-making, identifying the main idea, summarizing, predicting, monitoring, and backtracking will be described in turn.

Goal-Setting

Research shows that young children do not set optimal reading goals for themselves. For example, instead of reading something to increase their knowledge about the topic or be entertained, young readers say that the goal of reading is to "pronounce all of the words properly." Other students act as if their goal is simply to "get the assignment done" (Paris et al., 1991). With these goals, students who read all words properly and finish reading an assigned passage will not be bothered if they fail to comprehend what they read. Over time children replace their suboptimal goals with more appropriate ones regarding meaning. Typically, however, this shift takes too many years to complete. It should be clear that teachers need to help students set more appropriate goals for themselves early on in the elementary grades.

Inference-Making

Given the fact that (a) schematized knowledge underlies inference-making and (b) schematized knowledge increases with age, it should not be surprising to learn that many studies have found that children in the later grades (i.e., fourth, fifth, and sixth grades) are more likely to make inferences than children in the earlier grades. For example, when reading the sentence "The soldier stirred his coffee," older students are more likely than younger students to infer that the soldier used a spoon (Paris, 1978).

But the common finding of developmental differences in inference-making should not imply that younger children are incapable of making inferences. Recent studies have shown that young children demonstrate very good inference-making skills when they are presented with stories about very familiar topics or are given instruction on how to make inferences (Dewitz, Carr & Patberg, 1987; Paris et al., 1991; Wasik, 1986). Thus, the natural course of inference-making can be altered by way of instruction or by using highly familiar content.

One good way of eliciting inferences is to stop in the middle of stories whenever an inference is required and ask questions. For example, when students read the popular Miss Nelson stories (about a teacher named Miss Nelson), they need to make the inference that a mean substitute teacher in the story named Viola Swamp is really Miss Nelson in disguise. Throughout the book, subtle clues are left to help readers make this connection. Young readers usually miss these clues, so it would be helpful to ask questions such as "What is Viola Swamp's dress doing in Miss Nelson's closet?" Over time, repeated questions that require inferences would ultimately help children make inferences on their own. However, since older students seem to make inferences without much prompting, focused instruction on inference-making is best for kindergartners through fourth graders.

Identifying the Main Idea

Children in the elementary grades have difficulty recognizing, recalling, and constructing the main idea in passages (Baumann, 1981; Johnston & Afflerbach, 1985; Paris et al., 1991). Moreover, there is evidence that this skill improves throughout the adolescent and early adult years. Once again, however, the identification of main ideas is more likely when familiar content is used (Sternberg, 1985) and when students are directly taught how to perform this strategy (e.g., Baumann, 1981).

Summarizing

As might be expected given the findings for identifying the main idea, there are clear developmental trends in the ability to provide a good summary. Whereas younger students (e.g., fifth graders) tend to create summaries by simply deleting statements and using the author's words, older students (e.g., high school students) tend to combine and reorganize ideas using their own words (Brown & Day, 1983; Paris et al., 1991; Taylor, 1986).

As was found for both inference-making and identifying the main idea, however, preadolescent children can be taught how to provide a good summary (Brown, Day & Jones, 1983; Rinehart, Stahl & Erickson, 1986; Palinscar & Brown, 1984). In the Rinehart et al. (1986) study, for example, children were taught four rules for summarizing over the course of five one-hour lessons: identify the main information, delete trivial information, delete redundant information, and relate main and supporting information. The teacher modeled each strategy and then asked students to practice the modeled strategy. They worked first at the paragraph level, and then moved up to combining paragraph summaries into a single summary for the whole text. When training was over, the researchers found that trained children showed better memory for what they read than untrained children.

Predicting

Studies have shown that although many students do not spontaneously make predictions when they read, they can be taught to do so. In support of the claim that good comprehenders make predictions when they read, these studies also show that children's reading comprehension improves after being told how to make predictions (Fielding, Anderson & Pearson, 1990; Hansen & Pearson, 1983; Palinscar & Brown, 1984; Pearson & Fielding, 1991).

One way to improve student predictions is to have them first look at the cover of a book and predict what the book will be about after examining the title and cover illustration (Pressley et al., 1994). Then, in the midst of reading the work, children can be asked to stop and make additional predictions as they read. Finally, after the reading is completed, children can be asked to examine their original predictions to see whether they were right. Pressley and his colleagues have shown that whereas first graders need a lot of prompting to make such predictions, older students need much less prompting after three years of such instruction.

Monitoring

As noted previously, the essence of reading comprehension is the extraction of meaning; that is, one reads *in order to* gain an understanding of a story or some topic area. If students read a story or an informational passage and do not come away with a good understanding of what they read, that means that they did not attain the central goal of reading (Baker & Brown, 1984; Paris et al., 1991). If it were to be found that many children do not detect their comprehension failures or do not try to fix a comprehension failure when it occurs, that would mean that reading instruction is seriously deficient. To see this, consider an analogy. What would we think about a vocational school that constantly produced car mechanics who could not detect or repair problems with a malfunctioning automobile? Just as the essence of car repair involves knowing the difference between a well-functioning and malfunctioning car (and knowing how to fix the latter), the essence of reading is knowing the difference between adequate and inadequate comprehension (and knowing how to fix the latter).

Unfortunately, many studies have shown that children in the early elementary and middle school years have difficulty detecting their own comprehension failures (Baker & Brown, 1984; Garner, 1987; Paris et al., 1991). For example, in a classic study, Markman (1979) showed how even sixth graders can fail to detect logical inconsistencies in expository passages. In one passage, several lines pointed out that there is no light at the bottom of the ocean and that it is necessary to have light in order to see colors. After these lines were presented, the very next line stated that fish who live at the bottom of the sea use color to select their food. Even with explicit instructions to find such problems in passages, a sizable number of sixth graders could not find them. Using similar materials, this finding has been replicated many times with other age groups (e.g., Baker, 1984).

Overall, the developmental research on monitoring has revealed the following trends: (a) in the elementary grades and somewhat beyond, children often operate on automatic pilot when they read and seem oblivious to comprehension difficulties (Duffy & Roehler, 1987); (b) whereas younger readers tend to use a single standard for judging the meaningfulness of what they have read (e.g., problems with a single word), older readers use multiple standards for judging meaningfulness and consistency (Baker, 1984; Garner, 1981); and (c) older students are more likely to construct coherent representations of texts and benefit from instruction that helps them form such representations (Paris et al., 1991).

Backtracking

In her review of the literature, Garner (1987) argued that backtracking develops substantially between the sixth and tenth grades. There are at least three reasons younger readers tend not to reread a portion of text: (a) they sometimes think that it is illegal to do so, (b) they may not realize that they have a comprehension problem (see the above section on monitoring), and (c) they are often unfamiliar with text structure and cannot, therefore, use text structure to help guide their search for clarifying information. In addition, since many young readers think that the goal of reading is not to construct meaning but to sound out words properly, they would not be troubled by a comprehension failure (Paris et al., 1991). Thus, if some meaningless portion of a text were sounded-out properly, there would be no need to reread it.

Summary

With age, children seem to develop both structural and functional competencies that help them process what they are reading. In particular, research shows that older children demonstrate better reading comprehension than younger children because they are more likely than younger children to have: (a) extensive schematized knowledge of topics, (b) structural knowledge of the different kinds of texts (e.g., stories and expository texts), and (c) functional knowledge of reading strategies such as inference-making and backtracking.

In addition, three themes emerge from the research on schemata and strategies. First, it takes considerable time for children to develop schemata and strategies on their own. In the absence of explicit instruction, many middle school and high school students (who have been learning to read for more than five years) fail to make use of schemata and strategies to guide their comprehension. Second, instruction can substantially decrease the amount of time it takes for children to develop schemata and strategies. In particular, a large number of instructional studies have shown that explicit instruction on schemata or strategies can improve the comprehension of even elementary students. Third, children's prior knowledge of a topic can influence the degree to which they use their schemata or strategies to enhance their comprehension. Familiarity can compensate for a lack of knowledge of prose structure and can also enhance the chances that strategies will be deployed. Indeed, several recent studies of poor-reading adults show that people who are very knowledgeable about some topic (e.g., baseball) can show excellent comprehension of a passage on that topic (Recht & Leslie, 1988; Walker, 1987).

Individual Differences in Reading Comprehension

Researchers who have investigated individual differences in reading comprehension have attempted to answer questions such as: (a) Why do certain children obtain higher scores on standardized comprehension tests than other children in the same grade? and (b) Do "good" and "poor" comprehenders in the same grade differ in terms of their schemata for narratives, schemata for expository texts, and reading strategies? The goal of the present section is to try and provide answers to these questions.

If the theory presented near the beginning of this chapter is correct (i.e., that adult readers have reading strategies as well as schemata for topics and various types of texts), then it would be expected that (a) poor comprehenders would have less knowledge of the structure of stories and prose passages than same-aged good comprehenders, and (b) poor comprehenders would also be less likely to have or use reading strategies than same-age good comprehenders.

For the most part, the research confirms these expectations. For example, in terms of story schemas, Montague, Maddux, and Dereshiwksy (1990) found that when given narratives to recall, normally achieving students from three grades recalled more total ideas and more of the internal responses of characters than same-aged learning disabled (LD) students. In terms of expository texts, Meyer et al. (1980), Taylor (1980), and McGee (1982), all found that good comprehenders not only recalled more ideas than poor comprehenders, but the former were also more likely to organize their recalls in terms of top-level (i.e., superordinate) ideas. Finally, there is a wealth of studies that show how poor comprehenders are less likely to have knowledge of and use reading strategies than good comprehenders (Paris et al., 1991).

More support for the claim that poor comprehenders are deficient in their structural and strategic knowledge comes from a variety of instructional studies. In the case of narratives, Dimino et al. (1990) found that the comprehension level of ninth-grade, poor comprehenders could be improved by teaching them how to identify the main components of a story. Gurney et al. (1990) had similar success with LD students in high school. In the case of expository texts, Geva (1983) and Slater et al. (1985) found that teaching low-ability students how to identify certain text structures improved their comprehension. In the case of reading strategies, it has been shown that poor readers can be successfully taught how to: (a) make inferences (Hansen & Pearson, 1983), (b) identify the main idea (Schunk

& Rice, 1989), (c) summarize (Palincsar & Brown, 1984), (d) predict (Fielding et al., 1990), (e) monitor (Miller, Giovenco & Rentiers, 1987), and (f) backtrack (Garner et al., 1987).

Before moving on to the final section on instructional implications, however, it is important to note that while it is true that good and poor readers differ in terms of schemata and strategies, it is best to think of these differences as a *consequence* of earlier reading problems rather than as the primary cause of their later reading problems. As discussed in Chapter 5, the primary variables that distinguish between good and poor readers in the elementary grades are the abilities to (a) recognize words automatically, (b) recognize words quickly, and (c) interrelate graphic representations together with phonemic representations (Stanovich, 1986). Whereas good readers gain mastery over these abilities by the end of the third grade, poor readers do not. As a result, only the former are given multiple opportunities by their teachers to read longer segments of text and only the former have the experiences necessary to acquire higher-level schemata and strategies. Hence, the rich get richer and the poor get poorer.

Instructional Implications

A truly constructivist way to help you know how to translate theory and research about reading comprehension into practice is to provide a set of somewhat general, but not too abstract, guidelines as opposed to a set of highly prescriptive and concrete procedures (Pressley et al., 1994). And yet, to the inexperienced, it is often helpful to see an example of research-based instruction to make the application process easier. So, we shall end this chapter by first examining some general guidelines and then walking through an example of how reading theory can be implemented in the classroom.

General Guidelines

After an unusually brief period in the 1970s in which descriptive studies were conducted to examine the extent of schemata and strategies in students, researchers took what they had learned and tried to increase students' comprehension levels. The main approach was to implant schemata and strategies in both normally achieving and low-achieving students. In a recent review of this research, Pearson and Fielding (1991) summarized the findings as follows:

1. Students benefit when their teachers help them to recall, identify, or construct narrative and expository text structures. Successful teachers have used a variety of approaches to help their students identify common relations among ideas. These methods include questioning, modeling, and webbing.

2. Students' comprehension is improved when their teachers draw relationships between their students' background knowledge and the content of their readings. This may be accomplished through (a) evoking appropriate knowledge before reading, (b) asking students to explain, infer, or predict during reading, or (c) asking inferential questions after reading.

3. A crucial aspect of acquiring and using schemata and strategies is the ability to monitor one's comprehension. The only way to detect a common structure across stories or expository passages is to *comprehend* them correctly in the first place (because comprehension entails seeing the relationships that the author intended). Moreover, only people who recognize that they have comprehension problems develop and use strategies for overcoming these problems. Studies show that children can be taught how to become more active, discerning, and aware comprehenders.

4. Students can be taught how to discriminate between important and less important information and also how to create succinct summaries. Those students who acquire these skills improve their comprehension considerably.

5. Although the successful approaches have used a variety of methods and focused on a variety of structural skills, they all have the following component in common: they help students *transform* ideas in one form or another. Pearson and Fielding (1991) suggest that this transformation process makes ideas more memorable because they make the author's ideas become the *reader's* ideas.

6. Finally, a new trend emerged in many of the successful instructional studies. In order to transfer reading skills to students so that they use these skills independently, teachers engaged in a two-phase process of (a) modeling a skill and sharing cognitive secrets about this skill as they perform it (i.e., saying what should be done, why it works, when it should be used, etc.), and (b) gradually turning responsibility over to students until they can perform it independently (i.e., "fading").

A Concrete Example: Project SAIL

In Montgomery County, Maryland, a program called SAIL (Students Achieving Independent Learning) illustrates how reading theory and research can shape instructional practice in an effective way. The goal of SAIL is to get children to use reading strategies regularly and appropriately. Beginning in the first grade, children are taught how to think aloud, set goals for reading, predict, visualize, make associations between what they are reading and what they know, and summarize what they read.

Most instruction is carried out in small reading groups. In the early grades, the names of reading strategies are written on cards and spread out in front of the children. The teacher selects a card, models the strategy on the card, and explains what she is doing using a think-aloud procedure. For example, to relate what she is reading to what she knows, she may say, "This story must be about people who live in Washington, D.C." when she encounters the word *Georgetown* in a story she is reading. She continues this process each time she encounters a word that she can relate to what she knows. After the teacher finishes modeling the strategy, each student in the group takes a turn. With beginners, the teacher has to use a lot of scaffolding to elicit adequate strategy use in children (see the section on Vygotsky in Chapter 2). With older students, she no longer needs the cards and she has to use much less prompting, because children seem to internalize the strategy after three years of being in the SAIL program.

Apart from illustrating the importance of prior knowledge and strategies, examination of the SAIL program reveals that it illustrates four other important things. First, teachers clearly teach differently to younger students than they do to older students. Thus, these teachers obviously comprehend the notion of development. Second, many of the SAIL classrooms are in schools that receive Chapter 1 funding and contain a number of minority students. Thus, we see that theory-based instruction can particularly benefit low-income, minority children. Third, SAIL teachers never seem to teach the same lesson twice. In particular, even when they use the same book and plan to ask the same questions, the fact that children are asked to make their own predictions and summaries of what they read means that lessons will always have a unique and constructivist quality.

Chapter 7

Writing

Summary

1. Writers rely on four kinds of knowledge when they write: knowledge of topics, knowledge of audiences, knowledge of genres, and knowledge of language. In addition, they engage in three main processes: planning, translating, revising.

2. Developmental studies show that, with age, children become more knowledgeable about topics, audiences, genres, and language. However, the major change that seems to occur is not so much the acquisition of these forms of knowledge as much as children's ability to consciously reflect on and manipulate this knowledge.

3. Developmental studies also reveal that older children are more likely to create goals for their writing than younger children. This increased focus on goals prompts older children to (a) produce text that is consistent with their goals and (b) revise their writing when it fails to fulfill their goals.

4. Good writers are usually good readers. In addition, good writers are better at manipulating verbal information than poor writers, and also have a larger vocabulary and repertoire of syntactic constructions than poor writers. Finally, good writers are more likely to plan and revise than poor writers.

5. Research shows that girls tend to be more fluent in their writing than boys and tend to deviate from standard usage less often than boys. In addition, girls are more likely than boys to revise and fulfill the minimum requirement of writing tasks.

Imagine that you have an instructor who recently gave you a B for his course, but you feel that your performance warrants an A. You think that the reason for the discrepancy is that the instructor just does not like you. When you complain to the dean of the instructor's college, he asks you to follow your university's standard policy for contesting a grade: Write an essay that explains why you think that the grade is unfair and why you should be given an A. He tells you that the essay will then be read by a committee composed of faculty and students who make recommendations about whether the grade should stand or be changed. In addition, you are told that your instructor will be given a copy of the essay and will be asked to respond to it.

Given such a task, what might your essay say? What would you say first? How would you end the essay? Try writing such an essay now. Stop when you think that you have a version that is good enough to send to the committee.

Finished? Now imagine that your dean is new and made a mistake. He informs you that your instructor will not see the essay and that the committee is supposed to be comprised exclusively of students. Given this new information, would you leave your essay as it is or would you change certain parts? Would you have the same goals for both essays? (i.e., what does your first line accomplish? Your second? etc.).

As we shall see in subsequent sections, this essay example is useful for illustrating the major processes involved in writing. We shall refer back to it often as the components of writing are described, so it might be helpful to be reflective now about what thoughts went through your mind as you were writing it.

In what follows, we shall examine the research on writing in four sections. In the first section, you will learn about what writers know and what they do when they write. In the second section, you will learn about developmental trends in the acquisition of writing knowledge and skills. In the third section, you will learn about individual differences in writing ability. In the final section, you will learn about the instructional implications of the research on writing.

The Nature of Writing

The goal of the present section is to provide a reasonably complete answer to the following question: "What are the component processes involved in writing?" The best way to answer this question is to examine current models of writing (e.g., Hayes & Flower, 1986; Scardamalia & Bereiter, 1986) and distill major writing processes from these models. Such an examination reveals that successful writers have specific kinds of *knowledge* and engage in specific *processes* when they write. Let's examine these two aspects of writing in turn.

Knowledge Needed for Writing

There are four main types of knowledge that successful writers have: knowledge of topics, knowledge of audiences, knowledge of genres, and knowledge of language (Glover, Ronning & Bruning, 1990; Scardamalia & Bereiter, 1986).

Topic Knowledge

In your own experience, you may have noticed that it is much easier to write a paper when you know a lot about the topic than when you know little about it. The same is true for even the most skilled writers. Knowledge helps you generate ideas and organize them effectively. To see this, imagine that you were given the assignment of writing an essay on the nature of writing. It should be clear that you would have an easier time writing such a paper after you read this section than before you did (unless you were already familiar with the literature on writing). As another example, imagine that you were writing the essay regarding an unfair grade for a friend rather than for yourself. If you did not take the class with the friend and experience things the way he or she did, it would be harder to write the essay than if the unfair grade were given to you.

Knowledge of Audiences

Being knowledgeable about a topic is certainly necessary for writing a good piece, but it is not sufficient. Writers also have to be able to get inside their reader's minds in order to be successful. That is, they need to be able to answer questions such as "What do my readers already know? What do they want to hear? How would they probably react to my statements?" In the extreme, writers who fail to understand what their readers know and believe could produce a variety of unwanted responses in them. For example, poor writing could make readers feel: (a) confused (if the level is too high), (b) belittled or bored (if the level is too low), or (b) angry (if the author's stance runs contrary to their beliefs). In most cases, readers want to learn something new or form a connection with something they read. Readers will not learn anything new if the material is either too familiar or too unfamiliar, and will not have their beliefs confirmed by someone who challenges their opinions.

Knowledge of Genres

If someone asked you to write an argumentative essay, a textbook, a story, and a poem, would you know how to write something in each of these genres? As we have seen in Chapter 6, genres have their own distinctive structure that good readers come to know. For example, we saw that stories have a narrative structure involving components such as settings, characters, and outcomes. Given the fact that there are standard ways of organizing ideas in specific genres and that readers come to expect this standard format when they read a work in that genre, writers need to stick close to this standard format in order to maximize the chance that their readers will like and comprehend what they have read. Of course, the task of writing something in a particular genre is made easier when a writer has a *schema* for that type of work.

Knowledge of Language

Although having knowledge of topics, audiences, and genres is important to writing well, an absolutely indispensable component of good writing is knowledge of your audience's native language. Writers need to know how to place specific words in specific grammatical constructions in order to convey just the right meaning. That is, writers need to have (a) a good vocabulary, (b) knowledge of grammatical rules, and (c) knowledge of the *pragmatics* of a language (e.g., knowing how to be polite, sarcastic, etc.).

To see how important knowledge of language is, consider the following example: A French psychologist who is editing a book on cognitive theories asks an American expert on Piaget's theory to contribute a chapter about Piaget to this volume. The American is told that the readers of this book will be non-English-speaking French undergraduates. Even if the American knew a lot about Piaget's theory, knew a lot about how French undergraduates think, and also had a schema for chapters, it should be obvious that she would be unable to write a good chapter if she were not sufficiently fluent in French.

Writing Processes

Good writing, of course, requires more than simply having knowledge; it also requires *using* this knowledge to create some text. That brings us to the second major aspect of writing: writing processes. In contemporary theories of writing, writers create texts by engaging in three main processes: planning, translating, and revising (Hayes & Flower, 1986; Scardamalia & Bereiter, 1986). Let's examine each of these processes in turn.

Planning

Planning is the process of thinking about what you will write next. Writers plan throughout the construction of some written work. In particular, they plan before they produce a single word, after they have written some portion of the work, and after they have inspected a completed first draft. According to the Flower and Hayes model, planning is said to include three subprocesses: goal-setting, generating, and organizing.

Goal-Setting.   In thinking about what they will write, writers first ask themselves, "What am I trying to accomplish with this line? (or this section)." What you end up writing depends very much on the goals you set. Let's go back to our example essay about the unfair grade to illustrate. In writing the letter to the committee, you might form the following goals:

> G1: I want to give them all of the evidence that demonstrates why I should get an A.
>
> G2: I want to give them a little bit of evidence that supports the idea that the instructor does not like me.
>
> G3: I want to present the evidence in a nonhostile, matter-of-fact way.
>
> G4: I want to be as articulate as possible, so that I can impress them with my competence.

Close inspection of these four goals shows that whereas the first two have to do with *what* you will say, the last two concern *how* you will say it. It should be clear that if you delete one or more of these goals, the letter that you would write would turn out differently with each deletion. For example, if you keep all four goals, you might write:

> I received A's on all four of Dr. Jones's assignments and never missed a class. Dr. Jones apparently gave me a B because of a personality conflict of some

sort. Several of my classmates noticed his irritation when I frequently asked him to clarify several of the points he made in class.

In contrast, if you deleted G3 and G4, you might write:

There is no way I should get a B! I got A's on *all* assignments and went to every one of his boring classes! Look, the guy just does not like me!

Generating. The second subprocess of planning involves the actual generation of things to say. Writers generate ideas based on the goals they construct. For example, in order to generate ideas in response to G1 above, you might say to yourself, "What would be good evidence to support the idea that I deserve an A?" Using goals to think of things to say is called *heuristic search* (Scardamalia & Bereiter, 1986).

Organizing. The third subprocess of planning involves taking the ideas that are generated and organizing them into a coherent, sequential pattern. In addition to simply asking yourself, "What should I say?" you also need to ask questions such as "What should I say first?" "How should I follow up that idea?" and "How should I group my ideas?"

Translating
So far we have seen that writers create goals in order to generate and organize their ideas. In practice, these generated goals and ideas serve as a writer's mental blueprint for writing something. To move beyond the point of simply having well-defined plans, however, a writer needs to use this blueprint to actually write some text. That brings us to the second major writing process: translating.

It can be argued that translating is an absolutely central aspect of good writing. To see why, consider the following analogy. A general contractor buys two copies of a blueprint for a well-designed house. He gives one copy to the best construction company in town and the other copy to the worst company. The companies differ primarily in the skills of their employees. Although both companies work from the same blueprint, only the good construction company succeeds in creating a well-built house. Writing skills, it turns out, are much like construction skills. Just as a well-built house can only be produced by someone who can take a blueprint and perform the proper carpentry actions (e.g., measuring, sawing, and hammering), a well-written work can only be produced by someone who can effectively translate mental plans into written words.

To get a sense of how writers translate plans into text, it is useful to make a distinction between the meaning of a portion of text and its interpretation (Barwise, 1989; Perfetti & McCutchen, 1987). Anything that has been written is inherently ambiguous because it has a range of possible interpretations. To illustrate, consider the sentence "Visiting relatives can be a nuisance." Let's say that the author of this line wanted to make the point that traveling to visit one's relatives is not fun. We can call this point the *meaning* that she wanted to convey.

However, someone who reads the sentence above *interprets* the sentence to mean that it is not fun when your relatives come to visit you. To avoid such a misinterpretation, the author would have been better off using the words, "It can be annoying to visit your relatives." Thus, good writing involves knowing how to choose words and grammatical constructions in such a way that only one of several possible interpretations of a sentence is fixed in a reader's mind.

Revising

Revising is the process of reconsidering and reconfiguring aspects of the writing process. Revision can take place both before and after a segment of text is produced. For example, even before they write anything down, writers often revise their plans or revise mental first drafts of the sentences they are about to write. Then, after they have actually written something, writers examine what they have produced to see if it (a) fulfills their plans and (b) is likely to fix the right interpretation in their readers' minds. If not, they attempt to substitute one word for another, or one grammatical construction for another until a satisfactory segment of text has been produced.

Given this account, it should be clear that there are three reasons writers would not revise:

1. They are not writing from mental plans;
2. They are unaware of the fact that any sentence can have a range of possible interpretations;
3. They have no internal standards for what makes an acceptable construction.

Summary

So far, we have seen that writers have specific kinds of knowledge and engage in specific processes when they write. With respect to knowledge, we learned that successful writers know a great deal about topics, genres, audiences, and language. With respect to processes, we learned that writers plan, translate, and revise. In the next section, we shall examine developmental trends in the acquisition of writing knowledge and skills.

The Development of Writing Ability

Now that we have a sense of what writers know and do, we are in a better position to ask questions about the development of writing ability. For example, given what we just learned about a writer's knowledge, we can ask questions such as "Do older children know more about topics, genres, audiences, and language than younger children?" Similarly, given what we learned about the processes in which writers engage, we can ask questions such as, "Do older children plan or revise more effectively than younger children?"

The goal of the present section is to provide answers to these questions. In keeping with the organization of the previous section on the nature of writing, we shall first examine the developmental literature regarding writing knowledge and then examine the literature regarding development in writing processes.

The Development of Writing Knowledge

Large-scale and small-scale studies have found that children become better writers with age (e.g., Applebee et al., 1990). One reason older students write better is that they have more of the knowledge needed for writing than younger students. As we have seen, writers can have knowledge of topics, genres, audiences, and language. Let's now examine the developmental literature to see whether there are age differences in these forms of knowledge.

Topic Knowledge

When asked to write a paper on some topic, younger children tend to generate fewer ideas than older children and adults (Scardamalia & Bereiter, 1986). This age difference in the amount of ideas generated derives, in part, from the fact that younger children usually have less topic knowledge than older children and adults. Sometimes age differences are even found within samples of students who are labeled "experts" on some topic. For example, in her study of the effects of knowledge on writing, McCutchen (1986) found that even in a group of children labeled "high knowledge," her high-knowledge eighth graders still had more pertinent knowledge than her high-knowledge fourth or sixth graders. Thus, it is usually safe to assume that for any given topic, older children will know more than younger children. As a result, the latter will have a greater resource of ideas to tap into.

However, studies have also shown that children seem to generate fewer ideas than their knowledge would warrant. In particular, researchers have found that simply prompting children to think of additional ideas causes them to generate many more things to say (Scardamalia et al., 1982). Why do children generate fewer ideas than they are capable of? The first reason seems to be that whereas younger students use a somewhat random method of associative thinking to generate ideas, older students use heuristic search to guide their generation of ideas (Hayes & Flower, 1986; Scardamalia & Bereiter, 1986).

The difference between associative thinking and heuristic search can best be described by way of an analogy. Imagine that your knowledge is stored in the form of a mental filing cabinet and that each piece of your knowledge (e.g., the fact that dogs bark) is a folder in the cabinet. Imagine next that if two ideas are highly associated, their folders are connected by way of a fairly strong string. If you pull out one idea (i.e., folder), it pulls out the other idea (i.e., folder). Ideas that are weakly associated are connected by weak strings. In an associative memory search, you go to some main folder for a topic and pull it out. As you do, you find that you pull out all of those ideas that are connected by strong strings, one-by-one, until there are no more folders attached by strings or until some of the weak strings break (leaving their folders behind).

In an heuristic search, in contrast, you first think about *categories* of information and then go to sections of the cabinet to pull out an entire set of folders for all of the ideas related to specific categories. For example, if you are writing an essay about the status of American education and you are trying to think of things to say, you might locate a section of your mental cabinet that groups together folders on the problems with the education system. Or, you might think of your ideas as indexed in some way (e.g., metaphorical red dots on folders for things you are good at) and your heuristic search uses this indexing to find specific folders (e.g., "Let's see, let me think of all of the things I'm good at."). Thus, a heuristic memory search is neither random nor purely associative; Rather, it is logical and *directed*. Of course, heuristic searches can also be supplemented by associative thinking, and such associations help add additional things to say (Scardamalia & Bereiter, 1986).

The second reason younger students generate fewer ideas than they are capable of is that they tend to retrieve only those ideas at the highest levels of hierarchically arranged knowledge (McCutchen & Perfetti, 1982; Scardamalia & Bereiter, 1986). When writing about animals, for example, younger writers might generate ideas immediately connected to the top-level node *animal* and fail to retrieve ideas below that level (e.g., information associated with different types of animals such as dogs and cats). Prompting seems to move them farther down a hierarchy to retrieve more detailed information (e.g., ask them "What can you tell me about different types of animals such as dogs or cats?").

Knowledge of Genres

In Chapter 6, we learned that extensive reading seems to cause children to acquire schemata for various types of texts (e.g., stories and expository texts). If children do acquire such schemata over time, it would be expected that when they are asked to write something in a particular genre, older children would be more likely than younger children to write something that conforms to the ideal structure for that genre. Let's examine the literature on three common genres (i.e., stories, expository texts, and argumentative essays) to see if this expectation is supported.

Story Writing.   The literature on story-writing suggests there is a developmental lag between being able to recognize a good story and being able to write one. In particular, even though five-and six-year-olds seem to have good knowledge of the canonical structure of stories (Stein, 1982), studies show that much older students (e.g., fourth, fifth, and eighth graders) sometimes have trouble composing stories that conform to this canonical structure. For example, in the most recent National Assessment of Educational Progress (NAEP), 65 percent of fourth graders were found to have an understanding of the basics of story-telling, but only 15 percent were able to write well-developed stories that had both a setting and at least one episode (Applebee et al., 1990). It is important to note, however, that students were given a short amount of time to compose their stories in this study.

In a study in which children were given several class periods to compose and potentially revise their stories, Freedman (1987) found that there was development between the fifth and twelfth grades in the degree of realization of the ideal form of a story. In the fifth and eighth grades, only 34 percent and 45 percent of children, respectively, wrote stories about true personal experiences that included some setting information and at least one complete episode. When asked to invent a story, however, these percentages rose to 55 percent and 70 percent, respectively. Finally, Langer (1986) found that whereas there were few differences between the stories of eight- and 14-year-olds in terms of structure, the stories of the 14-year-olds were more elaborated than those of the eight-year-olds. Comparing the NAEP study with the Freedman and Langer studies, then, we see that the size of the age difference can be large or small depending on nature of the writing task. But even in the best of circumstances, there still seems to be a lag of three to four years between using schemata to comprehend stories and using them to write stories.

Expository Writing. With respect to expository writing, we would expect an even larger developmental lag because of the findings for reading comprehension, which show that children seem to comprehend stories better than they comprehend expository texts (see Chapter 6). Several studies support this expectation of relatively poorer performance for expository writing. For example, Langer (1986) found a more marked difference between eight- and 14-year-olds for expository writing than for story-writing. At both grades, however, performance on the expository task was generally unimpressive. Similarly, in a highly structured task in which students were asked to complete a paragraph that already contained key elements (e.g., topic sentences and signals), Englert, Stewart, and Hiebert (1988) found that whereas sixth graders performed significantly better than third graders in the generation of textually consistent details (40 percent versus 37 percent, respectively) and main ideas (35 percent versus 22 percent, respectively), students at both grade levels tended to perform poorly on both of these expository writing tasks.

In summarizing the NAEP results for expository writing, Applebee et al. (1990) reported that:

> . . . about two-thirds of the eleventh graders were able to write from personal experience and supply adequate information for a job application, but only slightly more than half were able to write an adequate newspaper report from given information . . . For fourth and eighth graders . . . , the simpler and clearer the information provided, the more successful students were in summarizing and presenting it. More complex material required more complex writing strategies, which the majority of students seemed to lack (p. 25).

Over all grades, studies show that children are most successful when they write expository texts in the simple description format (i.e., taking some information and summarizing it). They have much more difficulty writing essays in the compare/contrast format or other formats that require them to *analyze* information rather than simply report it (Applebee et al., 1990; Englert et al., 1988).

Argumentative Writing.   Argumentative writing is a form of writing in which an author adopts the goal of convincing his or her readers that a particular point of view is a good one (Applebee et al., 1990). You engaged in argumentative writing when you wrote your essay about deserving an A. In judging the quality of an argumentative essay, researchers look for the presence of the key elements of a well-structured argument such as claims, data, warrants, recognition of an opposing point of view, and rebuttals (e.g., Knudson, 1992; McCann, 1989). Most developmental studies have shown than children write better argumentative essays with age.

For example, McCann (1989) asked sixth, ninth, and twelfth graders to write argumentative essays and found that the essays of the ninth and twelfth graders not only had more overall quality than those of the sixth graders, but they also contained significantly more claims and warrants. No significant grade differences emerged for the use of data to support a claim, however. In a similar study, Knudson (1992) found that fourth and sixth grade students used significantly fewer claims, data, and warrants than tenth and twelfth grade students. Thus, both studies showed that children are more likely with age to include the elements of good arguments.

However, the increased use of such elements does not imply that older students always produce high-quality arguments. In particular, the most recent NAEP for writing showed that only about 20 percent of students in each of the fourth, eighth, and eleventh grades wrote argumentative essays that were judged to be at the "adequate" level or better (Applebee et al., 1990).

Summary.   In sum, then, most students even in the high school levels have difficulty writing stories, expository reports, and argumentative essays. When development occurs, it is usually in the form of the increased use of key elements of a particular genre. In the case of stories, older students are more likely than younger students to include both a setting and a major episode in their stories. In the case of expository reports, older students are more likely to use superordinate structures (e.g., main ideas and supportive details) than younger students. In the case of argumentative essays, older students are more likely to use claims, data, and warrants than younger students. Although even elementary students have been found to use some structure in their writing, older students use more structure and tend to elaborate that structure more extensively.

Knowledge of Audiences

A major difference between writing and having a conversation is that when you have a conversation, you have an actual person to whom you speak. This individual reacts to your statements and also helps keep the conversation going by saying things back to you. When you write, however, you have no one to play these roles for you. As a result, you need to create your own imaginary audience and hypothesize about how these people would probably respond to your statements. Moreover, you need to be able to think about what you have written objectively to see whether someone else might have trouble understanding what you are trying to say. Writing, then, poses greater cognitive demands than having a conversation. If so, young children may be less effective writers than older children because the former have a harder time creating and writing to an imaginary audience than the latter (Bereiter & Scardamalia, 1982; Knudson, 1992).

In one of the few studies that investigated possible developmental differences in children's knowledge of how audiences affect what is written, Langer (1986) found that both eight-and 14-year-olds realized that a text would have to be modified if an audience were to change. However, whereas the younger children said that a shift in audience would mean that there would be different requirements regarding neatness and length, the older children argued that the changes would be reflected in terms of language and form. Obviously, more studies are needed to reveal the existence of other age differences in knowledge of audiences.

Knowledge of Language

Perfetti & McCutchen (1987, p. 130) define writing competence as "productive control over the grammatical devices of language in the service of some communicative intent." This definition nicely captures the central role played by a writer's knowledge of language. In order to have productive control over one's language and convey exactly what one wants to convey, a writer needs to have a good vocabulary and good command of syntax. Is there evidence that older students have larger vocabularies and greater command of syntax than younger students?

In the case of vocabulary, we noted in Chapter 5 that school children add about 3,000 new words to their vocabularies each year. Thus, the notion of *choosing just the right word* is more applicable to older children than younger children, since only the former are likely to have the range of words necessary to engage in such a selection process.

In the case of syntax, Loban (1976) and Hunt (1970) found that there is development in syntactic maturity throughout the school years. By *syntactic maturity*, it is meant that older children are more likely than younger children to group separate clauses together into single, more complex constructions. For example, instead of writing the three separate sentences in (1) below, older students are more likely to write the single construction in (2):

1. Philadelphia has a great baseball team. Philadelphia has a great football team. Philadelphia does not have a good basketball team.

2. Philadelphia has a great baseball team and a great football team, but it does not have a very good basketball team.

Moreover, even nine-year-olds seem to know that (2) is more acceptable than (1) when asked which is better. However, these same students could not imitate the constructions such as (1) or (2) when given parallel content (Scardamalia & Bereiter, 1986). Other researchers have found that high school students could not deliberately replicate the very same grammatical errors that they had made on a prior writing assignment. Thus, syntactic development during the school years seems to be the progressive attainment of *conscious control* over complex grammatical constructions.

A final aspect of language knowledge that seems to develop with age is the ability to use cohesive devices. By *cohesive devices*, it is meant such things as (a) using pronouns in one sentence to refer back to individuals named in earlier sentences, and (b) using the same or related words in several successive sentences. Sentence (3) below illustrates both of these devices. The words that create ties are italicized:

3. Mary was known as a popular girl. So *popular*, in fact, that *she* was named class president.

A variety of studies have shown that older children are more likely to use cohesive devices than younger children. McCutchen (1986), for example, found differences in coherence between younger (i.e., fourth graders) and older students (i.e., sixth and eighth graders) even when their knowledge of the topic was statistically controlled.

Summary

Across a variety of studies, older children were found to demonstrate greater knowledge of topics, genres, audiences, and language than younger children. The major change that seems to occur is not so much the acquisition of these forms of knowledge as much as children's ability to consciously reflect on and manipulate this knowledge (Perfetti & McCutchen, 1987; Scardamalia & Bereiter, 1986). In particular, with the exception of knowledge of audiences, children were always found to know more than they demonstrate in writing. In particular, children were found to generate less content than they know, comprehend texts of a particular type (e.g., stories) earlier than they can write texts of that type, and produce or recognize well-formed syntactic constructions before they can write such constructions themselves.

Development in Writing Processes

In the earlier section entitled The Nature of Writing, we learned that writers engage in three main processes: planning, translating, and revising. The questions of interest for the present section are, "Are older children more likely to carry out these processes than younger children?" and "If so, do older children carry out these processes more effectively?" Let's examine the developmental literature to see what the answers to these questions are.

Planning

Most developmental studies of writing show that children give very little evidence of explicit planning (Scardamalia & Bereiter, 1986). Although young writers may at times rehearse what they will eventually write in the form of partial or full sentences, these notes are probably early drafts of eventual lines rather than plans per se.

Instead of forming goals and writing to these goals, children are more likely to engage in what has been called knowledge telling (Scardamalia & Bereiter, 1986). Writers who engage in knowledge telling write down everything they know about a topic, in the order that ideas come to mind. Knowledge tellers stop writing when they feel that they have written down everything they know.

Because children do not write from goals and plans, they tend to generate ideas by way of associative thinking rather than heuristic search and often do not organize these ideas in any way. As a result, their stories, essays, and arguments often lack conceptual coherence.

Translation

In the earlier section of the development of writing knowledge, we learned that younger children have smaller vocabularies, a smaller repertoire of syntactic structures and cohesive devices, and less conscious control over these language forms than older children. As a result, they are less equipped for translating their personal meanings into precisely interpretable texts. That is, they produce "writer-based" texts rather than "reader-based" texts (Perfetti & McCutchen, 1987). Writer-based prose is *"full* of idiosyncratic phrases that are loaded with semantic content for the writer—meaning that is not, however, articulated for the reader" (Perfetti & McCutchen, 1987, p. 126). In reader-based prose, in contrast, ideas are well-articulated, there is little in the way of ambiguity, and there is a great deal of intersentence cohesion. In fact, the meaning is so well specified that most people who read a segment of the text would come away with the same interpretation of it.

Although few studies have shown that increases in vocabulary and syntax skills with age directly contribute to the production of reader-based prose, several studies have shown that older children are more likely to use a variety of intersentence cohesion devices than younger children. Moreover, the tendency to create more cohesive texts seems to increase linearly with age between the third grade and adulthood (Garner et al., 1986; McCutchen, 1986; Wright & Rosenberg, 1993).

Revising

The literature on developmental trends in revising has revealed four main findings. First, children, adolescents, and inexperienced college students do very little of it (Fitzgerald, 1987; Scardamalia & Bereiter, 1986). Second, when students do revise, the vast majority of changes are superficial rather than conceptual or organizational. That is, students are more likely to focus on specific words, spelling, or grammar than on deeper issues such as goals, plans, and overall intended meanings (Fitzgerald, 1987; Scardamalia & Bereiter, 1986). Third, the main reason children tend not to revise is that they have trouble detecting problems in the first place (especially in their own writings; Bartlett, 1982). When problems are pointed out to them, children can at times be quite good at making appropriate changes (e.g., Beal, 1990), though some studies have found that the changes do not always improve the quality of the text (Scardamalia & Bereiter, 1986). Fourth, a further constraint on children's revising may be that they lack sufficient memory capacity for dealing with multiple issues of content and quality at the same time. When an adult guides them through revisions in a scaffolded way, the quality of revisions improve (Scardamalia & Bereiter, 1986).

Summary

In sum, then, children not only gain more writing knowledge with age, but they also engage in writing processes more effectively as well. Knowledge and processes, of course, play equally important and interactive roles in the development of writing skills. For example, as children gain more knowledge of their language, they are more equipped for performing the process of translation effectively. Similarly, as they gain more knowledge of audiences, they become more skilled at detecting and correcting possible ambiguities in what they have written. Thus, it is best to think of the development of writing ability as the coalescing of knowledge and processes, rather than as the acquisition of separate components.

According to Berninger, Mizokawa, and Bragg (1991), there are three types of constraints that affect the rate at which writing knowledge and processes coalesce. First, there are neurodevelopmental constraints, which influence young children's writing by affecting the rapid, automatic production of letters and hand movements. These low-level constraints are thought to place restrictions on the so-called transcription process (i.e., writing down symbols) but not the central translation processes (i.e., converting ideas into potential text). After transcription processes have been mastered and automatized, linguistic constraints on words, sentences, and schemata have their effects. Finally, after transcription and translation processes have been sufficiently mastered, cognitive constraints on planning and revising may become evident. Thus, whereas neurodevelopmental constraints have their strongest influence on young writers, older children are influenced mostly by linguistic and cognitive constraints.

Individual Differences in Writing Ability

Having completed our discussion of how older students differ from younger students in their writing ability, we can now move on to the question "How do individuals of the same age differ from one another?" The research that provides answers to this question can be divided into those studies that have compared skilled writers to less skilled writers and those studies that have revealed the existence of gender and ethnic differences.

Comparisons of Skilled and Less Skilled Writers

The major findings of the studies which have compared same-aged good and poor writers are as follows:

1. Although good writers and poor writers do not differ in terms of grade point averages, achievement test scores, and short-term memory capacity, the former are better at manipulating verbal information than the latter (Benton et al., 1984). In particular, a study of college students showed that when students were asked to (a) reorder strings of letters into alphabetical order, (b) reorder words into a meaningful sentence, or (c) reorder sentences to make a meaningful paragraph, those students who showed good writing ability were faster and more accurate than their peers who wrote less well.

2. Good writers tend to be better readers than poor writers (Abbott & Berninger, 1993; Englert et al., 1988; Langer, 1986; Perfetti & McCutchen, 1987). In particular, studies show that there is a high correlation between a student's reading scores and his or her writing scores. Moreover, the same students who use their knowledge of the structure of genres to guide their reading comprehension also use this knowledge to help them write something in that genre (Wright & Rosenberg, 1993; Scardamalia & Bereiter, 1986). Writing and reading are not, of course, the same, but they do seem to rely on the same central knowledge structures (Perfetti & McCutchen, 1987).

3. Just as older writers are more likely than younger writers to use heuristic (i.e., goal-directed) search to retrieve ideas from long-term memory, good writers of a particular age group are also more likely to use heuristic search than poor writers of that age group (Scardamalia & Bereiter, 1986). When good writers lack knowledge on a particular topic and cannot retrieve information from memory, they may also use their heuristic search methods to delve into the published literature to find what they need (Glover, Ronning & Bruning, 1990). Few studies, however, have demonstrated this phenomenon. Finally, whereas expert writers usually elaborate on an assignment by building in issues, themes, and constraints, novice writers stick very close to the assignment (Scardamalia & Bereiter, 1986).

4. In terms of language competence, expert writers mainly differ from novice writers in two ways: (a) whereas spelling, punctuation, and grammar are largely automatized in the former, these processes are still somewhat effortful in the latter and (b) the former have a larger repertoire of sentence constructions and grammatical devices than the latter (Norris & Bruning, 1988; Perfetti & McCutchen, 1987; Scardamalia & Bereiter, 1986).

5. Whereas good writers spend a great deal of time creating goals and organizing their ideas before they write, poor writers show little evidence of explicit planning and goals. As a result, they tend to jump right into the task of writing, and their work demonstrates less sophisticated organization (Scardamalia & Bereiter, 1986). Experts are also more likely to comment on how their goals and plans change in the midst of writing.

6. Because expert writers are more likely than novices to create explicit goals and subgoals, the former are more likely to revise than the latter. Why? Deep-level revisions take place when one realizes that a segment of text does not meet the goals set for that segment (Scardamalia & Bereiter, 1986). For example, if you were writing to a friend to tell her that she does something offensive but you had the goal of being polite, you might say, in response to reading a draft, "Oh, that's no good. She might be offended by my saying that." In contrast, people who do not write from goals have nothing to compare the text to and will not, therefore, see the need to revise anything.

Furthermore, because good writers often change their goals and plans as they write, they will have a tendency to go back over what they have written and delete those portions that do not fit with the new plans and goals. Because poor writers tend not to change goals while writing, they will not engage in such wholesale revisions.

7. Finally, each of the six differences described above really concerns a difference in *metacognition* between good and poor writers. It is probably incorrect to say that poor writers do not have goals when they write or that they have little knowledge of genres or language. Instead, it is more correct to say that whereas good writers can consciously reflect on and manipulate their goals and knowledge, poor writers do not have the same conscious access to their goals and knowledge (Scardamalia & Bereiter, 1986).

Gender and Ethnic Differences

The literature on gender and ethnic differences in writing is less extensive than on good and poor writers. Nevertheless, it is still useful to examine the findings of these studies to have a sense of how students of various genders and ethnicities might differ from one another.

Gender Differences

Studies of schoolchildren have revealed gender differences for four aspects of writing: (a) fluency, (b) conformity to standard usage, (b) overall quality, and (d) the tendency to revise. In particular, Berninger and Fuller (1992) investigated whether boys and girls in the early elementary grades differ in their verbal fluency (i.e., speed with which they could name as many examples of something as they could), orthographic fluency (i.e., speed with which they could write the letters of the alphabet in the correct order), and compositional fluency (i.e., speed with which they could write stories and expository compositions). The results showed that whereas boys obtained higher scores for verbal fluency (effect size = .21; see Chapter 12 for an explanation of effect sizes), girls obtained higher scores for orthographic fluency (effect size = −.36) and compositional fluency (effect sizes = −.34 to −.83). Furthermore, of the 28 children who were in the lowest 5 percent of the distribution for compositional fluency, 23 (i.e., 82 percent) were boys.

Price and Graves (1980) obtained a similar gender split for the quantity of oral and written language. In particular, whereas boys produced more words in oral language than girls, the former were also twice as likely as the latter to make errors regarding double negatives, verbs, pronouns, and plural inflections in their writing and speech. Price and Graves labeled such errors "deviations from standard usage."

If gender differences in writing were limited to the quantitative differences revealed by Berninger and Fuller (1992) and Price and Graves (1980), there would be no reason to be concerned, because the quality of what one writes is usually more important than the quantity. But the most recent NAEP (1990) data for writing show that gender differences exist for the quality of writing as well. In particular, at each of the fourth, eighth, and eleventh grades, girls received higher overall scores than boys (Applebee et al., 1990). It should be noted, however, that children were given a fixed period of time to compose and that the average scores of boys and girls were not terribly high at any grade. Thus, the gender difference may once again reflect differences in fluency. Additional studies need to ascertain whether gender differences would remain or diminish if the time limit were removed.

As to gender differences in the tendency to revise, a small number of studies show that girls tend to engage in more extensive revisions than boys (Fitzgerald, 1987). It is not clear whether we should characterize this difference as one of quantity or quality, because the authors do not indicate whether the revisions actually improved what students had written.

Whereas gender differences have been found for four aspects of children's writing, parallel differences have not been reported for college students and professional writers. Instead, researchers have revealed what might be called stylistic and "word choice" differences. For example, some researchers argue that women are more likely than men to use qualifiers (e.g., "kind of"), hedges (e.g., "maybe"), and politeness terms to blunt the force of their assertions (e.g., Lakoff, 1973). Others have argued that there are gender differences in how well men and women write in specific genres because of a purported gender difference in world views (e.g., Flynn, 1988). In particular, a woman's "epistemology" is said to emphasize connectedness and interpersonal relations (Gilligan, 1982). As a result, they are better suited for writing personal narratives than argumentative essays. Males, in contrast, are thought to view the world in terms of impersonally denoted categories and competition. As a result, they are better suited for writing argumentative essays.

To test these hypotheses about the effects of world views on word choice and competence, Rubin and Greene (1992) asked college students to write a personal narrative and an argumentative essay. Once completed, the compositions were examined for the existence of 17 categories of terms and structures indicative of specific styles and world views. In contrast to the claim that there are definite male and female styles, the results showed that there were far more similarities between the genders than differences. In particular, of the 17 language categories, only five (i.e., 29 percent) revealed significant gender differences.

In sum, then, research with children reveals four trends: (a) girls tend to be more fluent in their writing than boys, (b) girls deviate from standard usage less often than boys, (c) girls are more likely to fulfill the minimum requirements of writing tasks than boys, and (d) girls are more likely to revise extensively than boys. With respect to adults, there is little evidence regarding similar quantitative and qualitative differences in writing. Instead, one finds widespread speculation that males and females have different writing styles. When empirical tests

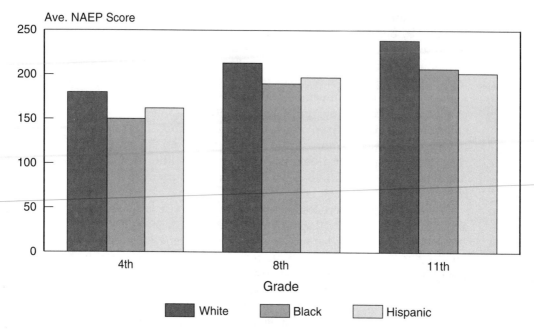

FIGURE 7.1   Ethnic Differences in Writing

Based on data provided in Applebee et al. (1990)

of stylistic differences have been conducted, however, one finds little evidence that they exist (Rubin & Greene, 1992).

Ethnic Differences

There is not much that can be said about the extent of ethnic differences in writing ability because so few studies have broken down writing performance by ethnicity. The one exception is the recent NAEP (Applebee et al., 1990). As can be seen in Figure 7.1, white students performed significantly better than Hispanic or Black students at each of the fourth, eighth, and eleventh grades. The unfortunate aspect of this data is that it is not at all clear *why* these differences exist. Are white students simply more fluent than minority students (i.e., can they generate more text in a shorter period of time)? Are white students more likely to plan or have greater knowledge of topics, genres, and language? It is essential that we learn the reasons for the performance difference, because one cannot create an effective intervention without knowing what causes a discrepancy in the first place. Explanations of ethnic differences in a variety of subjects are provided in Chapter 12.

Instructional Implications

There are two ways to approach the issue of how to teach writing to students. The first way is to propose instructional interventions that would eliminate each of the deficiencies in students' writing ability that have been revealed by research (as described above). Because many of these proposals have not been sufficiently verified by research yet, they should be treated merely as suggestions regarding how we should change the current practice of instruction. The second way to approach instruction is to summarize the results of studies that compared one form of writing instruction to another. We can then use the research on children's deficiencies to explain why certain approaches seem to be more effective than others. In what follows, research based on these two approaches is presented in turn. After examining the implications of these two approaches, we shall conclude this chapter by examining a case study of effective writing instruction that is based on contemporary theory and research.

Deficiency-Based Suggestions

Earlier we said that younger students and less skilled, older students had the following deficiencies that seem to lie at the heart of their writing problems: (a) a lack of explicit knowledge about the structure of specific genres, (b) inadequate knowledge of topics as well as ineffective strategies for retrieving the knowledge they do have, (c) a small vocabulary and a lack of awareness of grammatical structures and devices, (d) a failure to set goals or formulate plans, and (e) a failure to revise in more than a superficial way.

Given these deficiencies, one would expect that the following interventions would improve the quality of students' writing: (a) teaching them about the main elements of a particular genre (e.g., the seven parts of a good story), (b) having them write about highly familiar topics and teaching them how to use heuristic search procedures to access this knowledge, (c) providing instruction on vocabulary, grammatical structures, and cohesion devices, (d) teaching students how to set goals and write to those goals, and (e) teaching them how to revise. Are there studies that tried to see whether these interventions are effective?

In the case of teaching students about specific genres, a variety of authors report that the quality of student writing can be improved if students are taught about the elements of a genre. For example, Taylor and Beach (1984) found that instruction and practice in a hierarchical summary procedure had a positive effect on the expository writing of seventh graders. Similarly, Gambrell and Chasen (1991) found that explicit instruction on the structure of stories positively influenced the narrative writing performance of fourth and fifth grade below-average readers.

In the case of content generation, a number of different interventions have proved successful, including (a) having children write on topics about which they have a strong desire to express themselves (Graves, 1975), (b) engaging students in prewriting activities such as discussions (Boiarsky, 1982), (c) having children list words they might use after they have been assigned a topic (Bereiter & Scardamalia, 1982), (d) having students dictate rather than allocate too many attentional resources to the mechanics of writing (Scardamalia et al., 1982), and (e) prompting students to continue to say things by using statements such as "Is there anything else you could say?" (Scardamalia & Bereiter, 1986). But it is important to note that these approaches merely increase the number of ideas that come to mind. They do not teach children how to be self-directed, heuristic searchers.

In the case of teaching children language skills, it is difficult to find studies that show how vocabulary instruction or instruction on cohesive devices improves the quality of writing. But there are studies that show how syntax-based interventions such as "sentence combining" helps students to become more facile writers (Hillocks, 1989). In this technique, students are given separate sentences and asked to combine them into a single, more complex construction.

In the case of instruction designed to increase goal-setting in students, researchers have found two approaches that appear to work: (a) an "ending sentence" task in which students are given a sentence that their composition must end with, and (b) "conferencing" in which teachers help students articulate goals (Scardamalia & Bereiter, 1986). It is important to note, however, that neither approach lets students take responsibility for setting goals themselves. More research is needed in this area.

Finally, in the case of instruction on revision, there are studies that show that the quality of children's revisions can be significantly improved by removing the "executive control" aspect of revision. In particular, if children are walked through a fixed number of revision steps (e.g., stop, evaluate, diagnose, choose a tactic, and carry it out), they are able to revise more effectively than if left to their own devices (Scardamalia & Bereiter, 1986). Presumably, with enough practice, these routines could become internalized to the point that students could engage in them without the scaffolded support of their teacher.

In sum, then, most of the interventions that have attempted to remediate deficiencies in students' writing have been at least partially successful. However, a number of studies need to be conducted before firm conclusions can be made in this regard. Ideally, it would be useful to know (a) which of these interventions is the most effective, and (b) whether certain interventions should be conducted before others (e.g., goal-setting first, revision second, and so forth).

Comparing Instructional Approaches

The intervention programs described in the previous section were designed to remediate specific deficiencies in students' writing. In most cases, the emphasis was on improving the writing of a single group of students rather than on comparing one instructional approach to another. In the present section, the results of studies that compared specific approaches to the standard method of instruction will be described.

Before seeing which approaches are most effective, however, it might be useful to examine what this standard approach is. During any given day, most studies report that students spend very little time writing (Scardamalia & Bereiter, 1986). This finding is surprising, given that some teachers believe that drill and practice is the best method for improving writing (Langer, 1986). What we have, then, is the curious finding that the same individuals who feel that practice is important do not provide sufficient opportunities for practice! Of course, if students do not practice writing, two aspects of their competence will take an unnecessarily long time to develop: (a) automaticity in both lower-level and mid-level skills (e.g., transcription and translation), and (b) the acquisition of schemata for particular genres. Moreover, students typically are told what they should write about and are not given assignments in which they can set their own goals. Furthermore, the majority of comments that they receive from teachers (if they get any) are about lower-level mechanics such as grammar and spelling. Finally, students are typically not asked to revise a composition after it is turned in (Applebee et al., 1990; Scardamalia & Bereiter, 1986). In sum, then, we should not be surprised to learn that students do not write well, because they are not given the type of instruction that could foster the acquisition of writing knowledge and skills.

In a recent review that summarized the results of well-designed studies that compared the standard approach to other approaches, Hillocks (1989) found that the four most effective approaches were the "models" (*mean effect size = .22*), "sentence-combining" (*effect size = .35*), "scales" (*effect size = .36*) and "inquiry" approaches (*effect size = .57*). The "models" approach consists of presenting students with good examples of writing and helping them to identify the parts or features of the model. As such, there is an emphasis on the product rather than on the process of writing. The sentence-combining approach consists of teaching students how to combine two or more sentences into a single more complex sentence. In contrast to the models approach, the sentence-combining approach emphasizes the process of writing rather than written products (though students are given feedback about the correctness of their combinatory products). The scales approach consists of presenting compositions to students, teaching them how to evaluate the quality of these compositions, and asking them to revise the substandard ones. The emphasis on revision and evaluation makes the scales approach distinct from the models approach.

As indicated by the fact that it generates the largest effect size when it is contrasted with standard instruction, the inquiry approach seems to be more effective than any of the approaches described so far. The inquiry approach consists of presenting students with structured data and having them use the data in their writing. Responses to the data can range from simple reporting and describing to generalizing and hypothesizing. It is thought that the use of data probably helps students create plans, organize their thoughts, and circumvent problems associated with content generation.

Taken together, the results for comparative studies suggest that interventions work best when they (a) place a heavy emphasis on writing *processes* such as planning, translation, and revision, (b) use examples of both good and poor writing to gain insight into good *products*, and (c) have students do more of the intellectual work than teachers. Such approaches can be contrasted with approaches in which students passively learn about good grammar. Hillocks (1989) reports that heavy doses of grammar instruction actually engender *poorer* writing than the standard approach described earlier (effect size = −.30).

A Case Study

A good example of how to translate theory and research about writing into classroom practice is Graham and Harris' Self-Regulated Strategy Development model (Graham & Harris, in press). In this model, teachers provide writing instruction in seven stages. Let's illustrate these stages using the example of a fifth grade teacher who wants to show her students how to write good stories:

Stage 1: Initial Conference. The teacher begins by telling the entire class that she would like to teach them a strategy for writing stories. She asks students to say what they know about writing stories (e.g., the parts) and also discusses issues such as goals for learning the strategy and how learning the parts of a story can help someone write better stories. Finally, she points out that students will be collaborating with each other and that expending effort is necessary before the strategy will be mastered.

Stage 2: Preskill Development: Students are given a mini-lesson on the parts of a story (i.e., the setting and episode). They are also asked to identify examples of these story parts in books they are reading or stories they themselves have written.

Stage 3: Discussion of the Composition Strategy: Students are provided with a chart that lists the strategy steps for producing a story and a mnemonic for remembering questions for the parts of a story. The strategy consists of five steps: (1) think of a story you would like to share, (2) let your mind be free, (3) write down the "story part reminder," (4) make notes of your ideas for each part, and (5) write your story. The "story part reminder" is a mnemonic in which the student says "W-W-W, What = 2, How = 2." This mnemonic refers to three questions that start with "who," "when," and "where," respectively (hence, W-W-W), two "what" questions (hence, What = 2), and two "how" questions (hence, How = 2):

> Who is the main character?; Who else is in the story?
> When does the story take place?
> Where does it take place?
> What does the main character want to do?; What do other characters want to do?
> What happens when these characters try to do these things?
> How does the story end?
> How do the main and other characters feel?

After presenting the strategy, the teacher discusses the parts with them and solicits suggestions for how to carry out certain parts (e.g., freeing your mind).

Stage 4: Modeling. The teacher demonstrates and thinks aloud how to use the strategy to plan out the parts of a story. As she plans, she uses self-instructions to help her define the problem ("What am I trying to do here?"), plan ("First, I should try to develop the setting"), self-evaluate, self-reinforce, and cope ("Yeah, that works pretty well"). Here, the class discusses the importance of self-instructions and makes notes on things they might say to themselves. With the think-aloud procedure, they notice how the teacher frequently revises plans or parts as she writes.

Stage 5: Memorization of the Strategy and Mnemonic. Students practice the strategy and the mnemonic using whatever approach they want (e.g., alone or with a partner).

Stage 6: Collaborative Practice. As students attempt to use the strategy, the teacher works individually with them to guide them in an unobtrusive, though scaffolded way (e.g., "How's it going? What seems to be the problem? Maybe a different goal for that character would work . . ."). As students work, they are encouraged by the teacher to use goal-setting, self-monitoring, and self-reinforcement procedures.

Stage 7: Independent Performance. Students are encouraged to use the strategy again on a new story. This time, however, they do it largely on their own. Students who do not completely remember the steps of the mnemonic can write them down on the top of a page of paper as a reminder.

From what we learned earlier about the nature of writing, it should be clear why the Graham-Harris model would be effective. The strategy encourages all aspects of planning (goal-setting, generating, organization) and is built around a story schema. In addition, through modeling and think-aloud procedures, children see the pervasiveness and importance of revision. Finally, the method is effective because it is informed by current theories of self-regulation and motivation (see Chapter 11).

Chapter 8

Mathematics Learning

Summary

1. Contemporary math educators not only want students to acquire considerable knowledge and skill, they also want students to think like mathematicians.

2. Infants seem to show surprising appreciation of set size and simple operations (e.g., addition and subtraction).

3. By the age of four, many preschoolers become proficient counters and also seem to comprehend the unchanging cardinal value of small sets.

5. Between the first and fifth grade, children acquire a range of strategies for solving decon-textualized addition and subtraction problems. In addition, they progressively acquire schemata for word problems.

7. In the middle school period, rational numbers and integers pose both conceptual and procedural problems for children.

8. High school students have difficulty understanding the nature of algebraic entities such as variables and functions. They also have trouble (a) performing computations involving formulae and (b) solving algebra word problems.

9. Studies have revealed both gender and ethnic differences in mathematical performance.

Imagine that you have $600 and want to use this money to install a new hardwood floor in your home. The room has the shape and dimensions of that shown in Figure 8.1. The primary issue that concerns you is whether the flooring materials will cost more than $600. To find out, you go to a local flooring store and learn four important things: (a) each floorboard is 2 feet long by 3 inches wide, (b) each board costs $1.99, (c) boards are sold only in boxes containing 40 boards each, and (d) you can get only a store credit for the boxes you do not use (not a cash refund). Do you have enough money to install an entire floor?

It should be clear that it would be unwise to simply buy and install as many boards as you can for $600. If it is too little money, you could end up with a half-finished floor. If it is too much money, you could end up with unopened boxes or a store credit that you are unlikely to use. Take some time now to solve the problem.

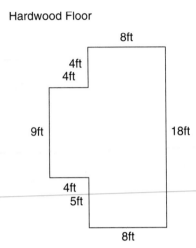

Hardwood Floor

FIGURE 8.1

As students move from the classroom into the world of adults, they confront problems similar to this one on a regular basis. If teachers fail to instill sufficient mathematical competence in their students, it would be extremely hard for students to adapt to the demands of contemporary society. It is for this reason that the primary goal of education has shifted from having students "know math" to having them *use* their math knowledge to solve problems effectively (National Council of Teachers of Mathematics, 1989).

In this chapter, we will examine the nature and development of important math skills. In the first section, we will get a sense of what mathematical knowledge entails. In the second section, we will trace the development of mathematical skills from infancy to adulthood. In the third section, we will examine individual differences in math skills. In the fourth section, we will explore the instructional implications of the research on mathematical thinking.

The Nature of Mathematical Knowledge and Skill

In this section, we consider the following question: What does it mean to be "good at math?" One way to answer this question is to say that people who are good at math have a lot of *mathematical knowledge*. A second way to answer it is to say that they engage in effective *mathematical thinking*.

Mathematical knowledge, like other kinds of knowledge, can be divided into two types: conceptual and procedural (Byrnes, 1992; Byrnes & Wasik, 1991; Hiebert, 1987; see Chapter 3). Examples of mathematical conceptual knowledge include: (1) comprehending the *referents* of symbols such as 5 and 1/2 (e.g., 5 refers to a set of 5 things); (2) comprehending the *relative numerosity* of several groups of objects (e.g., a group of seven apples is a smaller amount than a group of eight apples); (3) forming *categories* of mathematical entities (e.g., fractions, acute angles, etc.) and understanding the distinctions among different categories (e.g., acute angle versus right angle); (4) knowing a variety of mathematical *facts* (e.g., the sum of a triangle's angles is 180 degrees); and (5) knowing *why* the answer you found after you used a math algorithm or procedure is right or wrong (e.g., "$1/2$ plus $1/3$ equals $5/6$ because. . . ."). When thought of as being intuitions about numbers and their properties, conceptual knowledge has been called *number sense* (Markovits & Sowder, 1994).

In contrast to these conceptual ideas, procedural knowledge consists of knowing the steps required to attain specific goals. Examples of mathematical procedural knowledge include knowing how to: (1) count; (2) add, subtract, multiply and divide, (3) find the area of a polygon, (4) factor a polynomial, and (5) find the derivative of a function.

In essence, then, to say that someone has a lot of mathematical knowledge is to say he or she possesses a rich repertoire of mathematical concepts and procedures (Carpenter, 1987; Hiebert & LeFevre, 1987). But is having a rich network of knowledge all there is to being good at math? Most math educators would say "No." As alluded to earlier, mathematical ability also consists of being able to use your knowledge to solve problems (National Council of Teachers of Mathematics, 1989). That is, you not only have to "know math," you also have to "think like a mathematician." To illustrate the distinction between mathematical knowledge and thinking, we can return to the example of the hardwood floor. To solve this problem, you first need to determine how many boards you will need. To determine this number, you probably recognized that the area of the room has to be computed. Of course, the problem of finding the area would have been easy had the room been a straightforward shape like a rectangle or square, because you could simply have retrieved a formula from long-term memory to solve the problem (e.g., "area = length x width"). But the room is not shaped like anything to which a ready-made formula can be applied. As a result, someone could not solve this problem without resorting to some effective problem-solving techniques. One of these techniques can be stated as a general rule: "Take the larger problem and break it down into smaller subproblems." To illustrate, some of you may have subdivided the room into, say, two rectangles, found the area of each, and summed the areas to find the total area. If you did, you not only know math, you also thought like a mathematician.

The Development of Mathematical Skills

In this section, we shall chart the development of mathematical skills from infancy to adulthood. For each age group, we shall see different skills being mastered as well as specific topics that cause particular problems for children of that age group. It will become clear that the road to "thinking like a mathematician" is a long and difficult one at times.

The Infancy and Preschool Periods

Infancy

Why would anyone study mathematical thinking in infants or preschoolers? How can children have mathematical ideas before they are exposed to such ideas in school? The main reason researchers have examined math ideas in very young children is that the concept of *number* has often figured prominently in classical nature-nurture debates. Philosophers and psychologists who are nativists have argued that infants come into the world equipped with concepts such as number, space, and causality. Beginning at birth, infants are said to use these concepts to organize and make sense of their experiences. Nativists believe that if a very young infant could be shown to have a concept of number, that would be pretty strong evidence against nonnativist views such as empiricism or constructivism.

To test the presence of number concepts in young infants, however, researchers have had to be very resourceful. A six-month-old is neither verbal nor adept at pointing. To get around these obstacles, three main methodologies have been used. The first procedure, called *habituation*, involves an infant watching pictures being flashed on a screen. When the same picture is flashed on the screen repeatedly, the infant looks at it less and less (i.e., she habituates to it). The infant, in effect, is saying, "I've seen that before. I'm bored!" When a new picture is flashed, however, an infant will look at it for a long time, provided that she can tell the difference between the old and new picture. Let's say that picture 1 shows two dots and picture 2 shows three dots. If picture 1 is flashed 15 times and picture 2 is flashed on trial 16, a long look on trial 16 suggests that the infant can tell the difference between 2 and 3, and a short look means that she cannot tell the difference. Researchers have found that even six-month-olds will give longer looks when the set size changes after habituation has occurred (Starkey & Cooper, 1980). However, these findings do not hold up when the set size is larger than three (Strauss & Curtis, 1981).

What do the findings from habituation studies mean? Two interpretations have been offered. The first is that the ability to *subitize* is present very early and seems to be innate. *Subitizing* is the perception-based ability to rapidly determine the number of objects present without counting them. When there are four or fewer objects in view, most people can immediately "see" (i.e., subitize) how many there are. When there are more than four objects, most people have to count them to determine how many there are. The second interpretation of the habituation studies is that the data do not necessarily show that infants can subitize. Rather, the results only show that infants know that *something* differs between the two pictures. One need not infer that infants definitely know that the number of objects differs.

Using the second main technique (that can be called the *surprise* methodology), Wynn (1992) recently tried to show that five-month-olds can add and subtract small numbers. The methodology involved four phases. In the first phase, an object (e.g., a teddy bear) was placed on a small stage in front of an infant. In the second phase, a screen rose to hide the teddy. In the third phase, the infant saw a hand holding a second teddy go behind the screen and come out empty. The infant needs to infer that the second teddy was placed next to the first one behind the screen. In the fourth phase, either a "possible" or "impossible" event occurred. In the possible event, the screen was lowered and revealed two teddies. In the impossible event, the screen was lowered and revealed only one teddy (because the other was removed without the infant's knowing it). The results showed that infants looked longer at the more surprising impossible event than they did at the possible event, suggesting they were doing some mental addition.

The third main methodology involves a *visual expectation* procedure. Here, an infant sees a picture being flashed two or three times in a row on the left side of a screen. Then, the picture is flashed on the right side. Over time, the infant starts to follow the pattern with her eyes. If she fixates at the left side until the second one flashes, then moves her eyes to look for the picture to appear on the right, that seems to suggest that she is counting the ones on the left before looking to the right. Canfield and Smith (1993) found that five-month-olds fixated and shifted their eyes in a manner suggesting that they can count as many as three flashes before shifting their eyes.

What do all of the findings with infants mean? Once again, there are at least two possible interpretations. The first is that the nativists are right. That is, infants do seem to be born with math concepts (e.g., set size) and procedures (e.g., adding). The second is that infants really do not understand such high-level math ideas. Rather, they are similar to many animal species in that they possess brain structures that are implicitly sensitive to patterns in the environment. Even Skinnerian rats somehow learn that with a "Fixed Ratio 15" schedule of reinforcement, they need to press a bar 15 times before a food pellet is dispensed (Schwartz, 1976). Primitive and not-so-primitive brains can record environmental patterns (e.g., left-left-right), which can signal things like food. What might separate children from rats is that by the time children are five years old, they can abstract, consciously reflect on, and symbolically manipulate numerical patterns in their environment. Rats may be limited to nonsymbolic, neuron-based pattern detection. Which of the two possible interpretations of the infant data is right? Only additional research and theorizing will tell.

The Preschool Period

Most of the studies that have examined what preschoolers know have focused on one of two skills: (a) conservation of number and (b) counting. In what follows, the research on these two skills is summarized in turn.

Conservation was a key idea in Piagetian theory and can be defined as the understanding that the amount of something does not change when the objects involved are transformed in some way. In the case of number, Piaget (1965) was interested in discovering when children recognize that the *cardinal value* of a set of objects does not change after the objects are simply rearranged. To truly understand a number, he argued, a child needs to "abstract it" or "decontextualize" it from specific spatial arrangements. In his studies, Piaget found that conservation of number progressed through three phases. In the first phase, children say that two rows of objects only have the same number of objects if the rows look alike. These children do not use counting to verify their claims. Children in the second phase always need to re-count the rows when the objects in them are rearranged. Children in the third phase immediately realize that (a) the spatial arrangement of objects has no effect on the amount and (b) re-counting is not necessary after a rearrangement. For Piaget, only the children in the third phase have a "logical" concept of number and only they truly understand the cardinal value of a set.

Although Piaget's finding that most children enter the third phase at around age five or six has been replicated many times (Brainerd, 1978; Fuson, 1988), most contemporary researchers have challenged the claim that preschoolers lack insight into conservation and cardinal value. The most common criticism of Piaget's work is that his tasks underestimate what three- and four-year-old children know. To rectify this underestimation problem, researchers turned to a task that would provide more accurate assessments of early numerical competence: counting.

Counting is a form of procedural knowledge in that it involves performing a sequence of actions in order to achieve a goal. The goal of counting is to determine the numerosity or cardinal value of a set of objects. In essence, counting is an appropriate response to the question, "How many are there?"

Although counting is a form of procedural knowledge, children can use it to enrich or inform their conceptual knowledge. For example, earlier we said that the ability to understand that a group of seven objects is a smaller amount than a group of eight objects is a form of conceptual knowledge. In order to form such a judgment, however, a child has to first count the objects in each group. Similarly, counting may ultimately help a child come to understand that the cardinal value of a set of objects does not change when (a) the objects are arranged into a different spatial array (Piaget, 1965) and (b) one counts from left to right rather than from right to left (Briars & Siegler, 1984).

Similar to the research on infants' knowledge of number, the research on preschoolers' knowledge of counting is not without its ambiguities. If you ask a two-year-old to count to ten and he does it, does that mean he knows how many ten objects are? How do we know that he has not learned a behavior pattern by rote in the same way that he may have learned pat-a-cake? Thus, a child who says the right things may not really know how to count or understand numbers. To avoid misrepresenting what children know, researchers have endeavored to find more decisive ways of measuring counting knowledge in children. The central questions guiding this work are "What does a child need to know in order to count?" and "When do children understand the cardinal value of a set?"

In a seminal work, Gelman and Gallistel (1978) tried to answer these questions by formulating a set of five counting principles. The *one-one* principle reflects the knowledge that each object is assigned one and only one number word. The *stable order* principle involves knowing that number words should always be assigned in the same order (e.g., "one" first, "two" second, etc.). If a child seems to know that the last number assigned indicates the number of objects in the set, he or she is said to know the *cardinal* principle. The *order irrelevance* principle involves knowing that the order in which objects are counted is irrelevant. If a child recognizes that these four principles can be applied to any group of objects, he or she is said to comprehend the *abstraction* principle.

In judging whether a child knows these principles, either a lenient or strict criterion can be used. Consider the case in which you place a row of four chips in front of a child and ask her to tell you how many there are. She says, "One, three, four, nine—there are nine". You ask her to try again and she says the same thing. Using a lenient criterion, she might be given credit for the one-one, stable order, and cardinal principles because she applies just one word to each chip, always recites the four words in the same order, and uses the last number-word to say how many there are. Using a strict criterion, however, you might say that she should not be given credit for any of the principles because she did not use them correctly to accurately determine how many there are. Of course, the answer to the question "When do children seem to know the five principles?" depends on whether a lenient or strict criterion is used. But the answer also depends on the number of objects in a set. Using lenient scoring and sets of three or fewer objects, some three-year-olds and most four- and five-year-olds are credited with knowledge of the principles. Using the strict scoring and larger sets, only four- and five-year-old children are credited with knowledge.

Gelman and Gallistel's pioneering work was significant because it introduced counting skills overlooked by Piaget and because it revealed knowledge of cardinal value in children younger than five. Since that time, researchers have tried to build on these original findings using various methodologies. Some researchers had children comment on the accuracy of a puppet's counting rather than having them count themselves. The puppet's behavior either conformed to or violated the five counting principles. Other researchers simply asked children to give them a certain number of objects (e.g., "Give me four teddies"). Together, these latter studies showed that (a) between the ages of three and four, there is significant improvement in children's knowledge of counting and cardinal value and (b) four- and five-year-olds show considerable, though sometimes imperfect, skill in these areas (Briars & Siegler, 1984; Gelman & Meck, 1983; Ginsburg & Russell, 1981; Wynn, 1990).

So far, we have examined only the studies in which children were asked to count objects. Other researchers have also asked children to count as high as they can, without giving them objects to count. These studies show that even two-year-olds can usually count to three correctly. In the age range of 3.5 yrs. to four, the average child can count to 13 without making an error. In the range of 5.5 yrs. old to six, the average child can count to 51 without making an error (Fuson & Hall, 1983). Older preschoolers also extend the "one-to-nine" pattern to several decades beyond ten (e.g., 31, 32 . . . 39), but often fail to order the decades correctly. These age trends are generally quite similar across socioeconomic status (SES) groups, but occasionally a study reveals that up to 30 percent of low SES kindergartners cannot count to ten.

Given these findings, it should be clear that simplified math instruction could begin by age three for most children. In the absence of counting skills, three-year-olds could be asked to label sets of objects smaller than four using number words. Similarly, they could engage in tasks in which one-to-one correspondences between one set of objects and another are formed (e.g., setting the table for four dolls using four plates). Over time, mismatches and counting could be used to foster an early comprehension of whole numbers (e.g., using counting to figure out why one plate is left over when five plates are used with four dolls).

The Elementary School Period

Because many preschool children lack formal education, it may have been surprising to learn how much they know about numbers. Moreover, there is nothing obvious about their lives at home that would explain why there is a shift in numerical skills between the ages of three and four. From the elementary school period on, however, the developmental sequence of knowledge is not very surprising or mysterious because it largely follows the standard curriculum. That is, children master skills in the same order that these skills are presented in school. But, as we will see, children do not master all skills with equal facility and the reasons for their difficulties are not immediately obvious.

In elementary school, children are asked to learn the arithmetic skills of addition, subtraction, multiplication, and division of whole numbers. In what follows, we shall examine the research on those arithmetic tasks that have been given the most attention from researchers: (a) decontextualized computation problems and (b) word problems.

Decontextualized Computation Problems
Because most of the research on children's computation skills has focused on addition and subtraction, we shall only examine these two operations here.

Addition.   Instruction in addition usually begins with single-digit problems that have sums less than ten. Until recently, first graders encountered these problems in the form of decontextualized computation "sentences" such as "$3 + 7 = ?$". Whereas these problems may seem to be low level or easy, they pose quite a challenge to first graders. Why? The first reason is that first graders are often unfamiliar with the symbolic notation used in these sentences (Resnick, 1987). That is, children have to assign meaning to each of 3, +, and so on. To see the difficulty of this, imagine that you were asked to solve the following problem: "$X^{\#} \backslash\backslash Y^{\#-1} = ?$" What is the answer?

The second reason is that even after the formal sentence is decoded for them by a teacher, children may have no idea how to come up with the answer. To get them started, teachers usually provide explicit instruction in the form of the *count-all* strategy: Count out the number of objects indicated by the first number (e.g., put up three fingers), count out the number indicated by the second number (e.g., put up four more fingers), then count all of them (e.g., seven fingers total). Notice how first graders need to come to school being able to count. In most classrooms, children spend several weeks trying to solve addition sentences such as these and then move on to word problems that implicitly embed the same operations in them (e.g., "John has three apples. Bill gives him four more. How many does he have altogether?").

Before describing age trends in performance on decontextualized sentences, it is necessary to note that most math educators now feel that the approach of presenting decontextualized sentences first and word problems second is not the best way to go (NCTM, 1989). Why? The first reason is that because counting and addition are forms of procedural knowledge, they should be presented as things children can do to help them solve actual problems. In having children merely mimic a teacher ("Do this first, do this second . . . "), the goal-directed, problem-solving quality of these operations gets lost. The second reason is that children are asked to jump into the symbolic mode well before they may have built up meaningful referents for these symbols (e.g., *3* stands for three objects). That is, they are asked to learn procedures before they have acquired sufficient conceptual knowledge (Hiebert, 1987; Resnick, 1987). In order to avoid these problems, the NCTM recommends reversing the typical sequence of events. That is, they suggest beginning instruction on addition using simple, orally presented word problems. To build up conceptual referents for symbols, children should be given manipulatives such as poker chips or base-10 blocks. After the children have a good deal of practice with word problems, teachers should then progressively introduce the formal, symbolic mode.

Because this reversed sequence is a relatively recent trend, most of the research that has examined children's single-digit addition and subtraction derives from classrooms in which decontextualized sentences were taught in the traditional way. The primary goal of teachers who use the traditional approach is to move children from a reliance on counting to a reliance on direct retrieval of the answer. To see why, consider how tedious and inefficient the count-all strategy is. With large numbers, it would take a lot of time to come up with the answer and a child would soon run out of fingers and toes. To reach the goal of having students rely on direct retrieval, most teachers use a lot of repetition. In the first grade, for example, teachers spend a considerable amount of time having their students practice the 45 possible pairings of sums involving the numbers 1 to 9. From the second grade on, teachers reintroduce these pairs, but for fewer and fewer weeks.

Researchers who have studied children's addition strategies have mainly focused on two main questions: (a) What strategies do children use to solve single-digit addition problems? and (b) Do children use specific strategies at specific ages? Regarding the first question, it has not been easy to determine the strategies that children use. Why? In the first place, simple observation often is ambiguous. To see this, imagine that you ask a fifth grader to solve the problem "3 + 4 = ?". After being silent for a few seconds, he says "7." Do you know for sure that he definitely used direct retrieval and did not count? This assessment problem could not be easily overcome by simply asking children to tell you what they did because children often lack conscious access to what they are doing or misreport what they did (Karmiloff-Smith, 1984; Siegler & Jenkins, 1989). To discover what children do, then, researchers have had to resort to a variety of approaches including observation, interviews, and reaction-time experiments (Fuson, 1988; Resnick, 1983). These varied approaches revealed the following strategies:

1. *Count all*: Use fingers or other objects to count out the first addend, then the second addend, and then the total (e.g., for *3 + 7*, they say "1,2,3 . . . 1,2,3,4 . . . 1,2,3,4,5,6,7");
2. *Count on from first*: Start the count with the first addend and add on the number indicated by the second addend (e.g., "3 . . . 4,5,6,7").
3. *Count on from second*: Start the count with the second addend and add on the number indicated by the first addend (e.g., "4 . . . 5,6,7").
4. *Count on from larger* ("Min"): Start with the larger of the two addends and add on from there (e.g., "4 . . . 5,6,7").
5. *Derived facts*: Use known facts to construct the answer (e.g., a child might say "3 + 3 = 6, and 4 is one more than 3, so 3 + 4 = 7").
6. *Direct retrieval*: Retrieve the answer directly from memory.

A close examination of this list reveals that strategies become increasingly more efficient and dependent on prior knowledge as one moves from the first to the sixth strategy. Also worth noting is the fact that only the count-all and direct retrieval strategies are taught to children. Thus, the remaining strategies seem to be invented by children (Resnick, 1987).

The second question asked by researchers is whether there are age trends in the use of certain addition strategies. Given the standard instructional sequence described earlier, it might be expected that most first graders would use the count-all strategy and most fifth graders would use direct retrieval. It might be further expected that strategies 2 to 5 (see above) would be used by children in the second, third, and fourth grades. To examine these possibilities, two main approaches have been used. The first, called the *chronometric* approach, involves presenting addition sentences on a computer screen and asking children to give the answer as fast as possible. Then, children's strategies are derived from their reaction times. Although it may seem odd to use reaction times to determine strategy use, the chronometric approach is one way to get around the mismatch between what children say they do and what they actually do. Also, it is clear that the six strategies listed above can be rank-ordered in terms of how long they take to execute.

In line with expectations, the earliest chronometric studies suggested that first graders mostly use the count-all strategy and fifth graders mostly use the "min" and direct retrieval strategies (Ashcraft, 1982; Groen & Parkman, 1972; Siegler & Jenkins, 1989). But researchers soon questioned this conclusion because the chronometric approach did not perfectly account for children's performances. In addition, the approach averages across children and problems, thereby obscuring the fact that (a) children in the same grade may use different strategies and (b) an individual child may use different strategies at different times (Siegler & Jenkins, 1989).

The second approach, called the *microgenetic* approach, was designed to avoid some of the problems of the chronometric approach (Siegler & Jenkins, 1989). In a microgenetic study, an individual child is interviewed and observed for many weeks until he or she discovers a strategy. For example, a child who is taught the count-all strategy might be followed until she invents the count-on strategy on her own. Siegler and his colleagues have found that most children use multiple strategies instead of a single strategy. Moreover, first graders have been found to use direct retrieval for so-called "ties" (e.g., 1 + 1, 2 + 2, 3 + 3, etc.) and fifth graders have been found to use count-all when fatigued or uncertain. Thus, the "one child–one strategy" characterization implied by the chronometric approach appears to be incorrect. The proper characterization of performance seems to be a child deciding among *several* strategies.

In contrast to the large amount of research conducted with single-digit addition problems, very few studies have examined children's learning of two-digit addition problems such as "24 + 17 = ?". One recent study showed that even first graders can learn to solve two-digit problems that require regrouping when they are given considerable practice learning how to relate the addends to manipulatives (Fuson & Briars, 1990). Using Base–10 blocks, children were taught to relate digits in the ones column in a number (e.g., the 4 in 24) to small square blocks called "ones" and the digits in the tens column (e.g., the 2 in 24) to long, rectangular blocks called "tens." Base–10 blocks are such that ten "ones" stuck together in a column are the same length and width as a single "tens" block. The success of Fuson and Briar's study is somewhat surprising given that few people would have thought that first graders could handle the notion of *place value*.

Subtraction.   The research on single-digit subtraction sentences has revealed findings similar to those for single-digit addition sentences. Instruction on subtraction often begins near the end of the first grade and involves children using the "take away" method with fingers or manipulatives. The earliest chronometric and interview studies on subtraction revealed that children seem to use at least three mental counting procedures (Resnick, 1983). In the *decrementing* model, the child starts with the larger number (the minuend) and decrements by one as many times as indicated by the smaller number (the subtrahend). For example, with "7 – 3," the child holds up seven fingers and says "6–5–4 . . . 4." This decrementing approach is consistent with what teachers show children. In the *incrementing* model, the child starts with the subtrahend (e.g., 3) and increments it by one until the minuend is reached. For example, she holds up three fingers and says "4–5–6–7 . . . 4" as she progressively adds four fingers to the original three. In the *choice* model, the child decides which of the decrementing or incrementing strategies would produce the answer with the fewest steps. Reaction-time studies suggested that although most primary children use the choice model, many second graders seem to depend on the decrementing model. Using the microgenetic approach, however, Siegler (1989) found that children at all ages rely on multiple strategies when they solve subtraction problems.

In later grades, children progress to two-and three-digit subtraction problems and confront a new set of challenges. Consider several examples:

(a)   28   (b)   24
     – 17   – 17

The first issue that children need to deal with is the new vertical look of these problems. Additional issues arise when children are asked to solve problems that require regrouping (e.g., example (b) above). The standard algorithm of placing a dash through the left-hand number (e.g., the *2* in *24*) in order to add a ten to the right-hand number (e.g., make *4* into *14*) usually seems utterly meaningless and mysterious to children. As a result, they often make a number of procedural errors when they try to execute this algorithm.

Brown and Burton (1978) analyzed the types of errors that children make when they try to solve subtraction-with-regrouping problems. They found that an important source of errors was children's consistent tendency to omit key steps in the general subtraction algorithm. For example, when given a problem such as "205 – 26," children would place a dash through the *0* in *205*, change the *5* into a *15,* and change the *0* into a *9*. However, they would forget to make the *2* into a *1*. Thus, they would give the answer "*279*," a number larger than either the subtrahend or minuend! Brown & Burton called errors such as these "bugs," because they are like the missing steps in a faulty computer program. Table 8.1 lists several of the more common subtraction bugs.

Why are bugs so prevalent in regrouping problems? Many experts think that children make these errors because the standard "dashes" algorithm is presented in a meaningless, computational way (Resnick, 1987). As a result, few children understand what they are doing when they place dashes through numbers and decrement them by 1. A more meaningful way to present the subtraction algorithm is to expand out minuends and subtrahends into their constituent parts.

TABLE 8.1   Some of the More Common Subtraction "Bugs"

1. BORROW/FROM/ZERO
   For problems in which children need to borrow from a *0* (e.g., *205 – 26*), they write a *9* above the *0* but do not continue borrowing from the column to the left of *0* (e.g., answer given = *279*).

2. SMALLER/FROM/LARGER
   For problems in which a smaller number is above a larger number in a given column (e.g., *217 – 98*), children subtract the smaller from larger instead of borrowing (e.g., answer given = *281*).

3. DIFF/0 – N = N
   Whenever the top digit in a column is a *0*, children write the bottom digit instead of borrowing and subtracting (e.g., *306 – 13 = 313*).

From: Brown & Burton (1978)

Consider the problem "205 − 26" again. *205* can be written as *200 + 5* and *26* can be rewritten as *20 + 6*. After lining up digits by columns, children can readily see that they cannot take the 6 away from the 5, so they need to regroup the 200 into *190 + 10*. That way, the *10* and *5* can be combined into *15*. After children become familiar with the expanded format, they will begin to understand why you have to "skip" over the *0* in *205* to borrow the *1* from the *2*.

What is missing in the dashes algorithm, then, and is explicit in the expanded format is a meaningful representation of *place value*. The dashes algorithm suggests that the *2* in *205* represents a *2*, not a *200*. Once again we see the hazards of moving too quickly into computational algorithms before children have a sufficient understanding of concepts such as place value. In a recent study, seventh graders were taught to mentally transform numbers in multi-digit subtraction problems into the expanded format. This technique increased the speed and efficiency with which students performed the computations and also enhanced their "number sense" (Markovits & Sowder, 1994).

Word Problems

When confronted with word problems such as those in Table 8.2, most children have trouble (Carpenter, 1987). Math teachers are initially puzzled by children's difficulty with word problems because there does not seem to be a major difference between, say, the first word problem in Table 8.1. and the decontextualized problem "3 + 5 = ?". What is it about word problems that make them so difficult? Most theorists have tried to answer this question by proposing a set of cognitive operations that need to be performed in order for a problem to be solved. Errors are explained by saying that children failed to perform one or more of these operations correctly. In what follows, we shall examine some of the more central operations.

One of the first things that a child needs to do in order to solve a word problem is construct an accurate *situation model* (Kintsch & Greeno, 1985). A situation model is a mental representation of the state of affairs described in the problem. More specifically, it is a representation of the number of objects that each character has and what happens to each character's objects as the problem progresses. A situation model is "accurate" if it correctly reflects the underlying *semantic structure* of the problem (Carpenter & Moser, 1982; Riley et al., 1983). The notion of semantic structure refers to whether the problem involves increases, decreases, or comparisons of sets. (see Table 8.2 for illustrations of the three most common types). If something interferes with a child's ability to construct an accurate situation model for a word problem, he or she will not be able to solve it.

One factor that interferes with the construction of a situation model is the placement of the unknown in the problem. In "change" problems, for example (see Table 8.2), the unknown can be in the *start set* (e.g., "Julia has some cookies . . ."), the *change set* (e.g. "Julia has 3 cookies. Tommy gives her some more . . .") or the *result set* (e.g., ". . . How many does she have altogether?"). Children have much more difficulty creating a situation model when the unknown is the start set or

TABLE 8.2   Three Major Semantic Structures of Arithmetic Word Problems

1. *Change*

Julia has 3 cookies. Tommy gives her 5 more.

How many does she have altogether?

Julia has some cookies. Tommy gives her 5 more. Now Julia has 8. How many did she have to start with?

    Success Rate: 1st Grade (41–100%)[a]
                   5th Grade (67–100%)

2. *Combine*

Julia has 3 cookies. Tommy has 5 cookies. How many do they have altogether?

Julia has 3 cookies. Tommy has some cookies too. Together they have 8 cookies. How many does Tommy have?

    Success rate: 1st Grade (39–88%)
                   5th Grade (72–94%)

3. *Compare*

Julia has 3 cookies. Tommy has 5 cookies. How many does Tommy have more than Julia?

Julia has 3 cookies. Tommy has 2 more than Julia. How many cookies does Tommy have?

    Success rate: 1st Grade (6–81%)
                   5th Grade (60–86%)

---

[a]Note: Success rates derive from figures provided in Riley et al. (1983) and Morales et al. (1985). Success varies as a function of the placement of the unknown and wording of the question.

change set than when it is the result set (Morales, Shute & Pellegrino, 1985; Riley et al., 1983).

Young children's difficulty with undefined start sets or change sets has been attributed to their lacking a well-established *part-whole* schema for numbers (Resnick, 1983; Riley et al., 1983). With the development of the part-whole schema, a given number (the whole) is understood as being made up of multiple combinations of other numbers (the parts). Before the acquisition of a part-whole schema, a number such as 3 is conceptualized as a set of objects whose cardinal value falls between 2 and 4. After the part-whole schema develops, however, several things happen. First, a number such as 3 is now conceptualized as being partitioned into the following combinations: *0 3, 1 2,* and *2 1.* Second, addition is viewed as being the combination of parts (e.g., 1 + 2 = 3), subtraction is viewed as the removal of one part from the whole (e.g., 3 – 2 = 1), and addition and subtraction are viewed as inverse operations (e.g., 3 – 2 = 1 is the inverse of 1 + 2 = 3). In contrast, children who lack the part-whole schema solve addition and subtraction problems in a linear, "on line" way and fail to see a relationship between expressions such as "3 + 1 = 4" and "1 + 3 = 4." The reader may note that the part-whole schema would be quite useful for understanding the expanded forms of subtraction-with-regrouping problems.

If a child lacks a part-whole schema and tries to solve a word problem in a linear way, he will encounter an impasse when an unknown start set or change set is reached. For the fourth problem shown in Table 8.2, for example, he might say, "Julia has three cookies, so I should hold up three fingers. Tommy has some cookies, so I should hold up . . . Wait! How many is 'some'?" In contrast, unknown start sets and change sets cause fewer problems for a child who has the part-whole schema, because the unknown is simply seen as a missing element in a three-component schema. In effect, when they are given the fourth problem in Table 8.2, they might reason, "I know how many Julia has and how many they have altogether, so I need to find out how many Tommy has."

In addition to constructing an accurate situation model, the second thing children need to do in order to solve a word problem is understand what the author of a word problem is asking of them. For the first "compare" problem in Table 8.2, for example, children may not understand that the question "How many does Julia have more than Tommy?" is asking them to compare Julia's amount to Tommy's amount (Stern, 1993). Performance is often quite poor on compare problems because of this language factor.

After constructing an accurate situation model and determining what is being asked, children are finally in a position to use addition or subtraction to derive the answer. Which operation to perform, of course, will depend on the specific semantic structure of the problem and the placement of the unknown. For example, in "change" problems with an unknown result set (e.g., the first problem in Table 8.2), addition should be used. In "change" problems with an unknown change set (e.g., the second problem in Table 8.2), however, subtraction should be used.

Once the barriers to constructing situation models and understanding what is asked are overcome, continued practice is likely to foster the development of (a) *problem schemata* for the various types of word problems, (b) *action schemata* for the solutions to each of these problems (Riley et al., 1983), and (c) associative links between problem schemata and action schemata. The development of such schemata help children come up with correct answers more quickly and efficiently. That is, they would not have to reinvent the wheel each time they encounter a problem of a particular type.

Recently, teachers have tried to improve student performance on word problems by introducing them very early in the first grade. These days, first graders are given all types of word problems and manipulatives to help them create a partial situation model. For example, they might use poker chips to represent as many amounts as given in the problem (e.g., Julia's amount, Tommy's amount, etc.). Then, they are merely asked by their teachers to try to figure out a way to answer the problem using the chips. In a classical constructivist classroom, teachers would only provide hints and ask students to problem-solve on their own. Moreover, discussions of possible solutions would be encouraged, as would examining how peers have tried to solve the problem.

The Middle School Period

By the time they enter middle school, most children are quite proficient in their ability to execute various algorithms for addition, subtraction, multiplication, and division of whole numbers. But just when things are going so well, teachers introduce ideas such as *rational numbers* (e.g., fractions and decimals) and *integers* (e.g., +7, –4). They are told that a number such as 3 is no longer simply a set of three objects or the product of combinations such as "2 + 1." Now it is described as the rational number 3/1 or the opposite of –3. It should not be surprising to learn that most children find these ideas difficult to grasp. In what follows, we shall try to examine why rational numbers and integers are so hard to understand.

The difficulties children have with rational numbers and integers are both conceptual and procedural (Wearne & Hiebert, 1988). In the case of fractions, children have problems understanding concepts related to *cardinal*, *ordinal*, and *equivalence* relations (Byrnes & Wasik, 1991; Hiebert & Behr, 1988; Post, Wachsmuth, Lesh & Behr, 1985). That is, they have trouble (a) relating symbols such as $^3/_5$ to appropriate referents (cardinal relations), (b) understanding that $^1/_4$ is less than $^1/_3$ (ordinal relations), and (c) understanding that $^1/_2$ is the same amount as $^3/_6$ (equivalence relations). Procedurally, they have trouble learning the least common denominator method for adding fractions and the "invert and multiply" procedure for dividing fractions.

With respect to decimals and integers, children again have problems understanding concepts related to cardinal and ordinal relations. For example, they do not understand the role of zeros in decimals and fail to see how *.30* is larger than *.047* (Resnick et al., 1989). Similarly, they have trouble relating negative integers to concrete referents and fail to see how *–9* could be less than 2 (Byrnes, 1992). Procedurally, children do not understand (a) why they have to "line up the decimal points" when they add or subtract decimals (Wearne & Hiebert, 1988) or (b) how to compute answers to problems such as "3 + –2" and "–3 – –2" (Byrnes, 1992).

Why do children have such trouble with rational numbers and integers? Three explanations seem plausible. The first is that rational numbers and integers are more abstract than positive whole numbers. Consider how it is easier to conceptualize 5 as five dollars than to conceptualize –5 as "five dollars in the hole." Similarly, it is easy to relate 3 + 2 to concrete actions (e.g., two children adding their cookies together) but not so easy to relate division of fractions to concrete actions.

The second explanation is that the concepts and procedures related to rational numbers and integers are quite different from those related to positive whole numbers. For example, the procedure for adding "$^1/_3 + ^1/_2$" is nothing like the procedure for adding "3 + 2." Thus, children cannot simply assimilate information about rational numbers and integers to their existing knowledge of whole numbers. They have to create brand new schemata for these new classes of numbers.

Because information about rational numbers and integers is so discrepant from what they know about whole numbers, both Piagetian theory and Vygotskian theory would predict that children would either ignore this new information or distort it to fit with what they already know (see Chapters 2 and 3). Close examination of children's errors suggests that many children seem to distort what they are learning. Consider the case of fractions. Conceptually, a child wants $\frac{1}{3}$ to be less than $\frac{1}{4}$ because 3 is less than 4. Procedurally, he wants to simply add numerators and denominators (e.g. $\frac{1}{2} + \frac{1}{3} = \frac{2}{5}$) because that is how whole numbers are added. Similar "over-assimilations" exist for decimals and integers (Byrnes, 1992; Byrnes & Wasik, 1991).

The third explanation is that many teachers spend very little time teaching the conceptual underpinnings of procedures related to rational numbers and integers. Most of the time they teach procedures in a purely computational way (Byrnes, 1992; Hiebert & Behr, 1988). Children who lack conceptual knowledge are likely to make many computational errors. In support of this claim, Byrnes (1992) and Byrnes & Wasik (1991) found that children who had more conceptual knowledge of fractions and integers prior to instruction learned procedures for adding these numbers better than children with less conceptual knowledge.

The High School Period

Although many high school students take courses in algebra, geometry, trigonometry, and calculus, most educational researchers have focused exclusively on a single subject: algebra. As a result, only the research on algebra will be examined here. In what follows, the literature on students' comprehension of algebraic formulae is summarized first and that concerning their understanding of algebra word problems is summarized second.

Algebraic Formulae

Historically, mathematicians developed algebra to be "generalized arithmetic." That is, its formulae are abstractions across a large class of specific arithmetic "sentences." (Resnick, Cauzinille-Marmeche & Mathieu, 1987). For example, the expression "X + Y" is a generalization of specific arithmetic sentences such as "2 + 1," "3 + 2," and "9 + 7." One of the first things that children need to grasp in order to understand formulae, then, is the fact that X could stand for the 2, 3, or 9 of the three arithmetic sentences. In fact, X could stand for any number.

This notion of a *variable* is quite difficult for children to understand at first. In particular, research has shown that they seem to progress through several levels of understanding before they master it. At the lowest level, children immediately assign a number to X because they fail to grasp the notion of "unknown value." For example, when asked to "write a number that is 3 more than X," they first put a down a value for X (e.g., 5) and then write one that is 3 more than the value given for X (e.g., 8). At the second level, they think that X stands for a specific number that is not yet known. At the third level, X is considered to be a generalized number; that is, it can take on more than one value. At the fourth level, X is considered to be a variable that not only represents a range of values, but also is linked in a systematic way to a set of values represented by another variable such as Y (Herscovics, 1989; Kieran, 1989).

Of course, if students have trouble understanding the notion of variable, they will also have trouble dealing with algebraic expressions. When given an expression such as "$X + 3 - Y$" and asked "What is the value of Y?," children initially refuse to put the answer "$X + 3$" because they think that answers have to be a single, determinate value. In addition, children also have trouble combining variables within algebraic expressions. For example, some students do not understand why "$7a$" is the answer to "$2a + 5a$" and others make the error of assuming that "z" is the answer to "$2yz - 2y$" (Kieran, 1989).

Why do students make such errors? Four explanations can be offered. First, just as -5 is more abstract than 5, X is more abstract than either of the former two numbers (cf. Resnick et al., 1987). In particular, whereas any negative or positive number can be related to a specific concrete array of objects, variables must be related to an array of possible *numbers*. Second, algebraic operations cannot be easily assimilated to arithmetic operations. For example, although the expression $(3 + 2)^2$ is formally related to the generalization $(a + b)^2$, the "answer" to these two problems would be computed in distinct ways. In particular, few children would solve the former by first forming the expression "$(3 + 2)(3 + 2)$" and then using the "foil" method to generate "$3^2 + (2)(3*2) + 2^2$." Most would say "5 squared is 25." Third, algebraic operations are usually taught in a nonconceptual, computational way (Wagner & Kieran, 1989). If these first three explanations seem familiar, they should because they were offered earlier when rational numbers and integers were at issue.

The fourth explanation has to do with the notion of *malrules* (Matz, 1982; Resnick et al., 1987). According to this proposal, students construct prototype rules from which they extrapolate new rules. For example, after working with many distributivity problems such as "$3*(4 + 2) = 3*4 + 3*2$" and "$a(b + c) = ab + bc$," children form the prototype rule "$a \# (b @ c) = (a\#b) @ (a\#c)$." Then, when confronted with a problem such as "$\sqrt{b + c}$," they think it can be decomposed into "$\sqrt{b} + \sqrt{c}$."

Given the cognitive complexity of algebra, it may not be surprising to learn that many high school students perform poorly on the algebra items of large-scale national assessments (e.g, Carpenter et al., 1981). For example, when given the equation "$W = 17 + 5A$" and asked "According to this formula, for each year older someone gets, how much more should he weigh?," only 64 percent of 17-year-olds with two years of algebra gave the right answer of "5 pounds more each year." Similarly, when given a Table such as that below, only 80 percent of students who had two years of algebra could generate the missing numbers and only about a quarter of those students could generate the equation "$y = X + 3$" for this Table.

X:	6	4	5	8	1
Y:		7	8		4

One way to help improve children's performance in algebra is to help them develop more accurate "mental models" of variables and algebraic operations.

One straightforward way to help them acquire a clear sense of functions such as "y = f(x)" is to have them release a ball from different heights and measure how high it bounces. In this way, they can create two columns of drop points (i.e., *x* values) and their corresponding bounce heights (i.e., *y* values). They will see that the height with which something bounces is a function of the height at which it is released. They will also clearly see that there is a very large range of possible heights (eliminating the one-value interpretation of variables).

Algebra Word Problems

Simply put, students have considerable difficulty with algebra word problems (Chaiklin, 1989; Mayer, Larkin & Kaldane, 1984). In order to understand why this is so, most researchers have engaged in two phases of research. In the first phase, they proposed a model of the cognitive operations responsible for success on algebra word problems. That is, they gave an answer to the question, "What things do you need to do in your head in order to solve an algebra word problem?". In the second phase, they tried to identify the factors that interfere with a student's ability to execute one or more of the necessary operations.

Perhaps the most influential model of performance on algebra word problems is that proposed by Mayer, Larkin, and Kaldane (1984). Mayer et al. contend that students need to engage in four steps when they solve problems such as those in Table 8.3:

1. First, the problem must be *translated* into a fragmented internal representation. That is, a string of propositional knowns and unknowns must be constructed using linguistic and factual knowledge. For example, for the "astronaut" problem in Table 8.3, students need to create a string of mental propositions such as "OXYGEN PER ASTRONAUT PER DAY = 2.2; "NUMBER OF ASTRONAUTS = 3," and so on.
2. Second, the fragmented internal representation has to be reorganized into a coherent structure (e.g., "TOTAL OXYGEN = (OXYGEN PER ASTRONAUT PER DAY) × (NUMBER OF ASTRONAUTS) × (NUMBER OF DAYS) . . .). Once the coherent structure is formed, the problem is *understood*. Mayer et al. believe that schemata for specific types of problems help students reorganize propositions into coherent structures;
3. Third, a plan has to be developed for how to generate the answer (e.g., "Okay, first I need to figure out TIME so I can then use this number to figure out the total amount of oxygen . . ."). A student's existing *strategic knowledge* helps him or her construct an effective plan;
4. Fourth, the plan has to be *executed* using appropriate algorithms (e.g., carry out the computations such as "$2.2 \times 3 \times 5$"). The execution phase, of course, requires knowledge of various algorithms.

There are two primary reasons Mayer at al.'s model has credibility. First, it is based on successful computer simulations of algebra problem-solving (e.g., Paige & Simon, 1966). Second, it has received good empirical support in the psychological literature. For example, Mayer (1982) found that when college students

TABLE 8.3   Examples of Algebra Word Problems

The Astronaut Problem

An astronaut requires 2.2 pounds of oxygen per day while in space. How many pounds of oxygen are needed for a team of 3 astronauts for 5 days in space?

_____ 13.2   _____ 15.2   _____ 33   ____ 330

The Student-Professor Problem

Write an equation using S and P to represent the following statement: "There are six times as many students as professors at this university." Use S for the number of students and P for the number of professors.

The River Problem

A river steamer travels 36 miles downstream in the same time that it travels 24 miles upstream. The steamer's engine drives in still water at a rate of 12 miles per hour more than the rate of the current. Find the rate of the current.

Examples taken from Mayer et al. (1984).

tried to make sense of so-called relational statements in word problems (e.g., "the rate in still water is 12 mph more than the rate in the current"), they had a strong tendency to misinterpret them as so-called assignment statements (e.g., "The rate in still water is 12 mph). In addition, Clement (1982) found that only 63 percent of college students could write the proper formula for the "student-professor" problem in Table 8.3. The most common error was to translate "six times as many students" as $6S$ and put $6S = P$ as their answer. Of course, if students make such errors during the translation phase of problem-solving, they will not be able to come up with the right answer.

Additional empirical support for the four-step model comes from studies that show the importance of problem schemata. For example, Hinsley, Hayes, and Simon (1977) found that many students demonstrate an immediate recognition of types of problems (e.g., "Oh, that's one of those 'rate' problems"). Students who are familiar with a type of problem will, of course, have a very good idea how to set up a plan for solving it. Other studies show that (a) students have an easier time recalling word problems if these problems are of the type that occur frequently in their algebra textbook (Mayer et al., 1984) and (b) students seem to use their schemata for problems to discriminate between irrelevant and relevant details (Low & Over, 1993).

Summary

The last four subsections examined the development of mathematical skills from infancy to young adulthood. Three main themes emerged from this research. The first theme is that the more abstract math gets, the more children have conceptual and procedural problems. The second theme is that a number of children's problems seem to derive from the fact that traditional math instruction places far more emphasis on procedural knowledge than it does on conceptual knowledge. As a result, children make many "mindless" computational errors because they do not understand what they are doing. The third theme is that the acquisition of schemata greatly enhances children's understanding of, and success in, math.

Individual Differences in Mathematical Skills

If classrooms were homogeneous such that all students were fairly similar to each other, then math teachers would only have to read the literature on developmental trends in order to know what to expect when teaching a particular age group. But, of course, classrooms are not homogeneous and the differences among students often seem to overwhelm the similarities. Thus, to get a complete picture of the classroom, a teacher needs to know something about developmental differences *and* individual differences.

In examining individual differences in math performance, researchers have asked, "Given this age group, are there subgroups of children who behave differently than others?" Typically, three variables have been used to form and compare subgroups of children within math classes: gender, ethnicity, and strategy preference. In what follows, the research on these three variables is described in turn.

Before proceeding, however, it should be noted that in the perspective of this book, the to-be-reported differences are not the inevitable consequence of education. Rather, many of these differences are symptomatic of an educational system that is not sufficiently sensitive to the needs of subgroups of children. The differences between genders and ethnic groups are merely reported in this chapter. Explanations of why these differences occur can be found in Chapter 12.

Gender Differences

Take a moment to answer the following three questions:

1. Who has more natural ability in math, boys or girls?
2. Who gets better grades in math, boys or girls?
3. Who does better on math achievement tests and experimenter-made math tests, boys or girls?

The consensus among researchers is that the answer to the first question is "they both have the same," the answer to the second question is "girls," and the answer to the third is "it depends on factors such as age, type of test, and selectivity of the sample" (Halpern, 1992; Hyde, Fennema & Lamon, 1990; see Chapter 12). Unfortunately, the consensus among average Americans seems to be that the answer is "boys" to all three questions (Eccles et al., 1985). Most people, then, are apparently unfamiliar with the current research on gender differences.

Let's examine the research pertinent to the third question, because the data from achievement tests seem to play an important role in the average person's perceptions. Extensive reviews of many studies reveal that boys sometimes perform better than girls, girls sometimes perform better than boys, and sometimes there is no difference between boys and girls. In particular, gender differences favoring boys are only likely to emerge if the math test requires problem-solving *and* the students taking this test are either older than 14 or gifted. Gender differences favoring girls are likely to emerge in two situations: (a) when the math test requires computational skill *and* the students are below the age of 15 or (b) when the math test contains items that require knowing when you have enough information to answer *and* the students are gifted (Becker, 1990). However, few of these differences are large in absolute terms, and there are lots of cases in which no gender differences are found (e.g., on tests measuring math concepts; Hyde et al., 1990). Thus, the cultural belief that boys always do better in math is incorrect. The origins and social consequences of faulty belief about gender differences are discussed in Chapter 12.

Ethnic Differences

In contrast to gender differences, ethnic differences tend to be large at all grade levels and are found for all three kinds of math tests (computations, concepts, and problem-solving). More specifically, whereas most "effect sizes" for gender differences are .20 or smaller (Hyde et al., 1990), most effect sizes for ethnic differences are .40 or larger (e.g., Stevenson, Chen & Uttal, 1990; see Chapter 12 for an explanation of "effect size"). Moreover, if a difference exists between ethnic groups on one type of test (e.g., computations), a similar difference exists for other types of tests as well (e.g., problem-solving).

As to the specifics of ethnic differences, several conclusions can be drawn. First, as early as the first grade, White students tend to perform better than African-American or Hispanic students on math achievement tests (Alexander & Entwhistle, 1988; Johnson, 1989; Stevenson et al., 1990). Second, no clear or consistent differences emerge between African-American and Hispanic students; that is, sometimes African Americans do better than Hispanics (e.g., Stevenson et al., 1990), sometimes Hispanics do better than African Americans (e.g., College Board, 1988), and sometimes these groups perform about the same (e.g., Gross, 1993). Third, Asian-American students tend to perform better than White students, especially as children move into the middle school and high school years (Gross, 1993; College Board, 1988). On the SATs, for example, whereas the average math score for Asian students is 522, the average for White students is 490. For African-American and Hispanic students, the averages are 384 and 424, respectively. This means that Asian students get approximately 30 out of the 60 SAT items right (50 percent), White students get about 27 right (45 percent), Hispanic students get about 19 right (32 percent), and African-American students get about 14 right (23 percent).

A significant factor that seems to contribute to ethnic differences in performance is a student's socioeconomic status (SES). In particular, Stevenson et al.

(1990) found that performance differences in math between White, African-American, and Hispanic students disappear when one controls for SES. In addition, SAT scores seem to be highly related to family income. For example, for those students whose family income is less than $10,000, the average SAT math score is 418. For those students whose family income falls between $30,000 and $40,000, the average is 473. If family income is $70,000 or more, the average is 523 (College Board, 1988). In terms of percent correct, these SAT scores turn out to be 32 percent, 42 percent, and 50 percent correct, respectively. We shall examine the role of SES further in Chapter 12.

Before moving on, it is important to note that the largest ethnic differences arise for so-called formal mathematics; that is, ethnic groups differ in terms of how well they have learned the curriculum-based math ideas appropriate for their grade level. In contrast, few ethnic or cross-cultural differences arise for the "informal" mathematical ideas that children construct prior to school or outside of school (Ginsburg & Miller, 1981). In Ginsburg & Russell's (1981) study, for example, White and African-American preschoolers differed on only two out of 17 tasks that tap into informal math ideas (Ginsburg & Russell, 1981). In addition, low-SES African-American students performed similarly to middle-class White students on these measures. The fact that ethnic differences emerge by the end of the first grade suggests that school differences may be producing the ethnic differences described earlier.

Strategy Preferences

As discussed earlier in the section on arithmetic, microgenetic studies have revealed that children possess a range of strategies for solving addition and subtraction problems. What was not mentioned earlier was that this research also revealed subgroups of children who have almost traitlike tendencies to solve problems in characteristic ways. Siegler (1988) labeled these subgroups "perfectionists," "good students," and "not-so-good" students.

When presented with arithmetic sentences (e.g., "3 + 7 = ?"), perfectionists tend to use time-consuming counting strategies unless they are highly confident that they could retrieve the answer directly from memory (e.g., 90 percent sure). Good students seem to set a lower threshold for confidence than perfectionists (e.g., 70 percent sure), so they count less often and use direct retrieval more often than perfectionists. This preference for efficiency seemed to pay off because good students were often correct when they used direct retrieval. Not-so-good students were similar to good students in their greater reliance on direct retrieval over counting, but the answers they retrieved were often wrong.

If you had to predict which of these subgroups would show the most achievement in math, which one(s) would it be? Perfectionists will almost always be correct because they almost always use a foolproof method (i.e., counting). Good students should also do well because they seem to know when they should fall back on a foolproof method. Not-so-good students, in contrast, would probably not do well. In support of these expectations, Siegler (1988) found that perfectionists were at the eighty-fourth and eightieth percentiles on a standardized math test for computation and problem-solving, respectively. The corresponding figures for good students were 68 (computations) and 80 (problem-solving). For not-so-good students, they were 22 (computations) and 38 (problem-solving).

Instructional Implications

In what follows, we shall first examine some general guidelines for instruction. In contemporary constructivist theory, flexible teaching is assumed to ensue when teachers have a clear understanding of the causes of success and failure in mathematics, not when they are simply armed with "teacher-proof" techniques (see Chapter 1). The guidelines tap into the causes of success and failure implicated earlier in this chapter. After the guidelines have been presented, we shall examine a case study of effective instruction that illustrates many of these guidelines.

General Guidelines

The research on mathematical thinking suggests the following instructional implications:

1. Preschool experiences should be structured in such a way as to enhance children's existing mathematical knowledge, however informal or implicit it may be; in light of the importance of counting in early arithmetic, instruction that prompts children to induce and extend the five counting principles is also encouraged.

2. In line with the recommendations of the NCTM (1989), instruction in arithmetic should focus on building up children's conceptual referents for symbols using concrete, goal-directed activities; there should be no chasm between rote computation and problem-solving. All computations should be performed in the service of solving a problem. The emphasis on conceptual understanding holds true for whole numbers, rational numbers, integers, and algebraic expressions.

3. In line with Vygotskian and Piagetian theory (see Chapter 2), instruction should form bridges between children's informal math ideas and the formal mathematics presented in school (Allardice & Ginsburg, 1983). Early ethnic differences in school performance may well reflect differences in the way teachers can build such bridges.

4. Instructional activities should promote the acquisition of part-whole schemata for numbers as well as the schemata that underlie successful performance on word problems. Generally, this is accomplished by having students solve structurally similar problems and asking them to induce the similarities (Gick & Holyoak, 1983; Sweller & Cooper, 1985).

5. Teachers in the later grades should identify existing differences between subgroups of students and try to tailor instruction to the specific needs of these subgroups. Teachers in the early grades should try to avoid creating performance differences in the first place.

6. Teachers should strive to create as many "perfectionists" and "good students" as possible. High standards for accuracy are likely to promote the former grouping (See Chapter 11 for more on personal standards). Exercises that promote an accurate metacognitive understanding of when you do and do not know an answer is likely to promote the latter grouping.

7. Finally, there is no substitute for extensive practice. Even when teachers tie procedures to concrete referents or rely on meaningful problem-solving, students still make a variety of procedural errors (Byrnes, 1992; Peterson, Fennema, Carpenter, & Loef, 1989; Resnick & Omanson, 1987). Although there is no dichotomy between *meaning*, on one hand, and *repetition* on the other, many people often assume there is. The best approach, which can be labeled *meaningful repetition* is illustrated well by Fuson & Briars (1990). These researchers not only taught students how to link the digits in numbers to Base–10 blocks, they also gave children considerable practice in doing so. Hence, the linkage did not come quickly or easily.

A Case Study

To illustrate how teachers can translate contemporary theory and research on math learning to practice, we can give more detail to the study of Markovits and Sowder (1994) that was described earlier. These researchers worked closely with a classroom teacher to increase the "number sense" of her seventh grade students using a total of 76 lessons that were five to 50 minutes in duration. Let's examine a portion of one of these lessons that tried to help students increase their estimation skills.

There were three parts to this lesson. During the first part, the teacher discussed each of seven problems on a worksheet. The first problem on the sheet was "26 + 58 = 84. What happens if you add 1 to 26 and subtract 1 from 58?" The second was "$26 \times 58 = 1508$. What happens if you add 1 to 56 and subtract 1 from 58?" As students discussed these problems, the teacher helped them see and understand how adding or subtracting numbers to operands works differently with addition and multiplication.

During the second part of the lesson, students discussed their homework problems involving estimation. One problem asked them to add four numbers, each of which had three or four digits. The idea of such exercises is that when you estimate, it is important to round up and round down numbers in compensatory ways. If you round up all numbers, the answer will be way off. For example, the answer to "450 + 550 + 650 + 750" is 2400. If you round all numbers up to 500, 600, 700, and 800, respectively, you get the answer 2600 and you are off by 200. In contrast, if you round to get 500, 500, 700, and 700, you get exactly 2400.

In part three of the lesson, students were shown a problem and asked to say which of three answers would give the closest estimate. For example, given a problem similar to 42×73, and the choices 40×70, 42×70, and 40×73, students were led to see that 40×70 cannot be the closest because both numbers are rounded down. To decide between the other choices, students are asked to determine how much they would lose in each estimate. With 42×70, they come to see that they lose 3×42 or 126. With 40×73, they lose 2×73 or 146. The discussion was then followed with a card game in which students were asked to decide the closest estimates using similar multiplication problems.

The results of this study showed that students increased in their number sense and estimation skills for whole numbers, decimals, and fractions. What was particularly nice about this intervention was that students continued to use their flexible, conceptual strategies at a long-term follow-up. In addition, it is a good example of constructivism in the classroom.

$$C \ h \ a \ p \ t \ e \ r \quad 9$$

Science Learning

Summary

1. Scientists create theories to explain phenomena. Nonscientists also create theories, but these "lay" theories sometimes contain misconceptions.

2. People develop lay theories in response to their experiences. People who have different experiences usually develop different theories. Moreover, personal theories can be highly idiosyncratic.

3. Science education can be viewed as changing lay theories into their scientific counterparts. In general, theories become more accurate, elaborate, and metacognitive with age.

4. Scientists use their theories to form hypotheses. In addition, they use the "isolation of variables" technique to test their hypotheses. Nonscientists, in contrast, often conduct experiments in which variables are not systematically controlled. Moreover, they usually try to confirm their hypotheses rather than disconfirm them.

5. With age, there is a decrease in the tendency to conduct uncontrolled experiments and seek confirmation of one's hypotheses. Nevertheless, many adolescents and adults engage in imperfect scientific reasoning.

6. Whereas gender differences have been found on science achievement tests that require knowledge of facts, no gender differences have been found for hypothesis-testing, experimentation, and misconceptions.

Joe, a business executive, said to his colleague Mary, "I feel awful! I hope I'm not coming down with a cold." Mary replied, "Just take vitamin C three times a day for the next two days and you'll feel better." Joe did so, and sure enough, he never came down with a cold. From that point on, he always took vitamin C to stop a cold.

If you were Joe, would you have taken vitamin C? Is his reasoning sound? According to the norms of good scientific thinking, the answer to the second question would be "No." You may already know why Joe's thinking is flawed, but if you do not know why now, you will by the end of this chapter.

In what follows, the nature and development of scientific thinking will be described. In the first major section of this chapter, we will consider three structural aspects of scientific thinking: theories, scientific phenomena, and scientific mis-conceptions. In the second major section, we shall examine two functional or ac-tion-oriented aspects of scientific thinking: hypothesis-testing, and experimenta-tion techniques. Finally, in the third section, we will consider the educational implications of all of the research on structural and functional aspects of scien-tific thinking.

Structural Aspects of Scientific Thinking

In this book, "structural" aspects of performance are defined as those that have to do with conceptual knowledge (see Chapter 6). Three components of scientific conceptual knowledge are theories, scientific phenomena, and misconceptions. In what follows, we shall define each of these components in turn and describe in-dividual and developmental differences in them as well.

Theories and Scientific Phenomena

In order to truly understand scientific thinking, it is necessary to understand the guiding force behind a scientist's activities: his or her *theory*. Simply put, a theory is an *explanation* for why objects or people have the characteristics they do, or why objects and people behave as they do. Thus, we would create a theory to explain why Julia has blue eyes, why Harry is tall, and why diamonds are hard (charac-teristics). Similarly, we would create a theory to explain why Julia cries when she is left with a baby-sitter, why Harry has trouble learning math, and why dia-monds can cut glass (behaviors). All of these characteristics and behaviors qual-ify as *scientific phenomena* simply because someone could try to explain them.

Explanations are based on someone's *causal* beliefs; that is, explanations im-plicitly or explicitly refer to some causal *mechanism* that could have produced the characteristics or behaviors in question (Piaget & Garcia, 1974). A mechanism is a sequence of actions or processes that are responsible for an observed charac-teristic or behavior. For example, the mechanism of genetic transmission (i.e., meiosis, fertilization, etc.) is part of the explanation for why Julia has blue eyes. Similarly, to explain why Harry has trouble learning math, we might appeal to possible deficits in the mechanisms of attention, retrieval, and assimilation (see Chapters 2 and 3). Finally, mechanisms involving the movement of electrons and the combustion of gases would be part of the explanation for why an automobile starts up when someone turns the key.

But theories do more than explain phenomena that have happened already. They also permit *predictions* of phenomena that have not happened yet. For ex-ample, a political scientist might have a very simple theory for why people elect the presidents that they do: "If the economy is good, people will vote for the in-cumbent. If it's bad, they will vote for a challenger who seems to be the most likely to improve the economy." This theory most likely would have been created by the political scientist in order to explain the election of all past presidents.

However, he could easily use it to predict that the incumbent president will not be reelected in the next election. In sciences such as physics, those predictions that always turn out to be true are called *laws* (e.g., Newton's law that "A body at rest will remain at rest unless acted upon by some force . . .").

Whenever you read a book that describes someone's theory, then, what you will read is (a) a description of the phenomena that the scientist thinks he or she can explain, (b) his or her explanation of those phenomena, (c) his or her predictions, and (d) a summary of studies designed to test his or her predictions. For example, a book on Newton's theory of physics would describe phenomena (e.g., the trajectory of a ball shot from a cannon), Newton's explanation of these phenomena, predictions made possible by this theory, and summaries of experiments conducted by physicists who wanted to see if Newton was right.

Lest it be thought that only scientists have theories, a recent line of research has revealed that nonscientists (including children) have theories too (Carey, 1985; Gelman & Coley, 1991; Weiner, 1986; Wellman, 1990). Nonscientists try to explain many of the same phenomena that scientists have studied. However, nonscientists often develop incorrect theories because they have less education in the sciences. For example, a parent might develop the theory that solid food helps her infant sleep through the night because it is "heavy." A pediatrician would know that this view is incorrect, because it is inconsistent with scientific accounts of an infant's metabolism and because it has been disconfirmed in studies. Similarly, an adolescent might think that a dog who lost its tail in an accident would have offspring who lack tails too. A geneticist would know that this theory is incorrect, because she would say that experience of this sort does not alter genes and genes transmit traits between generations.

When someone has a theory for some phenomenon but lacks advanced education in a science, we say that this person has a "naive" theory. Thus, the explanations given by the parent or adolescent would be part of their "naive biologies." Naive theories function for nonscientists the same way that they do for scientists; namely, they explain phenomena and allow for predictions. Scientific theories, however, are more accurate, elaborate, and precise (particularly with respect to the nature of mechanisms). Some researchers prefer the term *alternative frameworks* over *naive theories* because the former has a less negative connotation than the latter (Eylon & Linn, 1988).

In addition to explaining and predicting things, theories also play a role in how we mentally group things. In particular, it is common for both scientists and nonscientists to group objects together into various categories after they have developed theories to explain the characteristics of these objects. For example, zoologists try to explain the characteristics of animals (e.g., mammary glands) and botanists try to explain the characteristics of plants (e.g., year-round green leaves). After finding adequate explanations of an animal's characteristics, zoologists created taxonomic categories of these animals (e.g., mammals, fish, crustaceans, etc.) and botanists did the same for plants (e.g., evergreens, deciduous trees, etc.). All major sciences include such taxonomic categories, but the categories that derive from some theories are not so obvious. For example, psychologists have created categories of children based on what they can do (e.g., "concrete operational" children, "learning disabled" children, etc.).

History has shown that whenever a theory changes, the categories change as well. For example, at one time, whales were considered fish until notions such as *self-regulating temperature* (i.e., warm-blooded) were developed in zoological theories. After the zoological theories changed and we knew more about whales, whales were recategorized as mammals.

Individual Differences

The discussion so far has examined the general characteristics of theories. In this section, we consider how theories might differ among individuals of the same age group. In addressing the issue of individual differences, one asks, "If we focus on just one age group, do all people in this age group have similar theories or do some people have different theories than others?" To answer this question, we can pose another question: "What could cause people of the same age to develop different theories?"

Research has shown that the answer to the second question is straightforward: Two peers will have different theories if they have had different personal experiences or different amounts of education in particular topics. To illustrate the first case, consider studies that have shown that women who have had children tend to have different "naive developmental psychologies" than women without children or even their husbands (Holden, 1988). To illustrate the second case, consider that experts have more elaborate and detailed theories than novices. For example, a 26-year-old graduate student in physics will have a vastly different theory of physics than a 26-year-old accountant (Chi, Glaser & Rees, 1982).

These claims regarding the role of experience and education in theory development have implications for gender differences in theories. Given that females tend to take fewer science classes in high school than males and tend to have fewer informal experiences related to physical sciences, it should not be surprising to learn that males perform better than females on science achievement tests (Linn & Hyde, 1989). That is, males tend to know more science facts than females (see Chapter 12).

One way teachers can elicit the naive beliefs of students is to present them with a phenomenon that requires an explanation (e.g., why a 12-ounce can of regular Coke sinks in a bucket of water when a 12-ounce can of Diet Coke does not). Then, they can ask small groups of students to devise a theory of the phenomenon. Teachers will find that nearly every group will come up with a theory that differs from those of other groups. Discussion can then ensue about how to decide which (if any) of these theories is right.

Developmental Differences

There are a variety of ways in which theories develop between infancy and adulthood. Early in development, theories seem to start off as a network of correlations between pairs of environmental events or pairs of characteristics (Keil, 1991). For example, a young child might notice the covariation between pushing her glass over (Event 1) and her milk splashing to the floor (Event 2), and that between having a deep voice (Characteristic 1) and being a man (Characteristic 2). Children seem to use the covariance rule that if one event frequently co-occurs with another, the two events are causally connected (Bullock, Gelman & Baillargeon, 1982). They also understand the "temporal order" rule, which specifies that the second event is caused by the first event. In addition, they are more likely to believe that there is a causal relation between two events if (a) the time gap between the first event and the second is short (the "temporal proximity" rule), and (b) the objects or people involved are close together or make contact (the "spatial proximity" rule) (Shultz, 1982).

In the case of characteristics or traits, three of the four causal rules would apply, because when an object always has the same two characteristics, one of the object's characteristics co-occurs with the other, the two characteristics are present at the same time, and they are spatially close together because they are part of the same object or person. Because one characteristic would not always precede the appearance of another, the "temporal order" rule would not apply and people would not necessarily think that one characteristic causes another. But, of course, the trait "has wings" does cause the trait "can fly" (Keil, 1991) and the trait "large Adam's apple" does cause the trait "deep voice."

Regardless of whether events or characteristics are at issue, children will attribute a causal relation when the four causal rules apply (i.e., covariation, temporal order, etc.). What is missing in their causal analysis, however, is knowledge of the mechanism responsible for the consistent covariation. In the absence of knowledge of causal mechanisms, children and adults will attribute causality anyway if what they observe conforms to the four causal rules (Keil, 1991; Piaget & Garcia, 1974). That is, they seem to form a belief such as "I know that these things are causally related, but I don't yet know how or why" (Keil, 1991; Gelman & Coley, 1991). For example, I and most people know very little about how a car engine works. Nevertheless, we all still believe that we cause our car to start up when we turn the key.

When we learn about mechanisms, our causal beliefs are strengthened considerably. Many teachers, for example, believe that their teaching techniques are effective but are not quite sure why. After learning about Piaget's theory or Schema theory, teachers often learn of the mechanisms responsible for their success. This knowledge in turn reinforces their original beliefs.

But there are occasions when things happen so quickly that we do not have time to consider temporal order, consistent co-occurrence, and so on. In fact, we do not need to experience things ourselves to attribute causality. All we need is information about mechanisms that makes sense to us. Some studies have shown, for example, that knowledge of causal mechanisms can be more important than the four causal rules when children and adolescents form causal judgments (Shultz, 1982; Koslowski & Okagaki, 1986). For example, someone who has never driven in a car or turned the key herself might nevertheless come to believe that turning the key starts up the car after taking a class that explains how a car engine works.

So early on in development, children use the four causal rules to create mental networks of correlated events and characteristics. They do not yet know the details of the causal mechanisms involved, but they suspect that there must be *some* mechanism involved. Over time, they invent mechanisms (Piaget & Garcia, 1974) or learn about them in school and add this information to the correlation network. In the absence of instruction, most of the mechanisms that children and adults invent are almost always incorrect. Thus, continued instruction ultimately causes children's and adult's theories to change from being "naive" to being "scientific."

The second major way that theories develop is that they move from being implicit or unconscious mental structures to conscious ideas that can be reflected upon (Karmiloff-Smith & Inhelder, 1974; Kuhn, 1992). In a sense, children become more metacognitive about their theories with age (Baker & Piburn, 1990). By *conscious* and *metacognitive* we mean that a child would come to understand what kind of evidence would show that her theory is wrong, and would also be able to compare the merits of her theory to the merits of someone else's theory. For example, consider our adolescent above who was thinking about dogs without tails. To think metacognitively about his genetic theory, he would have to know what kind of evidence would prove his theory right and wrong. He might say, "Well, if I surgically remove a dog's tail, my theory would be right if the dog's puppies are born without tails. It would be wrong if the puppies are born with tails." He would also be have to able to compare and contrast his genetic view with, say, the Darwinian view.

The third way that theories develop concerns mental categories: When theories change, the categories that a child constructs change as well (Carey, 1985; Gelman & Coley, 1991). Similar to how scientists recategorized whales as mammals when their zoological theories changed, children recategorize things when their theories change. For example, young children initially group things according to how similar these objects are to a prototype (Carey, 1985). For example, the prototypical animal is a dog. If something looks like a dog, children will categorize it as an animal. However, when they learn in school that animals are living things that can move themselves, have limited growth, and have nonphotosynthetic metabolism, children come to realize that people and insects are animals too. The ability to reason about categories has been found to relate significantly to science achievement in schools (Piburn, 1990).

The developmental work suggests, then, that both younger and older students could quickly learn the covariation between two events (a rubber ball becoming brittle after being dipped in liquid nitrogen), but only the older ones could probably understand the explanations of why things turned out as they did (e.g., why the ball became brittle and broke). The reason young students would have trouble with scientific explanations is that many are either too abstract or too discrepant from the naive explanations of students to be interpretable. It seems clear, then, that only those phenomena that have easy-to-visualize or easy-to-demonstrate causal mechanisms should be discussed in the elementary grades (e.g., the operation of gears in simple machines). Because so few explanations involve clearly understood mechanisms, it makes sense that elementary teachers avoid explanations and spend most of their time teaching classification schemes (e.g., animal families; types of trees; etc.). The problem with this approach, however, is that students will fail to see science as the problem-solving activity that it is.

Scientific Misconceptions

The topic of scientific misconceptions is currently one of the most popular research topics in science education. Studies in this area show that instead of coming to science class with a mind that is a "blank slate," students come to class with minds that are filled with a variety of informal or intuitive conceptions that do not square with the scientific concepts taught in class. For example, students come to class with their own concepts of *force* or *temperature* that are quite different from the concepts of *force* and *temperature* taught in their science classes (Linn, 1986). The conflict between their informal conceptions and those taught in class causes them to distort or forget the proper conceptualizations. Because a student's intuitive concepts deviate from the conceptions endorsed by a larger scientific community, the intuitive concepts are frequently called "misconceptions."

Before examining the research on misconceptions, it first is useful to understand how scientific concepts relate to theories. In most instances, a *concept* is a part of a scientific explanation. For example, concepts such as *force* and *gravity* are part of a physicist's explanation for why objects move the way they do. Similarly, *bonding, molecule, atom,* and *reaction* are part of a chemist's explanation of processes such as corrosion and fermentation. Finally, concepts such as *encoding* and *retrieval* are part of a psychologist's explanation for how people remember. In essence, then, a theory is made up of concepts. Therefore, when we say that a student has a misconception about a concept such as *force,* we are also saying that a portion of his or her naive theory of physics deviates from a scientific theory of physics.

To get a flavor of the way intuitive and scientific concepts differ, consider the tasks presented in Figures 9.1 and 9.2. For Figure 9.1, draw a line to indicate the trajectory of the ball when the string is cut just as the ball reaches Point A. For Figure 9.2, draw lines indicating all forces that are acting on the horseshoe when it is tossed toward the peg. Done? Now examine Figures 9.3 and 9.4, which show how the lines should have been drawn. If you are like most people, you drew a curved line for the ball, and forces other than the force of gravity for the horseshoe.

At present, there are literally hundreds of studies that were conducted to document the extent of misconceptions in students. Most studies reveal a wide range of misconceptions. For example, one study revealed 52 different misconceptions regarding atoms and molecules in a sample of twelfth graders (Griffiths & Preston, 1992). Some students believed that a water molecule was as big as a speck of dust and others thought that it became bigger when heated.

It would not be surprising to learn that students have misconceptions before they take a physics or chemistry class. It took brilliant scientists such as Newton

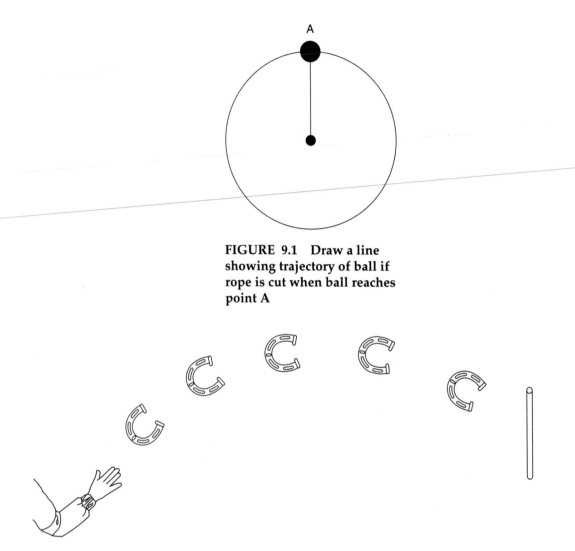

FIGURE 9.1 Draw a line showing trajectory of ball if rope is cut when ball reaches point A

FIGURE 9.2 Draw arrows for all forces acting on the horseshoe

many years to develop the proper conception of *force*. It is very unlikely that the average fifth grader would invent this concept on his or her own. And yet, standard instruction is not sufficient to eliminate misconceptions. Many studies show that certain misconceptions persist even after students take science classes (e.g., Abraham et al., 1992; BouJaoude, 1992; Clement, 1982; Garnett & Treagust, 1992; McCloskey, 1983).

Why do students have misconceptions? The principal reason seems to be that many science concepts have to do with abstractions or nonobservable entities.

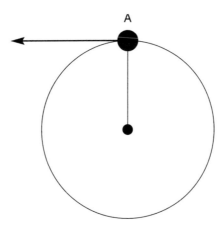

FIGURE 9.3 The trajectory of the ball if rope cut at "A"

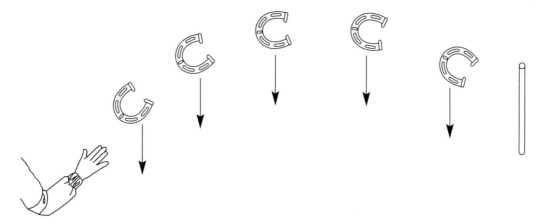

FIGURE 9.4 Arrows indicate that only the force of gravity is acting on the horseshoe

Consider the concept of density (i.e., mass per unit volume of a substance). By sight and feel, a 12-ounce can of regular Coke and a 12-once can of diet Coke seem to be the same. But if you put both in a tub of water, the diet Coke floats and the regular Coke sinks. This counter-intuitive result occurs because diet Coke is less dense than water (i.e., less mass per unit volume) and regular Coke is more dense. Students have difficulty with this concept because whereas you can see the can's size and feel its weight, you cannot directly perceive its density. Thus, if a teacher were to use the "Coke" task to elicit student theories, it is likely that many misconceptions about density would be revealed. In fact, any physical phenomenon is likely to reveal misconceptions in younger students because the true explanation probably involves abstract mechanisms.

The findings from the studies of misconceptions are significant for several reasons. First, studies show that teachers seem to be unaware that their students have misconceptions (e.g., Abraham et al., 1992). The mismatch between a teacher's perception and a researcher's perception probably arises from the fact that researchers ask children different questions than teachers do. In class, many science teachers are most concerned about children's learning the proper science "vocabulary" (e.g., what *photosynthesis* means) and usually teach "at" students (Carey, 1986; Roth, 1994). Although a child could get an *A* on a test by learning vocabulary and other facts by rote, such a child would probably not understand the concepts behind this information. Researchers, in contrast, ask questions that require deeper understanding, such as "Can a molecule be weighed by a scale?" and "Does a molecule get bigger when it is heated?" If teachers asked such questions and found out that their students did not truly understand what they presented, they would clearly try to modify their teaching. One way to modify things immediately is to spend more time asking questions of students rather than presenting information in a lecture format.

The second reason misconceptions are significant is that if the concepts that make up a person's theory are inaccurate, then he or she will make a number of inaccurate predictions. Moreover, a person with inaccurate concepts will attempt to control the wrong variables. For example, Newton and his followers espoused the concept of *ether* (a gaseous substance presumed to "fill up" the space between planets and other heavenly bodies). In the late 1800s, researchers finally gave up the idea of *ether* after studies repeatedly failed to find evidence of this substance.

Individual Differences

Although there are certain misconceptions that almost all students develop before instruction, there is a variety of other misconceptions that only one or two students in a classroom develop. Thus, studies show a wide range of individual differences in the number and type of misconceptions held by students (Griffiths & Preston, 1992; Heller & Finley, 1992). For example, Griffiths and Preston (1992) found that only six of a total of 52 misconceptions were held by more than half of their sample.

Even when a common misconception is revealed, studies show that people differ in terms of how strongly they cling to this misconception. For example, some students are very reluctant to give up the belief that energy flows through wires in an electrical circuit. Other students more readily give up this belief after instruction (Heller & Finley, 1992). Each student, then, seems to have "core" beliefs that are held with a high degree of certainty and "peripheral" beliefs that they readily change to defend their core beliefs (Linn, 1986; Kuhn et al., 1988).

At present, it is not at all clear why some misconceptions are held by many students and why some are held by only a few students. We also do not know why some beliefs end up as core beliefs and others end up as peripheral beliefs. The reason for this lack of knowledge is that we still do not have a clear sense of where misconceptions come from. Whereas there is some evidence that textbooks contribute to the problem (Abraham et al., 1992) and other evidence that many teachers have misconceptions (Heller & Finley, 1992), we still need more information on the various sources of misconceptions. Once all of these sources are identified, we can then try to determine how these sources contribute to individual differences.

Finally, of the hundreds of studies conducted on misconceptions, only a few studies report gender differences. Thus, males and females seem to form similar misconceptions and do so to a similar extent.

Developmental Differences

Most studies of misconceptions have revealed the faulty beliefs of a single age group, and only a handful of studies have considered whether children at different ages hold different misconceptions. As a result, it is difficult to draw developmental conclusions about this research. Perhaps the only conclusion that can be drawn is that misconceptions can be found at virtually all age levels. Most studies, however, have interviewed students either just before or just after they took a science course (e.g., physics). As a result, the majority of studies have interviewed middle school, high school, or college students. There is, then, a need for more developmental research in this area especially using preadolescent students as subjects.

Functional Aspects of Scientific Thinking

Whereas structural aspects of scientific thinking have to do with what people know about scientific concepts, facts, or phenomena, functional aspects have to do with what people do when they try to solve a scientific problem. Two functional aspects of scientific thinking are described next: hypothesis-testing and experimentation techniques.

Hypothesis-Testing

Hypotheses derive from a person's theory and are predictions about the way things will turn out if the theory is true. A common way to state a hypothesis is to use an "if . . . then" sentence (Piburn, 1990; Ward, Byrnes & Overton, 1990). For example, someone who believes in Einstein's theory of relativity might form the hypothesis that "If an astronaut in space had a watch and someone on Earth had one too, we'd find that the astronaut's watch would run slower." Similarly, someone who believes in Bowlby's theory of infant attachment might form the hypothesis that "If we placed a 12-month-old in a room with a stranger, she'd start to cry." If things turn out the way a scientist predicts (e.g., the watch in space does run slower), that means that a portion of his theory could well be correct. If things do not turn out as predicted, that means that a portion of his theory may not be correct. Thus, hypothesis-testing is an important way for scientists to know whether or not their theories are correct.

To assess the ability to test hypotheses, the first thing to do is to either (a) have students create their own hypotheses or (b) present them with ready-made hypotheses. To get them to create a hypothesis, you could ask them "what would happen if" questions (e.g., "What would happen if you rolled a ball off this table?"). After a hypothesis is either created or presented, the next step is to introduce evidence that either does or does not have a bearing on the accuracy of the hypothesis. Once again you could have them gather their own evidence through experimentation and observation (e.g., "Roll the ball off a few times and see if you are right.") or present them with evidence. Finally, you need to have them *evaluate* the evidence; that is, they need to judge whether their prediction was correct (e.g., "All right, here's what happened when someone rolled the ball. Was your prediction right?").

Early Studies of Hypothesis-Testing

Early studies did not attempt to link up a person's theories with his or her hypotheses. Instead, people were asked to form hypotheses about arbitrary relations of colors, shapes, or numbers. For example, Bruner, Goodnow, and Austin (1956) presented adults with a shape of a certain color and had them guess whether it "fit a rule." After subjects made a guess (e.g. "this red square fits"), they were told if they were right or wrong. If they were told that the shape did fit the rule, they had to form a hypothesis regarding the basis for grouping all shapes that received a "Yes." For example, subjects might be shown a variety of shapes and learn that a red circle, red square, and red triangle all received a "Yes." They might then form the hypothesis that the group consists of "red things." Thus, people were presented with evidence (i.e., the shapes) and then asked to create a hypothesis to account for the evidence.

Table 9.1 shows two other classic tasks that also involve relations that bear no relation to a person's scientific theories: the "4-card" and "2–4–6" tasks. Pre-

TABLE 9.1   Hypothesis Testing Tasks

The Four-Card Task

Rule: If there is a vowel on one side of a card, there is an even number on the other side.

| A | D | 7 | 4 |

Which of the four cards above would you definitely need to turn over in order to see whether the rule has been broken?

The 2–4–6 Task

I am using a rule to generate three numbers. Your job is to keep giving me three numbers that you think fit the rule I used. When you are sure that you know the rule, tell me what the rule is. O.K. Three numbers that fit the rule are 2–4–6. Now you give me sets of numbers that fit the rule. When you are sure know the rule, tell me what it is.

sumably, researchers who used all of these tasks were interested in *abstract* or *general* hypothesis-testing ability and did not want to help or artificially inflate adults' performances by allowing them to rely on their prior knowledge. What are the "right" ways of behaving on Bruner et al's task and the tasks in Table 9.1? According to philosophers of science (e.g., Popper, 1950), adults in these studies should not have sought evidence that would confirm (i.e., support the truth of) a rule. Rather, they should make sure that no evidence exists that *disconfirms* the rule. In this view, it makes little sense to keep trying to prove that an initial hypothesis is right by gathering data that supports or confirms this hypothesis, because things could continually turn out as you predict for the *wrong reasons*.

To illustrate this point using a meaningful example, suppose you have a theory that vitamin C helps people fend off colds. To test out this theory, you set up the hypothesis "If someone feeling a cold coming on takes vitamin C, that person will not get the cold." To prove this hypothesis, you ask three people you know who feel like they are getting a cold to take vitamin C for several days. After letting the vitamin C have a chance to work, you call you friends to see how things went. You find that all three did not get a cold. You conclude, "You see, I was right!"

What is wrong with this thinking? To show that vitamin C matters, you should have contacted a larger number of people and followed them for the same amount of time. Some of these people should have taken vitamin C and some should not have (see below). What you should be looking for is not so much the people who took the vitamin C and avoided the cold, but the people who took vitamin C but got a cold anyway. By trying to prove yourself wrong, you would have found data against your hypothesis. By trying to prove yourself right, you may not have discovered this disconfirming data and would probably not think of other reasons your friends failed to get colds (e.g., perhaps they really were not coming down with colds). The tendency to only look for confirming cases has been called the "confirmation bias."

Besides keeping you from thinking of other reasons the data turned out the way you expected, another problem with the confirmation bias is that even though a hypothesis turns out to be true right now, it could always be proved wrong in the future. Philosophers use the example of swans to illustrate this point. Consider a man named Harry who finds that every swan he has ever seen is white. It would be wrong for him to infer that "all swans are white," because there exists a species of black swans. It just happens that Harry has not encountered black swans yet. Consider next our vitamin C example again. It is possible that the first three people you contact and give vitamin C do not get colds, but the next ten who take vitamin C get the colds anyway. By stopping at the first three, you would never have encountered the last ten.

The confirmation bias has been found in a variety of experiments since the 1950s. Adults and children show a strong tendency to seek confirmation of their favorite hypotheses instead of trying to disconfirm their own or rival hypotheses (Schauble, 1990; Kuhn et al., 1988; Mynatt, Doherty & Tweney, 1977; Wason, 1983). For example, they choose just the *D* card in the four-card task (see Table 9.1), or continually generate three numbers that are consistent with a rule in the

2–4–6 task (e.g., 2–4–6, 6–8–10, 12–14–16, etc. for the rule "Even numbers that increase by 2").

According to philosophers of science in the logical positivist tradition, this persistent confirmation bias demonstrates that children and adults rarely show high levels of scientific thinking. Others, however, argue that the behavior of children and adults is perfectly appropropriate (e.g., Klayman & Ha, 1987; Koslowski and Maqueda, 1993). In the first place, it makes sense to first gather data to see if certain variables (e.g., the thickness of the ozone layer) correlate with certain other variables (e.g., the skin cancer rate). Once this covariation is established and a theory is developed to explain the relationship, one can then look for data that disconfirms the theory (e.g., historical times when the ozone was even thinner and the cancer rate was less than it is now).

Second, Koslowski and Maqueda (1993) argue that scientists often gather data that not only support the causal relation that they favor but also simultaneously disconfirm other, alternative explanations. For example, you might believe that the main causal determinant of a girl's math achievement is her parent's beliefs. In contrast, a rival scientist believes that parental beliefs do not matter, only genes do. To prove that you are right and your rival is wrong, you find pairs of identical twins who are separated at birth. Then, you find a subset of pairs in which one twin was raised by sexist parents and the other was raised by nonsexists. Finally, you discover that parental beliefs are more important than genes because only the twins who have sexist parents differed in math achievement. Koslowski and Maqueda argue that an outside observer who casually observes your experiment might think that you are just trying to prove the correctness of your own "parental belief" hypothesis. If the observer were to probe further, he or she would see that you are also falsifying the genetic account. Thus, Koslowski and Maqueda argue that many of the hypothesis-testing studies need to be reexamined in order to see whether children and adults were not trying to simultaneously confirm their own hypotheses while disconfirming other, rival hypotheses.

Notwithstanding these arguments, however, there is evidence that children and adults pay attention to only that data which is consistent with their theory and will distort or ignore evidence that is contrary to their favored theory (Karmiloff-Smith & Inhelder, 1974; Kuhn et al., 1988; Shustack, 1988). This, too, is indicative of a confirmation bias. Let's say that you have the hypothesis that left-handed females are good in math (because their brains are more like a male's brain). Frequently, you meet females with high levels of math ability, but only notice the left-handed ones because being left-handed is more salient than being right-handed. Thus, the left-handed ones stand out and make you think that left-handedness goes with good math ability.

In the midst of conducting experiments with their students, it is very important for teachers to point out disconfirming data to them. In fact, constructing labs so that the data generated in them will disconfirm existing misconceptions should be a central tactic in science classes. It is only through disconfirmation that theories and misconceptions can change.

Besides behaviors related to the confirmation bias, researchers have found other behaviors that seem to conflict with the proposals advanced by philosophers of science. For example, logical positivists argue that when evidence is found that suggests that your hypothesis is wrong, you should abandon this hypothesis and create a completely new one. Instead of doing so, however, children, adults, and scientists seem to cling to hypotheses even when disconfirming data arises. People are especially likely to do so if they feel certain that they are correct (Kuhn et al., 1988; Lakatos, 1971). For example, a scientist might observe the radiation coming from a distant planet and come to believe that the planet must have moons. She looks through her telescope, however, and sees no moons. Instead of abandoning her hypothesis, she continually builds stronger and stronger telescopes to find moons.

As was the case for the confirmation bias, the act of clinging to a hypothesis in the face of disconfirming data has been interpreted as being irrational by some scientists and perfectly reasonable by others (Koslowski & Maqueda, 1993; Nisbett & Ross, 1980). Koslowski and Maqueda, for example, argue that although most scientists tend to retain a working hypothesis after encountering data that disconfirms it, they also use the disconfirming data to *modify* rather than discard the hypothesis. Many important and less important discoveries would have been missed had an initial hypothesis been totally abandoned rather than modified. To illustrate, consider our vitamin C example above. It might be that a person needs to *both* have a specific antibody to cold viruses and take vitamin C in order to avoid a cold (because vitamin C speeds up the duplication of the antibody). If someone took vitamin C and got a cold anyway, it would be wrong to conclude that taking vitamin C has no effect on colds. Moreover, just as it makes sense to repeat an experiment to make sure a causal relationship exists, it makes sense to repeat an experiment to make sure a causal relationship does *not* exist. Problems arise only when a person clings to a hypothesis after numerous disconfirming cases or modifies it in implausible ways.

Individual Differences

The discussion so far has centered around hypothesis-testing behaviors that are characteristic of most people. In this section, we will examine ways in which one person differs from another. It is the case that some people demonstrate appropriate hypothesis-testing behaviors; that is, they try to (a) disconfirm rather than confirm their hypotheses, (b) take into account all evidence, not just that which is consistent with their views, and (c) modify or discard hypotheses when disconfirming data accumulate. Such people tend to be in the minority, but they clearly differ from individuals who demonstrate all of the biases described above. At present, we lack an explanation of why some people perform as they should and why some do not. Increased education seems to covary with higher levels of performance (e.g., Kuhn et al., 1988; Kuhn, 1992), but it is not at all clear why only *some* of the individuals with the same education demonstrate high levels of performance. It would be quite valuable to discover how certain individuals are able to take advantage of their education so that we could know how to elevate the performance of those who do not.

A second type of individual difference has emerged in several recent studies of hypothesis-testing. David Klahr and his associates (Klahr & Dunbar, 1988; Dunbar & Klahr, 1989) discovered that adults adopted one of two approaches when they hypothesized about the behavior of a small robot. The robot walked forward, turned, and made noises depending on which buttons on a control pad were pushed. For example, the → button told it to turn a certain number of degrees and the *hold* button told it to do nothing for a certain period of time. If someone pressed the sequence, → *15 hold 50 fire* 2 the robot would turn right, pause for 50 seconds, and then fire two shots. After learning how several buttons worked, subjects were next asked to discover how a repeat button worked. For example, imagine what might happen when the command "repeat 2" is added to the string of three commands above (making it the 4th and last command). Most people initially thought that the command "repeat 2" meant "do the three-action sequence twice." In reality, it meant "do the last two actions again (i.e. hold 50 and fire 2)."

About one-third of Klahr & Dunbar's subjects tested the first erroneous hypothesis until they encountered several instances of disconfirming data. After realizing that they needed a new hypothesis, they consulted their knowledge for other hypotheses and then engaged in new experiments. These subjects (whom Klahr & Dunbar called "theorists") seemed to say, "Huh! I guess the 2 doesn't mean do the whole thing 2 times. But what else could the 2 stand for? Maybe it stands for the second command. Maybe it stands for the last 2 commands . . ." Klahr and Dunbar called the remaining two-thirds of subjects "experimenters." Unlike the "theorists," "experimenters" did not discover the correct rule by relying on their knowledge. Rather, after realizing that their initial hypothesis was wrong, they first conducted a number of experiments and then induced a hypothesis that was consistent with the behavior of the robot.

The difference in style between theorists and experimenters did not result in one group's having more success than the other. All but one or two adults discovered how the *repeat* key worked. Instead, the difference between groups was manifested in how *efficient* they were in discovering how the *repeat* button worked. It took the experimenters twice as much time to discover the correct function because they conducted twice as many experiments as theorists.

In contrast to the findings regarding gender differences in theories, no gender differences have emerged in studies of hypothesis-testing (Kuhn et al., 1988; Meehan, 1984).

Developmental Differences

In general, the developmental research suggests that adults tend to have more hypothesis-testing skill than children. In particular, adults are more likely than children to (a) know what kind of evidence would support the truth of a hypothesis and what kind of evidence would disconfirm it (Overton, 1990), (b) seek evidence to disconfirm a favored hypothesis (Bruner et al., 1956), and (c) discard or modify a hypothesis on the basis of disconfirming evidence (Dunbar & Klahr, 1989; Koslowski & Maqueda, 1993; Schauble, 1990). Moreover, adults are less likely to demonstrate a confirmation bias than children or young adolescents. This is not to say that all adults engage in appropriate hypothesis-testing. Rather, it is best to say that a greater percentage of adults engage in appropriate hypothesis-testing than children do.

In addition, the size of the developmental differences depends on the meaningfulness of the content. Differences are smaller when adults and children have similar amounts of knowledge (Carey, 1985). Differences are larger when (a) hypotheses refer to arbitrary or abstract relations (e.g., Table 9.1) or (b) adults have more knowledge in the domain from which hypotheses derive. To illustrate the latter assertion, consider several studies of Dunbar and Klahr (1989). Whereas 95 percent of adults in their first experiment discovered the correct operation of the *repeat* key, only 5 percent of eight- to 11-year-olds in their third experiment did. Adults apparently knew from prior programming experience that numbers could refer to line numbers (e.g., "Go to 10" means "go to line 10"). Due to less experience and education, children apparently thought that a number could only refer to the number of times something occurred. Thus, they fixated on interpretations such as "*repeat 5*" means "perform all actions five times." In general, the more knowledge someone has, the greater number of hypotheses he or she can construct. Because adults tend to have more knowledge than children, they can generate a greater variety of plausible hypotheses. This ability in conjunction with their greater tendency to reject hypotheses in the face of disconfirming evidence means that adults will more often discover the correct relation among the variables under study.

The implication of this finding is that students should either be taught effective hypothesis-testing using moderately familiar material or spend a lot of time becoming familiar with a topic before they begin experimentation. Unfortunately, studies show that labs typically have little to do with the material concurrently presented in lectures or students' texts (Roth, 1994), so it once again makes sense that few students seem to demonstrate high levels of hypothesis-testing skills.

Experimentation Techniques

In addition to having an accurate theory and setting up hypotheses, good scientific thinking consists of knowing the best ways to gather data to test hypotheses. In most instances, this "best way" is a properly controlled experiment. Why? Consider our vitamin C example again. Imagine that the real factor that determines whether you will succumb to a cold is the existence of a particular antibody in your immune system. If you have this antibody, you will successfully fend off the invading virus. If you lack the antibody (or your immune system is under stress for some reason), you will catch the cold. Lets say that Joe has the antibody and takes vitamin C for three days. If he fends off the cold, it is really because he had the antibody, not because he took the vitamin C. Thus, Joe's belief that the vitamin C helped would be fallacious.

How could Joe have avoided this error? He should have done the following. First, he should take the vitamin C for this cold and document what happens. He should note whether he was under stress, had another ailment, was eating properly, and getting enough sleep. Second, he should wait until he feels another cold coming on and then repeat the entire procedure except for taking the vitamin C. If everything is the same except for the presence versus absence of vitamin C (i.e., he was under similar amounts of stress, slept the same, and so on), then this would constitute a reasonably conclusive test. If he fends off the cold with the vitamin C but gets a cold without it, he should conclude that vitamin C helps. Otherwise, he should believe that vitamin C does not matter. If Joe ever did conduct such a test, he would find that vitamin C does not help. Upon learning this, he should search for another factor that determines whether he gets sick (e.g., the antibody in his immune system).

The technique of varying one variable (e.g., vitamin C) while holding all other variables constant (e.g., the amount of sleep, etc.) has been given various labels, including the "isolation of variables scheme" (Inhelder & Piaget, 1958), "separation of variables scheme" (Martorano, 1975) and "controlling variables strategy" (Linn, Clement & Pulos, 1983). Regardless of the label, this technique is considered a central aspect of good scientific thinking, because scientists are always striving to distinguish between genuine causal relations and illusory causal relations. That is their job. If scientists do not conduct properly controlled experiments, they will often conclude that an illusory causal relation is a real causal relation. Hence, they will be performing their job poorly. Their false beliefs about a suspected causal relation will in turn engender many false or groundless theories, because theories are explanations of purported causal relationships. To see this, consider how a physician might uncritically accept flawed data about vitamin C and develop an elaborate theory of how vitamin C works in the body to prevent a cold.

Individual differences

Two factors have been found to produce individual differences in the tendency to control variables. The first is an individual's preexisting theories. When presented with a situation in which four or five variables could produce an outcome, people do not tend to control all of these presented variables. Instead, they use their preexisting theories to decide which variables *could* relate to an outcome and then control just those variables (Linn & Swiney, 1981; Kuhn et al., 1988; Schauble, 1990). People who have different theories would then control different variables. For example, pretend that you and a friend are asked to decide which of the following variables affects the gas mileage of a car: (a) how fast it is driven, (b) how heavy it is, (c) the type of muffler it has, and (d) its color. In conducting an experiment, you might think of controlling the first two variables while ignoring the other two. For example, to test the role of weight, you compare the gas mileage of a heavy car that is driven at 30 mph to a light car driven at the same speed (ignoring the color and type of muffler on each). You might do so because you think that a car's color and muffler have no effect on its gas mileage. You would be right in the case of color, but wrong in the case of the muffler. Your friend, in contrast, knew that mufflers relate to gas mileage so she controlled mufflers in her tests.

The second individual difference variable concerns the way people process visual information. Some people can appropriately perceive a certain visual stimulus even when other stimuli surrounding the stimulus are distracting. Such individuals are called "field independent." Individuals who cannot perceive the focal stimulus because they cannot overcome the distracting information are called "field dependent." Research has shown that field independent subjects are more likely to control variables than field dependent subjects, presumably because only the former perceive and control variables that have less obvious or subtle effects (Linn, 1978; Linn, Pulos & Gans, 1981).

Similar to the research on hypothesis-testing, essentially no gender differences have emerged in the studies that have examined the ability to control variables (Kuhn & Brannock, 1977; Meehan, 1984; Roberge & Flexer, 1979). Overton and Meehan (1982), however, found that females who were identified as "learned helpless" performed worse than nonhelpless males and females on an isolation of variables task.

Developmental Differences

The first wave of developmental research tried to substantiate Inhelder and Piaget's (1958) claim that the "isolation of variables" scheme does not emerge until age 11 or 12. What these researchers found was both good news and bad news for Piagetians. The good news was that children below the age of ten seldom controlled variables when given the same tasks that Piaget used (e.g., the pendulum task). Although adolescents and adults did control variables on these tasks, the bad news was that only about 40 percent of them did (Keating, 1980). Thus, most of the subsequent research in this area did not try to answer the basic question "When does the isolation of variables scheme first emerge in development?" Rather, the question became "Why do so few adolescents and adults control variables and is there anything we can do to improve their performance?"

The research that tried to answer the second question revealed that the performance of adolescents and adults can be greatly affected by (a) the content of the task, (b) the questions asked, and (c) training or feedback (Kuhn et al., 1988; Linn, 1978; Linn et al., 1983; Linn, Pulos & Gans, 1981; Stone & Day, 1978). For example, whereas only 40 percent of subjects control variables when given a pendulum and asked "Which factor affects the rate of oscillation, the weight or the length of string?", 90 percent will control variables when asked to determine which of two types of seeds produces a bigger plant. In addition, multiple-choice questions produce a greater percentage of correct answers than free-response questions, especially in older adolescents. Finally, short training sessions or simple forms of feedback can elevate the performance of adolescents and adults up to 90 percent correct.

Variations in content and questions tend to have little effect on the performance of children below the age of ten. However, it is possible to reveal the isolation of variables schema in gifted eight-year-olds (Case, 1974) and average ten-year-olds (Siegler & Liebert, 1975) by using more intensive, longer-term training and by reducing the number of variables to control. For example, after training, gifted eight-year-olds will come to recognize that a comparison between a short thin rod and a long fat rod is not "a fair test" of the role of length in the rod's flexibility. Of course, recognizing an unfair test after training and devising a controlled experiment *on one's own* are two separate things. It is not difficult to elicit the latter skill in adolescents and adults, but it is distressing that many tend not to control variables unless prompted to do so.

What all of this research means is that, in everyday contexts, children younger than ten years of age and 60 percent of adolescents and adults are likely to believe that certain variables (e.g., vitamin C) are causally related to certain outcomes (e.g., avoiding a cold), when in fact they are not. The prevalence of such faulty reasoning can have serious consequences. Consider how a math teacher might see the covariation between high SAT math scores on one hand, and being male on the other. This data might lead him to believe that there is a genetic component to math ability. This belief may in turn cause him to favor boys in his class and treat girls as if they were unintelligent. Had he conducted a properly controlled experiment (or examined the literature to find one), he might find that his behavior toward his female students is unwarranted because his belief in the genetic component is not well established (see Chapter 12).

Summary

In this chapter we learned that scientists (a) create theories in order to explain scientific phenomena, (b) use their theories to form hypotheses (i.e., make predictions), and (c) conduct controlled experiments in order to verify the accuracy of their predictions. Nonscientists differ from scientists in that the former have "naive" (as opposed to "scientific") theories and frequently fail to conduct controlled experiments. As a result, nonscientists often form and retain faulty causal beliefs (e.g., about the value of vitamin C), and frequently make inaccurate predictions.

We also learned that there are individual differences with respect to theories, hypothesis-testing, experimentation, and misconceptions. Most of these differences center around the idiosyncratic beliefs held by students and different styles of experimentation or hypothesis-testing. Gender differences have been found only on achievement tests requiring knowledge of scientific vocabulary and facts. Essentially no gender differences have been found for hypothesis-testing, experimentation, and misconceptions.

Finally, we found that there were developmental differences in several aspects of scientific thinking. In particular, children's theories tend to be less elaborate and accurate than adults' theories. In addition, children are more likely to demonstrate confirmation and perseveration biases than adults when they test hypotheses. Third, children can recognize the difference between a fair and unfair test after training but show little evidence of being able to employ the isolation of variables scheme to devise a multivariate, controlled experiment of their own. Although many adolescents and adults often fail to conduct controlled experiments in the absence of prompting, they will show high levels of skill when given feedback and prompting.

Implications for Teaching

As you might expect given previous chapters in this book, we shall end by first considering some general implications of the research on scientific thinking and then examine a case study of effective instruction that illustrates some of these guidelines.

General Guidelines

In many science classrooms, teachers have the goal of getting their students to master a series of facts and a specific scientific vocabulary. Little attempt is made to get children to think and act like scientists (Carey, 1986; Linn & Songer, 1993; Roth, 1994). In taking a "content mastery" approach, teachers convey the idea to children that scientific knowledge is fixed and absolute, rather than constantly changing. Many educators argue that this approach to science instruction is the reason students demonstrate confirmation biases, fail to spontaneously conduct controlled experiments, and hold many misconceptions. It is clear, then, that science education is in need of reform.

One promising way to reform science education is to move from the content mastery model of instruction to an *apprenticeship* model of instruction (Brown, Collins & Duguid, 1989; Linn & Songer, 1993; Roth, 1994). The primary goal of the apprenticeship model is to have students progressively internalize the beliefs and practices of working scientists. Ideally, the apprentice model should begin as soon as science instruction begins. Instead of mastering facts, students would observe scientific phenomena, propose explanations of these phenomena, and conduct controlled experiments to see if their theories are correct. In this way, laboratory exercises would not be totally divorced from everyday classroom lectures. Instead, labs would be at the *center* of instruction.

The role of teachers in the apprenticeship model is to help children construct experiments and point out how the data generated from experiments either support or contradict children's current theories. Teachers would not present vocabulary in isolation but would present scientific terms in the context of conversing with children about scientific phenomena or the results of experiments. That way, children would acquire a scientific vocabulary in the same way that they acquire other words in their natural language. If any lecturing is done, it would be historical in nature, pointing out how some of the misconceptions held by students were held by scientists many years ago (e.g., the "impetus" conception of force). Historical perspectives would also allow children to see that scientific knowledge is constantly changing.

In addition to these general implications, the research on scientific thinking has more specific instructional implications:

1. Teachers need to acknowledge the fact that their students have naive theories. Education should have the effect of changing students' naive theories into scientific theories. One of the best ways of effecting this change is to help children acquire a more accurate understanding of various theoretical mechanisms. Instruction should, therefore, focus directly on mechanisms.

2. Confirmation and perseveration (as in repetition) biases are fairly natural tendencies or "habits of mind" when students test hypotheses. These biases can be overcome if teachers repeatedly point out how to avoid them when experimental data is interpreted in class. But it should be noted that instruction that is limited to helping students avoid biases will not help them become better hypothesis-testers. Even if they avoid biases, students still need to have an accurate theory if they want to be successful at predicting outcomes.

3. With respect to experimentation, elementary students should be taught how to control variables in the manner of Case (1974) and Siegler and Liebert (1975); that is, they should have multiple experiences designing "fair tests." Due to information-processing limitations (see Chapter 2), these tests should involve only two variables. By the time these students enter middle school or high school, they probably will not need training or feedback to conduct a controlled experiment with two or more variables.

4. With respect to misconceptions, the main strategy should be to diagnose, confront, and remediate them. Teachers who are unaware of misconceptions and who simply lecture about science topics will not reduce or eliminate misconceptions in their students.

One promising strategy for remediating misconceptions is the use of "bridging" analogies (Brown, 1992). Bridging analogies were devised for cases in which the gap between an idea that you want your students to understand and those ideas that they already understand is too large to make a connection. To get a sense of this phenomenon, try to answer the following two questions: (a) When you put a book on a table, does the table exert a force on the book? and (b) When you press down on a spring with your hand, does the spring exert a force back on your hand? You may know that the answer to both questions is "Yes" but only really believe it is for the second one. Often teachers try to use examples like the one with the spring to help students understand the one about the book. However, the gap between the situations is too large for students to see a connection.

The logic behind bridging analogies is to progressively modify an example that students already understand (e.g., the spring example) until you have transformed it into the example that you want them to understand (e.g., the book example). For example, you could first ask the question above about the spring. Then, you could ask, "If you put a book on a spring, does the spring exert a force back on the book?" Next, you could ask, "If you put the book on a flexible board suspended over two sawhorses, would the board exert a force back on the book?" And finally, you would present them with the example of a book on a table. Brown (1992) found that this approach greatly reduced misconceptions about the concept of force in high school students.

A second approach to remediating misconceptions is to help learners become dissatisfied with their existing conceptions and find new, more accurate concepts to be intelligible, plausible and fruitful (Stofflett, 1994). To make new concepts more intelligible, it is important to make analogies to what students already know and understand. To make them more plausible, learners have to find them potentially believable and consistent with their experiences (experiences they are not thinking of). To be fruitful, learners have to recognize how new practical applications or experiments can arise from the new conceptions.

In all, there is a great deal that needs to be done in science classrooms in order for children to ultimately think and behave as scientists. Although achievement tests and many studies reveal flaws in students' thinking, a number of studies show that students can reveal scientific competence given sufficient amounts of advanced education. The emphasis now is on having students demonstrate proficiency well before they reach graduate school.

A Case Study

A study conducted by Hewson and Hewson (1983) illustrates many of the instructional implications of the research on scientific thinking described above. The students in their study were mostly Black ninth graders from Soweto, South Africa, who held many misconceptions about mass, volume, and density. Hewson and Hewson wanted students to become dissatisfied with their misconceptions and find the correct conceptions to be more intelligible, plausible, and fruitful. At the point at which instruction began, students had been taught the proper conception twice in previous years but still held on to the misconceptions.

There were three major segments to the instructional sequence. In the first part, the authors identified students' existing conceptions of, and misconceptions about, mass, volume, and density. Once they were identified, the goal was to have the students eliminate the misconceptions and replace them with correct conceptions.

For example, many students defined *density* as the packing of particles of different materials. Through discussion, the teacher had students exchange this definition for the definition that *density* involves both the packing of particles *and* the mass of the packed particles. Through workbook exercises, students also came to differentiate their idea that density is simply "crowdedness" into the idea that density involves the number of objects *per unit area*. In order for this differentiation and exchange of ideas to take place, the discussion and worksheet had to make the new ideas intelligible and plausible (e.g., by helping students envision the definition using metaphors such as the number of boxes in a room). Following these experiences, two discussions and three experiments were conducted. In the discussions, students were told about the facts that (a) density is the mass of something per unit volume (e.g., grams per cubic centimeter), (b) all matter has density, and (c) all matter has mass and volume. Through experiments, students came to characterize the relative density of objects (that one object is more dense than another) and that it is the density of an object and not its weight or volume that determines whether it will float. The floating experiments helped students see that something that is lighter may nevertheless sink while something that is heavier may nevertheless float. After being shown these contradictions, students became dissatisfied with their misconceptions and came to see how the correct conception was more fruitful (i.e., applicable to more cases).

Hewson and Hewson (1983) found that this new approach, which focused on misconceptions, was far more effective in promoting accurate conceptions of mass, volume, and density than standard instruction. In a recent study with preservice teachers using the intelligibility-plausibility-dissatisfaction (IPDF) model, Stofflett (1994) had similar success in changing student misconceptions about the nature of science teaching. In light of what we know about constructivism, Piagetian theory, and Schema theory (see Chapters 1 and 2), the success of these studies should not be surprising.

Social Studies Learning

Summary

1. The primary goals of social studies education are to help students (a) become knowledgeable and active citizens, (b) get in touch with their personal identities and values, and (c) develop a sensitivity to other cultures and values. Some of the core disciplines that comprise the social studies include history, geography, economics, and civics.

2. History educators want students to know the chronology of significant events and to understand why these events occurred and why they were significant. Moreover, they want students to see that historians interpret rather than merely record history. Research shows that although these tasks are progressively mastered by children as they move through school, many students do not attain high levels of competence by the time they leave high school.

3. Among other things, geography educators want students to be able to interpret maps as well as locate major land forms, bodies of water, regions of natural resources, and major cultural groups. Research shows that although map skills and location skills improve with age, many high school seniors and college students perform at mediocre levels.

4. Economics educators want students to be able to comprehend important concepts such as *profit* and *scarcity*. Research shows that children seem to pass through various levels of understanding of these concepts.

5. As far as civics is concerned, national tests show that students do not gain mastery over knowledge of our government and the rights and responsibilities of citizens until they are in the twelfth grade.

6. Many social studies educators argue that children's performance on social studies assessments would improve if we did not wait until the fourth or fifth grade to teach social studies in a significant way.

7. Although there are gender differences in some aspects of social studies knowledge, the differences between males and females are much smaller than those between White students and minority students.

Over the years, there have been many debates about the issue of which disciplines make up the social studies (Armento, 1986; Brophy, 1990). Whereas some experts limit the selection to geography, civics, and political science, others want to include history, psychology, and sociology as well. Thus, it is not currently possible to propose a definition of "the social studies" that everyone will agree with. Nevertheless, it is not a good idea to begin a chapter with only a vague sense of what it will be about. Therefore, let's propose a reasonable definition to gain some initial clarity: The social studies consist of an interrelated set of topics related to the history, environment, economics, lifestyles, and governments of peoples who live in this and other regions of the world. In this chapter, we will examine the literature on developmental and individual differences in students' learning of this kind of information.

Before delving into the literature, however, it is important to answer the following question: Why do students need to take classes in the social studies? Most experts agree that the content of social studies classes should help students do at least three things: (a) become knowledgeable and active citizens, (b) get in touch with their personal identities and values, and (c) develop a sensitivity to other cultures and values (Brophy, 1990).

To see the importance of this knowledge, consider what would happen if we never instilled it in students. Without an informed and active electorate, government officials would be free to do as they please. Moreover, many of the most important changes in society would not have taken place if it were not for volunteer citizen groups (e.g., the civil rights movement). Furthermore, without knowledge of other cultures and values, students might develop or retain biases against certain ethnic or religious groups and be inclined to impose their values on others.

In what follows, we shall examine the nature and development of social studies expertise. In the first section, we shall define social studies knowledge and skill. In the second section, we shall explore the development of this knowledge and skill. In the third section, we shall explore individual differences in social studies learning. In the fourth and final section, we shall explore the instructional implications of all of this work.

Expertise in the Social Studies

The model of education that seems to be driving many of the current educational reform movements is one that suggests that students should be encouraged to emulate professionals in specific fields. For example, we learned in Chapter 8 that math educators want students to be able to think like mathematicians by the time they leave the twelfth grade. Similarly, in Chapter 9 we saw that science educators want students to think and act like practicing scientists. Although many experts in the field of social studies education also argue that the goal of social studies instruction is to get students to think and act like social scientists, others argue instead that curricular decisions in the social studies should be guided more by the needs of students and society (Brophy, 1990). By emphasizing *citizen education*, the goal of social studies education becomes one of helping students make appropriate and informed *decisions* about public-policy issues.

Nearly all Americans live in a community and many of them are parents. As a result, most need to be well informed about a great variety of issues that could affect them. For example, consider some issues that Americans have been grappling with for many years:

1. Should there be a national health plan that guarantees health insurance to all Americans?
2. Should America send troops to help a democratic ally that has fallen prey to a military coup?
3. Should we impose a ten-cents-a-gallon tax on gasoline to reduce the federal deficit?
4. Should we allow prayer in public schools?
5. Should we impose fines on people who pollute?

Take some time now to provide a reasoned answer to each of these questions.

It should be clear that taking an appropriate stance on any of these issues requires considerable knowledge on your part. Individuals who are ignorant of certain facts (e.g., the number of American soldiers, other soldiers, and civilians who would be killed in an invasion) might adopt a stance that they would later regret.

But effective decision-making involves *values* in addition to knowledge (Slovic, 1990). To see this, imagine the situation in which a congressman holds a "town hall" meeting to get input from his constituents about invading a foreign country to restore democracy there. Imagine next that two of his constituents are both armed with the same information: 350 Americans would probably lose their lives during the invasion. If one constituent believes that no loss of life is justifiable, he might urge the congressman to vote against the invasion. If the other believes that 500 lives are expendable if the lives of one million people would be better, she might urge the congressman to vote for the invasion. Thus, people who have the same knowledge but different values will choose different options.

Social studies educators hope that by teaching students about the history, economics, lifestyles, and governments of this and other countries, students will have the knowledge they need to make informed decisions about public-policy issues. In many private and public schools, there is also an emphasis on instilling certain values in students as well (e.g., love of country; respect for others). Some schools, however, do not try to instill values as much as help students get in touch with the values they already have (Brophy, 1990).

When can students understand the facts they need to be good citizens and decision makers? Do certain groups gain more social studies knowledge than others? We shall address these questions in the next two sections.

The Development of Social Studies Knowledge

In what follows, we shall examine the development of social studies knowledge by looking at age trends within four of the disciplines that comprise the social studies: history, geography, economics, and civics.

History

It is safe to say that we not only want our students to know certain historical facts, but we also want them to *comprehend* the significance of these facts (Brophy, 1990). For example, in addition to simply knowing *that* the Boston Tea Party occurred, we want students to (a) understand *why* it occurred, (b) understand *why* it was a significant event (according to historians), and (c) know its place in the chronology of significant events in American history.

What does it take to understand historical events in this way? Three cognitive abilities seem to be indispensable. The first is the ability to order events in time. The second is the ability to understand causal relations among events. The third is the ability to recognize that historians do not merely record reality, they *interpret* it and are selective in what they choose to interpret. Let's examine the development of these subskills further. After doing so, we shall examine age trends in performance on national assessments of history knowledge.

Concepts of Time

Clearly, we would be fighting a losing battle if we tried to teach history to students who could neither understand the difference between the past and the present nor mentally arrange past events into a sequence. Fortunately for elementary school teachers, considerable development occurs in these abilities during the preschool period. Beginning at about two years of age, children's language suggests that they distinguish between things that are happening now and things that happened earlier (Friedman, 1990; Nelson, 1991). Moreover, two-year-olds can imitate a sequence of events as long as the sequence is familiar to them and involves just two actions. By the age of four, these event representations develop into extended, multiple-sequence "scripts" (e.g., a "lunchtime script," see Chapter 2 or Nelson, 1986).

However, whereas young children can comprehend the difference between the past and present and also arrange events into short sequences, Friedman (1990, p. 93) notes that

> . . . their sense of past and future probably differs markedly from our own . . . lacking both knowledge of long-scale patterns and of conventional frameworks . . . young children undoubtedly experience a far less differentiated past. Probably past events can only be located within islands of structure . . . without any appreciation of where the islands lie relative to one another.

It should also be noted that children's early successes with respect to temporal notions derive from their own activities. It is more difficult to conceptualize a series of events that happened to someone else than to recall a series of events in which you participated.

In reviewing the extant research, Friedman (1990) argues that whereas older preschoolers can represent a span that extends about 24 hours into the past, most six- and seven-year-olds can correctly order sets of cards that represent seasons or holidays, suggesting that they can comprehend annual patterns. Moreover, they can order the days of the week and months of the year. Between eight years of age and adolescence, children's conceptualizations of temporal patterns increase in span and uniformity. Adolescents are also more likely than younger children to comprehend the conventional quality of time (e.g., understanding daylight saving time).

It would appear, then, that whereas attempts to teach a "timeline" of historical events would clearly not be successful for preschoolers, it would also not be successful for children in the early elementary grades either. This assumption seems to be endorsed by most school districts, because many have limited social studies instruction to the "expanding communities" framework for children in the fourth grade and below (Brophy, VanSledright & Bredin, 1992; Wyner & Farquhar, 1991). In this framework, instruction focuses on the self in kindergarten, the family in the first grade, the neighborhood in the second grade, the community in the third grade, and the state in the fourth grade. A systematic focus on American history and western civilization usually does not start until the fifth grade or later. For young children, then, "history" becomes their own personal history (i.e., they focus events that have happened to them and on their family "tree") and progressively shifts toward the history of their neighborhood, community, and state.

And yet, it is a truism that children learn what they are taught. Many researchers are rejecting the idea of waiting to teach American and western history until the fifth grade because they question the Piagetian research on which this delay was originally based (Levstik & Pappas, 1987). Some reviewers contend that when earlier instruction has been tried, it has met with some success (Alleman & Rosaen, 1991). Moreover, the research that shows that children become more facile with clocks and calendars with age makes sense given the fact that children are exposed to these instruments in school.

One way to help children acquire an earlier understanding of history is to have them play-act a series of historical events in the proper order. By engaging in the behaviors themselves, children might get a better sense of motives and could also develop "scripts" for the events. However, since the formation of scripts requires a certain amount of consistency and repetition, perhaps they could repeat the same play-act sequence several years in a row (e.g., kindergarten, first, and second grade).

Causal Notions

As several researchers have noted, the essence of a comprehensive historical perspective is being able to understanding *why* certain events took place and *how* these events affected the course of history (Hallden, 1986; McKeown & Beck, 1990). We know from research that infants and preschoolers can comprehend simple causal relations (see Chapter 9), but does that mean that somewhat older students can understand why events such as the Boston Tea Party occurred and what effect such events had on subsequent events in American history?

At a minimum, students would need to understand abstract concepts such as *taxation* and *representation* in order to understand why the Boston Tea Party occurred (McKeown & Beck, 1990). Moreover, they would need to understand the motivations and belief systems of significant individuals as well as comprehend significant aspects of group behaviors and processes. Hence, they would need to understand causal principles of psychology, philosophy, sociology, and political science (because these sciences explain the behaviors of individuals and groups). Given the abstract and sophisticated nature of these principles, it should not be surprising to learn that, despite the best efforts of teachers, students often simplify the causes of events down to the level of the personal motives of individuals (Hallden, 1986). Moreover, given the absence of causal explanations in many history textbooks, it should also not be surprising to learn that students' historical knowledge is often characterized by simple associations and unconnected structures (McKeown & Beck, 1990).

One way to test students' causal understanding is to have them engage in *counterfactual reasoning*. Someone who can engage in counterfactual reasoning can envision what would have happened if certain events had *not* occurred. To see how this works, try answering the following questions:

1. Would there have been a Protestant Reformation if the Catholic Church had given a divorce to Henry VIII and rectified the problems identified by Martin Luther?
2. Would we have pulled out of Vietnam if President Kennedy had not been assassinated?

According to Piagetian theory, children cannot engage in counterfactual reasoning until they are ten or 11 years old (see Chapter 2). We know that Piaget underestimated the abilities of young children sometimes, so it remains to be seen whether research would show that younger children could not engage in counterfactual reasoning under some circumstances. But, of course, in order to understand what would happen if something did not occur, you first need to understand why things happened as they did. Since we just argued that this is not an easy task for students, perhaps counterfactual reasoning would be hard for elementary students as well.

Historians As Interpreters

A sophisticated understanding of history not only requires the ability to construct mental timelines and understand causal relations, it also requires the ability to understand that historians are people who have pet theories and biases that cause them to look at events in interpretative ways. Several studies have shown that young children think that there is only one "reality" that we all see in the same way (Kuhn, Amsel & O'Loughlin, 1988). When told about two historians who witnessed the same event (e.g., the same battle in the Civil War), young children often think that the historians would necessarily record the events in the same way. As an adult, you have a better sense of how these accounts could differ. In particular, you would clearly recognize how a historian from a southern U.S. university could see things differently from a historian from a northern U.S. university.

Although above-average fifth graders have a rudimentary sense of the notion of biased interpretations (Brophy et al., 1992), a fully mature conception of multiple interpretations is not evident until students are college age and beyond (Kuhn et al., 1988). Thus, most elementary students take all information presented in history classes as immutable facts. Once again, though, because textbooks and teachers may present the information in this way, perhaps instruction could foster an earlier appreciation of multiple perspectives than has been found to date. One strategy might be to have children form teams and ask them to create a seasonal display (e.g., for Thanksgiving). After telling them that the team with the best display wins, you then appoint two judges, one from each team to rate the display. Children will soon learn that observers can be biased.

Age Trends on National Assessments

In 1988, Educational Testing Service (ETS) conducted a large-scale study of the history knowledge in fourth, eighth, and twelfth graders. From the items used on this test, they derived four levels of performance. Table 10.1 describes the four levels and Figure 10.1 shows the percentage of students who scored at these

---

TABLE 10.1   Level of Understanding on the 1988 NAEP for History

---

Level 200: Knows Simple Historical Facts

Students at this level know some historical facts of the type learned from everyday experiences. For example, they can identify a few national holidays and patriotic symbols. They can read simple timelines, graphs, charts, and maps.

Level 250: Knows Beginning Historical Information and Has Rudimentary
Interpretive Skills

Students at this level know a greater number and variety of historical facts of the type commonly learned from historical studies. For example, they can identify a number of historical figures, events, and terms. They are developing a sense of chronology and can interpret timelines, maps, and graphs.

Level 300: Understands Basic Historical Terms and Relationships

Students at this level have a broad knowledge of historical terms, facts, regions, and ideas. They have a general sense of chronology and can recognize characterizations of particular time periods in history. These students have some knowledge of the content of primary texts in U.S. political and constitutional history, such as the Declaration of Independence and Constitution. They are familiar with certain historically significant economic and social developments and have some awareness of different social and cultural groups. These students are beginning to comprehend the historical significance of domestic governmental policies and also the international context of U.S. history. They show an emerging understanding of causal relationships.

Level 350: Interprets Historical Information and Ideas

Students at this level are developing a detailed understanding of historical vocabulary, facts, regions, and ideas. They are familiar with a wider array of texts such as the Articles of Confederation and Federalist Papers. They are aware of the religious diversity of the United States and recognize the continuing tension between democratic principles and social realities such as poverty and discrimination. They have a rudimentary understanding of the history of U.S. foreign policy and are beginning to relate social science concepts (e.g., price theory, separation of powers) to historical themes and can evaluate causal relationships.

Source: David C. Hammock et al. (1990), *The U.S. History Report Card.* Princeton, NJ: National Assessment of Educational Progress.

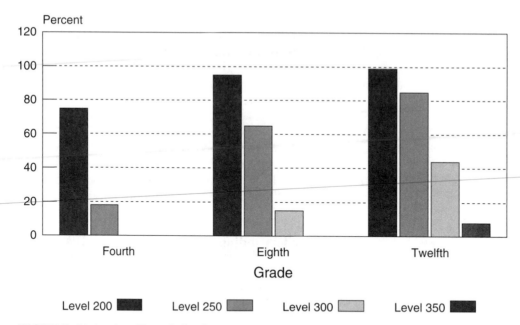

FIGURE 10.1   Age Trends in the 1988 History NAEP

levels. As you can see, whereas nearly all students at all ages knew simple historical facts (Level 200), very few seemed to understand basic historical terms and relationships (Level 300) and fewer still could interpret historical information and ideas (Level 350). The largest shifts in knowledge occurred between the fourth and eighth grades for Level 250 knowledge (which includes a conception of time-lines), and between the eighth and twelfth grades for Level 300 knowledge (which includes a beginning comprehension of causal relationships). The authors of a summary report conclude that although factual knowledge clearly increases with age, " . . . the assessment results indicate that across the grades, most students have a limited grasp of U.S. history" (Hammock et al., 1990, p. 10). What is not clear at present is whether the poor performance of younger students reflects the fact that they are conceptually incapable of the reasoning required at Levels 300 and 350 or that they were taught in inappropriate ways (e.g., they were never asked to think at higher levels).

Geography

Geography texts present a variety of topics that can be grouped under the headings "geographical skills" (e.g., map reading), "human geography" (e.g., location of major cultural groups) and "physical geography" (e.g., location of the world's natural resources) (Farrell & Cirrincione, 1989). Teachers, however, consider the topics having to do with map skills and locations as being the most important to cover (see Table 10.2). It is useful, therefore, to examine the literature to see if there are developmental trends in children's learning of these topics.

TABLE 10.2   **Geography Topics Judged Most Important by Social Studies Teachers**

	Rating
1. Map interpretation	4.32
2. Location of major land forms and bodies of water	4.30
3. Global interdependence	4.29
4. Location and distribution of natural resources	4.24
5. Finding places on maps and atlases	4.23
6. Conservation of natural resources	4.17
7. Location of major cultural regions	4.15
8. Location and distribution of major cultural groups	4.14
9. Location and characteristics of major global political divisions	4.11
10. Relations between political decisions and land use	4.06

Adapted from Farrell, R.T. & Cirrincione, J.M. (1989). The content of Geography curriculum—a teachers perspective. *Social Education, 53,* 105–108; Rating scale ranged from "not very important (1) to "very important" (5).

Map Skills

In order to comprehend the meaning of a map, students need to be able to do at least three things: (a) recognize and differentiate among cartographic or pictographic symbols (e.g., see the difference between the star for the capital of a state and a dot for other cities in the state), (b) understand that these symbols refer to real, three-dimensional counterparts (e.g., actual cities), and (c) project the spatial arrangement of symbols on the map (e.g., the symbol for Pennsylvania is above that for Maryland) on to the real physical world (e.g., recognize that the state of Pennsylvania is north of the state of Maryland) (Bluestein & Acredolo, 1979; Liben & Downs, 1993). In addition, students need to be able to use the map even when it is not aligned to their own perspective (as is the case with many "you are here" maps found in shopping malls).

Studies show that many preschoolers possess rudimentary map-reading skills. For example, when a two-dimensional drawing of a room is used to show children where a teddy bear is hidden, 50 percent of three-year-olds and nearly all four-and five-year-olds can use the map to find the bear (Bluestein & Acredolo, 1979; Presson, 1982). However, when a more complex map of a classroom is used and they need to indicate on the map the location of a person in the room, five-year-olds indicate the correct location about 43 percent of the time. Success rates increase to 65 percent and then again to 85 percent by the first and second grades, respectively (Liben & Downs, 1993). In addition, whereas rotating the map 180 degrees away from the child's perspective has no effect on children's performance in the fifth and sixth grades, performance drops considerably for younger children.

Thus, even young children can understand that a map "stands for" an actual set of locations and that they can use the map to find a particular location. After the preschool period, map skills continue to improve. In particular, children become more able to deal with unaligned maps, maps of places they have never been, and maps that use abstract symbols that do not resemble their real-world counterparts (Liben & Downs, 1993).

An important contributor to this increasing skill is the development of spatial abilities that were originally identified by Piaget. In particular, studies show a consistent correlation between success on Piagetian spatial tasks and map-reading tasks (Liben & Downs, 1993; Muir, 1985). But in the Piagetian perspective, skills are constructed through experience. It is possible that by increasing map use in schools (e.g., to find a "treasure" hidden in the schoolyard), children will become more facile. To help with comprehending more difficult aspects of maps, these exercises should substitute abstract symbols for realistic symbols (e.g., a star for a drawing of a tree, a square for a sand box) and use misaligned maps to teach children how to mentally rotate their perspective.

Identifying Locations

As might be expected from the increasing emphasis on social studies with age, older children can identify locations on a map of the world better than young children. In one study of about 2,800 students, Herman, Barron, Hawkins, and Berryman (1988) found that the percentages of correct placements of ten countries were 30 percent for fourth graders, 40 percent for fifth graders, and 44 percent for sixth graders. Children at all grades were most successful locating Mexico (43 percent, 63 percent, 63 percent correct, respectively) and least successful at locating Venezuela (18 percent, 31 percent, and 34 percent correct, respectively). In a study of college freshman, Cross (1987) found that students showed an overall success rate of only 39 percent for the locations of the following 11 countries: China, Cuba, Great Britain, El Salvador, Ethiopia, India, Iran, Lebanon, Poland, South Africa, and the Soviet Union. Students were most successful in identifying the Soviet Union (73 percent) and Cuba (65 percent) and least successful in identifying Lebanon (11 percent) and Poland (12 percent). Overall, then, the data suggest that whereas there is improvement with age in location skills, performance is mediocre at best even in college students. Such findings for location skills are consistent with the findings of the National Assessment of Educational Progress (NAEP) for geography, which showed that twelfth graders score about 300 on a scale that ranges from 0 to 500 (Digest of Educational Statistics, 1990). These findings are intriguing in light of the fact that teachers think it is very important to teach children how to identify locations (Farrell & Cirrincione, 1989).

One could dismiss the poor performance of students by saying, "Who cares. Only airline pilots need to know where places are." However, locations are an important aspect of understanding world events. For example, Poland's unfortunate history relates to the fact that it is a neighbor to both Germany and Russia. In one sense, locations can only be learned through repetition. But there are a variety of memory strategies that could improve retention (e.g., imagery; see Chapter 4) as well as incentives that improve motivation. Have you ever noticed that you learn locations and use a map better when you want to go somewhere? (e.g., drive several states away for a spring break vacation).

Economics

In any given society, there are people who have certain wants and needs (e.g., thirst, hunger, movement) and resources that can be used to fulfill these needs (e.g., water, food, and transportation). Economics is the study of how people try to balance their personal needs with limited and shared resources (Sunal, 1991). In trying to describe this situation and explain how the balance is struck, economists have created concepts such as *scarcity, monetary value, profit, consumption, production,* and *economic inequality.* Educational researchers have tried to determine when children can comprehend such abstract concepts.

In most studies, researchers used Piagetian methods to assess economic understanding. In particular, it has been common to use concrete stimuli to elicit responses (e.g., play money in a pretend shop) and then propose stages in children's economic conceptions (Schug, 1987; Sunal, 1991).

Although the number and details of the stages vary by concept, several common age trends emerge across studies. In the early grades, children possess a very limited understanding of economic notions. For example, young children think that everyone usually gets what he or she needs and that shopkeepers do not sell items at a higher price than they bought them for. Moreover, any exchange of money at a store is seen as a merely a ritualistic behavior (Sunal, 1991).

With age, children acquire a progressively more accurate understanding of concepts such as *scarcity* and *profit* but do not integrate ideas into a system of related notions. For example, students may not realize that shops exist because we have needs and that shopkeepers earn a living (i.e., make a profit) by helping us meet our needs. Ultimately, concepts become integrated into a system such that by adolescence, students seem to understand basic economics ideas in the manner described by economists (Schug, 1987).

As with other social studies domains, a number of experts recently have called into question the idea that younger children are incapable of understanding basic economics notions. Most have argued that young children lack insight into certain ideas because they lack experience. When children engage in school-based "mini-economies," they show a greater understanding than the stagelike accounts suggest (Schug & Walstad, 1991).

Civics

In order to be able to participate in a democracy, students need to learn about the responsibilities of government (e.g., national defense, education of children, etc.), the responsibilities and rights of individuals (e.g., voting and freedom of speech), and the interrelations between citizens and their government. Civics educators strive to instill this knowledge in students. Are they successful?

National assessments show that whereas students do acquire more civics knowledge with age, even twelfth graders lack sufficient knowledge to fully participate in a democracy. For example, one study showed that the percentage of students who understand (a) governmental responsibilities, (b) the relations among citizens and government, and (c) individual rights were 10 percent, 61 percent, and 89 percent, for fourth, eighth, and twelfth graders, respectively. The corresponding percentages for understanding the structures, functions, and powers of the American government as defined in the Constitution were 0 percent, 13 percent, and 49 percent, respectively (Digest of Educational Statistics, 1990). Moreover, other studies show that students have at best a superficial understanding of civics "facts" and also have serious misconceptions of how our government works (Patrick & Hoge, 1991).

Summary of Developmental Trends

Two themes emerge from the research that has examined age trends in children's learning of history, geography, economics, and civics. The first is that whereas factual knowledge in these subjects increases between the fourth and twelfth grades, many students leave high school with only a superficial understanding of important social studies concepts. The second is that the poor performance of younger students may have more to do with lack of experience than with a basic inability to learn the material. Either way, there seems to be something fundamentally wrong with the way students learn social studies.

It might be added that all of the developmental research described above only shows how much knowledge students have acquired (or have not acquired). It does not tell us whether twelfth graders who have acquired knowledge make better decisions about public-policy issues than students with less knowledge. It also does not indicate whether knowledgeable twelfth graders are more likely to be active citizens than less knowledgeable twelfth graders. Given that making decisions and being an active citizen are two major goals of social studies education, additional research needs to be done to see if these goals have been met. Most people do not participate beyond voting (Ferguson, 1991), so clearly a lot needs to be changed.

Individual Differences in Social Studies Knowledge

Having discussed global age trends, we next turn to the issue of how same-aged individuals differ from one another. Research has revealed four variables associated with individual differences in social studies knowledge and skill: gender, socioeconomic status (SES), ethnicity, and expertise. Let's examine the research on these four variables in turn.

Gender Differences

History and Geography
Figure 10.2 displays the average scores of twelfth grade males and females on the 1988 NAEP exams for history and geography. As can be seen, whereas males performed better than females on both assessments, the differences are not ter-

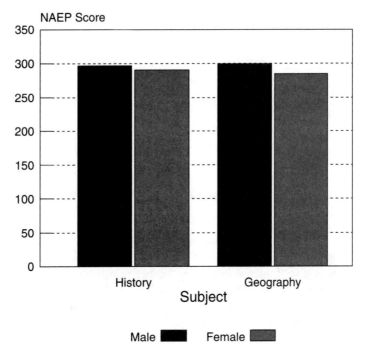

FIGURE 10.2   Gender Differences in 12th Graders

ribly large. In the case of history, for example, the male score is only 2 percent higher than the female mean. For geography, the male mean is only 5 percent higher. For comparison purposes, it might be helpful to note that the male score on the math subtest of the SAT is typically 10 percent higher than the female score (see Chapter 8).

The 5 percent difference on the NAEP geography exam is consistent with the findings of Herman et al. (1988) for location skills. In particular, the percentages of boys and girls in the fourth to sixth grades who could correctly locate countries were 40 percent and 35 percent, respectively.

The one exception to the typically small gender difference in performance is Cross's (1987) study of the location skills of students attending a satellite campus of the University of Wisconsin. In this study, the percentages of correct locations identified were 48 percent for males and 31 percent for females. What is particularly troubling about this latter finding is the fact that many of the females in this study were education majors.

Economics

Reviews of research on economics learning show that there are consistent, though small, gender differences at the elementary, secondary, and college levels (Schug & Walstad, 1991). Most of the studies that showed gender differences, however, involved multiple-choice tests. When essay tests have been used, females have performed better than males.

Civics

The story for civics is similar to what has been said so far for history, geography, and economics: When there is a difference favoring males, it is not terribly large. Figure 10.3 shows gender differences for two components of the most recent NAEP exam for civics: (a) understanding the nature of our political institutions and (b) understanding specific government structures and functions. As can be seen, whereas females performed slightly better on the items comprising the former component of the test (2 percent higher), males performed better on the items comprising the latter component (Digest of Education, 1990).

Summary

For each of history, geography, economics, and civics, there is a consistent tendency for males to perform better on assessments than females. The size of the gender gap does not appear to be age-related (i.e., it is the same size from about the fourth grade on), but it is usually small at all ages. In addition, there is some suggestion that females can be more knowledgeable than males for certain types of social studies information and also perform better when they have a chance to exercise their writing skills.

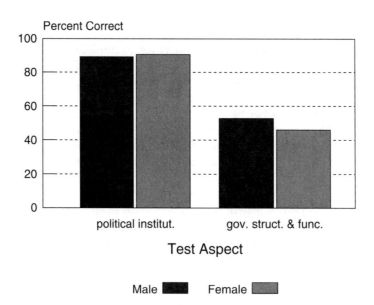

FIGURE 10.3   Gender differences on 1988 NAEP Civics

Note: Results are for 12th graders only.

Socioeconomic Status (SES)

In many of the studies described earlier in this chapter, researchers examined the relation between a student's socioeconomic status (SES) and his or her performance. In assigning students to various SES levels, researchers often created a composite index based on their household characteristics as well as the income, education level, and occupation of their parents. It has generally been found that students from lower SES levels perform more poorly than students from higher SES levels.

For example, in their study of the location skills of fourth, fifth, and sixth graders, Herman et al. (1988) found that high-and middle-SES students correctly identified more countries than low-SES students (percents correct = 45 percent, 42 percent, and 32 percent, for high, middle, and low SES groups, respectively). Similarly, the 1988 NAEP for geography showed that the scores of twelfth graders varied by their parents' level of education and the amount of reading materials in their home. For example, if students had parents who graduated from college or provided four types of reading materials in the home, they scored around 300 on the exam. In contrast, if their parents were high school dropouts or provided two or fewer types of reading materials, students scored about 270 on the exam (Digest of Educational Statistics, 1990).

For the 1988 NAEP for history, the findings were quite similar. At each of the fourth, eighth, and twelfth grades, students scored about ten points higher for each successive level of education that their parents attained. At the twelfth grade, for example, the average score for children of high school dropouts was 274. If their parents were high school graduates, the average score was 285. When their parents attended some college or graduated from college, the scores were 297 and 306, respectively (Hammock et al., 1990).

Summary

In contrast to gender, then, SES seems to be a powerful determinant of performance on social studies assessments. If children come from homes in which their parents are educated, make a good income, and provide numerous reading materials, results show that they perform better on national assessments and tests than children who come from lower SES homes. At present, however, it is not clear whether these home factors are causally responsible for success on social studies tests or whether the differences reflect differences in the quality of education received by children in different SES groups. After all, children from more affluent homes often have access to the best education available.

Ethnic Differences

As might be expected from the fact that SES often covaries with ethnicity, differences in performance among ethnic groups mirror those found for SES levels. In particular, the average scores of White, Hispanic, and Black twelfth graders on the 1988 geography NAEP were 301, 272, and 258, respectively (Digest of Educational Statistics, 1990). For the 1988 history NAEP, the average scores of White, Hispanic, and Black twelfth graders were 301, 274, and 274, respectively. In both cases, then, White students performed substantially higher than Black or Hispanic students.

Unfortunately, the ethnic differences found for geography and history assessments have also been found on the 1988 NAEP civics exam. At all grade levels, the percentage of White students who demonstrated an understanding of political institutions and governmental functions was always about 20 points higher than the percentages for Black and Hispanic students who demonstrated such an understanding. In comparison to the 2 percent to 7 percent difference between males and females, then, the discrepancy between White students and minority students for the civics NAEP is three to ten times larger.

Novice-Expert Differences

As discussed in Chapter 4, differences between novices and experts become apparent when they are asked to solve problems. James Voss and his colleagues have used this problem-solving approach to reveal expertise-related differences on political science problems (e.g., Voss, Tyler & Yengo, 1983).

One of the problems they have used is the following. Try solving it now in order to get a better understanding of the results of this work:

> Assume you are the head of the Soviet Ministry of Agriculture and assume that crop productivity has been low over the past several years. You now have the responsibility of increasing crop production. How would you go about doing this?

This example is representative of many problems in the social science area in that the "problem" is an undesirable state of affairs that needs to be improved or eliminated. In such cases, it is common for people to identify the cause of the undesirable state of affairs and propose solving the problem by eliminating the cause. Voss and his colleagues refer to this strategy as the "Identify and Eliminate Causes" (IEC) solution.

Voss et al. (1983) have found that whereas both experts and novices use the IEC strategy to propose solutions to the crop-productivity problem and other problems, they go about it in different ways. In particular, experts did not immediately identify causes of a problem. Rather, they first embellished what they had been told by thinking about aspects of the former Soviet agricultural system that would interfere with the implementation of most solutions. Voss et al. called these perceived interferences "constraints." To illustrate how experts build in constraints before they even begin to entertain causes, consider the beginning of one expert's response:

> I think that as minister of agriculture, one has to start out with the realization that there are certain kinds of special agricultural constraints within which

you are going to work. The first one, the most obvious one, is that by almost every count only ten percent of the land in the Soviet Union is arable . . . And secondly, even in that arable ten percent of the total land surface, you will still have climate for instance, problems over which you have no direct control. Okay, so that is sort of the overall parameter in which we are working (p. 215).

This expert went on to add several other constraints as well.

In contrast, novices rarely mentioned constraints. Instead, they engaged in a strategy of simply citing causes and proposing solutions based on these causes. For example, one novice proposed a total of 12 causes and 12 distinct solutions. For each cause that the novice identified (e.g., outdated farm machinery), he or she proposed a solution that would eliminate that cause (e.g., providing new machinery to the workers).

Besides the recognition of constraints, a second difference between experts and novices was the abstractness of the proposed causes. Whereas novices proposed specific and concrete causes, experts proposed more abstract causes. For example, instead of blaming low productivity on outdated machinery, one expert attributed the problem to inadequate technology at many levels of production (e.g., machinery, irrigation, fertilization, computerization, etc.).

The third major difference concerned the tendency of experts to spend most of their time justifying one or two solutions rather than spending their time rattling off many solutions. The tendency of experts to justify their solutions may be due to the fact that they were *social* scientists. Unlike the fields of physics or mathematics in which problems can be said to have a single, agreed-upon solution, problems in the social sciences often have no definite solution. Moreover, there is no clear way to assess whether a solution has worked. Take the crop-productivity problem, for example. If a solution is implemented, how far does productivity have to rise in order for the solution to be thought of as effective? Clearly, there could be disagreements about an acceptable level. The social scientists in Voss et al.'s study may have been very used to arguing about hard-to-implement and hard-to-evaluate solutions.

The three differences between novices and experts seem to derive from two main sources: (a) experts' greater knowledge and (b) experts' greater experience practicing in the discipline. Knowledge helped experts think of constraints as well as data that could be used to bolster claims. Moreover, knowledge helped experts to group causes together into more abstract categories. Experience in researching and writing about political issues helped them recognize the complexities of solutions (i.e., nothing is simple or perfect) and the need to justify one's proposals (because the readers of their work often challenged what the experts have written).

In support of these claims, Voss and his colleagues found that social scientists who were not experts on the Soviet Union nevertheless built in constraints and tried to justify their solutions the same way that Soviet experts did. Professional chemists, on the other hand, gave responses similar to those of novices.

Thus, this data suggests that helping novices to think like experts requires more than coursework. Whereas traditional coursework will increase knowledge, it will not promote the development of a generalized problem-solving *approach* to issues (e.g., "think about constraints and remember to justify your solutions"). To attain this goal, students would need lots of practice thinking through hypothetical problems.

Instructional Implications

In what follows, we shall examine the instructional implications of the research on social studies learning in two ways. First, we shall examine several general guidelines for how to approach social studies instruction. Then, we shall examine a case study that illustrates many of the principles described in the general guidelines.

General Guidelines

The results of the research on developmental and individual differences in social studies learning suggest that something is seriously wrong with the way students are taught social studies. Even when we are talking about twelfth graders or groups within a grade who are performing better than others (e.g., males or Whites), performance is only mediocre at best.

Why do students perform so poorly? Experts suggest that there are two main causes: (a) an emphasis on fact learning over comprehension, application, and decision making in the classroom (Brophy, 1990) and (b) the use of textbooks that include unnecessary detail and do not provide explanations of events and issues (McKeown & Beck, 1990). These two deficiencies in the classroom suggest the first two instructional implications:

1. In teaching social studies, it is more important to stress major principles and generalizations and focus on a few illustrative examples than to give shallow coverage to a large number of facts. Using examples of history and geography, for example, Brophy (1990, p. 404) suggests,

> [teachers should] emphasize the basic economic, social, or political forces that have shaped [a country's] development (not just a chronology of noteworthy events), linking these to discipline based concepts, generalizations, and principles (such as colonization and modernization). Similarly, in focusing more specifically on [a country's] geography, [teachers should] stress the relationships between its climate and natural resources, its economy, and its location and power vis-a-vis other countries as determinants of its past history and current status, not just descriptive and statistical facts.

Of course, in emphasizing higher-order thinking over shallow coverage, students will not necessarily perform better on national assessments, because most require recall of facts. We would still have many 17-year-olds, then, not knowing the dates of the Civil War. And yet, we would possibly have a more impressive group of 17-year-olds who could recognize a current event (e.g., an invasion of a country) as another example of a general principle that they learned in class. Moreover, we might have a larger percentage of active citizens.

If it is desirous to have students recall factual information, there are techniques such as "elaborative interrogation" that have been found to be more effective for geographic facts than other approaches (e.g., Martin & Pressley, 1991). Using this technique, one asks students *why* some fact is true (e.g., "Why is Saskatchewan the province that produces the most apples in Canada?") instead of asking them to learn the fact by rote. Wood et al. (1993) found elaborative interrogation to be effective for even preschoolers and elementary students.

2. If teachers will be placing an increased emphasis on explanation, comprehension, application, and generalization, textbooks have to be altered to be in syncrony with this new approach. Current textbooks are rife with facts (often inaccurate or irrelevant) and low on causal explanation.

The remaining instructional implications derive from the outcomes of the research on developmental and individual differences:

3. Theories and research on cognitive development suggest that certain concepts (e.g., a timeline of events, abstract causal relations, etc.) might be too difficult for younger elementary students to comprehend. And yet, children have cognitive capacities that teachers can exploit to help them gain at least partial insight into these difficult ideas. For example, children can form mental "scripts" of common activities by repeatedly engaging in these activities. They should be able to form scripts for historical events in the same way. The formation of such scripts through plays and so forth would be more effective in helping children develop a timeline of events than verbal description. Also, young children are quite capable of analogical reasoning (Brown, 1989) and teachers can rely on analogies to help children grasp somewhat foreign or difficult ideas. For example, teachers can have students relate and compare their own family experience to that of other families in this and other countries. Finally, simulated experiences such as "mini-economies" and "mini-governments" can go a long way in helping students understand their real-life counterparts. In sum, then, the standard "expanding communities" framework could be augmented with all of these activities.

4. The research on individual differences suggests that the most troublesome findings pertain to low SES and minority students. The fact that SES covaries with success on achievement tests could mean that a great deal of social studies knowledge is acquired outside of school, or that high SES children attend more effective schools than low SES children (or both). If only the former is true, three things could be tried. First, it would be important to create extracurricular activities for low SES students (e.g., after-school, summer, or weekend "academies"). Second, large-scale parent education efforts could begin. Third, perhaps watching educational TV programs might be required of students (e.g., *Carmen Sandiego*).

If the second possibility is true, it is essential that deficiencies in schools that service low SES students be identified. If the principals and teaching staff need professional development (e.g., to learn about new teaching techniques), efforts should begin in that regard.

5. Finally, the proposal mentioned in the first implication about improving comprehension could be augmented by asking students to solve hypothetical problems. Teachers could provide mild criticism of solutions offered by students and instruct them on how to provide justifications for their tentative ideas. In this way, students would emulate practicing social scientists and potentially develop a scripted approach to thinking about problems in the social studies.

A Case Study

If indeed we want students to use social studies knowledge to make decisions and solve problems, then it makes sense to ask them to learn social studies facts to make decisions and solve problems. An interesting way to achieve this goal is illustrated by the ICONS project created by Judith Torney-Purta and her colleagues at the University of Maryland. Students who participate in ICONS are placed into teams and asked to pretend that they are the foreign ministers of various countries. For example, some students take on the role of being the foreign ministers of France, some form a Russian team, and some form a Brazilian team. Then, each team is asked to represent its country in a simulated international conference in which it is confronted with contemporary world problems. During one conference, for example, students were asked to develop a consensual policy about how to coerce South Africa into abandoning its apartheid policy as well as thinking about how to solve Mexico's enormous foreign debt. At other conferences, they delved into issues such as global warming and the war in Bosnia.

To be able to effectively participate in this process, students had to learn a great deal about the country they were trying to represent. For example, students who formed a South African team had to learn about the origins of apartheid and why some South Africans supported this policy. Similarly, students who formed the Russian team had to learn enough about Russia to say how its foreign ministers would respond to the problem of apartheid. Thus, they learned facts about these countries not to simply know the facts but to know how to formulate a national policy.

Each team was supervised by teachers who served more as resources than directive authoritarians. That is, they collected appropriate reading materials and helped students locate information that the students learned they would need. They also coordinated within-teams discussions about a country's response, once enough information about a country and the issue at hand was collected. In trying to reach consensus, students learn a great deal about effective forms of negotiation and compromise. Teachers play a role in teaching students how to solicit opinions and operate on the principles of democracy.

After each team has forged a proposed way to deal with a problem, the members sit down at a networked computer terminal and confer with other countries via computer messages. That is, teams are always in different rooms and very often even from different schools in the states of Maryland and Pennsylvania.

As a result of the ICONS experience, students are substantially more conversant about foreign countries and contemporary issues than students who learn the same material using the standard lecture format. In addition, students are motivated to learn the material and construct their own understanding of it through readings, discussions, and inter-group arguments.

Chapter *11*

Motivation

Summary

1. Motivation is a construct used to explain the initiation, direction, and intensity of an individual's behavior.

2. If we want to fully explain students' motivation in a situation, we need to appeal to their (a) goals, (b) knowledge of how to meet goals, (c) personal standards for what is good enough, (d) beliefs about their abilities and possible emotional states, (e) interests, and (f) values.

3. People who are intrinsically motivated engage in a task as an end in itself; people who are extrinsically motivated engage in a task as a means to an end.

4. Because of a variety of factors that conspire together, older children tend to have less achieve-ment motivation for school-related tasks than younger children.

5. Within any classroom, individual differences can be found along any of the aspects of motivation. Students differ in terms of their goals, knowledge, tendency to monitor, personal standards, ability beliefs, interests, and values. These differences greatly affect how hard students try, how long they persist, and the emotions they feel when confronted with tasks.

6. Teachers and classroom environments can affect student motivation in significant ways. Sometimes the shift from one set of teachers and environments to another can cause a sharp drop in student motivation.

As mentioned in Chapter 1, the present book was written to provide answers to the following question: Why do some students learn more in school than others? So far, two main answers to this question have emerged from the research presented in Chapters 2 to 9: (a) students with more knowledge learn more than students with less knowledge and (b) people who use strategies learn more than people who do not use strategies. In this chapter, we will examine another variable that greatly affects how much students learn: motivation.

To get an initial sense of the importance of motivation, answer the following questions:

1. Have you ever received a good grade in a course even though you found the course material to be dull or boring?

2. When you had a chance to take elective courses, why did you choose the ones you did?
3. Why are you reading this book right now?
4. Do you find that you get better grades and have better attendance in courses that you find interesting?

Questions such as these get at the heart of motivation. By the end of this chapter, you will know how they do.

Following the format of many other chapters in this book, we shall examine motivation in four sections. In the first section, motivation will be defined. More specifically, you will learn about the constituent parts of motivation. In the second section, you will learn how these constituent parts develop with age. In the third section, you will learn about individual differences in motivation. In the fourth and final section, the instructional implications of the research on motivation will be drawn.

The Nature of Motivation

Let's begin our discussion of motivation by giving a definition: Motivation is a construct used to explain the initiation, direction, and intensity of an individual's behavior in a particular situation (Stipek, 1993; Wigfield & Eccles, 1992). Thus, the notion of motivation is useful for answering questions such as "Why did she start doing that?" "Why did he choose that way of doing it instead of another way?" "Why is she trying so hard?" "Why did he give up so easily?"

In attempting to answer questions such as these, motivation theorists have identified a large number of constructs. Instead of examining these constructs one by one, we shall examine them in three groupings: goal-related constructs, knowledge-related constructs, and metacognitive constructs. Then, we gain closure on the description of motivation by drawing the distinction between intrinsic and extrinsic motivation.

To help you understand how all of the parts of motivation fit together, Figure 11.1 is provided. For simplicity, this figure shows a time line ranging from the point at which someone first thinks about what to do, to the point at which he or she experiences the consequences of the course of action he or she has chosen. Each of the parts of motivation (e.g., goals, ability beliefs, etc.) are placed along the timeline at a spot which illustrates the role this part plays in motivation.

Goals

In what follows, we shall examine goals in three parts. First, we shall describe the nature of goals. Then, we shall examine the various types of goals. Finally, we see how goals affect student motivation and learning.

The Nature of Goals

Goals have to do with the *reasons* people do what they do. More specifically, goals specify something that a person would like to accomplish by engaging in a par-

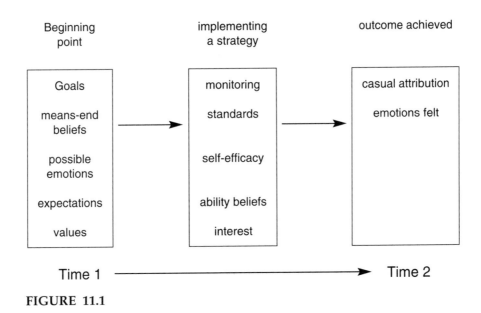

FIGURE 11.1

ticular activity (Stipek, 1993; Wentzel, 1991). In specifying how things should turn out, goals tend to direct or guide behavior.

In many situations, goals often remain implicit until someone asks questions such as "Why did you go to class?" or "Why are you taking this course?" Answers to such questions usually start with phrases such as "I have to . . ." or "I want to . . ." Regardless of whether you have to do something or want to do something, all goals have to do with personal *desires* (Searle, 1983). Sometimes you have the desire to do what you are told because you have found that circumventing rules can lead to undesirable consequences (e.g., you would get into trouble). Other times you are not trying to avoid problems as much as seek out desirable things (e.g., set a goal of making dinner when you are hungry).

Goals are inherently *cognitive* in that they are mental representations of some future state of affairs (Bandura, 1986). Thus, motivation theorists who espouse goals tend not to be strict behaviorists, because they argue that people control their *own* behavior by thinking about some desirable outcome and then performing actions that might bring about this desired outcome. Given the a priori character of goals, they are shown in Figure 11.1 at the very start of the time line.

Although goals specify how things might turn out, they often start off being somewhat vague. For example, the first time that people set career goals for themselves, they tend to say such things as, "I'd like to make a lot of money" or "I'd like to work with people." Such goals are not very helpful or directive, since there are several ways to make a good salary and there are many jobs that involve interactions with people. Goals only start directing people in a meaningful way when they become more specific.

Types of Goals

An examination of the research on motivation shows that researchers have proposed three dichotomies and one trichotomy of goal types. The first dichotomy is the "learning versus performance goal" dichotomy (Dweck & Leggett, 1988; Stipek, 1993). People who have *learning* goals (also called "mastery" or "task" goals) engage in behaviors in order to understand something, gain mastery over a skill, enjoy themselves, or feel competent. In contrast, people who have *performance* goals (also called "ego" goals) engage in behaviors in order to gain the approval of others, look better than others, gain rewards, or avoid criticism.

The second dichotomy of goals pertains to the distinction between proximal and distal goals (Bandura & Schunk, 1981; Schunk, 1991). *Proximal* goals are short-term goals such as "I want to get an A on the test next week." *Distal* goals are long-term goals such as "I want to get a 4.0 by the end of next year." In Information Processing theory terms (e.g., Siegler, 1983), proximal goals can be said to be subgoals of an overall, superordinate goal. In effect, they seem to be steps along a longer path. Distal goals, in contrast, tend to be of the superordinate variety.

The third dichotomy has to do with the distinction between *academic* and *social* goals (Wentzel, 1991). Research shows that in addition to having academic goals such as being a successful student, learning new things, understanding things, doing the best you can, and getting things done on time, students also have social goals, such as earning approval from others, having fun, making friends, helping others, being dependable, and being responsible.

In addition to the dichotomies of goals described above, there is also a trichotomy of goals that comes from the work on the cooperative learning approach (e.g., Johnson & Johnson, 1987; Slavin, 1990). Advocates of this approach suggest that classrooms can have one of three *goal structures*: individualistic, competitive, and cooperative. When a classroom is arranged in such a way that anyone has the opportunity to get the rewards of the classroom (e.g., good grades), students tend to set the goal of doing as well as they can (an individualistic goal structure). Such students are often indifferent to how well other students do (e.g., "As long as I get my A, who cares."). When only a certain number of students can get the best grade (e.g., just the top ten), students start thinking about doing better than other people in class (not only about doing generally well). Moreover, they want other students to perform poorly. Both of these desires reflect a competitive goal structure. When a classroom is arranged such that the assignment of rewards is based on how well a small group of students perform as a whole, students not only want themselves to do well, but they also want the other students in their own group to do well (a cooperative goal structure).

Effects of Goals on Motivation and Learning

Researchers have discovered five main ways that goals affect student behavior. As we shall see, three of these outcomes derive from the research on the "learning versus performance goal" dichotomy, one outcome derives from the research on the "proximal versus distal goal" dichotomy, one outcome derives from the "academic versus social goal" dichotomy, and the final one derives from cooperative learning theory.

First, whereas students who have learning goals seek challenging tasks that help them develop their competencies, students with performance goals choose tasks that will make them look competent to others (Dweck, 1986; Nicholls, 1983). In order to look good all of the time, of course, you need to do things that you are already good at. Thus, students with performance goals would be expected to rarely challenge themselves and to develop expertise in an area at a slower rate than students with learning goals.

Second, whereas students with learning goals see their teacher as a resource or guide, students with performance goals see their teacher as an evaluator who will either reward or punish their behavior (Stipek, 1993). Thus, it would be predicted that students with learning goals would seek help from their teachers more often than students with performance goals. Inasmuch as teachers can be a valuable resource for information and strategies, it would be further expected that students who seek help appropriately would show greater achievement than students who do not (Wentzel, 1991).

Third, goals can affect what students pay attention to in a learning situation. Students who care more about how they look than what they are learning will tend to learn less than students who are mastery-oriented. In support of this claim, research shows that students do not process information at a deep level when they are overly concerned about evaluation or looking bad (Graham & Golan, 1991; Nicholls, 1983; Stipek, 1993).

Fourth, research has found three ways that proximal goals help students more than distal goals: (a) proximal goals provide more frequent and continual feedback, (b) the feedback provided when proximal goals are met gives students a constant sense of progress and mastery (Schunk, 1991), and (c) it is easier to keep proximal goals in mind than distal goals (i.e., students are more likely to forget distal goals).

Fifth, social goals such as being helpful, responsible, and compliant have been found to be strongly related to academic achievement (Wentzel, 1989, 1991). Why should this be the case? It seems that students who know how to get along with others and who are helpful, responsible, and compliant have more frequent and positive interactions with their teachers and peers. The more interactions one has with teachers and competent peers, the more likely one is to achieve (Vygotsky, 1962; Wentzel, 1991). Of course, not all social goals relate to success in school. For example, students who strongly endorse the goal of having fun in school have been found to have low GPAs (Wentzel, 1989).

Finally, the type of goal structure fostered within individual classrooms has predictable consequences on student learning and achievement. Whereas student achievement is higher when cooperative learning programs have both cooperative and competitive elements (Slavin, 1990), competitive goal structures discourage students from helping each other, set up a pecking order in the classroom, and create a situation in which low achievers have little chance of success (Ames, 1986; Johnson & Johnson, 1987). In thinking about the type of classroom they would like to design, teachers have to decide whether the higher achievement fostered by competition outweighs its negative consequences.

Knowledge

Although goals are crucial to getting the ball rolling, there are several other factors that help you attain your goals. For instance, in addition to knowing what you want (e.g., to be rich), you also need to know how to get what you want (e.g., how to get rich). That brings us to the second key component of motivation: knowledge.

In several contemporary motivational accounts, beliefs related to how-to knowledge have been called *means-end* beliefs (e.g., Skinner, Chapman & Baltes, 1988). Because means-end beliefs have to do with knowing how to do things to reach certain goals, we can simply say that there is very little difference between means-end beliefs and *procedural knowledge* (See Chapters 3 and 9 for discussions of procedural knowledge). Thus, beliefs about how to add fractions, conduct an experiment, and decode a word are all examples of means-ends beliefs (and procedural knowledge). Examples in the social realm include knowing how to make friends or persuade others.

So far, then, we have accumulated two possible explanations of someone's behavior. In particular, in response to motivation-related questions such as "Why is she going to graduate school?", we can say such things as "She wants to earn a good salary" (referring to her goals) or "She thinks that getting an M.B.A. will help her get a high-paying job" (referring to her means-ends belief/procedural knowledge). Similarly, we can account for someone's lack of motivation for something (e.g., not finishing high school) by arguing that he or she lacks certain goals or lacks appropriate procedural knowledge.

Metacognitive Processes

The research on motivation reveals that people engage in a variety of monitoring and appraisal activities. Given the self-reflective quality of both monitoring and appraisal (Bandura, 1986), these activities are grouped under the single heading "metacognitive processes" in this book. In what follows, we shall examine three aspects of metacognition related to motivation: (a) monitoring of progress, (b) appraisal of actions, and (c) appraisal of outcomes.

Monitoring of Progress

Although some goals can be attained quickly with a single action (e.g., scratching one's head to relieve an itch), many other goals involve a series of actions and take some time to fulfill. As a result, it is often necessary to examine how far one has progressed towards one's goals (Bandura, 1986). To see the utility of occasionally taking stock of one's progress, consider the case of a dieter who sets the goal for himself of losing five pounds by the time he goes to his ten-year college reunion (two months away). After seeing several glowing endorsements by celebrities, he decides to use a popular liquid diet to achieve this goal (a means-end belief). It should be obvious that in order to maximize his goal of losing the five pounds within two months, our dieter should weigh himself occasionally to see whether the liquid diet is working. By engaging in monitoring, he could switch diets in sufficient time to lose the weight if he finds out early on that the liquid diet is not working (i.e., he could switch to Plan B).

In a sense, then, humans have the capacity to envision a "path" leading from where they currently are (e.g., five pounds too heavy) to some ultimate goal state (e.g., five pounds lighter). The path is a set of intermediate states of affairs that connect the initial state to the goal state (Newell & Simon, 1972). Apparently, this path is a natural consequence of setting a goal and deciding on a particular strategy for attaining the goal. Without this capacity for creating mental paths, we would have no way of knowing how far we have progressed in some endeavor.

Appraisal of Actions

The use of the term *appraisal* is meant to capture notions such as *evaluation* and *estimation*. Thus, when we speak of the appraisal of actions, we are referring to the processes of (a) evaluating actions that have been already performed (e.g., they were performed well; what I am doing is working; I am enjoying myself, etc.) and (b) estimating the likelihood that actions will be performed in a particular way in the future (e.g., it is likely that they will be performed well; it is likely that such-and-such strategy will work; it is likely that I will enjoy myself).

The appraisal of past and future actions often occurs in the midst of monitoring your progress. Whenever you pause to reflect upon your progress, you think about what you have done and whether it is a good idea to continue that course of action. Thus, appraisal is often what we do when we monitor our progress. Having said that, let's now examine three types of beliefs that play an important role in the appraisal process: personal standards, self-efficacy beliefs, and ability beliefs. Then, we shall examine an additional dimension along which we judge actions: interest.

Personal Standards.   Personal standards refer to beliefs about what is "good enough." Recall that when you monitor your progress, you stop and think about how well things are going. In order to form such a judgment, you have to compare your actual progress to some standard (Bandura, 1986). Let's say that you are dieting and you find that you have lost one pound a week for the last three weeks. Is that good enough? Is it too fast? Is it too slow? Or, let's say that you are devoting a certain amount of time and effort to your courses. After getting your midterm exam grades, you might think about whether your grades are good enough. Should you study harder next time or do something different? Thus, standards have to do with issues of quality and often involve considerations of *rate* of change or progress. Obviously, one's standards play an important role in the process of deciding whether to continue a course of action or switch to a new one.

Self-Efficacy Beliefs.   Self-efficacy pertains to an individual's belief that he or she can succeed in a particular type of task (Bandura, 1986). In order to feel self-efficacious about something, the individual must first know which actions to perform to do well (a means-end belief) and also how well these actions need to be performed by *anyone*. But self-efficacy has to do with the person's belief that *he* or *she* has the ability to perform these actions well enough to succeed. For example, in the midst of a basketball game, I might know that I would have to shoot a basketball through the hoop in order to earn the two points that my team needs to win (a means-end belief), but nevertheless believe that I lack the skill necessary to make that shot under pressure. Bandura's (1986) notion of self-efficacy is quite similar to Skinner et al.'s (1988) notion of *agency beliefs* (i.e., beliefs about being able to personally control successes).

How would self-efficacy beliefs affect the monitoring/ appraisal process? Consider our dieting and studying examples again. If our dieter tried extremely hard to lose weight and discovers that he lost three pounds in three weeks, his decision to stay on the liquid diet would be affected by his sense of self-efficacy and by his standards. If he has high self-efficacy about dieting (i.e., he thinks that he has the self-control and pain tolerance needed to diet), and he is dissatisfied with his weight loss, he would be expected to find an even stricter diet. If he has low self-efficacy, however, he would be expected to discontinue dieting altogether.

Similar predictions would be made about studying. Someone with high self-efficacy about their ability to study who got disappointing midterm grades would try to find better study habits and expend more effort next time. Someone with low self-efficacy would tend to lose interest in studying.

In a variety of laboratory studies, researchers have shown that self-efficacy relates to effort, persistence, and quality of problem-solving on tasks (Bandura, 1986; Bandura & Wood, 1989). In addition, studies of schoolchildren show that about 14 percent of the variance in academic achievement is accounted for by self-efficacy (Berry & West, 1993).

Ability Beliefs.   Ability beliefs are closely related to, though somewhat distinct from, self-efficacy beliefs. Whereas a self-efficacy belief is a judgment about your ability to be successful in a particular task in a particular situation, an ability belief is a general sense of your skill in an area or set of areas (Stipek, 1993; Berry & West, 1993). Thus, whereas an example of a self-efficacy belief would be "I can get an A on that history test tomorrow," an example of an ability belief would be "I'm pretty good in social studies" or "I'm a very good student."

Most students have a large number of ability beliefs about school subjects, sports, social relations, and their appearance. Researchers have found that the ability beliefs, which comprise a student's *self-concept*, seem to be mentally arranged into a hierarchy. At the top of the hierarchy, there is a general self-concept that is an overall sense of how competent one feels (e.g., "I'm pretty good at most things"). Just below the general self-concept, beliefs subdivide into academic and nonacademic self-concepts (e.g., "I do pretty well in school" versus "I make friends easily"). Then, the academic self-concept is further divided into lower-level beliefs about abilities in specific subjects (e.g., math, science, and reading), and the nonacademic self-concept is further divided into social, emotional, and physical self-concepts (Marsh, 1989; Harter, 1985). Support for this hierarchical framework comes from studies that show that people who generally feel good about themselves can nevertheless feel that they are not very good in certain things (e.g., math). Similarly, researchers have found a near-zero correlation between verbal and math self-concepts (Feather, 1988; Marsh, 1989).

In addition to discovering that people have specific and general beliefs about their abilities in academic subjects, researchers have also found that students develop one of two conceptions of their intelligence. Students who hold an *entity view* of their intelligence believe that (a) intelligence is a fixed capacity that does not increase or decrease over time and (b) smart people learn things effortlessly and rarely make errors. In contrast, student who hold an *incremental view* of their intelligence believe that intelligence is not a fixed capacity. In fact, they feel that each time one learns a new skill, one becomes that much smarter. Moreover, they recognize that when one is learning a new skill, expending effort and making mistakes are all part of the game (Dweck & Elliot, 1983).

In sum, then, we have very specific beliefs about our abilities in certain areas (e.g., math, sports, social relations) as well as more general conceptions about our overall abilities and intelligence. How do these ability beliefs affect our motivation? It seems that ability beliefs play a role in the appraisal process similar to that played by self-efficacy beliefs. In particular, people who feel good about their ability and who have an incremental view of their intelligence would be expected to expend more effort and persist more after failure than people with less positive views of their skill or people who hold an entity view of their intelligence.

But in addition to affecting the way people behave midstream in their quest for goals, ability beliefs and views of intelligence also affect the initial goals people set for themselves. For example, when given a choice between easy and hard tasks in an area (e.g., science), people who feel more competent about their skill in that area would be more likely to choose the harder task than people with less positive views of their skill. Thus, similar to students who have learning goals (see above), students who have positive views of their ability and who hold an incremental view of their intelligence would be more likely to challenge themselves than students with less positive views of their ability or students with an entity view of their intelligence (Dweck & Elliot, 1983).

Interest.   A final factor that plays a role in the process of appraising actions is interest. Interest is conceptualized as a quality of a person-object interaction that can show itself in the form of prolonged, relatively effortless attention and feelings of pleasure and concentration (Renninger, Hidi & Krapp, 1991). Thus, interest involves a blending of cognitive processes (i.e., attention) and emotional processes (i.e., feelings of pleasure and enjoyment). Interest has been viewed both as a traitlike tendency of individuals (e.g., having a long-standing interest in science) as well as a property of objects that capture the attention of most people (e.g., a novel that most people find interesting).

Similar to ability beliefs, interest can affect both early and midstream processes in the motivation system. Early on, interest can affect the choices people make and goals they set for themselves (Wigfield & Eccles, 1992). When people monitor their progress, interest can play a role in judgments of how things are going. One student might find an activity to be particularly interesting and another might find it to be boring. Interest can affect the degree to which a student persists in an activity, even when the student has high self-efficacy or positive ability beliefs for a skill. For example, a college student who has a 4.0 GPA in engineering and who has positive ability beliefs might nevertheless switch his major to music education because he finds the latter topic to be more interesting than the former.

Appraisal of Outcomes

In addition to monitoring their progress and appraising their actions midstream, people also estimate the likelihood that certain future events will occur and evaluate their performance after their goals have been met. The idea that people think about what will happen next has been implicit in many of the things said so far. For example, when people monitor their progress, they not only think about how well things are going, they also think about how well things will go in the future. Moreover, people with high self-efficacy for a task (e.g., a math problem) believe that although they might be still far from their goal, they can still reach it if they try something else or double their efforts.

In this section, we will examine how people evaluate outcomes both before they occur and after they occur. In particular, we will examine the factors that influence the judgments people make when they ask themselves forward-looking questions such as "What will happen next?", "Why will it happen?", and "How will I feel about it if it does happen?" as well as backward-looking questions such as "What happened?", "Why did it happen?" and "How do I feel about it?". As we shall see, these questions pertain to four components of motivation: expectations, causal attributions, values, and emotions.

Expectations.   An expectation is a belief about the likelihood of something happening in the future. In theories of motivation and decision making, the expectations that have received a lot of scrutiny are those pertaining to outcomes (Atkinson, 1964; Slovic, 1990). Some examples of expectations for outcomes include statements such as "It probably won't rain today," "It is pretty likely that I will get a 4.0 this semester," and "I think I will find my ideal mate."

When people form judgments about the likelihood that an outcome will happen, they consider both internal and external factors. By internal factors, it is meant such things as (a) how much skill it would take to attain the outcome and whether they have the skill and (b) how much effort it would take to reach their goals and whether they are likely to expend the necessary effort. By external factors, it is meant those things that are not under the control of the person (e.g., weather patterns, the number of A grades given by some teachers, and the number of unmarried, desirable adults that you normally encounter). So, when a person feels that there is only a 20 percent chance that he or she will get a 4.0 this semester, a portion of this estimate could derive from the perceptions of internal factors (e.g., "I have to work really hard to get an A") and the remainder could derive from the perceptions of external factors (e.g., "I have to take Dr. Jones next semester and he does not gives many A's").

Causal Attributions.   In contrast to expectations that are forward-looking, causal attributions are initially backward-looking. In particular, causal attributions are made after an outcome has occurred. When someone makes a causal attribution, he or she assigns causality to some factor that seems to be responsible for the outcome (Weiner, 1986). For example, consider the situation in which two students get a C on the same test. One student might attribute this outcome to ineffective study strategies and the other might attribute it to poor teaching on the part of the instructor.

When trying to explain achievement-related outcomes, research has shown that people tend to attribute their successes and failures to one of two main factors: ability or effort. For example, when students do poorly on a test, one might say "I'm not very good in math" (attributing the outcome to low ability) and another might say "I didn't try very hard" (attributing the outcome to low effort). But students also have been found to cite bad luck, poor teaching, and a variety of other idiosyncratic factors in explaining why they got the grade they did (Weiner, 1986).

Weiner (1986) argues that causes such as ability and effort vary along three dimensions: stability, controllability, and locus. Whereas stable causes reflect a permanent aspect of a person or situation, unstable causes reflect a transient or variable aspect. Depending on the person, some people might consider their ability to be a stable attribute (if they have an entity view of their intelligence) and effort to be an unstable attribute (if they often apply themselves in a variable way). Other people might view their ability to be an unstable attribute (if they have an incremental view) and effort to be a stable trait (if they consider themselves to be "naturally lazy").

The perceived stability of a cause plays an important role in performance expectations. In particular, if people attribute their performance to a stable cause, it is normal for them to raise their expectations following success and lower their expectations following failure (Weiner, 1986). For example, consider the case of a student who thinks that there is a 60 percent chance that he will get a B on a test. If he (a) ends up getting a C on the test, (b) attributes his failure to low ability, and (c) believes that ability is a stable trait, he will probably think that he has less than a 60 percent chance of a B on the next test. However, if he attributes his failure to a temporary lapse of effort, he might continue to think that he has a 60 percent chance of a B on the next test.

In addition to viewing causes as being stable or unstable, students also consider some causes to be controllable (e.g., how hard they try) and other causes to be uncontrollable (e.g., how smart they are). Moreover, some causes of success and failure are believed to be internal (e.g., effort and ability) and others are external (e.g., teacher bias, bad luck, and hard tests).

Values.   In theories of motivation and decision making, values have to do with the desirable and undesirable aspects of outcomes (Feather, 1988; Slovic, 1990; Wigfield & Eccles, 1992). What makes something desirable or undesirable, of course, depends on the person. Some people think that it is important to be rich and others think that it is important to be well liked.

In a recent analysis, Wigfield & Eccles (1992) argued that there are four different types of values that influence achievement behaviors: *attainment value, intrinsic value, utility value,* and *cost.* Attainment value has to do with whether it is important to do well on the task. To see the attainment value of something, ask yourself questions such as "Do I care how well I do on this? Is it important to me to do well?" The intrinsic value of a task concerns the enjoyment you would feel if you engaged in the task. To see the intrinsic value of something, ask yourself the following question: "Would I find it to be enjoyable or interesting?" Note that interest seems to play a role when people appraise actions (see above) and when they appraise outcomes. The utility value of a task concerns the relation between the task and future goals. To see the utility value of a task, ask yourself the question "Will doing this help me meet my goals?" The cost of a choice concerns all of the negative aspects of performing a task including negative emotions (e.g., embarrassment or anxiety) and the amount of effort needed. To see the cost of something, ask yourself, "What would I lose if I engaged in this task?"

Values affect behavior in the following way: People tend to seek out desirable outcomes and avoid undesirable outcomes. By *desirable,* it is meant an outcome judged to be important, interesting, useful, or "low cost" (Wigfield & Eccles, 1992). By *undesirable,* it is meant unimportant, uninteresting, useless, or costly outcomes.

Although values are an important reason people make the choices they do, values alone do not determine achievement behavior. In particular, people try to attain desirable outcomes only if there is a reasonably good chance that they can attain them (Slovic, 1990; Wigfield & Eccles, 1992). For example, whereas most students will tell you that getting an A is more desirable than getting a B, only those students who think that is it possible to get an A will try to get it. Thus, *both* expectancies and values affect motivation.

Emotions.   In addition to expectancies, attributions, and values, the final factor that affects how an outcome is appraised is the emotion associated with it. Whereas the attainment of some outcomes is likely to engender positive emotions in the person who attains them (e.g., joy, pride, or self-esteem), other outcomes are likely to engender negative emotions (e.g., anxiety, guilt, or shame). Clearly, most people want to experience the positive emotions more often than the negative emotions. Thus, we would expect that people would try to attain outcomes that engender positive feelings and avoid those outcomes that engender negative feelings.

Of all the emotions that may affect motivation, there are four that have received the most attention from motivation researchers: anxiety, shame, pride, and self-esteem. Let's examine the two negative emotions first and the two positive emotions second.

Anxiety is a complex emotion that is closely related to fear and worry. Researchers have identified both a self-evaluative component and a somatic/physiological component of anxiety (Wigfield & Eccles, 1989). The self-evaluative component consists of negative cognitions about being able to do well on something (e.g., "I'm afraid I'll probably flunk the exam"), and the somatic component involves the actual emotional and bodily reaction associated with thinking about the potential failure. Studies show that the self-evaluative component of anxiety relates more strongly to school performance than the somatic component.

Shame is an emotional response that is engendered when an individual feels responsible for poor behavior (Weiner, 1986). Students are most likely to feel shame when they attribute their failures to low ability. When students attribute their poor performance to low effort, they are more likely to feel guilty than embarrassed.

In sum, then, the two negative emotions come into play when students are thinking about possible failure in the future or when they are thinking about failures that occurred in the past. As we shall see, the two positive emotions are the consequences of successes rather than failure.

When students feel that they are responsible for their successes through hard work or ability, they are likely to feel *pride*. In a sense, they say, "What I did was good and I am entirely responsible for it." *Self-esteem* is a generalized sense of pride and competence that is accrued across many episodes of success.

As mentioned above, emotions play a role in assessments of the desirability of outcomes. Students think that outcomes that engender happiness or pride are more desirable than outcomes that engender anxiety, guilt, or shame. Thus, emotions play a role in decisions regarding which outcomes to go after. In addition, we have seen that some negative emotions play a debilitating role when people are in the middle of trying to attain outcomes. Anxiety can promote maladaptive coping behaviors (e.g., avoiding academic situations; thinking about failure rather than studying properly, etc.).

Instrinsic versus Extrinsic Motivation

Before moving on to a consideration of developmental and individual differences in motivation, it is important to examine one final issue that in many ways captures a lot of what has been said so far: the distinction between intrinsic and extrinsic motivation. People who engage in behaviors to receive praise, gain tangible rewards, or avoid punishment are *extrinsically* motivated (e.g., a fourth grader who works on his science project to win the prize for best project). People who engage in behaviors to feel competent, gain mastery over some skill, or satisfy their curiosity are *intrinsically* motivated (e.g., a fourth grader who continues to work on a science project after the science fair is over to tinker with it further). In effect, when you are intrinsically motivated, you are the one making yourself do something and you are engaged in an activity for that activity's sake (e.g., read for the sake of reading). When you are extrinsically motivated, someone else is in control of how you behave. Overall we can say that intrinsic motivation concerns engaging in a task as an end in itself; extrinsic motivation concerns using a task as a means to an end (Deci & Ryan, 1985).

Researchers who have examined intrinsic motivation suggest that people are naturally inclined to seek feelings of competence, gain control over their environment, set challenges for themselves, and satisfy their curiosities (Berlyne, 1966; Deci & Ryan, 1985; Stipek, 1993). That is, no one has to make you want to feel competent and so forth, you just naturally want to. Researchers have found that feelings of competence naturally follow successes, particularly if a student believes she controlled the success. When given a choice of an easy, moderately difficult, or hard task, most people choose the moderately difficult one. Finally, the introduction of novelty, surprise, or events that lack an explanation seems to engender attention and sustained interest.

It is relatively easy to make someone who is intrinsically motivated into someone who is extrinsically motivated. The key factors in this shift are the frequent introduction of external rewards (e.g., prizes, personal recognition) or punishments, as well as the use of competition and social comparison in the classroom (Ames, 1986; Deci & Ryan, 1985).

Given what has been said so far, we can see that learning goals, the incremental view of intelligence, self-efficacy, interest, and values all have to do with intrinsic motivation. In contrast, performance goals, the entity view of intelligence, and the behaviorist notions of reinforcement and punishment have to do with extrinsic motivation.

Summary

We have seen that motivation constructs can be grouped under three main headings: goals, knowledge, and metacognitive processes. A goal is a future-oriented specification of what someone wants. Knowledge has to do with knowing how to make things happen. The metacognitive processes include (a) monitoring of progress, (b) using your beliefs and preferences to appraise ongoing actions, (c) evaluating the likelihood and desirability of outcomes, and (d) explaining why outcomes occurred. In addition, we have found that people can either be intrinsically or extrinsically motivated. Given this description of the nature of motivation, we would expect to find that motivated individuals would have different goals and knowledge than less motivated individuals, and would also engage in metacognitive processes differently. In the next two sections, we shall examine whether this is the case.

The Development of Motivation

So far we have examined the constituent parts of motivation. In this section, we shall examine the literature to see whether there is evidence that these constituent parts change over time. That is, we shall attempt to answer questions such as "Do older students have different goals than younger students?" "Do older students have different means-end beliefs than younger students?" and "Do older students engage in the metacognitive aspects of motivation differently from younger students?"

Goals

Researchers who have examined motivational goals have not made a large number of developmental comparisons. As a result, little is known about developmental trends in the "natural" expression of learning, performance, proximal, distal, academic, or social goals. There is, however, some reason to believe that whereas younger children might be more likely to engage in a task for its own sake (i.e., adopt learning goals), older students might be more likely to do so because they believe they should or because they want to get a good grade (i.e., adopt performance goals) (Dweck & Elliot, 1988; Nicholls, 1983). Similarly, there is reason to suspect that whereas social goals might become more important with age, academic goals might become less important with age. If a number of studies were to confirm these expectations, it would mean that students would be less likely to challenge themselves or go after high grades with age.

Although motivation researchers have not compiled extensive evidence in support of the claim that goals change with age, researchers who study other topics have. For example, researchers who study reading comprehension have found that older and younger children have different goals when they read (Paris & Byrnes, 1989). Researchers who study writing have revealed similar findings (Scardamalia & Bereiter, 1986).

Knowledge

Unlike the goals component that concerns the *reasons* students engage in specific behaviors, the knowledge component has to do with *what* they do. As mentioned in the previous section, older students and younger students often engage in the same behaviors (e.g., read) but do so for different reasons (e.g., to pronounce words properly versus to learn something). But it is also true that older students could have the same goals as younger students (e.g., get an A) but nevertheless try to attain these goals in different ways (e.g., using different studying techniques). In the present section, we are concerned with the latter possibility.

We have seen in many of the chapters in this book that older students are more likely than younger students to have more accurate and extensive procedural knowledge. In particular, the latter know more math procedures, scientific problem-solving techniques, reading strategies, and writing skills. In addition, they are more likely to know effective memory and study strategies.

Metacognitive Processes

We have seen so far that there are two possible answers to questions of the form "Why are older children doing X and younger children doing Y?". The first would be that older children have different goals than younger children. The second would be that older children have different means-end beliefs than younger children. In this section, we will examine some additional answers that focus on the three subdivisions of metacognitive processes that we examined earlier: monitoring of progress, appraisal of actions, and appraisal of outcomes.

Monitoring of Progress

Research has shown that older children are more likely to monitor their performance than younger children (e.g., Baker & Brown, 1984; Markman, 1981). It turns out that this developmental trend has both positive and negative consequences for younger children. Because they do not monitor how far they have progressed toward a goal, younger children cannot become discouraged by the realization that they have not progressed very far. As a result, it may not matter what their standards are or how highly they think of themselves. All young children would probably continue with the same course of action that they started with. But whereas young children gain something by not being discouraged as often as older children, they lose something in that they will not fix a strategy that is not working.

Appraisal of Actions

Personal Standards and Self-Efficacy. Very few studies have examined the possibility of developmental differences in personal standards or self-efficacy. Bandura (1986) suggests that personal standards become progressively internalized as children interact with parents, peers, and teachers. Both direct instruction and modeling play a role in this internalization process. From this account, we can speculate that older students might be more likely to have standards than younger students. We cannot, however, say whether the former have higher standards than the latter.

With respect to self-efficacy, children develop a sense that they have control over successes by virtue of having many experiences in which their actions produced success and proportionately fewer experiences of failure (Bandura, 1986). Given the standard curriculum in which certain skills are reintroduced year after year, one would expect that older children would feel more self-efficacious than younger children when asked to think about the same types of tasks (because the latter have had more practice with these tasks). In support of this claim, Zimmerman & Martinez-Pons (1990) found that mean levels of self-efficacy for both verbal skills and math skills increased significantly from the fifth to eleventh grades.

If personal standards stay the same over time and more and more children come to believe that they can be successful, it would be predicted that older children as a group would have more motivation than younger children. If standards increase over time, we would expect the levels of motivation of older children to be that much more enhanced. However, if children lower their standards at the same rate that they increase in their sense of self-efficacy, we would expect roughly similar levels of motivation in younger and older students. Clearly, given the complex interactions among goals, standards and self-efficacy, more developmental research is needed to sort out developmental trends in overall motivation levels.

Ability Beliefs.   Research has revealed three ways in which ability beliefs change over time. First, children's self-concept becomes increasingly differentiated with age. That is, the gap between their academic and nonacademic beliefs becomes wider, as does the gap between their math and verbal self-concepts (Marsh, 1989). Concretely, this would mean that whereas younger students would hold themselves in high regard for all subject areas, older students would feel that they are better in some areas than others.

Second, there appears to be a curvilinear trend in which the self-concept declines during preadolescence and early adolescence, levels out in middle adolescence, and then increases in late adolescence and early adulthood (Marsh, 1989). These first two trends would suggest that whereas elementary students would show high levels of motivation and persistence for all subjects, middle school students would show generally less motivation overall. In addition, middle school students would apply themselves only in those subjects for which they have higher ability beliefs. During high school and beyond, motivation levels should return for most subject areas. But again, there is much more to motivation than ability beliefs, so research is needed to examine the patterns.

Third, whereas older students make a clear distinction between effort and ability, younger students seem to think that effort and ability are the same (Nicholls, 1983; Stipek, 1993). Thus, younger students tend to think that someone who is "really smart" is someone who "tries really hard." In contrast, once students acquire an entity view of intelligence, they come to believe that smart people do not have to try very hard (i.e., "things come easily to them").

Interest.   There are only a few studies that have examined the development of interests over time, because researchers have often viewed interest as an individual difference variable rather than a developmental difference variable. In one study, Wigfield et al. (1989) asked first, second, and fourth graders to rate their enjoyment of various school subjects. They found that whereas there were no grade differences in children's liking of math or computers, there were differences in their liking of reading, music, and sports. In particular, both first and second graders liked reading more than fourth graders. The gap in ratings for reading between the first and fourth grades represented about a 15 percent drop. Also, whereas there was a 9 percent decline in children's liking of music over time, there was an 11 percent increase in their liking of sports over time. At all grade levels, children liked computers the best (average rating = 6.3 out of 7) followed by sports (average rating = 6.0), music (average rating = 5.25), reading (average rating = 5.25), and math (average rating = 5.0). Thus, the ratings for math were about 21 percent lower than those for computers.

Because elementary children are not given much choice over the subjects they learn, these age differences would probably affect other aspects of school performance besides course selection, such as attention, effort, and persistence. For example, during reading or music lessons, fourth grade teachers would be more likely to find their students having problems with attention and persistence than first grade teachers. Also, the overall average ratings suggest that math would not capture the attention of even the first graders.

In a study involving older students, Wigfield et al. (1991) asked children to rate their liking of social activities, sports, math, and English both before and after they made the transition to junior high school. Whereas students' liking of social activities and English stayed about the same over time, there was a 6 percent drop in interest in sports and a 10 percent drop in interest in math. In addition, there were large differences in what students found interesting. Students rated social activities and sports substantially (i.e., 25 percent) higher than math or English.

Appraisal of Outcomes

Expectancies and Attributions.   Research shows that young children are generally quite optimistic about things working out in their favor (Stipek, 1993). Part of their optimism stems from how they view their ability, another part derives from their attributions of success and failure, and still another part comes from their inability to differentiate between luck and skill (Nicholls, 1983). If young children hold an incremental view of their intelligence and feel that effort is their key to success, they will tend to be optimistic even after experiencing multiple failures. In particular, after performing poorly, they might say, "Oh, well, I'll just have to try harder next time." Moreover, if luck and skill are not sufficiently differentiated in their minds, they would feel that they have some influence over things that are out of their control (e.g., what will be on a test). Over time, social comparison, feedback from teachers, and other forms of experience inform children about the nature of ability as well as what they can control and what they cannot. As a result, many children will come to feel that they can no longer control success and will lose their initial sense of optimism.

Values.   As mentioned earlier, a central component of children's values is the importance they attach to different topics (Wigfield & Eccles, 1992). In their study of first, second and fourth graders, Wigfield et al. (1989) found that whereas there were no grade differences in the perceived importance of learning math, reading, social skills, or sports, grade differences emerged for learning computers and music. Both computers and music were judged to be less important with age.

In their study of children making the transition to junior high school, Eccles et al. (1989) found that there were significant drops ranging from 3 percent to 6 percent in the perceived importance of math, sports skills, and social skills between the sixth and seventh grades. The perceived importance of English was found to be lower at the start of the seventh grade but rebounded by the end of that year.

Taken together, these two studies show that many subjects lose their value for students between the first and seventh grades.

Emotions.   In the earlier section, The Nature of Motivation, we learned that anxiety, shame, and pride are emotions that play an important role in the motivation system. Here, we shall examine developmental trends in these emotions.

Most theorists assume that students develop test anxiety in response to repeated failure in evaluative situations (Stipek, 1993; Wigfield & Eccles, 1992). Research shows that young students who do poorly on tests do not become anxious right away. Rather, it is not until the end of elementary school that a consistent tendency to be anxious emerges in students.

The key to understanding student anxiety lies in how they define *failure.* Most students define a D or an F as a failure, so D students and F students would be expected to be more anxious about tests than B or A students. And yet, students with high ability can also develop test anxiety, especially if they hold unreasonably high standards for themselves (Stipek, 1993). For example, a student who always gets 95 percent correct on tests might nevertheless treat such performances as failures if he or she feels that only 100 percent is good enough.

Personal standards seem to develop from three main sources: (a) parental expectations, (b) teacher behaviors and classroom structure, and (c) social comparisons (Mac Iver, 1987; Wigfield & Eccles, 1992). When parents and teachers are relatively "transparent" about what they want, when they hold very high standards for performance, and when classrooms are arranged such that it is easy for students to compare their performance to each other's, students are more likely to develop anxiety than when the opposite is true.

Besides anxiety, the other emotion that often emerges in response to repeated failure is shame. Students who feel that they are responsible for performing poorly are likely to feel ashamed (Covington & Omelich, 1981; Weiner, 1986). Anyone who has experienced shame knows how uncomfortable it is to feel that way.

Pride, of course, is the opposite of shame and is felt when a student feels responsible for a successful performance. Both pride and shame emerge during the preschool period soon after children develop a clear sense of self (Stipek, Recchia & McClintic, 1992). Thus, children enter elementary school with a preexisting capacity to feel pride when they are successful. Given the age trends for monitoring of performance, conceptions of ability, and internalization of standards, it would be expected that only some students in the later elementary grades would consistently feel pride (i.e., those students who consistently do well on tests). In contrast, it would be expected that the majority of younger students would feel pride for a whole range of behaviors (e.g., being polite, trying hard, etc.).

Besides feeling emotions when they experience success or failure, children also become increasingly sensitive to the emotions expressed by their teachers. For example, whereas children as young as five recognize the link between teacher anger and low effort on the part of students, only students nine years of age and older comprehend the link between teacher pity and low ability attributions (Graham, Doubleday & Guarino, 1984).

Summary

The overall impression one gets from the developmental literature on motivation is that there are many reasons older children show less motivation than younger children. First, older children are likely to have different goals than younger children (e.g., social goals versus academic goals). Second, older children are more likely to monitor their performance and gauge it against standards than younger children. Third, students in the period ranging from late elementary school to early high school are more likely to have differentiated conceptions of their abilities as well as an overall lower sense of competence than students in the early elementary years. Fourth, students are more likely to encounter failure with age. Those older students who attribute their poor performance to low ability and who think that failure is unavoidable are likely to have low expectations for future success as well as negative emotional reactions such as anxiety, shame, and learned helplessness. At the very least, these students will not try very hard and will engage in a variety of avoidance behaviors (e.g., truancy). Finally, certain topics have been found to be not very interesting to students even in the first grade (e.g., math) and others that start off interesting become less interesting with age (e.g., reading). This is not to say, of course, that all students become less motivated with age. The most successful students will generally increase in their confidence level with age. The decrease in motivation will probably be limited to the least successful students in a grade.

Individual Differences in Motivation

Having described some general trends in the development of motivation, we can now turn our attention to the issue of individual differences. More specifically, we can ask, "Why do some students in a grade have more motivation than other students in that same grade?" As we shall see, individual differences can be found along most dimensions of motivation. Sometimes these differences covary with a student's gender or ability level, and sometimes they do not.

Goals

The first way that students differ concerns their goals. In particular, some students in a class have learning goals and others have performance goals (Dweck

& Elliot, 1983; Nicholls, 1983). Moreover, some set proximal goals, some set distal goals, and some set no goals at all (Bandura, 1986; Zimmerman & Martinez-Pons, 1990). Finally, some students focus more on their social goals than on their academic goals, and others focus more on their academic goals than on their social goals (Wentzel, 1989).

Differences among goals do not seem to covary with gender, but they are related to achievement levels. In particular, high achievement is associated with having learning goals and setting proximal goals for oneself. In addition, high achievers are adept at coordinating both their academic and social goals. That is, they are not only interested in learning information, they are also interested in working toward cooperative arrangements with their teachers and peers (Wentzel, 1991).

Knowledge

Within any given grade, students differ with respect to their means-end beliefs. For example, memory studies show that students will often disagree about which memory strategies are the most effective (Fabricious & Hagen, 1984). Students also differ in their beliefs about the utility of note-taking, studying, and help-seeking behaviors (Pintrich & DeGroot, 1990; Newman, 1991). As was the case for goals, variations among means-ends beliefs seem to covary more with ability level than with gender.

So far, then, we have two possible explanations for why one student in a class might be busily working at an assignment while the student seated in front of him or her is not. The engaged student might have different goals, different means-ends beliefs, or both.

Metacognitive Processes

Monitoring of Progress
The main factor that seems to predict which students in a classroom will monitor their progress and which will not is their ability level. Whereas older, high-achieving students monitor their progress, their same-aged low-achieving and learning-disabled peers do not (Baker & Brown, 1984; Paris & Byrnes, 1989).

Appraisal of Actions

Personal Standards
Research shows that whereas some people are "perfectionists," others are "satisficiers" (Simon, 1956; Siegler, 1988). Perfectionists set very high standards of performance and seem to be satisfied only when they have performed nearly flawlessly. "Satisficiers," in contrast, have lower standards than perfectionists and operate on the principle of performing "good enough." Of course, it is possible to be a high achiever and still be a "satisficier." For example, consider the situation in which students need to get at least 90 percent of test questions right in order to get an A. Whereas a perfectionist would be happy only with a 99 or

100, a "satisficing" student would be content with a 90 or 91. Both students, however, would be given an A.

Self-Efficacy.   Across a variety of domains, studies have revealed that when students in a particular grade are confronted with the same task (e.g., a math or vocabulary task), only some of these students feel highly self-efficacious for that task. Why do some students feel efficacious and others do not? Bandura (1986) suggests that there are four sources of self-efficacy judgments. The first is actual experience with success or failure in that task. Successful people (i.e., high achievers) will tend to feel more efficacious than less successful people (though not always). The second is vicarious experiences in which an individual observes the performance of someone else. Vicarious judgments have their most important effects in those situations in which a student lacks experience in a task and when some other person who has the experience is seen to be similar by the student (e.g., a peer of similar ability). The third is verbal persuasion. Here, the comments of influential others can affect the degree to which an individual feels he or she can control his or her success in a task. The fourth is physiological arousal. Emotional reactions such as anxiety can prompt a student to lose confidence. According to Bandura's (1986) account, individual differences among students in the same classroom could arise from each of these four sources.

It is hard to say at present whether there are gender differences in self-efficacy, because the results are somewhat mixed. In a study of both gifted and nongifted fifth, eighth, and eleventh graders, Zimmerman and Martinez-Pons (1990) found that boys surpassed girls in their verbal self-efficacy (i.e., their certainty about being able to give the correct definition of words) but not in their mathematical self-efficacy (i.e., their certainty about being able to correctly solve a set of math problems). In a sample of engineering students, Hackett et al. (1992) found no significant gender differences in school-related and career-related self-efficacy beliefs. These findings can be contrasted with those of Randhawa et al. (1993) and Betz and Hackett (1983) who found that males felt more self-efficacious than females about being able to (a) solve "everyday" math problems, (b) solve math problems at school, and (c) do well in math courses. The difference between the last two studies and the former two appears to be the fact that the students in the Randhawa et al. and Betz and Hackett studies were older than those in Zimmerman and Martinez-Pons (1990) (i.e., had more time to be exposed to failures, vicarious experiences, and verbal persuasion) and contained proportionately fewer talented students than either Zimmerman and Martinez-Pons (1990) or Hackett et al. (1992). Talented students are more successful than nontalented students and are likely to feel more self-efficacious (regardless of their gender). This explanation of the discrepancies among studies is supported by Kelly (1993) who found that achievement was a more powerful predictor of the career self-efficacy perceptions of ninth and eleventh graders than gender.

Ability Beliefs.   Research on ability beliefs have revealed a number of gender differences. In particular, studies of students in the first through eleventh grades have shown that whereas boys have more positive beliefs about their math and sports abilities than girls, girls have more positive beliefs about their reading and writing skills (Eccles et al., 1993; Marsh et al., 1984; Marsh, 1989; Wigfield et al., 1991).

At first blush, the findings for ability beliefs seem to contradict those for self-efficacy described above in which few gender differences were found for math-related performance. Viewed in a certain way, however, the two data sets may not be contradictory. In particular, self-efficacy only has to do with a sense that you can be successful. Even if you think you have less ability than someone else, you can nevertheless think that you can be successful (e.g., through hard work). Students may, however, decide that it is not worth the effort to continue a course of actions.

Before moving on to research on interests, it is worth noting that students' *perception* of their abilities seems to play a larger role in their motivation-related behavior than their actual performance. As was noted in the chapters on reading, writing, and math (Chapters 4, 5, 6 and 8), girls routinely get better grades than boys in all of these subjects. Differences only arise in math during adolescence on SATs and they are not terribly large. Conversely, gender differences favoring girls in verbal skills are extremely small as well. Given their actual performance, then, we can say that boys and girls either overestimate their ability or underestimate it. However, girls seem to be more "unrealistic" than boys because the correlations among beliefs and teacher ratings of ability are higher for boys than for girls (Eccles et al., 1989; Harter, 1985).

Interests.   Interest is, perhaps, the paradigmatic example of an individual-difference variable. Although there are things that nearly all people find interesting (e.g., a car wreck on the side of a highway) or large subgroups of people find interesting (e.g., boys and sports), it is the norm for people to have their own idiosyncratic tastes and preferences (Renninger, 1991). Nevertheless, gender differences in interests are pervasive enough to influence student motivation and, therefore, warrant some discussion. In both younger and older students, the same pattern emerges: Whereas no gender difference emerges for interest in math, boys report liking sports more than girls and girls report liking reading and English more than boys (Wigfield et al., 1989; Wigfield et al., 1991). Also, older girls report liking social activities more than boys.

Appraisal of Outcomes

Expectancies.   Below the third grade, boys and girls generally do not differ significantly in their expectations for success and failure (Parsons & Ruble, 1977; Stipek & Hoffman, 1980). They begin tasks at an equally high level of optimism and seem equally indifferent to failure experiences. Although slightly older boys and girls also begin tasks with similar levels of optimism, failure seems to affect these older girls more strongly than boys. In particular, whereas boys become only slightly less optimistic after several failures, girls become dramatically less optimistic. Then, when children are nine to 11 years of age, gender differences are apparent even before the task begins, with girls being less optimistic about success than boys.

Attributions.   Within any given classroom, there are individual differences with respect to attributions for success and failure. Some students attribute their performance to their ability (or lack thereof), others attribute it to effort, others attribute it to the ease or difficulty of tests, and still others attribute it to luck (Stipek, 1993; Weiner, 1986).

Beyond these general differences among individuals, consistent gender differences have also been found. In particular, girls are less likely than boys to attribute their successes to high ability and more likely than boys to attribute their failures to low ability (Sohn, 1982; Stipek, 1993). These differences in attributions have been argued to underlie the gender differences in expectations described in the previous section.

Values.   When asked to say what is important to them, it is common for individuals to disagree. For example, whereas some people think that it is important to be ambitious, others think that it is more important to be honest. Similarly, whereas some people think that it is important to be intellectual and logical, others think that it is more important to be forgiving and helpful (Rokeach, 1973). In the academic realm, studies have shown that individuals disagree about the importance of subjects such as math and English (Feather, 1988; Wigfield & Eccles, 1992).

All of these differences have been hypothesized to affect the choices people make and several studies suggest that they do. For example, Feather (1988) found that having values such as being loving and forgiving predicted the importance that college students placed on English, which in turn predicted their enrollment decisions. Similarly, values related to being clean, obedient, polite, responsible, and self-controlled related to the importance placed on math, which in turn affected enrollment decisions in math related-fields. However, subsequent analyses showed that only math and English values predicted course enrollment when factors such as social class, age, and gender were controlled.

As might be expected from previous sections, gender differences have also been found with respect to values. For example, Feather (1988) found that college men valued math more than college women. The reverse was true for English. When asked to assess the usefulness of math, Betz and Hackett (1983) found that college males rated math higher than females did. In a study of first, second, and fourth graders, Eccles et al. (1993) found that whereas boys valued sports activities more than girls did, girls valued reading and music more than boys did. No gender difference was found for math in these young children.

Emotions.   Given the fact that boys are more likely to attribute their successes to their own ability than girls are, it would be expected that boys would be more likely to feel proud after being successful than girls. Conversely, girls should be more likely to feel ashamed or embarrassed after failing than boys because girls are more likely than boys to attribute their failures to low ability. As plausible as these hypotheses may seem, few studies have attempted to verify them. Thus, firm conclusions about gender differences in the expression of pride and shame await future study.

Gender differences have, however, been found for both test anxiety and learned helplessness. In particular, girls are not only more likely to develop test and math anxiety than boys (Betz & Hackett, 1983; Wigfield & Eccles, 1989), they are also more likely show a learned helpless pattern of behavior following a period of prolonged failure (Stipek, 1993; Dweck et al., 1978; Wigfield & Eccles, 1989).

Summary

Within any given classroom, individual differences can be found along any of the aspects of motivation. In particular, students differ in terms of their goals, means-end beliefs, tendency to monitor, standards, self-efficacy, ability beliefs, interests, expectations, and values. Moreover, those who are successful and who view their successes and failures in particular ways tend to experience positive emotions quite often. All other students tend to experience negative emotions quite often.

These overall differences among students also tend to covary with a student's gender. In particular, whereas no gender differences have been reported for goals, means-end beliefs, monitoring, and standards (though they may exist), gender differences have been found for the remaining seven constructs (i.e., 64 percent). Apart from explaining why males and females differ in their choices and levels of persistence in certain activities, these differences mean that school may be a more positive experience for males than for females.

Instructional Implications

As in many previous chapters, we shall first examine some general instructional guidelines suggested by the research on motivation. Then, we shall focus on a specific case study in which researchers examined the effect of classroom structures on student motivation.

General Guidelines

Teachers should:

1. *Help students acquire and coordinate appropriate goals* (e.g., learning goals, proximal goals, social and academic goals);

2. *Empower students with appropriate means-end beliefs* (e.g., not only demonstrate skills but explain why they work);

3. *Provide devices to help them monitor their progress* (e.g., charts and other forms of feedback);

4. *Provide numerous experiences in which children of all skill levels feel successful and competent, but also challenged* (e.g., individualized instruction to just beyond each student's skill level). *Moreover, explicitly point out to students that they controlled the successes that just occurred.* Together, such experiences help students develop appropriately high standards, expectations, feelings of self-efficacy, and advantageous attributions.

5. *Adopt and communicate the incremental view of ability to students* (i.e., that intelligence is not fixed but increases as new skills are acquired; errors are normal in the early phases of learning, etc.);

6. *Point out to students the value and importance of learning certain skills, using authentic and convincing argumentation* (e.g., why it is important to learn long division or learn about other cultures);

7. *Frequently introduce novelty and information that cries out for explanation.*

Case Study

Jacqueline Eccles, Allan Wigfield, and their colleagues have tried to determine why there is a sharp drop in motivation as students make the transition from elementary school to junior high school. In a large-scale study of 12 school districts in Michigan, they identified six differences between elementary classrooms and junior high classrooms that seem to accelerate the already declining motivation of students (Eccles et al., 1993). First, teachers in junior high classrooms place greater emphasis on control and discipline and provide fewer opportunities for student choice than teachers in elementary classrooms. Eccles et al. have found that providing students with choice enhances their intrinsic motivation. Second, there are fewer positive or personal teacher-student interactions in junior high than there are in elementary school. Eccles et al. have found that when students perceive there to be less support from their teachers, students tend to value the subjects taught by these teachers less and find the subjects less interesting. Third, teachers in the junior high tend to use whole-class activities, between-class ability grouping, and public evaluation more often than teachers in elementary schools. Moving from small groups to whole classes makes the environment less personal. Between-class ability grouping and public evaluation promote concerns about evaluation and also make competition more likely. Fourth, junior high teachers feel less efficacious than elementary teachers about their teaching abilities (especially for helping low-achieving students do better). Eccles et al. have found that when teachers do not feel efficacious, their students soon acquire low expectations for themselves as well. Fifth, junior high teachers often assign classwork to first year students that requires a lower level of cognitive skills than the work these students were assigned a year earlier in elementary school. Sixth, junior high teachers use a higher standard in grading than elementary teachers (i.e., it is harder to get an A). The fifth and sixth factors together can have a disastrous effect when a student gets, say, a B for the first time for work on tasks that are perceived as not that challenging. Eccles et al. have found that there is no stronger predictor of a student's sense of self-efficacy than the grades he or she receives. Thus, the harder grading would be expected to produce a new wave of students who suddenly no longer feel efficacious.

This line of research clearly shows that classroom contexts play an important role in student motivation. If you were asked to "fix" this problem in Michigan junior high schools, what would you propose?

Explaining Individual Differences

Summary

1. To make comparisons across studies of gender or ethnic differences easier to interpret, we can use either percent corrects or effect sizes.

2. Studies show that whereas females perform better than males on reading comprehension and writing tests as early as the first grade, males perform better on math, science, and social studies tests beginning in adolescence. The largest differences are found for writing fluency and quality at all age levels (favoring females) and for math problem-solving during adolescence (favoring males).

3. There are four theories that have been proposed to explain gender differences in cognitive performance: the genetic/physiological view, the socialization view, the differential course work/experience view, and the cognitive process view. Each of these theories has its shortcomings.

4. The findings for ethnic differences are quite consistent across subject areas: White students perform substantially better than both African-American and Hispanic students, and Hispanic students perform slightly better than African-American students.

5. There are three main explanations of ethnic differences in cognitive performance: the cognitive deficit view, the contextual view, and the cultural incongruity view. Each of these views has its shortcomings.

6. Each of the theories of gender and ethnic differences provides clues as to how to remediate the differences. However, the fact that we have not developed a fully adequate account of either gender or ethnic differences means that attempts at remediation may not be especially effective.

In Chapters 5 to 11, you were told about a variety of performance differences between subgroups of children in the same grade (e.g., males versus females), but you were not told *why* these subgroups may have differed. In the present chapter, possible explanations of these differences are provided. For the sake of brevity, however, we shall limit the focus to just two types of individual differences that were reported in nearly every chapter: gender differences and ethnic differences.

This chapter is organized as follows. In the first section, we shall define a key construct that has been used to quantify the size of gender and ethnic differences: an effect size. In the second section, we shall examine and evaluate explanations of gender differences in cognitive performance. In the third section, we shall examine and evaluate explanations of ethnic differences. In the final section, the instructional implications of the work on gender and ethnic differences will be drawn.

Effect Sizes

If you were given the assignment of locating all of the studies in which gender differences were found for cognitive skills, you would find a large number of studies. If asked, "On average, how large is the difference between men and women?" you would immediately recognize that this question is hard to answer because the authors of these studies all seemed to use a different test. For example, in one study, researchers may have given a 20-item spatial test to men and women and found that, on average, men got 15 right and women got ten right. Another study might have given a 60-item math test (e.g., the SAT math) to men and women and found that, on average, men got 28 right and women got 22 right. Is the five-item difference on the spatial test big or small? How about the six-item difference on the SAT? Which of these differences are bigger?

The main reason these questions are hard to answer is that the differences are not on the same scale. One way to make all of the differences be on the same scale is to convert everything to percents correct. For example, for the spatial test, we would say that men got 75 percent correct and women got 50 percent correct. For the math test, we would say that men got 47 percent correct and women got 37 percent correct. Once scores were converted in this way, we could find the average size of the difference in percents correct. The average of a 25 percent difference (i.e., 75 percent – 50 percent) and a 10 percent difference (i.e., 47 percent – 37 percent) is a 17.5 percent difference.

The reader will note that in this book, individual differences were often reported in terms of a difference in percents correct. Although this practice solves our problem of putting things on the same scale, it does not tell us whether an average difference is big or not. Since there do not appear to be any existing conventions in this regard, we shall have to devise our own metric. To do so, we can use a classroom analogy as a guide. In many courses, students who get 90 percent correct or greater on a test get an A. Those who get 80 percent to 89 percent, get a B, and so on. In this metric, a 10 percent difference is a whole letter grade (e.g., an A versus a B). If so, then a 5 percent would be half of a letter grade (e.g., an A versus an A+). Let's say that any difference in scores of 10 percent or greater is fairly substantial. Anything 5 percent or less is fairly small and inconsequential, because the scores would probably be the same letter grade.

Besides converting scores to percents correct, a second way to make everything be on the same scale is to convert mean differences to *effect sizes*. To create an effect size, you need to compute the *mean* score on some test for each of the two groups as well as the *standard deviation* for each group on that test. In a very rough sense, a standard deviation can be thought of as the average amount that a person's score differs from the group score. If we use the formula (found in any basic statistics book) for determining the standard deviation for females on the SAT and find that it is, say, 118, then we can say that most women who took the SAT got a score that differed, on average, about 118 points from the group mean of 453 points. So, for example, Mary Jones may have received a 603 (+150), Sarah Parker may have received a score of 335 (–118), Marsha Fensterbach may have received a score of 557 (+104) and Julia Smith may have received a score of 353 (–100). On average, these women differed about 118 points from the female mean of 453.

After we find the means for the two groups of interest (e.g., men and women) and compute standard deviations, we then use the formula, "(Mean^1 – Mean^2)/standard deviation^2" to find the effect size. For our SAT example, if the male mean is 500, the female mean is 453, and the female standard deviation is 118, then we have an effect size of (500 – 453)/118, or .40. What this value of .40 means is that the groups differ by four-tenths of a standard deviation. Had the male mean been 571 and the female mean been 453, then we would say that they differed by one full standard deviation (i.e., 118/118 = 1.0). Effect sizes can either be positive or negative and can sometimes be larger than 2.0.

Why would anyone go to the trouble of computing effect sizes when percents correct seem to work just as well? The reason is that effect sizes can tell us many things that a difference in percents correct cannot. In the first place, standard deviations helps us see who is performing in the average range on some test, who is performing above average, and who is performing below average. In particular, if you take the mean score for a group and create a range of scores starting from one standard deviation below that mean and ending at one standard deviation above it, you will often find that 66 percent of people fall in this range of scores. Using our SAT example again for women (i.e., a mean of 453 and a standard deviation of 118), we would find that 66 percent of the women in this study scored between 335 (–118) and 571 (+118). The remaining 34 percent would split evenly into either the 0 to 334 range (i.e., below average) or the 572 to 800 range (i.e., above average).

From this perspective, we can say that any woman whose SAT score is one standard deviation or higher above the mean is doing quite well relative to her peers. In fact, her score is probably better than 83 percent of her peers (i.e., the 66 percent in the average range added to the 17 percent in the below average range). Analogously, if we find an effect size of 1.0, that tells us that the people in the higher group (e.g., males) who scored right at their mean are performing better than 83 percent of the lower group. In other words, with an effect size of 1.0, someone in the higher group who is average relative to his or her own group is well above average relative to the comparison group. It is for this reason that effect sizes are thought to be big when they get closer to 1.0. The closer they are to zero, the smaller they are thought to be. For example, our hypothetical effect size

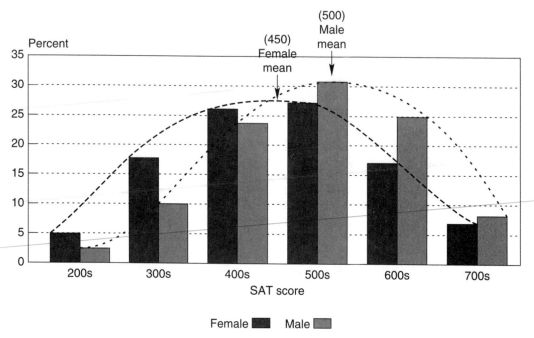

FIGURE 12.1a   SAT-Math Scores, 1991–1992

Source: College Entrance Examination Board, National Report on College Bound Seniors, 1991–92.

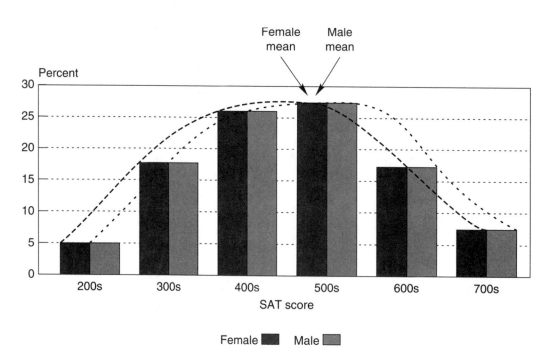

FIGURE 12.1b   SAT Distributions If Effect Size Were Zero

of .40 for SATs is closer to zero than it is to 1.0, so we might call it small or moderately sized, (depending on our bias, perhaps).

The other thing effect sizes tell us is the degree of overlap between two "bell-shaped" distributions of scores. When we get an effect size of 0, that not only indicates that means for the comparison groups are identical (e.g., (500 – 500)/118), it also tells us that the two distributions of scores for the groups completely overlap and lie on top of each other. To get a pictorial sense of this notion, take a look at Figure 12.1. The one figure illustrates the usual 47-point difference in, and distribution of, SAT scores (Digest of Educational Statistics, 1993) and the other hypothetical one illustrates how the distributions would overlap if the male and female means and distributions were the same.

Because effect sizes are more informative than percents correct, they have been used as often as possible in this book. Percents correct have been used only when pertinent information has not been provided the authors of the reviewed study (e.g., standard deviations). Either way, we shall use the convention that a large difference approaches a 1.0 effect size or a difference of 10 percent or greater in scores.

Explaining Gender Differences

Because it is difficult to remember all of the specifics of the gender differences revealed in previous chapters, we shall begin with a summary and partial expansion of the findings. Then, we shall examine explanations of these differences.

Summary of Gender Differences

Reading
The average effect size for seven studies of early reading (first to third graders) is d = −.18 (favoring females; not quite one-fifth of a standard deviation). For reading comprehension in older students, the 1990 National Assessment of Educational Progress (NAEP) found that nine-, 13- and 17-year-old females obtained scores that were 3 percent to 5 percent higher than those of males. On the SAT verbal, females have scored slightly higher than males for many years. In recent years, however, males have scored about 8 points (i.e., 4 percent) higher. The SAT involves vocabulary and verbal reasoning in addition to reading comprehension. With the exception of the SAT, then, females tend to perform slightly better than males. Some suggest that these differences are so small, they are hardly worth talking about (e.g., Hyde & Linn, 1988).

Writing
In the elementary grades, moderate (−.30s) to fairly large (−.80s) effect sizes (favoring girls) have been found for both orthographic fluency and compositional fluency. In addition, one study found that 82 percent of the students in the

lowest 5 percent of the distribution for compositional fluency were boys. In a recent NAEP for writing, fourth, eight, and eleventh grade girls received scores that were 9 percent to 11 percent higher than boys' scores. Thus, females tend to perform considerably better than boys on writing.

Math

No gender differences are typically found for preadolescent students. At around age 15, a small to moderate difference appears when problem-solving is at issue, especially when talented students are under investigation. Gender differences for younger students are found only when mathematically precocious students are studied. The average effect size for all types of math tests and students of d = .20 (favoring boys) is similar in size to that for reading comprehension (favoring girls). The largest effect size for average students occurs for the SAT math (d = .40). Since 1967, there has been a 47-point (i.e., 10 percent) difference in SAT math scores favoring males. However, females consistently tend to obtain higher grades in math courses than males at all grade levels (d's ranging from −.09 to −.35; Kimball, 1989).

Science

Males have been found to perform better than females on science achievement tests. A recent NAEP showed that whereas the difference between genders amounted to less than 1 percent in 9-year-olds, it increased to 3 percent in 13-year-olds, and 5 percent by the end of high school (favoring males). Such differences are half as large as those found for math and can be considered fairly small.

Social Studies

Research shows that males perform about 2 percent to 5 percent better than females on tests of economics, history, and geography. For the recent NAEP on civics, however, females performed slightly better on one section of the test and males performed better on the other. Either way, the differences are on the small side.

Summary

In sum, then, whereas females perform better on reading comprehension and writing tests as early as the first grade, males perform better on math, science, and most social studies tests beginning in adolescence. The largest differences are found for writing fluency and quality at all age levels (favoring females) and for math problem-solving during adolescence (favoring males, especially among students with academic talent). The other differences are considerably smaller and suggest that the distributions of scores for the genders largely overlap.

Theories of Gender Differences

Now that we know *how* the genders differ in the different subject areas, and *when* these differences start to emerge, we can begin to address the issue of *why* these differences emerge as they do. Four views have been proposed regarding the origin of gender differences in cognition: (a) the genetic/physiological view, (b) the socialization view, (c) the differential course work view, and (d) the cognitive process view. Let's examine and evaluate each of these views in turn.

The Genetic/Physiological View

Over the last 100 years, neuropsychologists have attempted to discover the nature of the brain's morphology and how this morphology relates to human performance. Although there are clear disagreements about the specifics of what we now know (Gardner, 1983; Halpern, 1992; Squire, 1987), there is nevertheless an emerging consensus about how structures in the brain are arranged and function. This consensus can be summarized as follows:

1. Different types of information (e.g., visual, verbal) seem to be processed and stored in different regions of the brain; that is, there is a certain degree of *localization* of function and storage. Some functions seem to cluster, more or less, to different hemispheres of the brain (left or right). This left-right clustering is called *lateralization*.
2. Although specific regions seem to handle specific tasks (e.g., pattern recognition), any complex skill (e.g., overall vision) involves a whole series of these regions. It is for this reason that damage to one processing area may have little overall effect on function. To make an analogy, automobiles are assembled in different stages in different regions of a factory. If one region shuts down (e.g., the one responsible for painting), it still may be possible to produce a car that works reasonably well. Of course, certain regions of the brain are crucial to overall functioning, and damage to these regions may produce an obvious deficit.
3. Despite the localization and lateralization of functions, the brain is nevertheless highly interconnected. Almost any region connects and communicates with any other. Thus, we can say that a certain region *mainly* performs certain tasks, but we cannot say that it only does that task or that no other region participates in the task.

Researchers who adopt the physiological view all assume that there is an optimal morphology for high-level performance. For example, some assume that having a highly lateralized brain is better than a brain that spreads tasks out over both hemispheres. Researchers differ, however, in terms of their beliefs about which mechanisms are responsible for achieving this optimal morphology. Some researchers appeal to genetics and suggest that male genes specify a different brain morphology than female genes. These geneticists would explain the male superiority in math and the female superiority in writing to differences in brain organization and function.

Others start with genes but suggest that hormones are the agents that directly alter the brain. Research with rats show that male and female hormones alter the morphology of brain structures such as the hypothalamus and corpus callosum. At present, there is no research with humans that demonstrates similar, unequivocal differences in brain structure. There are merely suggestive pieces of evidence, such as the fact that male students who are extremely precocious in math ability are more often left-handed than people in the average population (Benbow, 1988). Handedness is an index of the dominance of one hemisphere over the other and is an index, therefore, of greater lateralization.

Although a number of people find the physiological view compelling, there are several important problems with it. In the first place, we are still quite far from understanding the nature of brain morphology, let alone describing the optimal version of this morphology. The brain is just too complex and the data are far from "clean." Second, it is not at all clear which regions of the brain are responsible or especially important for success on the SAT or other tasks. Third, many studies have shown that experience can alter brain morphology (Squire, 1987). So, if the genders differ in brain morphology (and that is a big if still), it is not clear whether this difference has arisen due to genes, hormones, or experience. Fourth, males and females may have the same morphology but use different strategies when they solve tasks (Byrnes & Takahira, 1993; Halpern, 1992). These strategies might show up as different regions of the brain "firing" when problem-solving is under way, but such a difference in activity does not mean that male and female brains are "naturally" more or less lateralized (or better organized, etc.). If all students are taught to use the same strategy, then the same regions of the brain would probably be active in all students.

The Socialization View

The polar opposite of the genetic view is the socialization view. Researchers who adopt this view assume that gender differences in cognitive performance arise from the values inherent in society that are transmitted to students by their family, peers, and teachers (Eccles, 1983; Halpern, 1992; Parsons, Kaczala & Meece, 1982). Certain domains (e.g., math and science) are stereotyped as "male" domains and others (e.g., reading and writing) are stereotyped as "female" domains. Such stereotypes are likely to affect the achievement-related beliefs of students in a variety of ways. In the first place, girls would be less likely than boys to find math interesting or important, and would be more likely than boys to form low expectations for how well they will perform in math. In addition, girls would be less likely to (a) try hard in math classes, (b) believe they have high math ability, (c) pursue math-related careers, and (d) take the additional math courses required for such careers.

Many studies have supported these predictions. In fact, as reviewed in Chapter 11, gender differences in beliefs can be found as early as the first grade. Thus, it is clear that students do seem to internalize cultural values. The question is, however, whether gender differences in beliefs are causally responsible for the gender differences in achievement found for reading, writing, math, science, and social studies.

What is needed to support such an assertion is a comprehensive theory that links beliefs to those behaviors that serve as intermediaries to successful performance on achievement tests. For example, one theory might be that interest promotes active, engaged listening in class (rather than passive listening coupled with "spacing out"). Moreover, prior to taking classroom tests, students who value math and believe that they have talent in math will study harder and more effectively than students who do not. Over time, the former students will gain more expertise in a subject area than the latter students. Then, when students are not forced to take certain classes anymore (e.g., math in high school), only the interested and self-efficacious student will take electives in that domain. These additional classes, in turn, would promote still greater knowledge and skill. With greater knowledge and skill, students can perform quite well on achievement tests.

Such an account could effectively explain the gender differences reported earlier. Perhaps girls like to read and write more than boys. Perhaps boys like math, science, and social studies better. All of this sounds reasonable, but as was the case for the genetic/physiological view, the socialization view runs into problems.

In the first place, it is hard to find a study that demonstrates the longitudinal relations between interest, type of engagement, amount of studying, and so forth described above. Instead, we have only piecemeal, often low (i.e., .30), correlations among one or two variables from cross-sectional studies. Second, we have the fact that girls routinely get better grades than boys in subjects such as math and science. Girls think that math is more difficult than boys do and value it less (Parsons et al., 1982; Wigfield et al., 1991), so why are girls trying so hard to get better grades? If we assume that good grades mean that they are learning something, girls must be acquiring a considerable amount of skill over time, are they not? Third, studies of mathematically precocious students show no gender differences in beliefs, yet 13-year-old precocious boys perform significantly better than 13-year-old precocious girls on the SAT (Benbow, 1988). Finally, whereas gender differences in beliefs can be found in the first grade, some gender differences in achievement test performance do not occur until adolescence. As yet, advocates of the socialization view have not adequately dealt with these issues.

The Differential Coursework View. The differential coursework view was originally proposed by Pallas and Alexander (1983) to explain the gender difference on the SAT math. They showed that taking courses such as algebra, geometry, and calculus was a good predictor of success on the SAT. This predictive relation makes sense in light of the fact that the SAT requires knowledge of arithmetic, algebra, and geometry (but not calculus). In addition, Pallas and Alexander showed that the usual 47-point gender difference could be statistically reduced to 13 points when prior coursework is controlled. In a related vein, Byrnes and Takahira (1993, 1994) found that knowledge of arithmetic, algebra, and geometry topics was a good predictor of success on SAT items. Typically, one gets such knowledge by way of courses.

In one sense, the differential coursework view can be thought of as a subtheme of the socialization view. Recall that the socialization view predicts differential coursework on the part of high school boys and girls. And yet the former is distinct from the latter because the former merely says that course work matters. It does not specify why students chose the courses they did.

Despite the empirical support it receives from Pallas and Alexander and Byrnes and Takahira, the differential coursework view has its problems. In the first place, the gender difference in math and science starts either just before (i.e., age 13) or right after girls and boys start taking different classes (i.e., 15). For coursework to have an effect, one would think that several years of different course-taking has to pass. Second, performance on calculus courses predicts success on the SAT, but calculus material is not part of the test. Third, gender differences in reading and writing occur from the beginning of schooling, not after boys and girls have taken different courses for years. Fourth, the 1986 NAEP for science showed that a similar number of males and females took biology (i.e., 88 percent, 89 percent, respectively) and chemistry courses (i.e., 44 percent, 40 percent, respectively) in high school. Taking the latter two courses did improve student scores considerably, but it improved the scores of *both* males and females to the same extent. For example, the scores of males who took chemistry were 16 percent higher than the scores of males who did not take chemistry. The same 16 percent improvement was found for females. Hence, one could not explain the 5 percent gender gap in NAEP science scores in 11th graders by saying that males took more science courses or that they were helped more by these courses than females. Finally, gifted 13-year-olds who have not attended high school still show the usual gender difference in SAT performance.

Of course, one may revise the differential coursework view so as to accommodate these problems. In what can be called the "differential experience" view, knowledge and skill can be acquired either in school or out of school. Moreover, formal courses may be less important than experiences within specific courses. For example, perhaps boys and girls receive different amounts of reading and writing experiences in the preschool years. Similarly, perhaps gifted children receive more instruction in algebra and geometry in elementary school than the average seventh graders get (and the latter do get some). Finally, perhaps boys and girls have different amounts of informal exposure to science in their home lives. In support of the latter claim, Table 12.1 shows the percent of boys and girls who had informal experience with scientific instruments. Males clearly had more experience with some of these instruments than females. In fact, the percentage gap in use of instruments far exceeds the 5 percent gap on NAEP science scores. Nevertheless, before the value of the differential experience view can be fully assessed, additional studies need to be conducted that carefully document experience differences such as these.

The Cognitive Process View.   All of the views presented so far have included either proximal or distal variables in their explanation of gender differences. By *proximal*, it is meant that explanatory variables are closely connected to performance in space or time. By *distal*, it is meant that explanatory variables are somewhat removed from actual performance. For example, in a chain of events such as,

genes → hormones → lateralization → SAT performance,

TABLE 12.1   Percentages of Students Engaging in Science-Related Activities

Have you ever used a . . .	Grade		
	3	7	11
Yardstick			
male	68	–	–
female	67	–	–
Scale to weigh			
male	67	–	–
female	72	–	–
Magnifying Glass			
male	68	–	–
female	71	–	–
Microscope			
male	**51**	92	98
female	**37**	90	97
Telescope			
male	**58**	80	85
female	**45**	64	71
Barometer			
male	–	30	51
female	–	20	41
Electricity Meter			
male	–	31	49
female	–	**10**	**17**

Note: Data from the 1986 NAEP for Science; blank entries mean that students in the age group were not asked about those instruments. The largest differences have been bolded.

the variable genes would be viewed as somewhat distal because it is three steps removed from performance. In contrast, given the chain of events depicting the differential coursework view,

beliefs → course work → SAT performance,

the variable coursework would be considered to be proximal because it is just one step removed.

The cognitive process view involves variables that are even more proximal than those of the differential coursework view, because the former's variables would be inserted between the coursework and SAT performance steps in the chain above. Researchers who have adopted the cognitive process view have tried to identify the key processes responsible for success on an achievement test. After delineating these processes, they try to determine which processes seem to clearly differentiate the two groups of interest (usually high scorers and low scorers).

To illustrate, Byrnes and Takahira (1993, 1994) used the cognitive process approach to explain success on SAT items. They argue that students have to successfully execute the following processes in order to perform well on the SAT:

(*a*) define the problem (i.e., determine what the author of the item wants him or her to do),

(*b*) access prior knowledge (i.e., retrieve item-specific concepts and procedures from long-term memory),

(*c*) assemble an effective strategy (i.e., arrange prior concepts and procedures into an effective sequence of problem-solving steps),

(*d*) perform computations without error (i.e., solve for unknowns using arithmetic and algebra),

(*e*) avoid being seduced by misleading alternatives, and

(*f*) carry out operations (a) to (e) quickly enough that each problem can be solved in one minute or less.

After identifying the key processes in this way, Byrnes and Takahira (1993) tried to see whether males performed any of these processes better than females. More specifically, they used a statistical procedure called "regression" to see which processes predict success. In this procedure, a computer program determines which variables predict success and which do not and includes predictive variables into an algebraic equation. Variables that are included in the equation are unique predictors in the sense that they are not confounded with other variables. Byrnes and Takahira asked the computer which of the following variables were good predictors: (a) prior knowledge of specific arithmetic, algebra, and geometry concepts and procedures, (b) the strategies subjects used, (c) their math grade point average, and (d) the student's gender. What they found was that whereas prior knowledge and strategies were unique and strong predictors of success on the SAT, the variable "gender" was not. In other words, success was more a function of one's knowledge and skill than one's gender (because some successful students were knowledgeable and strategic females and some unsuccessful students were unknowledgeable and unstrategic males).

The value of the cognitive process approach is that the findings immediately suggest the causes of failure in the group that is performing less well (e.g., they are using suboptimal strategies). Once these causes have been identified, a training program can be implemented to improve performance (e.g., training them to use better strategies).

Like the other approaches, the cognitive process approach has its problems. The main defect is that it fails to specify *why* males and females may differ on the processes identified. For example, it does not tell us why females have less knowledge, or use suboptimal strategies, or fall prey to misleading alternatives.

Of course, one way to solve this problem is to combine the socialization, differential experience, and cognitive process views. Try to create your own synthesis of these views to see how the synthetic view could answer the question of why males and females differ with respect to specific variables.

Explaining Ethnic Differences

As in the section on gender differences, we shall first refresh our memories about the nature of ethnic differences in cognitive performance and then examine explanations of these differences. Of principal concern in this chapter are the differences among White, African-American, and Hispanic students, because these differences have been most often reported in the studies described in earlier chapters (presumably because the latter two groups are the largest minority groups in the country).

Summary of Ethnic Differences

Reading
For early reading, one study revealed effect sizes ranging from −.42 to −1.05 (favoring White students). This same study showed that ethnic differences remained even after the effects of SES were statistically controlled. Using a large sample of nine-, 13-, and 17-year-olds, the 1990 NAEP for reading found that the reading scores of White students were 8 percent to 15 percent higher than those of same-age minority students. Within minority students, the scores of Hispanic students were 1 percent to 4 percent higher than those of African-American students.

Writing
The most recent NAEP for writing revealed ethnic differences that were as large as or larger than those found for reading. In particular, the scores of White students were 7 percent to 20 percent higher than the scores of African-American and Hispanic students. Hispanic students scored 4 percent to 9 percent higher than African-American students.

Math
Studies have found that most effect sizes are −.40 or larger beginning in the first grade for both computation and problem-solving measures. For the SAT math, the scores of Asian students are 5 percent higher than those of White students, 18 percent higher than those of Hispanic students, and 27 percent higher than those of African-American students. The scores of White students are 13 percent higher than those of Hispanic students and 22 percent higher than those of African-American students.

Science

The 1986 NAEP for science showed that the scores of White students were 17 percent to 20 percent higher than those of African-American students, and 14 percent to 16 percent higher than those of Hispanic students. The scores of Hispanic students were about 3 percent to 5 percent higher than those of African-American students.

Social Studies

On each of the geography, history, and civics NAEPs, the scores of White students were around 20 percent higher than those of African-American and Hispanic students.

Summary

In sum, then, the findings are quite consistent across subject areas: White students perform substantially better than both African-American and Hispanic students, and Hispanics perform slightly better than African-American students. If we assume that the gender difference of 10 percent on the SAT math is large enough to cause concern, we clearly should be concerned about ethnic differences, because most of the White-minority differences are 10 percent or larger. In what follows, we shall examine possible explanations of these large differences.

Theories of Ethnic Differences

There are three main explanations of ethnic differences in cognitive performance. In this book, they are called (a) the cognitive deficit view, (b) the contextual view, and (c) the cultural incongruity view. Let's examine and evaluate each of these views in turn.

The Cognitive Deficit View

From the perspective of cognitive deficit view, minority children are thought to possess hard-wired (i.e., physiologically based) deficiencies in reasoning and analytical ability that are difficult to overcome (Ginsburg & Russell, 1981). Researchers who espouse the cognitive deficit view fall into one of two camps depending on their beliefs about what causes the presumed hard-wired differences: geneticists (e.g., Jensen, 1969; Herrnstein & Murray, 1994) and environmentalists (e.g., Hunt, 1964; Pollit et al., 1993).

Whereas the genetic view is self-explanatory (i.e., genes specify a suboptimal morphology), the environmental position needs further explication. Instead of assuming that genes produce different brain morphologies, these researchers assume that all ethnic groups probably start of with the same morphology (or potential for the same morphology) early in development but that factors such as prenatal insult, postnatal nutrition, and postnatal impoverishment change the initially healthy morphologies of minority children into a suboptimal variety.

To bolster their claims, these researchers appeal to four sets of findings. First, there is the well-established fact that growth in the size of brain neurons begins prenatally and continues postnatally. Second, they appeal to studies with animals that suggest that nutrition can have a powerful effect on the rate and extent of neuronal growth. Third, they cite studies that show how brain cells need to be stimulated in the first few years of life in order for vital functions to emerge (e.g., vision) and how enriched environments can actually alter brain physiology. Finally, they appeal to studies showing that children begin life with three times as many brain cells and synaptic connections as they need. Over time, excess cells are preprogrammed to die and redundant connections become "pruned" in the absence of stimulation. Environmentalists speculate that too many cells die and too many connections are pruned in undernourished and understimulated infants.

Why would minority children be more likely to be affected by prenatal insult and less likely to receive adequate nutrition and stimulation? It turns out that a large proportion of mothers who live in poverty or who have a drug dependency are of an ethnic minority. The children of these mothers become part of national samples of students who take national assessments and are thought by environmentalists to pull the overall mean of minority students down.

Because of their differences about the cause of ultimate brain differences, the geneticists and environmentalists also disagree about the effectiveness and utility of intervention programs. The geneticists would argue that no intervention would eliminate ethnic differences because students start off with different brain morphologies (even before they experience the environment). In contrast, the environmentalists would argue that certain types of interventions would work (e.g., enriched nutrition and enhanced stimulation during the first two years of life). If interventions begin too late (e.g., after age three), however, the environmentalists would also agree that little could be done to eliminate ethnic differences.

Having described both of the cognitive deficit views, we are now in a position to evaluate the overall approach. Four points can be made. First, at present, we cannot specify the optimal brain morphology for performance, so we obviously cannot say what a suboptimal morphology would look like. In other words, we could not "see" the difference if we examined the brains of White and minority children because we do not know what we are looking for. This is a serious problem, because there is no way to verify the physiological claims that lie at the heart of this approach. Second, achievement test scores covary considerably with the SES of parents. In the case of reading, for example, NAEP scores increase by 10 to 20 points for each education or income level surpassed by students' parents. Poorer, less-educated parents may not only provide less adequate nutrition and stimulation during infancy (supporting the cognitive deficit camp), but, as we said in Chapter 5, they also read considerably less to their children than richer, better-educated parents (supporting other views we will describe later). Since both things are true of a large subgroup of minority families, we cannot know which factor has caused the ethnic differences in reading performance. However, one could select out high-income minority children and compare them to high-income White children to see what happens to the performance gap. Third, a number of studies have shown that the performance of minority children *can* be substantially elevated using tutoring, cooperative learning, and other approaches (Slavin, Karweit & Wasik, 1994). This improvement would seem to be impossible if there were some unalterable physiological deficit interfering with success.

The Contextual View

Researchers who espouse the contextualist view place very little emphasis on physiological differences. Instead, they assume that skill development is entirely a function of *opportunity* and *emphasis* (Laboratory of Comparative Human Cognition, 1983). In particular, they argue that highly skilled students come from cultures that (a) provide multiple opportunities for learning these skills and (b) place a high value on these skills. In other words, you learn what your culture wants you to learn.

How do cultures provide opportunities for learning? Consider the fact that parents decide how their preschool children will spend their time. If preschool children are awake 14 hours a day, their parents could allow them to watch TV or play alone for ten of these hours and spend the rest of the time eating. Conversely, parents could verbally interact with them for five hours (e.g., joint play, conversations, joint reading), place them in preschool programs for three hours, and allow them to watch educational TV programs for four hours. Studies clearly show that parents differ in how much time they let their children engage in various activities (Adams, 1990).

After they enter school, cultures have their effects once again (Stevenson & Lee, 1990). School boards and other officials decide which subjects are taught in school and for how long. Subjects that are thought to be more important (e.g., math, reading) are given more time than subjects that are thought to be less important (e.g., music, the arts). Note that in the America 2000 proposal for reforming American schools, the only subjects that are referred to are science and math. It is clear that our country values certain subjects more than others.

Thus, powerful individuals in a culture (e.g., parents, teachers, and the people they respond to) play an important role in the *selection*, *arrangement*, and *duration* of contexts. From the perspective of the contextual view, ethnic differences in most of the subject areas derive from the fact that powerful individuals in the ethnic subcultures select different contexts, arrange them differently, or allow them to last for different amounts of time. For example, for economic and other reasons, middle-class White children are probably the largest consumers of books and make up the largest percentage of students in elite private preschool programs. In addition, there may be differences in the degree of emphasis placed on different subjects among schools that have different populations (e.g., largely White versus largely minority schools).

Thus, the ethnic differences in school readiness and actual performance in school are to be expected given differences in the types of contexts experienced by White and minority students. But it should be noted that the fact that White students tend to have more formal school knowledge by the time they graduate from high school than minority students does not mean that minority students are somehow completely unknowledgeable or unskilled. On the contrary, the contextualists would suggest that minority students acquire a variety of skills that are valued within their culture (e.g., story-telling, monetary skills) that often are not valued within the traditional classroom. It is for this reason that the contextualists often prefer the label "cognitive difference" to "cognitive deficit" to explain ethnic differences in cognition (Ginsburg & Russell, 1981). The notion of *cognitive difference* is meant to imply that all ethnic groups know a lot, but they know different things. It so happens that White students know more things that are valued by the powers that be in the larger culture (e.g., government officials and school boards).

How would ethnic differences be eliminated? According to the contextual view, we would have to homogenize the selection, arrangement, and duration of contexts across White, African-American, and Hispanic subcultures. Because such an experimental intervention has not been carried out, this proposal is speculative. Whereas programs such as Head Start were designed to eliminate contextual differences, it is not at all clear whether a Head Start classroom functions the same way that a middle-class family would or could. Thus, we currently cannot evaluate the contextual view, since many studies have to be conducted to test some of its claims. Of the few studies that bear on the claims, some pose problems for the contextual view, because White and minority parents do not seem to differ in terms of their goals and values about education (Stevenson, Chen & Uttal, 1990). Thus, differences may not have to do so much with *what* parents want for their children and what they value, as much as *knowing how* and *being able to* acquire them.

Cultural Incongruity View

The cultural incongruity view is related in many ways to the contextual view in terms of its basic assumptions. For example, cultural incongruity theorists emphasize the importance of cultural beliefs and practices in shaping ethnic differences. Moreover, they do not place much stock in the physiological explanation of ethnic differences. Where the two views differ is in terms of explaining how cultural differences lead to performance differences.

Whereas the contextual view emphasizes ethnic differences in values, the cultural incongruity view emphasizes ethnic differences in *communication patterns* and *participation structures* as well as the incompatibility between the ways these patterns and structures are manifested at home and the way they are manifested at school. Studies show differences, for example, between the way White, Native-American, African-American, Hispanic, and Hawaiian children communicate and interact with their parents. The nature of turn-taking, wait time for answers to questions, and so forth differs among ethnic groups (Gay, 1991). In traditional classrooms, one person talks at a time and is given about one second to answer a question. This pattern is similar to the way people communicate in White homes. A child who comes from an environment in which many people talk at once and people are given several seconds to answer a question would find the traditional classroom difficult to cope with.

In support of this view are the studies that show how student performance significantly improves after teachers are taught how to communicate, ask questions, and structure participation in a way that is more compatible with the way these activities are carried out in their students' homes (e.g., Boggs et al., 1985). Unlike the contextual view, which seems to imply a homogenizing of parent and student values to eliminate differences, the cultural incongruity view places the onus on teachers to change and allow for diversity.

Because this approach is still in its infancy, it is hard to say how it will ultimately be evaluated. Only time will tell. Two potential criticisms of this approach are that (a) it seems to work best for classrooms in which all children are of one ethnicity and the teacher is of a different ethnicity (what about classrooms that contain mixtures of ethnicities?), and (b) students would not learn the communication patterns and participation structures that predominate in the Anglo-dominated work world.

Instructional Implications

There are several themes that cut across the work on gender differences and ethnic differences. For example, physiological and environmental explanations have been offered for each type of difference. Within the environmental explanations, the notion of values has played a prominent role. With these similarities in mind, we can simplify the instructional implications somewhat by considering gender and ethnic differences together:

1. Research has revealed a range of differences between genders and between ethnic groups. Some of these differences are small, some are moderate, and some are large. For practical reasons, we should devote all of our time and energy to dealing only with the moderate and large differences (Hyde & Linn, 1988). In this book, we have characterized moderate or large differences as being at least a 10 percent difference in percents correct, and an effect size that is .40 or larger. In the case of gender, then, we should try to do something about the gender difference in writing that occurs at all age levels and the gender difference in math problem-solving found in gifted samples and average students older than 15. We should not be troubled by the small differences in reading, early math, science, or social studies. In the case of ethnicity, large differences exist for all subject areas. Hence, much of our resources should be devoted to remediating the pervasive differences between White, African-American, and Hispanic students.

2. The various explanations of individual differences described earlier provide a number of suggestions for how to eliminate gender and ethnic differences. For example,

   a. The environmental version of the cognitive deficit view would suggest that nutrition and stimulation programs should be targeted at low-income children.
   b. The socialization view of gender differences and the contextual view of ethnic differences suggest the creation of societal mechanisms that foster the adoption of the same values in all students, parents, and teachers. These mechanisms might include presentations in the media (e.g., atypi-

cal role models such as female or African-American engineers on TV shows), parent education programs, and workshops for teachers.

c. The differential experience view of gender differences and the contextual view of ethnic differences would suggest making the same learning contexts available to both genders and all ethnicities. This would mean occasionally selecting young girls as candidates for a math program for gifted students as well as finding scholarship funds for minority children to attend prestigious preschool programs.

d. The cognitive process view would suggest that school systems should engage in a two-step remediation program. During the first phase, the cognitive source of failure on achievement tests could be identified (e.g., insufficient conceptual and procedural knowledge). During the second phase, training programs should be designed that target the deficiencies identified during the first phase.

e. Finally, the cultural incongruity view would suggest teacher workshops and other professional development experiences that inform teachers about the communication patterns and participation structures of their students' home lives.

References

Abbott, R. D. & Berninger, V. W. (1993). Structural equation modeling of relationships among developmental skills and writing skills in primary- and intermediate-grade writers. *Journal of Educational Psychology, 85,* 478–508.

Abraham, M. R. Grzybowski, E. B., Renner, J. W., & Marek, E. A. (1992). Understandings and misunderstandings of eighth graders of five chemistry concepts found in textbooks. *Journal of Research in Science Teaching, 29,* 105–120.

Adams, M. J. (1990). *Beginning to read: Thinking and learning about print.* Cambridge, MA: MIT Press.

Alba, J. W. & Hasher, L. (1982). Is memory schematic? *Psychological Bulletin, 93,* 203–231.

Alexander, K. L. & Entwistle, D. R. (1988). Achievement during the first two years of school: Patterns and processes. *Monographs of the society for research in child development* (No. 218).

Allardice, B. S. & Ginsburg, H. P. (1983). Children's psychological difficulties in mathematics. In H. P. Ginsburg (Ed.), *The development of mathematical thinking* (pp. 319–353). New York: Academic Press.

Alleman, J. E. & Rosaen, C. L. (1991). The cognitive, social-emotional, and moral development of students: Basis for elementary and middle school social studies. In J. P. Shaver (Ed.), *Handbook of research on social studies teaching and learning* (pp. 121–133). New York: MacMillan.

Ames, C. (1986). Effective motivation: The contribution of the learning environment. In R. S. Feldman (Ed.), *The social psychology of education.* Cambridge: Cambridge University Press.

Anderson, J. R. (1983). *The architecture of cognition.* Cambridge, MA: Cambridge University Press.

Anderson, J. R. (1990). *Cognitive psychology and its implications* (2nd edition). New York: Freeman.

Anderson, J. R. (1993). Problem solving and learning. *American Psychologist, 48,* 35–44.

Anderson, J. R. (1995). *Learning and memory: An integrated approach.* New York: Wiley.

Anderson, J. R. & Schooler, L. J. (1991). Reflections on the environment in memory. *Psychological Science, 2,* 396–408.

Applebee, A. N., Langer, J. A., Mullis, I.V.S., and Jenkins, L. B. (1990). *The writing report card, 1984–1988: Findings from the national assessment of educational progress.* Princeton, NJ: ETS.

Arlin, P. (1981). Piagetian tasks as predictors of reading and math readiness. *Journal of Educational Psychology, 73,* 712–721.

Armento, B. (1986). Research on teaching social studies. In M. C. Wittrock (Ed.), *Handbook of research on teaching* (p. 942–951). New York: MacMillan.

Ashcraft, M. H. (1982). The development of mental arithmetic: A chronometric approach. *Developmental Review, 2,* 213–236.

Atkinson, J. W. (1964). *An introduction to motivation.* Princeton, NJ: Van Nostrand.

Atkinson, R. C. & Shiffrin, R. M. (1968). Human memory: A proposed system and its control processes. In K. W. Spence & J. T. Spence (Eds.), *The psychology of learning and motivation: Advances in research and theory* (Vol. 2). New York: Academic Press.

Baddeley, A.D. (1990). *Human memory: Theory and practice.* Boston: Allyn & Bacon.

Baker, D. & Piburn, M. D. (1990). Teachers perceptions of the effects of a scientific literacy course on subsequent learning in biology. *Journal of Research in Science Teaching, 27,* 477–491.

Baker, L. (1984). Spontaneous versus instructed use of multiple standards for evaluating comprehension: Effects of age, reading proficiency, and type of standard. *Journal of Experimental Child Psychology, 38,* 289–311.

Baker, L. & Brown, A. L. (1984). Metacognitive skills and reading. In P. D. Pearson, M. Kamil, R. Barr & P. Mosenthal (Eds.), *Handbook of reading research* (Vol. 1, pp. 353–394). White Plains, NY: Longman.

Bandura, A. (1986). *Social foundations of thought and action: A social cognitive theory.* Englewood Cliffs, NJ: Prentice-Hall.

Bandura, A. & Schunk, D. (1981). Cultivating, competence, self-efficacy, and intrinsic interest through proximal self-motivation. *Journal of Personality and Social Psychology, 41,* 586–598.

Bandura, A. & Wood, R. (1989). Effect of perceived controllability and performance standards on self-regulation of complex decision making. *Journal of Personality and Social Psychology, 56,* 805–814.

Bartlett, E. (1982). *Children's difficulties in establishing consistent voice and space/time dimensions in narrative text.* Paper presented at the meeting of the American Educational Research Association.

Barwise, J. (1989). *The situation in logic.* Stanford, CA: Center for the Study of Language and Information.

Baumann, J. F. (1981). Effect of ideational prominence on children's reading comprehension of expository prose. *Journal of Reading Behavior, 13,* 49–56.

Beal, C. R. (1990). The development of text evaluation and revision skills. *Child Development, 61,* 247–258.

Becker, B. J. (1990). Item characteristics and gender differences on the SAT-M for mathematically able youths. *American Educational Research Journal, 27,* 65–87.

Benbow, C. P. (1988). Sex differences in mathematical reasoning ability in intellectually talented preadolescents: Their nature, effects, and possible causes. *Behavioral and Brain Science, 11,* 169–232.

Benton, S. L., Glover, J. A., Kraft, R. G., & Plake, B. S. (1984). Cognitive capacity differences among writers. *Journal of Educational Psychology, 76,* 820–834.

Benton, S. L., Glover, J. A., Monkowski, P. G. & Shaughnessy, M. (1983). Decision difficulty and recall of prose. *Journal of Educational Psychology, 75,* 727–742.

Bereiter, C. & Scardamalia, M. (1982). From conversation to composition: The role of instruction in a developmental process. In R. Glaser (Ed.), *Advances in instructional psychology* (Vol. 2, 1–64). Hillsdale, NJ: Erlbaum.

Berlyne, D. (1966). Curiosity and exploration. *Science, 153,* 25–33.

Berninger, V. W. & Fuller, F. (1992). Gender differences in orthographic, verbal, and compositional fluency: Implications for assessing writing disabilities in primary grade children. *Journal of School Psychology, 30,* 363–382.

Berninger, V. W., Mizokowa, D. & Bragg, R. (1991). Theory-based diagnosis and remediation of writing disabilities. *Journal of School Psychology, 29,* 57–79.

Berry, J. M. & West, R. L. (1993). Cognitive self-efficacy in relation to personal mastery and goal setting across the life span. *International Journal of Behavioral Development, 16,* 351–379.

Betz, N. E. & Hackett, G. (1983). The relationship of mathematics self-efficacy expectations to the selection of science-based college majors. *Journal of Vocational Behavior, 23,* 329–345.

Bialystok, E. (1988). Aspects of linguistic awareness in reading comprehension. *Applied Psycholinguistics, 9,* 123–139.

Bloom, B. S., Englehart, M. B., Furst, E. J., Hill, W. H., & Krathwohl, O. R. (1956). *Taxonomy of educational objectives: The classification of educational goals. Handbook 1: The cognitive domain.* New York: Longman.

Bluestein, N. & Acredolo, L. (1979). Developmental changes in map-reading skills. *Child Development, 50,* 691–697.

Boggs, S. T., Watson-Gegeo, K. & McMillan, G. (1985). *Speaking, relating and learning: A study of Hawaiian children at home and at school.* Norwood, NJ: Ablex.

Boiarsky, C. (1982). Prewriting is the essence of writing. *English Journal, 71,* 44–47.

Bond, G. L. & Dykstra, R. (1967). The cooperative research program in first-grade reading instruction. *Reading Research Quarterly, 2,* 10–141.

Bornstein, M. H. (1989). Stability in early mental development: From attention and information processing in infancy to language and cognition in childhood. In M. H. Bornstein & N. A. Krasnegor (Eds.), *Stability and continuity in mental development: Behavioral and biological perspectives.* Hillsdale, NJ: Erlbaum.

BouJaoude, S. B. (1992). The relationship between students' learning strategies and the change in their misunderstandings during a high school chemistry course. *Journal of Research in Science Teaching, 29,* 687–699.

Bower, G. H., Black, J. B., & Turner, T. J. (1979). Scripts in memory for text. *Cognitive Psychology, 11,* 177–220.

Brainerd, C. J. (1978). The stage question in cognitive-developmental theory. *Brain and Behavioral Science, 2,* 173–213.

Bransford, J., Sherwood, R., Vye, N., and Rieser, J. (1986). Teaching thinking and problem-solving. *American Psychologist, 41,* 1078–1089.

Briars, D. & Siegler, R.S. (1984). A featural analysis of preschoolers' counting knowledge. *Developmental Psychology, 20,* 607–618.

Brophy, J. (1990). Teaching social studies for understanding and higher-order applications. *Elementary School Journal, 90,* 351–417.

Brophy, J., Van Sledright, B. & Bredin, N. (1992). Fifth graders' ideas about history expressed before and after their introduction to the subject. *Theory and Research in Social Education, 4,* 440–489.

Brown, A. L. (1989). Analogical reasoning and transfer: What develops? In S. Vosniadou & A. Ortony (Eds.), *Similarity and analogical reasoning* (pp. 369–412). Cambridge: Cambridge University Press.

Brown, A. L., Bransford, J. D., Ferrara, R. A. & Campione, J. C. (1983). Learning, remembering, and understanding. In J.H. Flavell & E.M. Markman (Eds.), *Handbook of Child Psychology: Vol.3. Cognitive Development* (pp. 263–340). New York: Wiley.

Brown, A. L. & Day, J. D. (1983). Macrorules for summarizing texts: The development of expertise. *Journal of Verbal Learning and Verbal Behavior, 22,* 1–14.

Brown, A. L., Day, J. D. & Jones, R. (1983). The development of plans for summarizing texts. *Child Development, 54,* 968–979.

Brown, D. E. (1992). Using examples and analogies to remediate misconceptions in physics: Factors influencing conceptual change. *Journal of Research in Science Teaching, 29,* 17–34.

Brown, J. S. & Burton, R. B. (1978). Diagnostic models for procedural bugs in basic mathematical skills. *Cognitive Science, 2,* 155–192.

Brown, J. S., Collins, A. & Duguid, P. (1989). Situated cognition and the culture of learning. *Educational Researcher, 18,* 32–42.

Bruner, J. S., Goodnow, J. J. & Austin, G. A. (1956). *A study of thinking.* New York: John Wiley.

Bryant, P. E., MacLean, M., Bradley, L. & Crossland, J. (1990). Rhyme and alliteration, phoneme detection, and learning to read. *Developmental Psychology, 26,* 429–438.

Bullock, M., Gelman, R, & Baillargeon, R. (1982). The development of causal reasoning. In W. J. Friedman (Ed.), *The developmental psychology of time.* New York: Academic Press.

Byrnes, J. P. (1992a). Categorizing and combining theories of cognitive development and learning. *Educational Psychology Review, 4,* 309–343.

Byrnes, J. P. (1992b). The conceptual basis of procedural learning. *Cognitive Development, 7,* 235–257.

Byrnes, J. P. & Takahira, S. (1993). Explaining gender differences on SAT-math items. *Developmental Psychology, 29*, 805–810.

Byrnes, J. P. & Takahira, S. (1994). Why some students perform well and others perform poorly on SAT-math items. *Contemporary Educational Psychology, 19*, 63–78.

Byrnes, J. P. & Wasik, B. A. (1991). Role of conceptual knowledge in mathematical procedural learning. *Developmental Psychology, 27*, 777–786.

Calfee, R. & Drum, P. (1986). Research on teaching reading. *Handbook of Research on Teaching* (3rd Edition, pp. 804–849). New York: Holt, Rinehart & Winston.

Canfield, R. L. & Smith, E. G. (1993). *Counting in early infancy: Number-based expectations.* Presented at the Meeting of the Society for Research in Child Development, New Orleans, LA.

Carey, S. (1985). *Conceptual change in childhood.* Cambridge, MA: MIT Press.

Carey, S. (1986). Cognitive science and science education. *American Psychologist, 41*, 1123–1130.

Carpenter, T. P. (1987). Conceptual knowledge as a foundation for procedural knowledge. In J. Hiebert (Ed.), *Conceptual and procedural knowledge: The case of mathematics* (pp. 113–132). Hillsdale, NJ: Erlbaum.

Carpenter, T. P., Corbitt, M. K., Kepner, H. S., Lindquist, M. M. & Reys, R. E. (1981). *Results from the second mathematics assessment of the National Assessment of Educational Progress.* Reston, VA: National Council of Teachers of Mathematics.

Carpenter, T. P. & Moser, J. M. (1982). The development of addition and subtraction. In R. Lesh & M. Landau (Eds.), *Acquisition of mathematical concepts and processes* (pp. 42–68). New York: Academic Press.

Carver, R. P. (1973). Reading as reasoning: Implications for measurement. In W. H. MacGinitie (Ed.), *Assessment problems in reading.* Newark, DE: International Reading Association.

Case, R. (1974). Structures and strictures: Some functional limitations on the course of cognitive growth. *Cognitive Psychology, 6*, 544–573.

Chaiklin, S. (1989). Cognitive studies of algebra problem solving and learning. In S. Wagner & C. Kieran (Eds.), *Research issues in the learning and teaching of algebra* (pp. 93–114). Reston, VA: National Council of Teachers of Mathematics.

Chall, J. S. (1967). *Learning to read: The great debate.* New York: McGraw Hill.

Chall, J. S. (1983). *Stages of reading development.* New York: McGraw Hill.

Chi, M.T.H., Glaser, R. & Rees, E. (1982). Expertise in problem-solving. In R. Sternberg (Ed.), *Advances in the psychology of human intelligence* (Vol 1). Hillsdale, NJ: Erlbaum.

Chi, M.T.H., Hutchinson, J. E. & Robin, A. F. (1989). How inferences about novel domain-related concepts can be constrained by structured knowledge. *Merrill-Palmer Quarterly, 35*, 27–62.

Clay, M. (1985). *The early detection of reading difficulties.* Auckland, New Zealand: Heinemann

Clement, J. (1982). Algebra word problem solutions: Thought processes underlying a common misconception. *Journal for Research in Mathematics Education, 13*, 16–30.

Cobb, P., Yackel, E. & Wood, T. (1992). A constructivist alternative to the representational view of mind in mathematics education. *Journal for Research in Mathematics Education, 23*, 2–33.

College Entrance Examination Board (1988). *1988 profile of SAT and achievement test takers.* New York: Author.

Collins, A. M. & Loftus, E. F. (1975). A spreading-activation theory of semantic processing. *Psychological Review, 82*, 407–428.

Covington, M. & Omelich, C. (1981). As failures mount: Affective and cognitive consequences of ability demotion in the classroom. *Journal of Educational Psychology, 73*, 796–808.

Craik, F.I.M. & Lockhart, R. S. (1972). Levels of processing: A framework for memory research. *Journal of Verbal Learning and Verbal Behavior, 11*, 671–684.

Cross, J. A. (1987). Factors associated with students' place location knowledge. *Journal of Geography, 86*, 59–63.

Cuban, L. (1984). Policy and research dilemmas in the teaching of reasoning: Unplanned designs. *Review of Educational Research, 54,* 655–681.

Danner, F. (1976). Children's understanding of intersentence organization in the recall of short descriptive passages. *Journal of Educational Psychology, 68,* 174–183.

de Bono, E. (1983). The direct teaching of thinking as a skill. *Phi Delta Kappan, 64,* 703–708.

Deci, E. & Ryan, R. (1985). *Intrinsic motivation and self-determination in human behavior.* New York: Plenum Press.

Department of Education (1990). *Digest of Educational Statistics.* Washington, DC: Author.

Dewitz, P., Carr, E. & Patberg, J.P. (1987). Effects of inference training on comprehension and comprehension monitoring. *Reading Research Quarterly, 22,* 99–121.

Dimino, J., Gersten, R., Carnine, D. & Blake, G. (1990). Story grammar: An approach for promoting at-risk secondary students' comprehension of literature. *The Elementary School Journal, 91,* 19–32.

Duffy, G. & Roehler, L. (1987). Improving classroom reading instruction through the use of responsive elaboration. *Reading Teacher, 40,* 514–521.

Dunbar, K. & Klahr, D. (1989). Developmental differences in scientific discovery processes. In D. Klahr & K. Kotovsky (Eds.), *Complex information processing: The impact of Herbert A. Simon.* Hillsdale, NJ: Erlbaum.

Durkin, D. (1979). What classroom observations reveal about reading comprehension instruction. *Reading Research Quarterly, 14,* 481–533.

Dweck, C. (1986). Motivational processes affecting learning. *American Psychologist, 41,* 1040–1048.

Dweck, C., Davidson, W., Nelson, S. & Enna, B. (1978). Sex differences in learned helplessness II: The contingencies of evaluative feedback in the classroom, and III: An experimental analysis. *Developmental Psychology, 14,* 268–276.

Dweck, C. & Elliot, E. (1983). Achievement motivation. In P. H. Mussen (Ed.), *Handbook of Child Psychology, Vol IV: Socialization, Personality, and Social Development* (pp. 643–691). New York: John Wiley.

Dweck, C. & Leggett, E. (1988). A social-cognitive approach to motivation and personality. *Psychological Review, 95,* 256–273.

Eccles, J. (1983). Expectancies, values, and academic behavior. In J. T. Spence (Ed.), *Achievement and achievement motives: Psychological and Sociological Approaches* (pp. 77–146). San Francisco: Freeman.

Eccles, J., Adler, T. F., Futterman, R., Goff, S. B., Kaczala, C. M., Meece, J. L., & Midgley, C. (1985). Self-perceptions, task perceptions, socializing influences, and the decision to enroll in mathematics. In S. F. Chipman, L. R. Brush, and D. M. Wilson (Eds.), *Women and mathematics: Balancing the equation* (pp. 95–121). Hillsdale, NJ: Erlbaum.

Eccles, J. S., Midgley, C., Wigfield, A., Flanagan, C., Buchanan, C. M., Reuman, D. & Mac Iver, D. (1993). Development During Adolescence: the impact of stage-environment fit on young adolescents' experiences in school and families. *American Psychologist, 48,* 90–116.

Eccles, J. S., Wigfield, A., Flanagan, C., Miller, C., Reuman, D., & Yee, D. (1989). Self-perceptions, domain values, and self-esteem: Relations and changes at early adolescence. *Journal of Personality, 57,* 283–310.

Eckler, J. A. & Weininger, O. (1989). Structural parallels between pretend play and narratives. *Developmental Psychology, 25,* 736–743.

Englert, C. S., Stewart, S. R., & Hiebert, E. H. (1988). Young writer's use of text structure in expository text generation. *Journal of Educational Psychology, 80,* 143–151.

Ennis, R. H. (1962). A concept of critical thinking. *Harvard Educational Review, 32,* 81–11.

Ericsson, K. A., & Smith, J. (1991). *Toward a general theory of expertise: Prospects and limits.* Cambridge: Cambridge University Press.

Erli, L. & Wilce, L. S. (1987). Cipher versus cue reading: An experiment in decoding acquisition. *Journal of Educational Psychology, 79,* 3–13.

Eylon, B. & Linn, M. C. (1988). Learning and instruction: An examination of four research perspectives. *Review of Educational Research, 58,* 251–301.

Fabricius, W. V. & Hagen, J. W. (1984). The use of causal attributions about free recall performance to assess metamemory and predict strategic memory behavior in young children. *Developmental Psychology, 20,* 975–987.

Farrell, R. T. & Cirrincione, J. M. (1989). The content of the geography curriculum—teachers perspective. *Social Education, 53,* 105–108.

Feather, N. T. (1988). Values, expectancies, and course enrollment: Testing the role of personal values within an expectancy-valence framework. *Journal of Educational Psychology, 80,* 381–391.

Ferguson, P. (1991). Impacts on social and political participation. In J. P. Shaver (Ed.), *Handbook of Research on Social Studies Teaching and Learning.* New York: Macmillan.

Fielding, L. G., Anderson, R. C. & Pearson, P. D. (1990). *How discussion questions influence children's story understanding* (tech. rep. No 490). Urbana: University of Illinois, Center for the Study of Reading.

Fitzgerald, J. (1987). Research on revision in writing. *Review of Educational Research, 57,* 481–506.

Flavell, J. H., Miller, P. H., & Miller, S. A. (1993). *Cognitive Development* (3rd edition). Englewood Cliffs, NJ: Prentice Hall.

Flynn, E. (1988). Composing as a woman. *College Composition and Communication, 39,* 423–435.

Freedman, A. (1987). Development in story writing. *Applied Psycholinguistics, 8,* 153–170.

Friedman, W. (1990). *About time: Inventing the fourth dimension.* Cambridge, MA: MIT Press.

Fuson, K. C. (1988). *Children's counting and concepts of number.* New York: Springer-Verlag.

Fuson, K. C. & Briars, D. J. (1990). Using a base-ten blocks learning/teaching approach for first- and second-grade place-value and multidigit addition and subtraction. *Journal for Research in Mathematics Education, 21,* 180–206.

Fuson, K. C. & Hall, J. W. (1983). The acquisition of early word meanings: A conceptual analysis and review. In H. P. Ginsburg (Ed.), *Children's mathematical thinking.* New York: Academic Press.

Gage, N. L. & Berliner, D. C. (1991). *Educational Psychology* (5th edition). Boston: Houghton Mifflin.

Gagne, E. D., Yekovich, C. W. & Yekovich, F. R. (1993). *The cognitive psychology of school learning.* New York: HarperCollins.

Gambrell, L. B. & Chasen, S. P. (1991). Explicit story instruction and the narrative writing of fourth-and fifth-grade below-average readers. *Reading Research and Instruction, 31,* 54–62.

Gardner, H. (1983). *Frames of mind.* New York: Basic Books.

Garner, R. (1987). Strategies for reading and studying expository texts. *Educational Psychologist, 22,* 299–312.

Garner, R., Alexander, P., Slater, W., Hare, V. C., Smith, T., & Reis, R. (1986). Children's knowledge of structural properties of expository text. *Journal of Educational Psychology, 78,* 411–416.

Garner, R., Hare, V. C., Alexander, P., Haynes, J., & Winograd, P. (1984). Inducing the use of a text lookback strategy among unsuccessful readers. *American Educational Research Journal, 21,* 789–798.

Garnett, P. J. & Treagust, D. F. (1992). Conceptual difficulties experienced by senior high school students of electrochemistry: Electrochemical (galvanic) and electrolytic cells. *Journal of Research in Science Teaching, 29,* 1079–1099.

Garrett, M. F. (1990). Sentence processing. In D. N. Osherson & H. Lasnik (Eds.), *An invitation to cognitive science, Vol. 1: Language* (pp. 133–175). Cambridge, MA; MIT Press.

Gay, G. (1991). Culturally diverse students and social studies. In J. P. Shaver (Ed.), *Handbook of research on social studies teaching and learning* (pp. 144–156). New York: Macmillan.

Gelman, R. & Gallistel, C. R. (1978). *The child's understanding of number.* Cambridge, MA: Harvard University Press.

Gelman, R. & Meck, E. (1983). Preschoolers' counting: Principles before skill. *Cognition, 13,* 343–359.

Gelman, S. A. & Coley, J. D. (1991). Language and categorization: The acquisition of natural kind terms. In S. A. Gelman & J. P. Byrnes (Eds.), *Perspectives on language and thought: Interrelations in development* (pp. 146–196). Cambridge: Cambridge University Press.

Geva, E. (1983). Facilitating reading comprehension through flowcharting. *Reading Research Quarterly, 18,* 383–405.

Gick, M. L. & Holyoak, K. J. (1983). Schema induction and analogical transfer. *Cognitive Psychology, 15,* 1–38.

Gilligan, C. (1982). *In a different voice: Psychological theory and women's development.* Cambridge, MA: Harvard University Press.

Ginsburg, H. & Russell, R. L. (1981). Social class and racial influences on early mathematical thinking. *Monographs of the Society for Research in Child Development, 46* (No. 193).

Glaser, R. & Chi, M.T.H. (1988). Overview. In M.T.H. Chi, R. Glaser, & M. Farr (Eds.), *The nature of expertise.* Hillsdale, NJ: Erlbaum.

Glover, J. A., Ronning, R. R. & Bruning, R. H. (1990). *Cognitive Psychology for Teachers.* New York: Macmillan.

Goodman, K. S. & Goodman, Y. (1979). Learning to read is natural. In L. B. Resnick & R. A. Weaver (Eds.), *Theory and practice of early reading* (pp. 51–94). Hillsdale, NJ: Erlbaum.

Goodman, Y. M. (1991). Comments in "Beginning to read: A critique by literacy professionals and a response by Marilyn Jager Adams." *The Reading Teacher, 44,* 375.

Graesser, A., Golding, J. M. & Long, D. L. (1991). Narrative representation and comprehension. In R. Barr, M. L. Kamil, P. Mosenthal, & P. D. Pearson (Eds.), *Handbook of reading research, Vol II* (pp. 171–205). New York: Longman.

Graham, S., Doubleday, C. & Guarino, P. (1984). The development of relations between perceived controllability and the emotions of pity, anger, and guilt. *Child Development, 55,* 561–565.

Graham, S. & Golan, S. (1991). Motivational influences on cognition: Task involvement, ego involvement, and depth of information processing. *Journal of Educational Psychology, 83,* 187–194.

Graham, S. & Harris, K.R. (in press). Teaching writing strategies within the context of a whole language class. In M. McIntyre & M. Pressley (Eds.), *Skills in whole language.* New York: Christopher Gordon Publishers.

Graves, D. H. (1975). An examination of the writing processes of seven-year-old children. *Research in the Teaching of English, 9,* 227–241.

Greene, R. L. (1986). Sources of recency effects in free recall. *Psychological Bulletin, 99,* 221–228.

Griffiths, A. K. & Preston, K. P. (1992). Grade-12 students' misconceptions relating to fundamental characteristics of atoms and molecules. *Journal of Research in Science Teaching, 29,* 611–628.

Groen, G. J. & Parkman, J. M. (1972). A chronometric analysis of simple addition. *Psychological Review, 79,* 329–343.

Gross, S. (1993). Early mathematics performance and achievement: Results of a study within a large suburban school system. *Journal of Negro Education, 62,* 269–287.

Gurney, D., Gersten, R., Dimino, J. & Carnine, D. (1990). Story grammar: Effective literature instruction for high school students with learning disabilities. *Journal of Learning Disabilities, 23,* 335–348.

Hackett, G., Betz, N. E., Casas, J. M. & Rocha-Singh, I. A. (1992). Gender, ethnicity, and social cognitive factors predicting the academic achievement of students in engineering. *Journal of Counseling Psychology, 39,* 527–538.

Hallden, O. (1986). Learning history. *Oxford Review of Education, 12,* 53–66.

Halpern, D. F. (1990). *Thought and knowledge: An introduction to critical thinking* (2nd Edition). Hillsdale, NJ: Erlbaum.

Halpern, D. F. (1992). *Sex differences in cognitive abilities* (2nd edition). Hillsdale, NJ: Erlbaum.

Hammock, D. C. et al. (1990). *The U.S. History Report Card.* Princeton, NJ: National Assessment of Educational Progress.

Hansen, J. & Pearson, P. D. (1983). An instructional study: Improving the inferential comprehension of good and poor fourth-grade readers. *Journal of Educational Psychology, 75,* 821–829.

Harter, S. (1985). Competence as a dimension of self-evaluation: Toward a comprehensive model of self-worth. In R. L. Leahy (Ed.), *The development of the self* (pp. 55–121).

Hayes, J. R. (1985). Three problems in teaching general skills. In J. Segal, S. Chipman, & R. Glaser (Eds.), *Thinking and learning, Vol. 2.* Hillsdale, NJ: Erlbaum.

Hayes, J. R. & Flower, L. S. (1986). Writing research and the writer. *American Psychologist, 41,* 1106–1113.

Heath, S. B. (1983). *Ways with words: Language, life*

and work in communities and classrooms. Cambridge: Cambridge University Press.

Heller, P. M. & Finley, F. N. (1992). Variable uses of alternative conceptions: A case study in current electricity. *Journal of Research in Science Teaching, 29,* 259–275.

Herman, W. L., Barron, M., Hawkins, M. L. & Berryman, C. (1988). World place location skills of elementary school students. *Journal of Educational Research, 81,* 374–376.

Herrnstein, R. J. & Murray, C. (1994). *The bell curve: Intelligence and class structure in American life.* New York: The Free Press.

Herscovics, N. (1989). Cognitive obstacles encountered in the learning of algebra. In S. Wagner & C. Kieran (Eds.), *Research issues in the learning and teaching of algebra* (pp. 60–86). Reston, VA: National Council of Teachers of Mathematics.

Hewson, M. G. & Hewson, P. W. (1983). Effect of instruction using students' prior knowledge and conceptual change strategies on science learning. *Journal of Research in Science Teaching, 20,* 731–743.

Hiebert, J. (1987). *Conceptual and procedural knowledge: The case of mathematics.* Hillsdale, NJ: Erlbaum.

Hiebert, J. & Behr, M. (1988). *Number concepts and operations in the middle grades.* Hilldale, NJ: Erlbaum.

Hiebert, J. & LeFevre, P. (1987). Conceptual and procedural knowledge in mathematics: An introductory analysis. In J. Hiebert (Ed.), *Conceptual and procedural knowledge in mathematics* (pp. 1–27). Hillsdale, NJ: Erlbaum.

Hillocks, G. (1989). Synthesis of research on teaching writing. *Educational Leadership, 44,* 71–82.

Hinsley, D. A., Hayes, J. R. & Simon, H. A. (1977). From words to equations: Meaning and representation in algebra word problems. In P. A. Carpenter & M. A. Just (Eds.), *Cognitive processes in comprehension.* Hillsdale, NJ: Erlbaum.

Hintzman, D. L. (1986). "Schema abstraction" in a multiple-trace memory model. *Psychological Review, 93,* 411–428.

Holden, G. W. (1988). Adults thinking about a childrearing problem: Effects of experience, parental status, and gender. *Child Development, 59,* 1623–1632.

Hunt, J. McV. (1964). *Intelligence and experience.* New York: Ronald Press.

Hunt, K. W. (1970). Syntactic maturity in school children and adults. *Monographs of the Society for Research in Child Development, 35* (No. 134).

Hyde, J. S., Fennema, E. & Lamon, S. J. (1990). Gender differences in mathematical performance: A meta-analysis. *Psychological Bulletin, 107,* 139–155.

Hyde, J. S. & Linn, M. C. (1988). Gender differences in verbal ability: A meta-analysis. *Psychological Bulletin, 104,* 53–69.

Inhelder, B. & Piaget, J. (1958). *The growth of logical thinking from childhood to adolescence.* New York: Basic Books.

Inhelder, B. & Piaget, J. (1964). *The early growth of logic in the child.* New York: Basic Books.

Iverson, S. & Tunmer, W. E. (1993). Phonological processing skills and the reading recovery program. *Journal of Educational Psychology, 85,* 112–126.

Janis, I. L. (1989). *Crucial decisions.* New York: The Free Press.

Jensen, A. R. (1969). How much can we boost IQ and scholastic achievement? *Harvard Educational Review, 39,* 1–123.

Jensen, A. R. (1987). The *g* factor beyond factor analysis. In R. R. Roning, J. A. Glover, J. C. Conoley, & J. C. Witt (Eds.), *The influence of cognitive psychology on testing.* Hillsdale, NJ: Erlbaum.

Johnson, D. W. & Johnson, R. T. (1987). *Learning together and alone.* Englewood Cliffs, NJ: Prentice-Hall.

Johnson, M. L. (1989). Minority differences in mathematics. In M. M. Lindquist (Ed.), *Results from the fourth mathematics assessment of the national assessment of educational progress* (pp. 135–148). Reston, VA: National Council of Teachers of Mathematics.

Johnston, P. & Afflerbach, P. (1985). The process of constructing main ideas from text. *Cognition and Instruction, 2,* 207–232.

Just, M. A. & Carpenter, P. A. (1987). *The psychology of reading and language comprehension.* Boston: Allyn & Bacon.

Kail, R. V. (1991). Developmental changes in speed of processing during childhood and adolescence. *Psychological Bulletin, 109,* 490–501.

Karmiloff-Smith, A. (1984). Children's problem-solving. In M. E. Lamb, A.L. Brown, & B. Rogoff (Eds.), *Advances in developmental psychology* (Vol. 3, pp. 39–90). Hillsdale, NJ: Erlbaum.

Karmiloff-Smith, A. & Inhelder, B. (1974). If you want to get ahead, get a theory. *Cognition, 3,* 195–212.

Keating, D. P. (1980). Thinking processes in adolescence. In J. Adelson (Ed.), *Handbook of adolescent psychology* (pp. 211–246). New York: Wiley.

Keil, F. C. (1991). Theories, concepts, and the acquisition of word meaning. In S. A. Gelman & J. P. Byrnes (Eds.), *Perspective on language and thought: Interrelations in development* (pp. 197–223). Cambridge: Cambridge University Press.

Kelly, K. R. (1993). The relation of gender and academic achievement to career self-efficacy and interests. *Gifted Child Quarterly, 37,* 59–64.

Kieran, C. (1989). The early learning of algebra: A structural perspective. In S. Wagner & C. Kieran (Eds.), *Research issues in the learning and teaching of algebra* (pp.33–56). Reston, VA: National Council of Teachers of Mathematics.

Kimball, M. M. (1989). A new perspective on women's math achievement. *Psychological Bulletin, 105,* 198–214.

Kintsch, W. (1974). *The representation of meaning in memory.* Hillsdale, NJ: Erlbaum.

Kintsch, W. (1982). Text representations. In W. Otto & S. White (Eds.), *Reading expository material* (pp. 87–102). New York: Academic Press.

Kintsch, W. & Greeno, J. G. (1985). Understanding and solving arithmetic word problems. *Psychological Review, 92,* 109–129.

Klahr, D. & Dunbar, K. (1988). Dual space search during scientific reasoning. *Cognitive Science, 12,* 1–48.

Klayman, J. & Ha, Y. (1987). Confirmation, disconfirmation, and information in hypothesis testing. *Psychological Review, 94,* 211–228.

Knudson, R. E. (1992). The development of written argumentation: An analysis and comparison of argumentative writing at four grade levels. *Child Study Journal, 22,* 167–181.

Koslowski, B. & Maqueda, M. (1993). What is confirmation bias and when do people actually have it? *Merrill-Palmer Quarterly, 39,* 104–130.

Koslowski, B. & Okagaki, L. (1986). Non-Humean indices of causation in problem-solving situations: Causal mechanism, analogous effects and the status of rival alternative accounts. *Child Development, 57,* 1100–1108.

Kreutzer, M. A., Leonard, C. & Flavell, J. H. (1975). An interview study of children's knowledge about memory. *Monographs of the Society for Research in Child Development, 40* (No. 159).

Kuhn, D. (1992). Piaget's child as scientist. In H. Beilin & P. Pufall (Eds.), *Piaget's theory: Prospects and possibilities* (pp. 185–210). Hillsdale, NJ: Erlbaum.

Kuhn, D., Amsel, E., & O'Loughlin, M. (1988). *The development of scientific thinking skills.* New York: Academic Press.

Kuhn, D. & Brannock, J. (1977). Development of the isolation of variable scheme in experimental and 'natural experience' contexts. *Developmental Psychology, 13,* 9–14.

Laboratory of Comparative Human Cognition (1983). Culture and cognitive development. In P. H. Mussen (Ed.), *Handbook of child psychology* (Vol. 4, *History, theory, and methods,* pp. 296–355). New York: Wiley.

Lakatos, I. (1971). Falsification and the methodology of scientific research programmes. In I. Lakatos & A. Musgrave (Eds.), *Criticism and the growth of knowledge* (pp. 91–180). Cambridge: Cambridge University Press.

Lakoff, R. (1973). Language and women's place. *Language and Society, 2,* 45–79.

Langer, J. A. (1986). *Children's reading and writing: Structures and strategies.* Norwood, NJ: Ablex.

Lasnick, H. (1990). Syntax. In D. N. Osherson & H. Lasnik (Eds.), *An invitation to cognitive science* (Vol. 1: *Language,* pp. 5–22). Cambridge, MA: MIT Press.

Levstik, L. S. & Pappas, C. C. (1987). Exploring the development of historical understanding.

Journal of Research and Development in Education, 21, 1–15.

Liben, L. S. & Downs, R. M. (1993). Understanding person-space-map relations: Cartographic and developmental perspectives. *Developmental Psychology, 29,* 739–752.

Liberman, I. Y., Shankweiler, D., Fischer, F. W., & Carter, B. (1974). Explicit syllable and phoneme segmentation in the young child. *Journal of Experimental Child Psychology, 18,* 201–212.

Linn, M. C. (1978). Influence of cognitive style and training on tasks requiring formal thought. *Child Development, 49,* 874–877.

Linn, M. C. (1986). Science. In R. F. Dillon & R. J. Sternberg (Eds.), *Cognition and instruction* (pp. 155–204). New York: Academic Press.

Linn, M. C., Clement, C. & Pulos, S. (1983). Is it formal if it's not physics? (The influence of content on formal reasoning). *Journal of Research in Science Teaching, 20,* 755–770.

Linn, M. C. & Hyde, J. S. (1989). Gender, mathematics, and science. *Educational Researcher, 18,* 17–27.

Linn, M. C., Pulos, S. & Gans, A. (1981). Correlates of formal reasoning: Content and problem effects. *Journal of Research in Science Teaching, 18,* 435–447.

Linn, M. C. & Songer, N. B. (1993). How do students make sense of science? *Merrill-Palmer Quarterly, 39,* 47–73.

Linn, M. C. & Swiney, J. (1981). Individual differences in formal thought: Role of expectations and aptitudes. *Journal of Educational Psychology, 73,* 274–286.

Lipman, M. (1985). Thinking skills fostered by philosophy for children. In J. W. Segal, S. F. Chipman, & R. Glaser (Eds.), *Thinking and learning skills: Vol. 1: Relating instruction to research.* Hillsdale, NJ: Erlbaum.

Loban, D. W. (1976). *Language development: Kindergarten through grade twelve* (Research Report No. 18). Urbana, IL: National Council of Teachers of English.

Low, R. & Over, R. (1993). Gender differences in solution of algebraic word problems containing irrelevant information. *Journal of Educational Psychology, 85,* 331–339.

Maccoby, E. & Jacklin, C. N. (1974). *The psychology of sex differences.* Stanford, CA: Stanford University Press.

Mac Iver, D. (1987). Classroom factors and student characteristics predicting students' use of achievement standards during ability self-assessment. *Child Development, 58,* 1258–1271.

Mandler, J. M. & Johnson, N. S. (1977). Remembrance of things parsed: Story structure and recall. *Cognitive Psychology, 9,* 111–151.

Markman, E. M. (1979). Realizing that you don't understand: Elementary school children's awareness of inconsistencies. *Child Development, 50,* 643–655.

Markman, E. M. (1981). Comprehension monitoring. In W. P. Dickson (Ed.), *Children's oral communication skills.* New York: Academic Press.

Markovits, Z. & Sowder, J. (1994). Developing number sense: An intervention study in grade 7. *Journal for Research in Mathematics Education, 25,* 4–29.

Marsh, H. W. (1989). Age and sex effects in multiple dimensions of self-concept: Preadolescence to early adulthood. *Journal of Educational Psychology, 81,* 417–430.

Marsh, H. W., Barnes, J., Cairns, L. & Tidman, M. (1984). The self-description questionnaire (SDQ): Age effects in the structure and level of self-concept for preadolescent children. *Journal of Educational Psychology, 76,* 940–956.

Martin, V. L. & Pressley, M. (1991). Elaborative-interrogation effects depend on the nature of the question. *Journal of Educational Psychology, 83,* 113–119.

Martorano, S. C. (1977). A developmental analysis of performance on Piaget's formal operations tasks. *Developmental Psychology, 13,* 666–672.

Matz, M. (1982). Towards a process model for high school algebra errors. In D. Sleeman & J. S. Brown (Eds.), *Intelligent tutoring systems* (pp. 25–50). New York: Academic Press.

Mayer, R. E. (1979). Twenty years of research on advance organizers: Assimilation theory is still the best predictor of results. *Instructional Science, 8,* 133–167.

Mayer, R. E. (1982). Memory for algebra story

problem. *Journal of Educational Psychology, 74,* 199–216.

Mayer, R. E. (1987). *Educational Psychology.* Boston: Little Brown.

Mayer, R. E. (1989). Models for understanding. *Review of Educational Research, 59,* 43–64.

Mayer, R. E., Larkin, J. H. & Kaldane, J. B. (1984). A cognitive analysis of mathematical problem-solving ability. In R. J. Sternberg (Ed.), *Advances in the psychology of human intelligence* (pp. 231–273). Hillsdale, NJ: Erlbaum.

McCann, T. M. (1989). Student argumentative writing knowledge and ability at three grade levels. *Research in the Teaching of English, 23,* 62–72.

McClelland, J. L. & Rumelhart, D. E. (1981). An interactive model of context effects in letter perception: I: An account of the basic findings. *Psychological Review, 88,* 375–407.

McCloskey, M (1983). Naive theories of motion. In D. Gentner & A. L. Stevens (Eds.), *Mental Models* (pp. 299–324). Hillsdale, NJ: Erlbaum.

McCutchen, D. (1986). Domain knowledge and linguistic knowledge in the development of writing ability. *Journal of Memory and Language, 25,* 431–444.

McCutchen, D. Perfetti, C. A. (1982) Coherence and connectedness in the development of discourse production. *Text, 2,* 113–139.

McDaniel, M. A., Einstein, G. O., Dunay, P. K., & Cobb, R. S. (1986). Encoding difficulty and memory: Toward a unifying theory. *Journal of Memory and Language, 25,* 645–656.

McDaniel, M. A., Waddell, P. J. & Einstein, G. O. (1988). A contextual account of the generation effect: A three factor theory. *Journal of Memory and Language, 27,* 521–536.

McGee, L. M. (1982). Awareness of text structure: Effects on children's recall of expository text. *Reading Research Quarterly, 17,* 581–591.

McKeown, M. G. & Beck, I. L. (1990). The assessment and characterization of young learners' knowledge of a topic in history. *American Educational Research Journal, 27,* 688–726.

McKeown, M. G., Beck, I. L., Omanson, R. C. & Perfetti, C. A. (1983). The effects of long-term vocabulary instruction on reading comprehension: A replication. *Journal of Reading Behavior, 15,* 3–18.

Meehan, A. M. (1984). A meta-analysis of sex differences in formal operational thought. *Child Development, 55,* 1110–1124.

Meyer, B.J.F. (1985). Prose analysis: Purposes, procedures, and problems. In B. K. Britton & J. B. Black (Eds.), *Understanding expository text* (pp. 11–66). Hillsdale, NJ: Erlbaum.

Meyer, B.J.F., Brandt, D. M., & Bluth, G. J. (1980). Use of top-level structure in text: Key for reading comprehension of ninth-grade students. *Reading Research Quarterly, 16,* 73–103.

Miller, G. A. (1956). The magical number seven, plus or minus two: Some limits on our capacity for processing information. *Psychological Review, 63,* 81–97.

Miller, G. E., Giovenco, A., & Rentiers, K. A. (1987). Fostering comprehension monitoring in below average readers through self-instruction training. *Journal of Reading Behavior, 19,* 303–317.

Montague, M., Maddux, C. D., & Dereshiwsky, M. I. (1990). Story grammar and comprehension and production of narrative prose by students with learning disabilities. *Journal of Learning Disabilities, 23,* 190–197.

Morales, R. V., Shute, V. J., & Pelligrino, J. W. (1985). Developmental differences in understanding and solving simple mathematics word problems. *Cognition and Instruction, 2,* 59–89.

Muir, S. P. (1985). Understanding and improving students' map reading skills. *The Elementary School Journal, 86,* 207–216.

Mynatt, C. R., Doherty, M. E., & Tweney, R. D. (1977). Confirmation bias in a simulated research environment: An experimental study of scientific influence. *Quarterly Journal of Experimental Psychology, 29,* 85–95.

Nagy, W., Herman, P. & Anderson, R. (1985). Learning words from context. *Reading Research Quarterly, 20,* 233–253.

National Council of Teachers of Mathematics (1989). *Curriculum and evaluation standards for school mathematics.* Reston, VA: Author.

Nelson, K. (1986). *Event knowledge: Structure and function in development.* Hillsdale, NJ: Erlbaum.

Nelson, K. (1991). The matter of time: Interdependencies between language and thought in development. In S. A. Gelman & J. P. Byrnes (Eds.), *Perspectives on language and thought: Interrelations in development* (pp. 278–318). Cambridge: Cambridge University Press.

Newell, A. & Rosenbloom, P. S. (1981). Mechanisms of skills acquisition and the law of practice. In J. R. Anderson (Ed.), *Cognitive skills and their acquisition.* Hillsdale, NJ: Erlbaum.

Newell, A. & Simon, H. A. (1972). *Human problem solving.* Englewood Cliffs, NJ: Prentice-Hall.

Newman, R. (1991). Goals and self-regulated learning: What motivates children to seek academic help? In M. Maehr & P. Pintrich (Eds.), *Advances in motivation and achievement, Vol. 7* (pp. 151–183). Greenwich, CT: JAI Press.

Newmann, F. M. (1990). Higher order thinking in teaching social studies: A rationale for the assessment for classroom thoughtfulness. *Journal of Curriculum Studies, 22,* 41–56.

Nicholls, J. (1983). Conceptions of ability and achievement motivation: A theory and its implications for education. In S. Paris, G. Olson, & H. Stevenson (Eds.), *Learning and motivation in the classroom* (pp. 211–237). Hillsdale, NJ: Erlbaum.

Nickerson, R. S., Perkins, D. N., & Smith, E. E. (1985). *The teaching of thinking.* Hillsdale, NJ: Erlbaum.

Nisbett, R. E. & Ross, L. (1980). *Human inference: Strategies and shortcomings of social judgment.*

Norris, J. A. & Bruning, R. H. (1988). Cohesion in the narratives of good and poor readers. *Journal of Speech and Hearing Disorders, 53,* 416–424.

Ornstein, P. A. & Naus, M. J. (1985). Effects of the knowledge base on children's memory strategies. In H. W. Reese (Ed.), *Advances in child development and behavior* (Vol. 19). New York: Academic Press.

Overton, W. F. (1990). Competence and procedures: Constraints on the development of logical reasoning. In W. F. Overton (Ed.), *Reasoning, necessity and logic: Developmental Perspectives* (pp. 1–32). Hillsdale, NJ: Erlbaum.

Overton, W. F. & Byrnes, J. P. (1991). Cognitive

development. In R. M. Lerner, A. C. Petersen, & J. Brooks-Gunn (Eds.), *Encyclopedia of adolescence* (Vol. 1 pp. 151–156). New York: Garland Publishing.

Overton, W. F. & Meehan, A. M. (1982). Individual differences in formal operational thought: Sex role and learned helplessness. *Child Development, 53,* 1536–1543.

Paige, J. M. & Simon, H. A. (1966). Cognitive processes in solving algebra word problems. In B. Kleinmuntz (Ed.), *Problem-solving: Research, method, and theory.* New York: Wiley.

Paivio, A. (1971). *Imagery and verbal processes.* New York: Holt, Rinehart & Winston.

Palincsar, A. M. & Brown, A. L. (1984). Reciprocal teaching of comprehension-fostering and comprehension-monitoring activities. *Cognition and Instruction, 1,* 117–175.

Pallas, A. M. & Alexander, K. L. (1983). Sex differences in quantitative SAT performance: New evidence on the differential coursework hypothesis. *American Educational Research Journal, 20,* 165–182.

Paris, S. G. (1975). Integration and inference in children's comprehension and memory. In F. Restle, R. Shiffrin, J. Castellan, H. Lindman, & D. Pisoni (Eds.), *Cognitive theory* (Vol 1). Hillsdale, NJ: Erlbaum.

Paris, S. G. (1978). Coordination of means and goals in the development of mnemonic skills. In P. A. Ornstein (Ed.), *Memory development in children.* Hillsdale, NJ: Erlbaum.

Paris, S. G. & Byrnes, J. P. (1989). The constructivist approach to self-regulation and learning in the classroom. In B. J. Zimmerman & D. H. Schunk (Eds.), *Self-regulated learning and academic achievement: Theory, research, and practice.* New York: Springer Verlag.

Paris, S. G., Wasik, B. A. & Turner, J. C. (1991). The development of strategic readers. In R. Barr, M. L. Kamil, P. B. Mosenthal, & P. D. Pearson (Eds.), *Handbook of reading research, Vol. II* (pp. 609–640). New York: Longman.

Parsons, J., Kaczala, C. & Meece, J. (1982). Socialization of achievement attitudes and beliefs: Classroom influences. *Child Development, 53,* 322–339.

Parsons, J. E. & Ruble, D. N. (1977). The development of achievement-related expectancies. *Child Development, 48,* 1075–1079.

Patrick, J. J. & Hoge, J. D. (1991). Teaching government, civics, and the law. In J. P. Shaver (Ed.), *Handbook of social studies teaching and learning* (pp. 427–436). New York: MacMillan.

Pearson, P. D. & Fielding, L. (1991). Comprehension instruction. In M. Barr, M. L. Kamil, P. B. Mosenthal, & P. D. Pearson (Eds.), *Handbook of reading research, Vol II* (pp. 815–861). New York: Longman.

Perfetti, C.A. (1985). *Reading ability.* New York: Oxford University Press.

Perfetti, C. A. & McCutchen, D. (1987). Schooled language competence: Linguistic abilities in reading and writing. In S. Rosenberg (Ed.), *Advances in applied psycholinguistics* (pp. 105–141). Cambridge: Cambridge University Press.

Peterson, P. L., Fennema, E., Carpenter, T. P. & Loef, M. (1989). Teacher's pedagogical content beliefs in mathematics. *Cognition and instruction, 6,* 1–40.

Piaget, J. (1952). *The origins of intelligence in children.* New York: International Universities Press.

Piaget, J. (1965). *The child's conception of number.* New York: Norton.

Piaget, J. (1969). *The child's conception of time.* New York: Basic Books.

Piaget, J. (1970). *Structuralism.* New York: Harper & Row.

Piaget, J. (1976). *The grasp of consciousness.* Cambridge, MA: Harvard University Press.

Piaget, J. (1980). *Experiments in contradiction.* Chicago: University of Chicago Press.

Piaget, J. & Garcia, R. (1974). *Understanding causality.* New York: Basic Books.

Piaget, J. & Inhelder, B. (1969). *The psychology of the child.* New York: Basic Books.

Piburn, M. (1990). Reasoning about logical propositions and success in science. *Journal of Research in Science Teaching, 27,* 887–900.

Pintrich, P. R. & DeGroot, E. V. (1990). Motivational and self-regulated learning components of classroom academic performance. *Journal of Educational Psychology, 82,* 33–40.

Pirie, S. & Kieran, T. (1992). Creating constructivist environments and constructing creative mathematics. *Educational Studies in Mathematics, 23,* 505–528.

Pollitt, E., Gorman, K. S., Engle, P. L., Martorell, R. & Rivera, J. (1993). Early supplemental feeding and cognition: Effects over two decades. *Monographs of the Society for Research in Child Development, 58* (No. 235).

Popper, K. R. (1959). *The logic of scientific discovery.* London: Hutchinson.

Post, T. R., Wachsmuth, I., Lesh, R. & Behr, M. J. (1985). Order and equivalence of rational numbers: A cognitive analysis. *Journal for Research in Mathematics Education, 16,* 18–36.

Pressley, M., Almasi, J., Schuder, T., Bergman, J., Hite, S., El-Dinary, P. B. & Brown, R. (1994). Transactional instruction of comprehension strategies: The Montgomery County Maryland SAIL program. *Reading and Writing Quarterly, 10,* 5–19.

Pressley, M., Borkowski, J. G. & Schneider, W. (1987). Cognitive strategies: Good strategy users coordinate metacognition and knowledge. In R. Vasta & G. Whitehurst (Eds.), *Annals of child development* (Vol. 5, pp. 89–129). Greenwich, CT: JAI.

Pressley, M., Johnson, C. J., Symons, S., McGoldrick, J. A. & Kurita, J. A. (1989). Strategies that improve children's memory and comprehension of text. *Elementary School Journal, 90,* 3–32.

Pressley, M., Levin, J. & Delaney, H. D. (1982). The mnemonic keyword method. *Review of Educational Research, 52,* 61–92.

Presson, C. C. (1982). The development of mapreading skills. *Child Development, 53,* 196–199.

Price, G. B. & Graves, R. L. (1980). Sex differences in syntax and usage in oral and written language. *Research in the Teaching of English, 14,* 147–153.

Randhawa, B. S., Beamer, J. E. & Lundberg, I. (1993). Role of mathematics self-efficacy in the structural model of mathematics achievement. *Journal of Educational Psychology, 85,* 41–48.

Recht, D. R. & Leslie, L. (1988). Effect of prior knowledge on good and poor readers' memory of text. *Journal of Educational Psychology, 80,* 16–20.

Renninger, K. A. (1991). Individual interest and development: Implications for theory and practice. In K. A. Renninger, S. Hidi & A. Krapp (Eds.), *The role of interest in learning and development* (pp. 361–396). Hilldale, NJ: Erlbaum.

Renninger, K. A., Hidi, S. & Krapp, A. (1991). *The role of interest in learning and development.* Hillsdale, NJ: Erlbaum.

Resnick, L. B. (1980). The role of invention in the development of mathematical competence. In R. H. Kluwe & H. Spada (Eds.), *Developmental models of thinking* (pp. 213–244). New York: Academic Press.

Resnick, L. B. (1983). A developmental theory of number understanding. In H. P. Ginsburg (Ed.), *The development of mathematical thinking* (pp. 109–151). New York: Academic Press.

Resnick, L. B. (1987a). Constructing knowledge in school. In L. S. Liben (Ed.), *Development and learning: Conflict or congruence?* (pp. 19–50). Hillsdale, NJ: Erlbaum.

Resnick, L. B. (1987b). *Education and learning to think.* Washington, DC: National Academy Press.

Resnick, L. B., Cauzinille-Marmeche, E., & Mathieu, J. (1987). Understanding algebra. In J. A. Sloboda & D. Rogers (Eds.), *Cognitive processes in mathematics.* Oxford: Oxford University Press.

Resnick, L. B., Nesher, P., Leonard, F., Magone, M., Omanson, S. & Peled, I. (1989). Conceptual bases of arithmetic errors: The case of decimal fractions. *Journal for Research in Mathematics Education, 20,* 8–27.

Resnick, L. B. & Omanson, S. F. (1987). Learning to understand arithmetic. In R. Glaser (Ed.), *Advances in instructional psychology* (Vol. 3, pp. 41–95). Hillsdale, NJ: Erlbaum.

Riley, M. S., Greeno, J. G. & Heller, J. I. (1983). Development of children's problem-solving ability in arithmetic. In H. P. Ginsburg (Ed.), *The development of mathematical thinking* (pp. 62–71). New York: Academic Press.

Rinehart, S. D., Stahl, S. A. & Erickson, L. G. (1986). Some effects of summarization training on reading and studying. *Reading Research Quarterly, 21,* 422–438.

Roberge, J. J. & Flexer, B. K. (1979). Further examination of formal operational reasoning abilities. *Child Development, 50,* 478–484.

Rokeach, M. (1973). *The nature of human values.* New York: Free Press.

Roller, C. M. (1990). The interaction between knowledge and structure variables in the processing of expository prose. *Reading Research Quarterly, 25,* 80–89.

Roser, N. & Juel, C. (1982). Effects of vocabulary instruction on reading comprehension. In J. Niles & L. Harris (Eds.), *New inquiries in reading research and instruction* (pp. 110–118). Rochester, NY: National Reading Conference.

Roth, W. M. (1994). Experimenting in a constructivist high school physics laboratory. *Journal of Research in Science Teaching, 31,* 197–223.

Rubin, D. L. & Greene, K. (1992). Gender-typical style in written language. *Research in the Teaching of English, 26,* 7–40.

Rumelhart, D. E. (1984). Schemata and the cognitive system. In R. S. Wyler & T. K. Srull (Eds.), *Handbook of social cognition* (Vol.1, pp. 161–188). Hillsdale, NJ: Erlbaum.

Salomon, G. & Perkins, D. N. (1989). Rocky roads to transfer: Rethinking mechanisms of a neglected phenomenon. *Educational Psychologist, 24,* 113–142.

Scardamalia, M. & Bereiter, C. (1986). Research on written composition. In M. C. Wittrock (Ed.), *Handbook of research on teaching* (3rd edition, pp. 778–803). New York: Macmillan.

Scardamalia, M., Bereiter, C. & Goelman, H. (1982). The role of production factors in writing ability. In M. Nystrand (Ed.), *What writers know: The language, process, and structure of written discourse.* New York: Academic Press.

Schacter, D. L. (1989). Memory. In M. I. Posner (Ed.), *Foundations of cognitive science* (pp. 683–726). Cambridge, MA: MIT Press.

Schauble, L. (1990). Belief revision in children: The role of prior knowledge and strategies for generating evidence. *Journal of Experimental Child Psychology, 49,* 31–57.

Schneider, W. (1985). Developmental trends in the metamemory-memory behavior relationship: An integrative review. In D. L. Forrest-Pressley, G. E. MacKinnon, & T. G. Waller (Eds.), *Cognition, metacognition, and performance.* New York: Academic Press.

Schug, M. C. (1987). Children's understanding of economics, *Elementary School Journal, 87,* 507–518.

Schug, M. C. & Walstad, W. B. (1991). Teaching and learning economics. In J. P. Shaver (Ed.), *Handbook of research on social studies teaching and learning* (pp. 411–419). New York: Macmillan.

Schunk, D. (1991). Goal-setting and self-evaluation: A social-cognitive perspective on self-regulation. In M. Maehr & P. Pintrich (Eds.), *Advances in motivation and achievement* (Vol. 7, pp. 85–113). Greenwich, CT: JAI Press.

Schunk, D. & Rice, J. (1989). Learning goals and children's reading comprehension. *Journal of Reading Behavior, 21,* 279–293.

Schwartz, B. (1976). *Psychology of learning and behavior* (2nd edition). New York: W. W. Norton.

Searle, J. (1983). *Intentionality.* Cambridge: Cambridge University Press.

Seidenberg, M. S. & McClelland, J. L. (1989). A distributed, developmental model of word recognition and naming. *Psychological Review, 96,* 523–568.

Segal, J. W., Chipman, S. F. & Glaser, R. (1985). *Thinking and learning skills* (Vols. 1 and 2). Hillsdale, NJ: Erlbaum.

Shapiro, L. R. & Hudson, J. A. (1991). Tell me a make-believe story: Coherence and cohesion in young children's picture-elicited narratives. *Developmental Psychology, 27,* 960–974.

Shultz, T. R. (1982). Rules of causal attribution. *Monographs of the society for research in child development, 47* (No. 194).

Shustack, M. (1988). Causal thinking. In R. Sternberg & E. E. Smith (Eds.), *The psychology of human thought.* Cambridge, MA: MIT Press.

Siegler, R. S. (1983). Information processing approaches to cognitive development. In P. H. Mussen (Ed.), *Handbook of child psychology: Vol 1: History, theory, and methods.* New York: Wiley.

Siegler, R. S. (1988). Individual differences in strategy choices: Good students, not-so-good students and perfectionists. *Child Development, 59,* 833–851.

Siegler, R. S. (1989). Hazards of mental chronometry: An example from children's subtraction. *Journal of Educational Psychology, 81,* 497–506.

Siegler, R. S. (1991). *Children's thinking* (2nd edition). Englewood Cliffs, NJ: Prentice Hall.

Siegler, R. S. & Jenkins, E. A. (1989). *How children discover new strategies.* Hillsdale, NJ: Erlbaum.

Siegler, R. S. & Liebert, R. M. (1975). Acquisition of formal reasoning by 10-and 13-year-olds: Designing a factorial experiment. *Developmental Psychology, 11,* 401–402.

Simon, H. A. (1956). Rational choice and the structure of the environment. *Psychological Review, 63,* 129–138.

Singly, M. K. & Anderson, J. R. (1989). *The transfer of cognitive skill.* Cambridge, MA; Harvard University Press.

Skinner, E., Chapman, M. & Baltes, P. (1988). Control, means-ends, and agency beliefs. A new conceptualization and its measurement during childhood. *Journal of Personality and Social Psychology, 54,* 117–133.

Slater, W. H., Graves, M. F., & Piché, G. L. (1985). Effects of structural organizers on ninth-grade students' comprehension and recall of four patterns of expository text. *Reading Research Quarterly, 20,* 189–202.

Slavin, R. (1990). *Cooperative learning: Theory, research, practice.* Englewood Cliffs, NJ: Prentice-Hall.

Slavin, R. E., Karweit, N. L. & Wasik, B. A. (1994). *Preventing early school failure: Research, theory, and practice.* Boston: Allyn & Bacon.

Slovic, P. (1990). Choice. In D. N. Osherson & E. E. Smith (Eds.), *Thinking.* Cambridge, MA: MIT Press.

Smith, E. E. (1989). Concepts and induction. In M. I. Posner (Ed.), *Foundations of cognitive science* (pp. 501–526). Cambridge, MA: MIT Press.

Smith, E. E. & Medin, D. L. (1981). *Categories and concepts.* Cambridge, MA: Harvard University Press.

Snow, R. E. (1994). A person-situation interaction theory of intelligence in outline. In A. Demetriou & A. Efklides (Eds.), *Intelligence, mind, and reasoning: Structure and development* (pp. 11–28). Amsterdam: North-Holland.

Sohn, D. (1982). Sex differences in achievement self-attributions: An effect size analysis. *Sex Roles, 8,* 345–357.

Spires, H. A., Gallini, J. & Riggsbee, J. (1992). Effects of schema-based and text structure-based cues on expository prose comprehension in fourth graders. *Journal of Experimental Education, 60,* 307–320.

Squire, L. R. (1987). *Memory and brain.* Oxford: Oxford University Press.

Squire, L. R. (1989). On the course of forgetting in very long term memory. *Journal of Experimental Psychology: Learning, memory, and cognition, 15,* 241–245.

Stahl, S. A. & Miller, P. D. (1989). Whole language and language experience approaches to beginning reading: A quantitative research synthesis. *Review of Educational Research, 59,* 87–116.

Stanovich, K. E. (1980). Toward an interactive-compensatory model of individual differences in the development of reading fluency. *Reading Research Quarterly, 16,* 32–65.

Stanovich, K. E. (1986). Matthew effects in reading: Some consequences of individual differences in the acquisition of literacy. *Reading Research Quarterly, 21,* 360–407.

Stanovich, K. E. (1988). The right and wrong places to look for the cognitive locus of reading disability. *Annals of Dyslexia, 38,* 154–177.

Stanovich, K. E., Cunningham, A. E. & Feeman, D. J. (1984). Intelligence, cognitive skills, and early reading progress. *Reading Research Quarterly, 29,* 278–303.

Starkey, P. & Cooper, R. G. (1980). Perception of numbers by human infants. *Science, 210,* 1033–1035.

Stein, N. L. (1982). What's in a story: Interpreting the interpretations of story grammars. *Discourse Processes, 5,* 319–335.

Stein, N. L. & Glenn, C. G. (1979). An analysis of story comprehension in elementary school children. In R. O. Freedle (Ed.), *New directions in discourse processing.* Norwood, NJ; Ablex.

Stein, N. L. & Policastro, T. (1984). The story: A comparison between children's and teacher's viewpoints. In H. Mandel, N. L. Stein & T. Trabasso (Eds.), *Learning and comprehension of text.* Hillsdale, NJ: Erlbaum.

Stern, E. (1993). What makes certain arithmetic problems involving the comparison of sets so difficult for children? *Journal of Educational Psychology, 85,* 7–23.

Sternberg, R. J. (1985). *Beyond IQ: A triarchic theory of human intelligence.* Cambridge: Cambridge University Press.

Stevenson, H. W., Chen, C. & Uttal, D. H. (1990). Beliefs and achievement: A study of black, white, and hispanic children. *Child Development, 61,* 508–523.

Stevenson, H. W. & Lee, S. Y. (1990). Contexts of achievement. *Monographs of the Society for Research in Child Development, 55* (No. 221).

Stipek, D. & Hoffman, J. (1980). Children's achievement-related expectancies as a function of academic performance histories and sex. *Journal of Educational Psychology, 72,* 861–865.

Stipek, D. J. (1993). *Motivation to learn: From theory to practice* (2nd edition). Boston: Allyn & Bacon.

Stipek, D., Recchia, S. & McClintock, S. (1992). Self-evaluation in young children. *Monographs of the Society for Research in Child Development, 57* (No. 226).

Stofflett, R. T. (1994). The accommodation of science pedagogical knowledge: The application of conceptual change constructs to teacher education. *Journal of Research in Science Teaching, 31,* 787–810.

Stone, C. A. & Day, M. C. (1978). Levels of availability of a formal operations strategy. *Child Development, 49,* 1054–1065.

Strauss, M. S. & Curtis, L. E. (1981). Infant perception of numerosity. *Child Development, 60,* 521–538.

Sulzby, E. (1991). Assessment of emergent literacy: Storybook reading. *The Reading Teacher, 44,* 498–500.

Sunal, C. S. (1990). *Early childhood social studies.* Columbus, OH: Merrill.

Sunal, C. S. (1993). Social studies in early childhood education. In B. Spodek (Ed.), *Handbook on the Education of Young Children.* New York: Macmillan.

Sweller, J. & Cooper, G. A. (1985). The use of examples as a substitute for problem solving in learning algebra. *Cognition and Instruction, 2,* 59–89.

Taylor, B. M. (1980). Children's memory for expository text after reading. *Reading Research Quarterly, 25,* 399–411.

Taylor, B. M. (1986). Summary writing by young children. *Reading Research Quarterly, 21,* 193–208.

Taylor, B. M. & Beach, R. W. (1984). The effects of text structure in the recall of expository material. *Reading Research Quarterly, 25,* 79–89.

Teale, W. H. (1986). Home background and young children's literacy development. In W. H. Teale & E. Sulzby (Eds.), *Emergent Literacy* (pp. 173–206). Norwood, NJ: Ablex.

Teale, W. H. & Sulzby, E. (1986). *Emergent literacy.* Norwood, NJ; Ablex.

Thorndike, E. L. (1913). *Educational Psychology.* New York: Teachers College Press.

Thorndike, E. L. & Woodworth, R. S. (1901). The influence of improvement in one mental function upon the efficiency of other functions. *Psychological Review, 8,* 247–261.

Tulving, E. & Psotka, J. (1971). Retroactive inhibition in free recall: Inaccessibility of information available in the memory store. *Journal of Experimental Psychology, 87,* 1–8.

Tunmer, W. E., Herriman, M. L. & Nesdale, A. R. (1988). Metalinguistic abilities and beginning reading. *Reading Research Quarterly, 23,* 134–158).

van Dijk, T. A. & Kintsch, W. (1983). *Strategies of discourse comprehension.* New York: Academic Press.

Vellutino, F. R. & Scanlon, D. M. (1991). The pre-eminence of phonologically based skills in learning to read. In S. A. Brady & D. P. Shankweiler (Eds.), *Phonological processes in literacy.* Hillsdale, NJ: Erlbaum.

Voss, J. F., Tyler, S. W. & Yengo, L. A. (1983). Individual differences in the solving of social science problems. In R. F. Dillon & R. R. Schmeck (Eds.), *Individual differences in cognition* (Vol. 1, pp. 205–232). New York: Academic Press.

Vye, N. J., Delclos, V. R., Burns, M. S. & Bransford, J. D. (1988). Teaching thinking and problem-solving: Instructional issues. In R. J. Sternberg & E. E. Smith (Eds.), *The psychology of human thought* (pp. 337–365). Cambridge: Cambridge University Press.

Vygotsky, L. S. (1962). *Thought and language.* Cambridge, MA: MIT Press.

Vygotsky, L. S. (1978). *Mind in society.* Cambridge, MA: Harvard University Press.

Waggoner, J. E., Meece, R. & Palermo, D. (1985). Grasping the meaning of metaphor: Story recall and comprehension. *Child Development, 56,* 1156–1166.

Wagner, S. & Kieran, C. (1989). *Research issues in the learning and teaching of algebra.* Reston, VA: National Council of Teachers of Mathematics.

Walker, C. H. (1987). Relative importance of domain knowledge and overall aptitude on acquisition of domain-related information. *Cognition and Instruction, 4,* 25–42.

Wallach, L., Wallach, M. A., Dozier, M. G. & Kaplan, N. E. (1977). Poor children learning to read do not have trouble with auditory discrimination but do have trouble with phoneme recognition. *Journal of Educational Psychology, 69,* 36–39.

Wallach, M. A. & Wallach, L. (1979). Helping disadvantaged children learn to read by teaching them phoneme identification skills. In L. A. Resnick & P. A. Weaver (Eds.), *Theory and practice of early reading* (Vol. 3, pp. 227–259). Hillsdale, NJ: Erlbaum.

Ward, S. L., Byrnes, J. P. & Overton, W. F. (1990). Organization of knowledge and conditional reasoning. *Journal of Educational Psychology, 82,* 832–837.

Wasik, B. A. (1986). *Familiarity of content and inference making in young children.* Unpublished doctoral dissertation, Temple University.

Wason, P. C. (1983). Realism and rationality in the selection task. In J. St. B. T. Evans (Ed.), *Thinking and reasoning: Psychological Approaches* (pp. 44–75). London: Routledge & Kegan Paul.

Wearne, D. & Hiebert, J. (1988). Constructing and using meaning for mathematical symbols: The case of decimal fractions. In J. Hiebert & M. Behr (Eds.), *Number concepts and operations in the middle grades* (pp. 220–235). Reston, VA: National Council of Teachers of Mathematics.

Weaver, C. A. & Kintsch, W. (1991). Expository text. In R. Barr, M. L Kamil, P. Mosenthal &

P. D. Pearson (Eds.), *Handbook of reading research* (Vol. II, pp. 230–245). New York: Longman.

Weiner, B. (1986). *An attribution theory of motivation and emotion.* New York: Springer-Verlag.

Weinstein, C. E. & Mayer, R. E. (1986). The teaching of learning strategies. In M. C. Wittrock (Ed.), *Handbook of research on teaching* (3rd edition). New York: Macmillan.

Wellman, H. M. (1990). *The child's theory of mind.* Cambridge, MA: MIT Press.

Wentzel, K. R. (1989). Adolescent classroom goals, standards for performance, and academic achievement: An interactionist perspective. *Journal of Educational Psychology, 81,* 131–142.

Wentzel, K. R. (1991). Social and academic goals at school: Motivation and achievement in context. In M. Maehr & P. Pintrich (Eds.), *Advances in motivation and achievement, volume 7* (pp. 185–212). Greenwich, CT: JAI.

Wertheimer, M. (1945). *Productive thinking.* New York: Harper & Brothers.

Wertsch, J. V. (1985). *Vygotsky and the social formation of mind.* Cambridge, MA: Harvard University Press.

Whitehurst, G. J., Falco, F. L., Lonigan, C. J., Fischel, J. E., DeBaryshe, B. D., Valdez-Menchaca, M. C. & Caulfield, M. (1988). Accelerating language development through picturebook reading. *Developmental Psychology, 24,* 552–559.

Whittlesea, B. W. A. & Cantwell, A. L. (1987). Enduring influence of the purpose of experiences: Encoding-retrieval interactions in word and pseudoword perception. *Memory and Cognition, 15,* 465–472.

Wigfield, A. & Eccles, J. S. (1989), Test Anxiety in elementary and secondary school students. *Educational Psychologist, 24,* 159–183.

Wigfield, A. & Eccles, J.S. (1992). The development of achievement task values: A theoretical analysis. *Developmental Review, 12,* 265–310.

Wigfield, A., Eccles, J., Harold-Goldsmith, R., Blumenfeld, P., Yoon, K. S., & Friedman-Doan, C. (1989). Gender and age differences in children's achievement self-perceptions during elementary school. Paper presented at the Biennial meeting of the Society for Research in Child Development, Kansas City, April.

Wigfield, A. W., Eccles, J., Mac Iver, D., Reuman, D. & Midgley, C. (1991). Transitions at early adolescence: Changes in children's domain-specific self-perceptions and general self-esteem across the transition to junior high school. *Developmental Psychology, 27,* 552–565.

Winograd, T. (1975). Frame representations and the declarative/ procedural controversy. In D. G. Bobrow & A. Collins (Eds.), *Representation and understanding: Studies in cognitive science* (pp. 185–210). New York: Academic Press.

Wood, D., Bruner, J. S. & Ross, G. (1976). The role of tutoring in problem-solving. *Journal of Child Psychology and Psychiatry, 17,* 89–100.

Wood, E., Miller, G., Symons, S., Canough, T. & Yedlicka, J. (1993). Effects of elaborative interrogation on young learners' recall of facts. *Elementary School Journal, 94,* 245–254.

Wright, R. E. & Rosenberg, S. (1993). Knowledge of text coherence and expository writing: A developmental study. *Journal of Educational Psychology, 85,* 152–158.

Wyner, N. B. & Farquhar, E. (1991). Cognitive, emotional, and social development: Early childhood social studies. In J.P. Shaver (Ed.), *Handbook of research on social studies teaching and learning* (pp. 109–120). New York: Macmillan.

Wynn, K. (1990). Children's understanding of counting. *Cognition, 36,* 155–193.

Wynn, K. (1992). Addition and subtraction by human infants. *Nature, 358,* 749–750.

Zimmerman, B. J. & Martinez-Pons, M. (1990). Student differences in self-regulated learning: Relating grade, sex, and giftedness to self-efficacy and strategy use. *Journal of Educational Psychology, 82,* 51–59.

Zinar, S. (1990). Fifth graders' recall of propositional content and causal relationships from expository prose. *Journal of Reading Behavior, 22,* 181–199.

Index